Ohio's Founding Fathers

Ohio's Founding Fathers

Fred J. Milligan

iUniverse, Inc.
New York Lincoln Shanghai

Ohio's Founding Fathers

iUniverse, Inc.

For information address:
iUniverse
2021 Pine Lake Road, Suite 100
Lincoln, NE 68512
www.iuniverse.com

ISBN: 0-595-29322-0 (Pbk)
ISBN: 0-595-75039-7 (Cloth)

Printed in the United States of America

To my father Fred J. Milligan, Sr., (1906-1997), who served as a member and president of the board of trustees and general counsel of the Ohio Historical Society and was instrumental in establishing the corporate limit marker program in Ohio and the passage of legislation requiring the teaching of Ohio history in the schools. He was passionate about Ohio history because he saw in it the source of the values that will preserve, protect, and inspire us in the future.

CONTENTS

Ohio County Boundary Lines

MAP SHOWING COUNTY BOUNDARIES AT TIME OF 1802 CONVENTION

Map from Randolph C. Downes, *Evolution of Ohio County Boundaries*, Ohio Historical Society, 1970, p. 22.

Ohio County Boundary Lines in 1803.

Map Showing County Boundaries Following Creation of New Counties by Ohio General Assembly in 1803

Map from Randolph C. Downes, *Evolution of Ohio County Boundaries, Ohio Historical Society, 1970, p. 25.*

Introduction

OHIO'S FOUNDING FATHERS

This is the story of the beginning of Ohio told through the lives of its founding fathers. Founding fathers include the thirty-five delegates to the convention held in Chillicothe in November, 1802, which decided that Ohio should become a state and then drafted its first constitution. Founding fathers also includes twenty additional men whose activities before and after the convention round out the story of the state's beginning. The time period covered by these lives begins with the first permanent settlement at Marietta in 1788 and extends through the election of William Henry Harrison as the first U.S. President from Ohio in 1840. History-telling can be about events, ideas or lives. This is a history of lives. Many of these people participated in the same events and shared the same ideas. The events and ideas are better understood when viewed from the perspective of several lives.

Many of the founders were from families who had been in America for several generations before they came to Ohio. Some were immigrants or sons of immigrants. Some had fought in the French and Indian War. Many had fought in the Revolutionary War. Many were in the Indian Wars. Many participated in the War of 1812. Several of the founding fathers were from prominent families of New England, Virginia, New Jersey and other eastern states and came to Ohio with superior education, valuable political and business connections in the east, and plenty of money to invest. Others were self-educated and self-made men. The founding fathers included land speculators and developers, surveyors, lawyers, doctors, ministers, teachers, farmers, businessmen, editors, and civil servants. Most were ambitious. Most had high character. Some had character flaws. Most were relatively lucky. Others were not. Most had successful lives. Some did not.

All shared one thing in common. They came to Ohio because they had "Ohio fever." An Ohioan in the 21st Century has difficulty understanding what "Ohio fever" was. However, "Ohio fever" was a household word throughout the eastern United States in the late 18th and early 19th centuries. It was a term people used to explain why normally sensible people left a comfortable civilized world to go off and seek their fortune in the wilderness. It was similar to the fever that caused many of their ancestors to come to America in the first place, but for most of them that was a long time ago and long forgotten. For those who had it Ohio Fever was the excitement of a fresh start, of new communities to be founded, of new farms on rich soil, of new businesses to be organized, of money to be made, of churches to be built, of new friends who shared the same excitement of a new beginning. There was also the joy of escaping the social restraints, limited opportunities, old quarrels, boredom, and pessimism of the eastern states. For some it was an escape from a hierarchical slave-owning society which they loathed. For others it was an escape from a puritanical and highly stratified New England culture. For others it was an escape from a society torn with dissension between rich and poor. The Revolution was a hard time in America which people endured because they had great hopes for the future, but after the Revolution came more hard times and a sense by many that the promise of the Revolution was not being realized. Of course Ohio Fever was not limited to the founding fathers. Everyone who came to Ohio had it. Not everyone kept it. Some became disillusioned and returned east. Others stayed but cursed the day they set foot in the state. Others caught another fever and headed west or south chasing a new dream.

The Revolutionary War experience was fresh in mind for the founding fathers. The revolutionary ideas which had emboldened them to declare independence from the crown and motherland were articles of faith. These ideas shaped how they saw the world. When Ohio became a state, the east was going through a second revolution, the Jeffersonian Revolution. It emboldened the people to reject the leadership of "their betters." The new enemy was not the king. It was "aristocrats". The government belonged to the people and should serve the people not the special interests of the privileged class. The founding fathers and people in Ohio were caught up in this second revolution, some on one side and some on the other. The ideas of this second revolution shaped how many of the founding fathers viewed the challenges they faced and how they portrayed them to the people they served. Many of the founding fathers lived to see and participated on one side or the other of a third revolution, the Jacksonian Revolution which occurred in the 1820s and 1830s.

Most of the founding fathers were devout Christians. Several were ministers. Others were deacons, elders or other church leaders. Many participated in the founding of congregations and erection of church buildings in their communities. They believed that the teaching and encouragement of morality was essential to a democratic government and that religion was the foundation of morality. They were Presbyterians, Methodists, Baptists, Congregationalists, Episcopalians, and Quakers. They believed government should encourage religion, but they also believed government had no business endorsing or dictating any particular Christian theology. These were times when there were ferocious theological battles between and within religious denominations. It was also a time when communities were divided between church goers and men who put their faith in their gun, their fists, and their own judgment for survival. During the constitutional convention, a proposal to impose a religious test on candidates for public office was overwhelmingly defeated. The first session of the General Assembly voted not to appoint a chaplain.

To the extent that "Founding Father of Ohio" is used as a title of honor, there are several persons who deserve the title whose lives are not the subject of this book because they were not Ohioans. Among those are the first three Presidents of the United States. Washington knew about Ohio fever. He had large investments in western lands and recognized that people were going west to settle regardless of what the government did. If the government provided protection for the settlers, they would remain a part of the United States. If it did not, these lands could very well end up under the control of Britain, Spain or France. Washington was able to muster the commitment and financial and military resources of the government to exercise control over the Ohio country. John Adams was on the team which negotiated the Treaty with Great Britain following the Revolutionary War. He is credited with insisting that Britain relinquish its claim to the Northwest Territory. Jefferson believed that the future of America was in the west. He conceived the plan of development of the Northwest Territory into states with equal status to the original states. His vision was the basis for the Ordinance of 1787, which established a governmental structure for the Northwest Territory as well as a plan for developing unsettled wilderness into co-equal states. The support of Jefferson and his allies in Congress was essential to Ohio becoming a state in 1803 with boundaries as they are known today. He recognized the importance of gaining control of the Mississippi so that Ohio and the other states in the Northwest Territory would have unimpeded access by water to eastern and international markets. Alexander Hamilton deserves the title for recognizing the importance of sale of western lands for liquidating the crushing debt of the Revolutionary War. George Rogers Clark deserves the title for seeing the strategic importance of seizing military control of the Northwest Territory during the Revolutionary War. He persuaded Virginia leaders to authorize and finance an expedition to seize the three French towns controlled by the British and his success in the venture served as the basis for persuading the

British to relinquish control of the Territory. Anthony Wayne deserves the title for his successful prosecution of the war against the Indians following St. Clair's defeat. His decisive victory at the Battle of Fallen Timbers in 1794 and his successful negotiation of the Treaty of Greenville the following year opened up Ohio to settlement. Ebenezer Zane also deserves the title. Zane persuaded the government to hire him to blaze a trail from Wheeling to Limestone (now Maysville), Kentucky. The road opened up the interior of the state and substantially increased the pace of settlement. Finally, the title should be conferred upon Manasseh Cutler. He persuaded the last Congress under the Articles of Confederation to adopt the Ordinance of 1787 creating a government for the Territory and to authorize the sale of a large tract of land at the mouth of the Muskingum to the Ohio Company.

The lives covered by this book show that there is more to creating a state than drafting a legal document called a constitution. Much work had been done before the constitution was drafted to create a governmental structure for Ohio. The constitution and early statutes built on the structures developed during the Territorial period. Following adoption of the constitution, much more work needed to be done to create effective governmental institutions at the state and local level. Important fundamental issues would have to be settled. The relationship between the state courts and the legislature was one of them. The relationship between the federal courts and the legislature was another. Control of elections through an exclusive secret organization was another. Federal and state control over banking was another. The extent to which the government should finance internal improvements to promote the economy was another. By 1825 the state had reached the political and economic maturity to accomplish three major reforms. It adopted a tax system which provided an equitable and stable financial basis for the government. It launched the canal system which when completed allowed farmers to get their products to market and import trade goods at a reasonable price. It established a state school system to assure that all children of the state would have an opportunity for a basic education. Many of the key persons in the 1825 reforms were founding fathers and some had been political enemies at the time of Ohio statehood.

The biographies of the founding fathers are organized by the counties which existed at the time of the Constitutional Convention of 1802. All of these counties were organized before Ohio became a state and their area was far more extensive than it is today. The counties are presented in the order of their legal settlement.

The story of early settlement is also the story of how the land was sold by the government. Unlike later states in the Northwest Territory, Ohio was the laboratory where the federal government experimented with different ways of subdividing and selling land. Here the system was developed which would guide federal land sales throughout the rest of the United States. Several of the founding fathers were intimately involved with the development of that system.

Chapter 1

FOUNDING FATHERS FROM WASHINGTON COUNTY

The Ohio Company Purchase

British colonists in America united to fight a War to win their independence from Great Britain. Promises of land were made to the soldiers who fought that War. Creditors who financed the War expected payment. National leaders looked to the lands northwest of the Ohio River as the national treasure to pay for the War. They persuaded the states to give up their individual claims to these lands so that they could be used for this purpose. Treaties were made to clear the Indian claims to land in the east and southern part of Ohio. Survey of the Seven Ranges on the east side of the Territory began in 1785 and townships were put up for sale in New York, but the sale was not successful. The sale was aimed at investors not settlers, and the investors lacked confidence that the government under the Articles of Confederation had anything to sell.

In 1785 the land was occupied by Indians who considered this their traditional hunting grounds and white squatters who saw no reason to pay for what they could take for free. The fact that Great Britain had surrendered its claim to these lands to the United States meant nothing if Congress under the Articles of Confederation was unable or unwilling to exercise dominion over them. Dominion meant financing a military force sufficient to subdue the Indians and intimidate the squatters. It meant establishing and financing a government for the Territory with authority to adopt and enforce laws to protect the settlers and their property. It meant establishing a plan for subdividing and sale of the land which encouraged investment and settlement, and it meant establishing an efficient organization to execute the plan.

1

1787 was a big year for the United States of America and for the future State of Ohio. A convention was held in Philadelphia that year which resulted in the drafting of the Constitution which created a federal government that commanded sufficient respect and possessed enough power to govern not only the thirteen states but also the western lands. A federal government was created which had sufficient resources and power to exercise dominion over the western lands. While the convention was meeting in Philadelphia, the final Congress under the Articles of Confederation met in New York and adopted the Ordinance of 1787 which created a government for the Northwest Territory and appointed its initial officers, men of stature and proven leadership ability. That Congress also authorized sale of a large tract of land in the southeast part of the future state to a New England investor group known as the Ohio Company and the sale of a large tract in the southwest part of the future state to a New Jersey investor group headed by John Cleves Symmes.

The Ohio Company purchase grew out of the promise made by the Continental Congress on September 15, 1776 to award bounty lands to soldiers who signed up for three year enlistments in the Continental Army. At the time the promise was made the Continental Congress had no lands. However, primarily as a result of the efforts of George Rogers Clark and his men, at the end of the War, the Americans were able to claim the Northwest Territory by conquest and persuade Great Britain to relinquish its claim. At the time the British relinquished their claim, the Northwest Territory was inhabited by Indians who had been repeatedly assured by the British that there would be no white settlement northwest of the Ohio River. Although the war with the British ended in 1783, the war with the Indians continued intermittently with surreptitious British aid until Wayne's victory at Fallen Timbers in August, 1794. The War resumed with the outbreak of war with the British and their Indian allies in 1812 and was concluded with Harrison's victory over the British and their Indian allies at the Battle of the Thames the following year.

At the end of the Revolutionary War the continental army gathered at Newburgh on the Hudson for the purpose of demobilization. Before returning to their homes, the men wanted their back pay. Since there was no money to pay them, they were given interest bearing certificates to be redeemed at some future time. Because of lack of confidence in the federal government's ability to pay, the certificates sold for one sixth of their face value in coin. The officers at Newburgh presented a plan to Congress to buy a large tract from the Indians in the west, create a new state, and sell the lands to veterans in exchange for their warrants. The officers persuaded Rufus Putnam to enlist the support of George Washington for recommending the plan to Congress. Putnam argued that adoption of the plan would protect the West from England, France and

Spain by establishing an armed population of military veterans, establish the credit of the government by reducing the debt represented by warrants to veterans, increase the value of the adjoining government-owned land, and protect the eastern settlements from the western Indians. Notwithstanding Washington's strong endorsement, Congress took no action on the plan. It first had to persuade the states to relinquish their competing claims to the Northwest Territory.

While the Congress attempted to resolve the claims of the states to ownership of the West and to adopt a plan for its development, the people were headed west. Some Indian traders and outfitters in Pittsburgh estimated that there were 110,000 squatters west of the mountains. They operated under no government and wanted none. Americans were going to settle in the west, and if they could not get protection from the United States, they might very well seek it from the British, French or Spanish.[1] If the thirteen eastern states failed to act, they would lose the opportunity to use the western lands to pay off the debts of the Revolutionary War, and the great hope for a new nation could founder in an acrimonious bankruptcy and divorce.

When Congress in 1785 directed that the survey of the Seven Ranges begin in eastern Ohio, it directed that a surveyor be appointed by each state and that the appointed surveyors proceed with the survey under the direction of Thomas Hutchins, the National Geographer. Rufus Putnam was appointed as surveyor from Massachusetts, but because of a surveying commitment in eastern Massachusetts, now Maine, he declined and recommended his good friend Benjamin Tupper. Tupper met Hutchins and the rest of the surveyors and chain carriers at Fort Pitt. The party moved west and on September 22, 1785, they began running their base line west from the Pennsylvania line. The surveys continued until attacks by Indians persuaded the men to return to the Ohio River. Notwithstanding the trouble with the Indians, Tupper was excited by what he saw and returned back to Massachusetts where he shared his observations and enthusiasm with Rufus Putnam. The two of them decided to found a colony in the Oho Country. They announced in several Massachusetts newspapers their plan to form an association by the name of the Ohio Company. They invited officers and soldiers who had served in the War and were entitled to bounty lands as well as other citizens desiring to become adventurers to meet and appoint county representatives who would join them at the Bunch of Grapes Tavern in Boston on March 1, 1786, to formulate the

---

1   William Donahue Ellis, *The Ordinance of 1787, The Nation Begins*, Landfall Press, Dayton, 1987 p. 17.

plan for the company. At the meeting they adopted a plan to raise up to a million dollars to purchase land from the government. Most of the money would actually be in the form of bounty land warrants. After a year of attempting to secure investors, they concluded that a land purchase in the Seven Ranges would not be acceptable because they could not secure one large compact tract; therefore, they decided to approach Congress with a proposal to purchase a large tract outside the Seven Ranges.[2]

Manasseh Cutler was selected as the representative of the Company to negotiate a land deal with Congress and to persuade them to adopt legislation for the governance of the Territory. Educated as a lawyer, minister, physician, and scientist, Cutler served as a chaplain during the Revolutionary War. Like Benjamin Franklin he was a renaissance man and like Franklin he was polished, charming and skilled in the art of politics.[3] As a result of his efforts, Congress adopted the Ordinance of 1787 to govern the Territory. The Ordinance provided an orderly plan for the transition of the territory from a colonial government to states admitted to the union with equal stature to the existing states. It also assured that slavery would be prohibited. These were essential requirements for the Ohio Company purchasers. In retrospect, it is rather remarkable that the representatives of the thirteen existing states agreed to this future diminution of their power and influence and that the southern states approved the slavery prohibition. As in the case of the delegates to the convention at Philadelphia which subordinated the interests of individual states to a new federal government, the representatives in Congress meeting in New York must have recognized that this was the last chance to salvage the dream of a new nation for which so many had fought and died.

Cutler negotiated a contract for the Company to buy 1,500,000 acres at $1.00 per acre with a cost reduction of one third for bad land. This meant that the price was actually sixty-six cents per acre. However, since the Company was allowed to pay with bounty land warrants and government securities which traded at substantially less than face value, the price in specie was actually eight and a half cents per acre. $500,000 was paid down and the balance was to be paid when the survey was completed. The company also received for free two

---

2   William Donahue Ellis, *The Ordinance of 1787, The Nation Begins*, Landfall Press, Dayton, 1987 pp. 53-61.

3   William Donahue Ellis, *The Ordinance of 1787, The Nation Begins*, Landfall Press, Dayton, 1987 pp. 61-62, 74-75.

townships for a university and a section in each township for support of schools and a section for the ministry.[4]

Cutler ended up with a contract for 5,000,000 acres, of which 1,500,000 acres would be allocated to the Ohio Company and the remainder to other well-connected investors who Cutler astutely enlisted to increase his leverage with reluctant members of Congress. The organizer of the "other investors" was William Duer, who served as secretary of the Board of Treasury, with whom Cutler negotiated the details of the contract.[5] Investors who passed up the opportunity to purchase townships in the Seven Ranges suddenly became interested in investing in the Ohio country. They were convinced that the Revolutionary War officers that led the Ohio Company would succeed in developing a successful settlement. They also were attracted by the terms which the Ohio Company had negotiated with Congress, which were superior to the terms offered in the Seven Ranges. Cutler appealed to Congress to make good on its promise to Revolutionary War veterans, and a number of investors saw an opportunity to get a good deal by joining forces with him. They used their influence to persuade the Congressional representatives whose Cutler's appeal to patriotism had not touched.

Cutler also won important political support by endorsing Arthur Saint Clair, the presiding officer of the Congress, for the office of Governor of the Territory. Saint Clair, whose home was in western Pennsylvania, recognized the opportunity in the West and the opportunity that the Governorship presented to influence its development. The authority of the office was similar to that of a colonial governor under the British regime.

Notwithstanding Cutler's concession to Saint Clair, he did want the assurance that the Ohio Company would have an important influence in the Territorial government. He was successful in persuading Congress to appoint two Ohio Company representatives as officers of the Territory. Major Winthrop Sargent was appointed secretary of the Territory and General Samuel Holden Parsons was appointed one of three judges of the Territory.

The Ohio Company land was located southwest of the Seven Ranges and included the mouth of the Muskingum River. Putnam felt this land was safer from Indian attack than land which the Company also considered in the Scioto Valley.[6] The Indian villages which had previously been situated in the

---

4   R. Douglas Hurt, *The Ohio Frontier*, Indiana University Press, 1996, p. 157.

5   William Donahue Ellis, *The Ordinance of 1787, The Nation Begins*, Landfall Press, Dayton, 1987 pp. 96-97.

6   William Donahue Ellis, *The Ordinance of 1787, The Nation Begins*, Landfall Press, Dayton, 1987, p. 61.

Muskingum Valley were gone as a result of the warfare between the tribes and the frontiersmen of western Pennsylvania and Virginia during and following the Revolutionary War, therefore, the area of settlement was located far away from the Indian population. Federal troops had constructed Fort Harmar at the mouth of the Muskingum in 1785, and the men formerly stationed at Fort Steuben in the Seven Ranges were stationed there. This provided federal protection for the area. Finally, the Muskingum Valley included land which seemed far superior to the land which New England farmers used to make their living.

Following Cutler's successful purchase, the representatives of the Ohio Company quickly developed plans for settlement with all the organizational skills which could be expected of experienced military officers. An advance party was selected with the necessary expertise to begin construction of the first settlement and to commence surveying the tract which the Company had purchased. Rufus Putnam was appointed superintendent of the affairs of the company and led the party west. Crossing the mountains they constructed a boat thirty miles above Pittsburgh and floated down the Ohio to the mouth of the Muskingum where they landed on April 7, 1788.[7] A town was surveyed, and cabins and a stockade constructed. The first legal settlement of Ohio was begun.

The government of the Northwest Territory was inaugurated with great fanfare on July 15, 1788, with the arrival of Governor Saint Clair. In his remarks to the gathered villagers, Governor Saint Clair described the challenges which lay before them in converting "a country from a state of nature to a state of civilization." However, he also described the excitement which he and the others shared by stating, "the gradual progress of improvements fills the minds with delectable ideas; vast forests converted to arable fields, and cities rising in places which were lately the habitations of wild beasts, give a pleasure something like that attendant on creation; if we can form an idea of it, the imagination is ravished, and a taste communicated of even the 'joy of God to see a happy world.'[8]

A second settlement was laid out down the Ohio from Marietta and settled in April, 1789. It was named Belpre. Most of the early settlers of Belpre had been officers in the Revolution.[9] As more settlers arrived, new settlements were established up the Muskingum and its tributaries.

---

7   Joseph Barker, *Recollections of the First Settlement of Ohio*, Marietta College, 1958, p. 3.

8   William Henry Smith, *St. Clair Papers*, Vol. II, 1882, p. 55.

9   S. P. Hildreth, *Pioneer History*, Cincinnati, 1848, p.p. 349-351.

In October, 1790, four hundred Frenchmen arrived at Marietta, who had been sold land by the Scioto Company, William Duer's investment group. Duer contracted with Rufus Putnam to erect cabins for them in a village located in the Ohio Company purchase which they named Gallipolis. Duer's group failed to meet its obligations under its contract with the government, and therefore, it never acquired title to the land which it had sold to the French. Furthermore, these French were mostly from Paris and were totally unprepared for life in the Ohio wilderness. Nonetheless many stayed and adapted to life in their new country. The Ohio Company sold them land at Gallipolis upon favorable terms, and Congress in 1795 gave 24,000 acres in Scioto County to the inhabitants of Gallipolis who were swindled by the Scioto Company. Duer filed bankruptcy and Putnam was never paid for erecting the cabins for the French settlers.[10]

On January 2, 1791, Indian hostility which had been simmering flared into open warfare when the Big Bottom settlement thirty miles north of Marietta was attacked. Most of the settlers were killed and their cabins burned.[11] Marietta was protected by Campus Martius, a fortification erected soon after the settlers arrived. At Belpre blockhouses were constructed and connected by palisades which the settlers named Farmers Castle.[12] Similar fortifications were constructed at other settlements. The settlers tended their field in parties with armed guards. Rangers were employed by the Company to patrol the area to detect signs of Indians approaching the settlements. Although most of the settlers survived, further extension of settlement in the Ohio Company purchase was suspended until the Indians were defeated at the Battle of Fallen Timbers in August, 1794, and the Treaty of Greenville signed in 1795.

The Ohio Company was unable to make its second payment to the government under its contract due to loss of company funds resulting from the bankruptcy of its treasurer and the expenses it incurred in defending the settlements from the Indians. Congress approved a renegotiation of the contract which gave the Company title to 964,285 acres instead of the 1,500,000 acres originally bargained for. In addition Congress gave them an additional 100,000 acres to be given free of charge in 100 acre lots to persons who would actually settle on the land. This was called the Donation Tract and was

---

10   S. P. Hildreth, *Pioneer History*, Cincinnati, 1848, p.p. 3271-272.
11   Beverly W. Bond, Jr., *The History of Ohio, The Foundations of Ohio*, Ohio Historical Society, Vol. I, p. 288.
12   S. P. Hildreth, *Pioneer History*, Cincinnati, 1848, p.p. 361-365.

intended to ease the impact of the Indian War by encouraging young men to join and help defend the settlement.[13]

Unlike other areas of settlement in the Ohio country, the development of Marietta and the Ohio country was tightly controlled by its leadership to protect the settlers from Indian attack and to assure that communities were developed in accordance with the founders' vision of a civilized community. Unlike other frontier towns that had a "wild west "character to them, Marietta was a New England town in the middle of the wilderness. Although there were deaths and injuries from Indian attacks, the settlers for the most part survived the War intact. Religion and education were attended to, and when hardship came in the form of hunger, disease, and Indian threats, it was dealt with in an organized manner which shared and minimized the pain. Although the quality of life may have been better in the settlements in the Ohio Company tract, the hierarchical, structured New England communities created by the Ohio Company were not attractive to many of the individualistic, egalitarian settlers streaming into the Ohio country. As a result of this and the availability of better land elsewhere, the settlement of this area did not keep pace with other newer areas of the Territory.[14]

Washington County

Washington County was established by Governor Saint Clair on July 27, 1788, as the first county in the Northwest Territory. It originally included all land in Ohio east of the Scioto River, North of the Ohio, and south of the Greenville Treaty Line and Lake Erie east of the Cuyahoga River.[15] By the time of the constitutional convention, Jefferson, Trumbull, and Fairfield had been taken from it and part had been attached to Hamilton and Adams. After the county was created by Governor Saint Clair, the leaders of the Ohio Company settlement were appointed the officials of the county and Marietta served as its

---

13   S. P. Hildreth, *Pioneer History*, Cincinnati, 1848, p.p. 305-307.

14   Andrew R. L. Cayton, *The Frontier Republic*, Kent State University Press, 1986, pp. 25-32.

15   Richard C. Knopf, *Transcription of the Executive Journal of the Northwest Territory*, Ohio Historical Society web page, pp. 27-28; Randolph C. Downes, *Evolution of Ohio County Boundaries*, Ohio Historical Society, 1970, pp. 5-10.

county seat. After statehood, Gallia, Columbiana, Muskingum, Athens, Monroe, Perry, Morgan, and Noble Counties were taken from it.[16]

Under the governmental structure of the Northwest Territory, the Governor appointed county officials. These included justices of the peace, judges of a Court of General Quarter Sessions, judges of the court of common please, a probate judge, a clerk for each of the courts, sheriff, and recorder. Justices of the Peace were responsible for maintaining the peace and hearing charges of petty offenses. The Court of General Quarter Sessions which included all of the Justices of the Peace had administrative responsibilities like county commissioners which included supervising local taxation, laying out roads, establishing township boundaries, and appointing township officials.[17] The Common Pleas Court heard more serious criminal and civil cases, and the Probate judge handled estates and guardianships. The Clerk kept the records of the court. The Sheriff served summons, subpoenas, orders, and warrants for the Courts and enforced the court's orders. The Recorder made a record of real estate transactions. In many cases, including Washington, the same persons held more than one office. Each county had its own militia and the Governor appointed its officers.

Washington County Delegates

RUFUS PUTNAM

Rufus Putnam was born April 9, 1738, in Sutton, Massachusetts. He was the great, great grandson of John Putnam of Wingrove, Rockinghamshire, Bucks Co., England, who immigrated with his wife Priscilla and children in 1634 and settled in Salem, Massachusetts. Rufus' father died when he was seven, and Rufus went to live with his grandparents where he attended school for two years. When his mother married Captain John Sadler, an Innkeeper in Sutton, Rufus moved into the Inn with his stepfather where he was put to work serving the customers. When he was sixteen, Rufus was bound out to a millwright. He taught himself mathematics and geography.

---

16   Randolph C. Downes, *Evolution of Ohio County Boundaries*, Ohio Historical Society, 1970, pp. 138-139.

17   Andrew R. L. Cayton, *The Frontier Republic*, Kent State University Press, 1986, pp. 27-28.

In March, 1757 at the age of nineteen he enlisted in the British Army and served in the French and Indian War as a ranger under his cousin Israel Putnam scouting for Indians around Fort Edward and Fort George.[18] He was at Fort William Henry when it was captured by the French and Indians under General Montcalm and returned home in February, 1758. He reenlisted later that year and joined General Abercrombie's campaign around Fort George. After returning home later that year, he reenlisted in the spring of 1759 and joined General Amherst's successful capture of Fort Ticonderoga. Returning home, he reenlisted a fourth time in the spring of 1760 serving at the outlet of Lake George until the end of the war. He became skilled in Indian warfare and acquired some knowledge of constructing fortifications. By the end of the war he attained the rank of ensign.[19]

After returning to New Braintree, in April, 1761 he married Elizabeth Ayers, but within a year both she and their child died. Four years later he married Persis Rice, his companion for more than fifty years.[20]

Between the French and Indian War and the outbreak of the Revolution, Putnam pursued mill construction, farming, and surveying. He joined an expedition of New Englanders sent to survey land for land grants to veterans in West Florida. They traveled by boat from New York around the coast of Florida to the mouth of the Mississippi and up that River a distance. Although the venture did not achieve its goal, Putnam learned about the Gulf of Mexico, the Mississippi River, and the West's potential trade with the West Indies and the east coast by way of river boat down the Ohio and Mississippi.[21]

After the battles at Lexington and Concord sparked the Revolution, Putnam enlisted as a lieutenant colonel in Colonel David Brewer's regiment at Roxbury, Massachusetts. He was assigned the job of fortifying Roxbury and areas nearby. After General Washington arrived to take command of the continental forces surrounding Boston, he viewed Putnam's work and was pleased. He assigned Putnam the job of fortifying Dorchester Heights overlooking Boston. The British were so impressed by the fortifications and the speed with which they were erected, they decided to leave Boston. He was next called upon to plan the fortifications for New York City, and on August 11, 1776, Washington appointed him Chief Engineer of the Continental Army with the

---

18   William Donahue Ellis, *The Ordinance of 1787*, Landfall Press, 1987, p. 34.

19   E.C. Randall, "Rutland: The Cradle of Ohio", *Ohio History* Vol.18, pp. 59-61.

20   E.C. Randall, "Rutland: The Cradle of Ohio", Ohio History Vol.18, pp. 61.

21   E.C. Randall, "Rutland: The Cradle of Ohio", *Ohio History* Vol.18, pp. 61-62.

rank of Colonel. During Washington's retreat from New York, he was responsible for fortifications at Washington's rear. In December, 1776, he resigned his position in Washington's army and became a colonel of a Massachusetts regiment serving in General Gates army and participated in the defeat of Burgoyne at Saratoga in October, 1777. In 1778 he was responsible for fortifying West Point and constructing nearby forts on the Hudson. He commanded a regiment in Anthony Wayne's brigade and participated in the battle at Stony Point and other battles during Wayne's campaign. On January 8, 1783, Putnam was made a brigadier general.[22]

Putnam was one of Washington's most trusted officers. When the officers at Newburgh developed a plan for erection of a new state in the west to satisfy the claims of war veterans, they enlisted Putnam to present the plan to Washington for his endorsement. Putnam prepared a summary of arguments for the plan. It would protect the west from England, France, and Spain by establishing a settlement of armed veterans. It would strengthen the credit of the government by satisfying the veterans' claims for land. Adjacent government land would become more valuable and generate cash for the government. It would create a protective barrier of armed veterans between the Indians and the eastern population centers. Although Washington strongly endorsed the plan, Congress was not ready to entertain it because of competing claims of states to the Ohio country.[23]

During the years he lived in Rutland, Putnam served as representative to the General Court, selectman, constable, tax collector, and member of a committee to lay out school lands and make repairs to the school building. He was also an Indian commissioner, and a founder and trustee of Leicester Academy. He served as a volunteer to put down Shay's rebellion.[24]

Following the War, Putnam was employed by the State of Massachusetts to survey its eastern province, which would subsequently become the State of Maine. Although chosen to join Hutchinson in his survey of the Seven Ranges in eastern Ohio, Putnam declined because of his commitment to complete his contract with Massachusetts. He recommended his good friend Colonel Benjamin Tupper.[25]

When the survey of the Seven Ranges was suspended by Hutchinson due to Indian troubles, Tupper returned to Massachusetts, arriving at Putnam's house

---

22   E.C. Randall, "Rutland: The Cradle of Ohio", *Ohio History* Vol.18, pp. 64-66.
23   William Donahue Ellis, *The Ordinance of 1787*, Landfall Press, 1987, pp. 37-38.
24   Martin A. Andrews, *History of Marietta and Washington County*, 1902, p. 865.
25   William Donahue Ellis, *The Ordinance of 1787*, Landfall Press, 1987, pp. 54-55.

in Rutland on January 9, 1786. After comparing their observations on the lands in Maine and the Ohio country and deciding that Ohio lands were far superior in quality to any known by New England farmers, they decided to organize a company to establish a settlement in the Ohio country. The company would build on the Newburgh plan proposed to Congress at the end of The Revolutionary War by providing veterans an opportunity to exchange their warrants for land in the west. The Ohio Company was organized and Manasseh Cutler was sent to Congress to negotiate a contract.[26] When Cutler returned to Massachusetts with the contract, planning and preparations began for the first settlement. Rufus Putnam was appointed superintendent of the venture. He led the men and supplies across the snow covered mountains to the Youghiogheny River where they built two large flat boats and three large canoes. With the melting of the snow, the party launched their boats and floated down the Youghiogheny to the Mongahela and down the Mongahela to the Ohio and down the Ohio to the Muskingum River, arriving at Fort Harmar on April 7, 1788.[27] Fort Harmar had been established in October, 1785 by Lieutenant Colonel Josiah Harmar whose task was to protect government surveyors, preserve the peace with the Indians, and keep squatters off of the government's land. The location of the fort across the Muskingum from the proposed site for their settlement was no doubt comforting to Putnam's party.

Putnam immediately set to work laying out and establishing Marietta, the first permanent settlement in the Northwest Territory. Trees were cleared and corn planted, cabins erected, and a garrison begun to provide refuge in case of Indian attack. Unlike later settlements up and down the river, Marietta was planned and built with all the organization, common sense and attention to detail that had characterized Putnam's military service. This was not a rag tag group of disorganized settlers, each motivated exclusively by self-interest. The creation of this settlement was organized like a military operation with assignment of individual responsibilities for the good of the community.

Governor Arthur Saint Clair arrived in July, 1788, and government for the Territory began. Just a few cabins in a small clearing in an endless wilderness, Marietta was the first evidence that American civilization was here to stay. Saint Clair created Washington County as the first county in the Territory on July 27, 1788. Recognizing his leadership of the community, Saint Clair appointed Putnam a justice of the peace and judge of the Court of General

---

26   Major E. C. Dawes, "The Beginning of the Ohio Company and the Scioto Purchase", *Ohio History*, Vol. IV, pp. 1-13.

27   William Donahue Ellis, *The Ordinance of 1787*, Landfall Press, 1987, pp. 57-61.

Quarter Sessions and also a judge of the Court of Common Pleas and the probate judge of the newly created County. In 1790 Putnam resigned as a county judge when he was appointed by President Washington as one of the three Territorial Judges, replacing Judge Parsons who had died. In 1796, Washington appointed his old friend Putnam Surveyor General of the United States. Throughout the Washington and Adams administrations, Putnam was a principal spokesman for the Federal government in Ohio and a principal advocate to those administrations for the Territory's needs. His judgment was respected and his opinion was sought on appointments to federal offices in the Territory. Putnam also served as the unchallenged, political leader of Marietta and Washington County throughout the Territorial period.[28]

Shortly after Marietta was established, war broke out with the Indians and continued until Wayne's victory at the Battle of Fallen Timbers in 1794. Putnam's military experience was important in planning the defense of Marietta and nearby settlements during the Indian War. His influence and advocacy with Washington and other members of his administration was important in winning the commitment of sufficient military force to defeat the Indians. Putnam was commissioned Brigadier General in the United States Army on May 4, 1792, and was appointed by President Washington as the government's commissioner to negotiate a treaty with the Indians on the Wabash River. On September 27, 1792, he successfully negotiated a Treaty at Vincennes with eight tribes in that area. The treaty kept these western tribes from joining with the Miami and Shawnee who were attacking the settlers in the Northwest Territory. Following the Treaty a group of chiefs was entertained at Campus Martius in Marietta on their way to a visit with the President at Philadelphia.[29]

From 1796 to 1803 Putnam served as Surveyor General of the United States. As Surveyor General he was responsible for government surveys in Ohio and the rest of the Northwest Territory. He developed and instituted the contract method of surveying which was followed for the next 110 years. Because surveying of the public lands was a big business in Ohio and Putnam controlled who received the work, his influence extended beyond the Ohio Company settlements. Many of the techniques and procedures he developed and improved were passed along to his successors.[30]

---

28   Andrew R. L. Cayton, *The Frontier Republic*, Kent State University Press, 1986, pp. 27-28, 31-50.

29   S. P. Hildreth, *Pioneer History*, Cincinnati, 1848, pp. 306-309.

30   Norman C. Caldwell, "Surveyor General Rufus Putnam", *Backsights Magazine*, Surveyors Historical Society.

Putnam's position as Surveyor General of the United States did not diminish his responsibility for leadership of the community. From 1801 to 1803 he served as chairman of the Town Meeting at Marietta.

Putnam was one of the leading advocates of Saint Clair's plan to divide the Territory at the Scioto River in order to postpone statehood and ensure that Marietta would be the capital of the first state admitted from the Territory. A leading Federalist, he believed that the territory was not ready for state government. The partnership between Marietta and the Federal government had been good for Marietta and for Putnam personally. From his perspective, the Virginians of the Scioto Valley leading the statehood movement were simply trying to advance their personal interests by increasing the value of their extensive land holdings around Chillicothe and securing lucrative offices in the new state government.

When Congress passed the Enabling Act calling for an election of delegates to a state convention to decide the question of statehood and adopt a constitution, Putnam and his Federalist allies held a county convention to select a slate of Federalist delegates. Although there was opposition from Washington County Republicans led by Meigs and Greene, the Federalist slate led by Putnam was elected as the county's delegates to the convention. After the results of the statewide election were announced, the Washington County delegates recognized that the Republicans had the votes for statehood. In order to increase their influence in the deliberations, Putnam and the other Washington County delegates, except Cutler, joined with the Republicans in voting for statehood. Putnam served on the committees appointed to draft article one on the legislature, article two on the executive, and article three on the judiciary. These were the three most important committees. He also served on the committees to draft an article on the militia and to consider the proposals made by Congress as a condition of admission to statehood.[31] Putnam voted for granting full civil rights to Negroes.[32]

Following the adoption of the constitution, elections were held for officers of the new state government. Republicans were triumphant throughout the state including Washington County. This represented a revolution in the county which overturned the political organization which had controlled the

---

31   "Journal of Convention", *Ohio Archaeological and Historical Society Publications*, Vol. V, pp. 88, 92, 93, 96, 101.

32   Helen M. Thurston, "The 1802 Constitutional Convention and the Status of the Negro", *Ohio History*, Vol. 81, p. 27.

county since its first settlement. In September, 1803, President Jefferson replaced Putnam as Surveyor General of the United States, and he retired from active politics.[33]

Although Rufus Putnam had little if any formal education himself, in 1797 he was one of the founders of the Muskingum Academy, a Greek and Latin School, which eventually became Marietta College.[34] He was also instrumental in the establishment of the Ohio University at Athens, the first college or university in the Northwest Territory. The contract of purchase between the Ohio Company and the government had provided that the government would give two townships for a university to be used in such manner as the future state would direct. In 1795, after the conclusion of the Indian war, Putnam led a party of surveyors to select the two townships. In 1799 he wrote to Manasseh Cutler seeking his assistance in drafting a charter for the university. After securing authorization from the first territorial legislature, he located and prepared a plat for the campus and for the town of Athens which was approved by the legislature in 1800. In the last session of the territorial legislature held in 1802, an act was passed establishing the university and its first board of trustees which included Rufus Putnam and other leaders of Washington County. Following statehood, the General Assembly in 1804 passed an act reestablishing the university and changing its name from American Western University to Ohio University. The Act included on the board of trustees Putnam as well as Governor Tiffin and Nathaniel Massie of Chillicothe, Bezaleel Wells of Steubenville, Joseph Darlinton of Adams County, Samuel Carpenter of Fairfield County, and Daniel Symmes of Hamilton County, all of whom are the subjects of biographies or mention in this book. Putnam served on the building committee and the committee to establish the first rules for the university. He recruited the first president. The university opened in 1808. In 1812 Putnam was given responsibility for the plans for a college building, and he hired an architect in Marietta to design it. He contributed the first $200 toward its construction. The building was completed in 1818. It has been restored and is now known as Cutler Hall on Ohio University's campus. Putnam served on the board for the remainder of his life.[35]

---

33   Andrew R. L. Cayton, *The Frontier Republic*, Kent State University Press, 1986, pp. 78-79.

34   Wayne Jordan, "Marietta College and the Ohio Company", *Ohio History*, Vol. 44, pp. 290-292; Martin A. Andrews, *History of Marietta and Washington County, Ohio*, 1902, p. 199.

35   Thomas Hoover, "The Beginnings of Higher Education in the Northwest Territory", *Ohio History*, Vol. 50, pp. 244-260.

Putnam believed in the future of Ohio and his investments showed it. In 1810 he owned 33 tracts of land totaling 3,120 acres.[36]

Putnam organized the Marietta Bible Society on October 22, 1812, and served as its first president.[37] The purpose was to raise funds to purchase Bibles for the poor. Manasseh Cutler had organized a Bible Society at Salem, Massachusetts in 1810 and another at Philadelphia a few years later which no doubt served as the inspiration for this effort.[38]

During his later years, Putnam lived with his daughter Elizabeth in Marietta. He died on May 4, 1824, at the age of 86.

Putnam's house at Marietta has been restored and preserved as part of the Campus Martius Museum operated by the Ohio Historical Society. The house which he owned before he came to Ohio is preserved as the General Rufus Putnam House, a bed and breakfast at Rutland, Massachusetts.

According to Henry Howe, "General Putnam was a man of strong, good sense, modest, benevolent, and scrupulous to fulfill the duties which he owed to God and man. In person, he was tall, of commanding appearance, and possessed a frame imminently fitted for the hardships and trials of war. His mind, though not brilliant, was solid, penetrating, and comprehensive, seldom erring in conclusions."[39]

EPHRAIM CUTLER

Ephraim Cutler was born April 13, 1767, in Edgartown, Massachusetts, the eldest son of Rev. Manasseh Cutler. His father had represented The Ohio Company in its successful negotiations with Congress for the Ohio Company tract. The Cutlers were descended from James Cutler of Norfolkshire, England who settled in Watertown, Massachusetts in 1634.[40] Ephraim was raised by his

---

36   Lee Soltow, "Inequality Amidst Abundance: Land Ownership in Early 19th Century Ohio", *Ohio History*, Vol. 88, p. 151.

37   Martin A. Andrews, *History of Marietta and Washington County, Ohio*, 1902, p. 199.

38   William Parker Cutler and Julia Perkins Cutler, *Life, Journals and Correspondence of Rev. Manasseh Cutler, L.L.D.*, Ohio University Press, Vol II, p. 320-321.

39   Henry Howe, *Historical Collections of Ohio*, Centennial Edition, 1908, Vol. II, p. 807.

40   William Parker Cutler and Julia Perkins Cutler, *Life Journals and Correspondence of Rev. Manasseh Cutler, L.L.D.*, Ohio University Press, Athens, Ohio, Vol 1, p. 1.

grandfather Hezekiah Cutler on the family farm at Killingly, Connecticut. He married Leah Attwood on April 13, 1787. Cutler and his family left Killingly for Marietta on June 15, 1795, and arrived at Marietta on September 18. Two of his children died during the trip.[41]

He initially settled at Waterford on the Muskingum where he kept a store. He then moved to land which he had purchased in Ames Township in what is now Athens County. He was the second settler in that township.[42] He cleared a farm and constructed a mill. While in Ames Township, he participated in the organization of the Western Library Association in 1803, the first public library in the Northwest Territory. The residents of the township agreed to raise money through the sale of furs to be used for the purchase of books. Cutler accompanied Samuel Brown to Boston where he purchased 51 books. This was the beginning of the collection which later was known as the "Coonskin Library."[43] He was elected to the offices of Overseer of the Poor and Township Trustee while living in Ames Township.[44] In 1806 he moved his family to Constitution, a village located on the Ohio River six miles below Marietta where he lived the remainder of his life.[45]

On September 9, 1800, Governor Saint Clair appointed Cutler a major in the Washington County militia.[46] He also served as a justice of the peace and judge of the court of quarter sessions and judge of the court of common pleas during the Territorial period.[47]

Cutler was elected as a representative from Washington County to the second territorial legislature which met from November 23, 1801 to January 23, 1802, at Chillicothe.[48] He participated in the enactment of the proposal to Congress to divide the Territory at the Scioto and the measure changing the seat of government from Chillicothe to Cincinnati, which resulted in a riotous protest by the townspeople of Chillciothe.

---

41   Henry Howe, *Historical Collections of Ohio*, Centennial Edition, 1908, Vol. II, p. 811.

42   *History of Hocking Valley, Ohio*, Interstate Publishing Co., 1883, p. 494.

43   *History of Hocking Valley, Ohio*, Interstate Publishing Co., 1883, p. 499-500.

44   *History of Hocking Valley, Ohio*, Interstate Publishing Co., 1883, p. 503.

45   Henry Howe, *Historical Collections of Ohio*, Centennial Edition, 1908, Vol. II, pp. 811-812.

46   Richard C. Knopf, *Transcription of the Executive Journal of the Northwest Territory*, Ohio Historical Society webpage, p. 541.

47   Martin A. Andrews, *History of Marietta and Washington County, Ohio*, 1902, p. 885.

48   William A. Taylor, *Ohio Statesmen and Annals of Progress*, State of Ohio, 1899, pp. 18-19.

Elected as a delegate to the convention as a Federalist, Cutler was the only delegate to vote against the formation of a state government and adoption of a constitution.[49] Unlike the other Federalist delegates, Cutler voted his conscience and refused to bow to political expediency in order to increase his influence in the drafting of the constitution. He served on the committee appointed to draft the bill of rights.[50] His father had insisted that The Ordinance of 1787 include a bill of rights and that it include a prohibition against slavery. Cutler's votes showed him to be strongly antislavery and a supporter of full civil rights for Negroes, and he no doubt was a strong advocate on these issues.[51]

It was later claimed that Cutler was responsible for the provision of the Constitution which prohibited slavery by casting a tie breaking vote. There is even a lake in Washington County called "Veto Lake" which supposedly commemorates his vote. However, the journal of the convention shows that there never was a close vote on the question of slavery. There was a close vote denying Negroes the right to vote with Edward Tiffin casting the tie breaking vote. There was also a close vote removing a provision which would have denied Negroes the right to hold office and other civil rights. This clause was removed as a result of John Milligan of Steubenville changing his earlier vote supporting the provision. In his biography, Cutler explains his role as follows: "I went to the convention and moved to strike out the obnoxious matter and made my objections as forcible I was able. Mr. McIntyre was absent that day, so there would be a tie unless we could bring over one more. Mr. Milligan had in the territorial legislature spoken against slavery, but in the convention had voted with the Virginia party. In the course of my remarks I happened to catch his eye, and the very language he had used in debating the question occurred to me. I put it to him, and when the vote was called, Mr. Milligan changed his vote, and we succeeded in placing the section in its original form. It cost me every effort I was capable of making, and it passed by a majority of one vote only."[52] Cutler's effort kept out of the constitution a provision which would certainly have been an embarrassment to later generations of Ohioans, but it did not prevent the legislature of the new state from promptly enacting laws restricting the civil rights of Negroes.[53]

---

49   "Journal of Convention", *Ohio History*, Vol. V, p. 88.

50   "Journal of Convention", *Ohio History*, Vol. V, p. 90.

51   Helen M. Thurston, "The 1802 Constitutional Convention and the Status of the Negro", *Ohio History*, Vol. 81, pp. 25, 27.

52   Cutler, *Life and Time of Ephraim Cutler*, 1890, pp. 75-77.

53   *Journal of the Ohio House of Representatives*, Second Session 1803-1804, pp. 37-38.

Cutler also played an important role at the convention in advocating inclusion of a clause providing that "schools and the means of instruction shall forever be encouraged by legislative provision."[54] In so doing he was following in the footsteps of his father who had strongly advocated support of education when the Ohio Company purchase was being negotiated.

Following the electoral triumph of the Republicans following statehood, Cutler's public responsibilities were suspended for a number of years. However, in 1819 Cutler was elected to the Ohio House of Representatives and served in the 1819-1820 session of the legislature.[55] He introduced a bill in the House which provided for the establishment of a system of common schools throughout the State. It passed the House but failed to pass the Senate.[56] However, his effort led to the passage of the first School Act for Ohio passed in January, 1821, which was largely ineffective because it left establishment of schools up to each township.[57] Cutler was reelected to the House for the 1822-1823 session and was appointed by the Governor to serve on a committee to devise a system of common schools.[58] He was elected to the Ohio Senate in 1823 and served during the 1823-1824 and 1824-1825 sessions. Following the report of the Schools Committee, an alliance was formed between those advocating state support for the schools and those advocating state support for a canal system. The School Act of 1825 was passed which provided for support of the schools through taxation for the first time.[59] This was also the session which launched the construction of the state canal system. Cutler not only contributed to the enactment of the first School Act, he also was instrumental in establishment of a new system of taxation which provided the financial basis for the schools and the canal system.[60] Under the new system taxation

---

54   Ohio Constitution of 1802, Article VIII, Section 3.

55   William A. Taylor, *Ohio Statesmen and Annals of Progress*, State of Ohio, 1899, p. 95.

56   Edward A. Miller, "History of Educational Legislation in Ohio from 1803 to 1850", *Ohio History*, Vol. 27, p. 14.

57   Edward A. Miller, "History of Educational Legislation in Ohio from 1803 to 1850", *Ohio History*, Vol. 27, p. 14.

58   William A. Taylor, *Ohio Statesmen and Annals of Progress*, State of Ohio, 1899, pp. 111-112.

59   Edward A. Miller, "History of Educational Legislation in Ohio from 1803 to 1850", *Ohio History*, Vol. 27, p. 17; Andrew R. L. Cayton, *The Frontier Republic*, Kent State University Press, 1986, p. 146.

60   Andrew R. L. Cayton, *The Frontier Republic*, Kent State University Press, 1986, p. 146.

was based on the value of property. Prior to the ad valorem tax system, taxation was based on a specified amount per acre or town lot, although land was placed in one of three classes depending upon a judgment as to its quality.[61]

Cutler also helped to organize and participated in the "Underground Railroad." This was a secret alliance of people opposing slavery which assisted escaped slaves travel northward across Ohio to Canada where slavery had been abolished. It was secret because Congress had passed a law requiring northern states to assist in recapturing fugitive slaves.[62]

Manasseh Cutler negotiated with Congress to have two townships donated for the purpose of establishing a university.[63] He considered it one of his most important achievements. His son Ephraim served on the Board of Trustees of the Ohio University from 1820 until his death. When Rufus Putnam left the Board, he assumed responsibility for assuring the success of the University.

Cutler was active in buying and selling land and in 1810 he owned 19 tracts totaling 2,498 acres.[64] Always a promoter of new projects to further economic development, he was supporter of the canals, roads, and railroads. In 1837 and 1839 he visited Baltimore for the purpose of advocating extension of a railroad to Marietta.[65] Successfully securing a post office for the Village of Constitution, he was appointed as its first postmaster and operated it from his house from 1842-1853.[66]

In 1828 he joined the Presbyterian Church at Warren shortly after it was organized and became an elder of the church. He was a member of the General Assembly in Pittsburgh in 1836 and at Philadelphia in 1837, where he witnessed the separation of the church into the "Old School" and "New School."[67] The division ended the Plan of Union adopted in 1801 under which the Congregationalist Churches of New England united with the Presbyterians to establish new churches in the West.

---

61   Caleb Atwater, *History of the State of Ohio*, Cincinnati, 1838, pp. 253-262.

62   Wilbur Henry Siebert, *Mysteries of Ohio's Underground Railroad*, Long's College Book Store, 1951, p. 119; Henry Robert Burke, "Judge Ephraim Cutler and Constitution" web page

63   William Parker Cutler and Julia Perkins Cutler, *Life, Journals and Correspondence of Rev. Manasseh Cutler, L.L.D.*, Ohio University Press, Vol II, pp. 321-322.

64   Lee Soltow, "Inequality Amidst Abundance: Land Ownership in Early 19th Century Ohio", *Ohio History*, Vol. 88, p. 151.

65   Martin A. Andrews, *History of Marietta and Washington County, Ohio*, 1902, p. 889.

66   Henry Robert Burke, "Judge Ephraim Cutler and Constitution", web page

67   Martin A. Andrews, *History of Marietta and Washington County, Ohio*, 1902, p. 889.

Cutler died July 8, 1853, at the age of 86. The County History states, "He was one of the busy workers, who at the right time and in their appointed sphere 'dug deep and laid broad the foundations of many generations.' Such labors may not be heeded, may even be desecrated and destroyed—but history must make their record 'well done.'

BENJAMIN IVES GILMAN

Benjamin Ives Gilman was born July 29, 1766, in Exeter on the coast of New Hampshire. He received his education at the Phillips-Exeter Academy. The Gilmans were a prominent family in Exeter and had produced several leaders of the community and state.[68] Benjamin came to Marietta in 1789 with his parents Joseph and Rebecca Ives Gilman. He returned to New Hampshire in 1790 to marry Hannah Robbins and then returned to Marietta with his bride.

Joseph Gilman had served as a member and chairman of the Committee of Public Safety and Correspondence during the Revolution and his home on the square in Exeter had frequently served as the meeting place for the leaders of the Revolution in New Hampshire. He was a merchant and had advanced most of his funds to pay for supplies for the state's troops. He received in exchange continental currency and promises to pay which depreciated in value resulting in his financial ruin. His reputation remained in intact and prior to departing for Marietta, he had served as Auditor of the State of New Hampshire. He responded to Putnam's call and became an associate of the Ohio Company.[69]

During the Indian War the Gilmans lived in a blockhouse above Fort Harmar.[70] While Benjamin was erecting a rail fence near the fort, a man working with him was shot by Indians who then pursued Gilman. He was swift of foot and outran them, or he also may have been killed.[71]

Recognizing that Joseph was a man of character and considerable experience, Governor Saint Clair appointed him as a justice of the peace and judge of the general court of quarter sessions and judge of the court of common pleas

---

68   Archer Butler Hulbert, *Records of the Ohio Company*, Marietta Historical Commission, 1917, Vol II, p. 59; "The Gilman Family," SeacoastNH web page

69   Archer Butler Hulbert, *Records of the Ohio Company*, Marietta Historical Commission, 1917, Vol I, p. 117; Joseph Barker, *Recollections of the First Settlement of Ohio*, Marietta College, 1958, p. 28; "The Gilman Family", SeacoastNH web page

70   S. P. Hildreth, *Pioneer History*, Cincinnati, 1848, p. 321.

71   S. P. Hildreth, *Pioneer History*, Cincinnati, 1848, pp. 340-341.

and probate judge.[72] The President appointed him as one of the three territorial judges in 1796 when Rufus Putnam resigned to accept the appointment as Surveyor General. He was Putnam's first recommendation for the position.[73] He served in this position until Ohio became a state.

Benjamin Ives Gilman established a store at Fort Harmar and became one of the leading merchants of the area. He also engaged in building ships for transport of freight and passengers down the Ohio and Mississippi. He was also one of Marietta's most active land speculators.[74]

Benjamin Gilman served as clerk of the courts of Washington County from 1795 to July, 1803.[75] As such he was responsible for the records of the court.

Gilman was elected as a Federalist delegate to the convention and he cast his votes with the other Federalists. He served with Rufus Putnam on the committees to draft article one on the legislature, article two on the executive and article three on the judiciary. He also served on the committee to draft article six on county officers.[76] He voted against slavery and he voted for giving suffrage and other civil rights to Negroes.[77]

Gilman was nominated by some of the Federalists for Governor, but he did not campaign. Most Federalists did not vote for Governor.[78] Gilman was deeply disappointed in the Republican sweep in the elections following the adoption of the Constitution. Although his name was offered in opposition to

---

72   Joseph Barker, *Recollections of the First Settlement of Ohio*, Marietta College, 1958, pp. 55, 56; Richard C. Knopf, *Transcription of the Executive Journal of the Northwest Territory*, Ohio Historical Society web page p. 370; Martin A. Andrews, *History of Marietta and Washington County, Ohio*, 1902, p. 431.

73   Andrew R. L. Cayton, *The Frontier Republic*, Kent State University Press, 1986, p. 49.

74   Kim M. Gruenwald, "Marietta's Example of a Settlement Pattern in the Ohio Country: A Reinterpretation", *Ohio History*, Vol. 105, p. 135; Joseph Barker, *Recollections of the First Settlement of Ohio*, Marietta College, 1958, pp. 28, 43; S. P. Hildreth, *Pioneer History*, Cincinnati, 1848, p. 321.

75   Martin A. Andrews, *History of Marietta and Washington County, Ohio*, 1902, p. 431.

76   "Journal of Convention", *Ohio History*, Vol. V, pp. 92, 93, 96.

77   Helen M. Thurston, "The 1802 Constitutional Convention and the Status of the Negro", Ohio History, Vol. 81, p. 27.

78   Alfred Byron Sears, *Thomas Worthington, Father of Ohio Statehood*, Ohio State University Press, 1958, p. 109.

Tiffin for Governor, Tiffin was elected unanimously.[79] In a letter dated February 14, 1803, he stated, "I am completely disgusted with the politics of the times; and confess that I have little expectation of any alteration for the better."[80]

Gilman's ambition for public office was frustrated by the Republican triumph. His investment in ship building for trade up and down the Ohio and Mississippi and in the Caribbean was destroyed by Jefferson's embargo of trade with Britain. In 1810 he was listed as the owner of 127 tracts totaling 22,128 acres, the most extensive holdings of any delegate to the convention.[81] The War of 1812, which Federalists bitterly opposed, severely diminished the value of land in the Ohio country and the ability of his buyers and tenants to make their payments. By 1813 his faith in the promise of the west was gone, and he moved to Philadelphia where be became a merchant and lived until his death in 1833. He was the only delegate to the convention to return to the east.[82]

JOHN MCINTIRE

John McIntire was born October 15, 1759, at Alexandria, Virginia. When he was thirty, he departed for the West and arrived in Wheeling with his cobbler's tools on his back. Ebenezer Zane hired him to repair the shoes of his large family. He and Zane's sixteen year old daughter Sally fell in love and were married in December 1789, despite the disapproval of her parents. After injuring his hand while loading his gun, McIntire went to work for a merchant and became a partner in the business. The Zanes reconciled their differences with McIntire, and he became their favorite son-in-law.[83]

---

79   Andrew R. L. Cayton, *The Frontier Republic*, Kent State University Press, 1986, p. 78.; William A. Taylor, *Ohio Statesmen and Annals of Progress*, State of Ohio, 1899, Vol I., p. 36.

80   Martin A. Andrews, *History of Marietta and Washington County, Ohio*, 1902, p. 105.

81   Lee Soltow, "Inequality Amidst Abundance: Land Ownership in Early 19th Century Ohio", *Ohio History*, Vol. 88, p. 151.

82   82 Kim M. Gruenwald, "Marietta's Example of a Settlement Pattern in the Ohio Country: A Reinterpretation", *Ohio History*, Vol. 105, p. 142.

83   Norris F. Schneider, *Y Bridge City*, The World Publishing Company, Cleveland, 1951, pp. 37-39.

Zane was the founder and leading citizen of Wheeling. In 1796 he proposed to Congress that he construct a road from Wheeling to Limestone (now Maysville, Kentucky). In exchange for his services in constructing the road, Congress agreed to allow him to use military warrants to buy a section of land where the road crossed the Muskingum, the Hocking, and the Scioto Rivers. Zane enlisted his brother Jonathan, an Indian scout, and his son-in-law John McIntire as partners in the venture. They began in 1796 and completed the road the following year.[84] The road was simply a horse trail blazed through the wilderness. It was not at that time built to accommodate wagon traffic. The trial was known as Zane's Trace. The Trace became the principal access for new settlers to the interior of the Ohio country.

When the trail was completed, Rufus Putnam, as Surveyor General, surveyed the three 640 acre tracts. Zane deeded the tract at the Muskingum to his brother Jonathan and his son-in-law McIntire for $100 and their services in helping construct the road. Settlement of the tract at the Muskingum began in 1797 and McIntire arrived the following year. He and Jonathan laid out a town in 1799, which they called Westbourne. McIntire constructed a double cabin to serve as his residence and an inn for travelers which was completed in 1800. His furniture and other possessions were brought from Wheeling by flatboat down the Ohio and up the Muskingum. The name of the town was changed to Zanesville in 1801.[85]

McIntire was nominated at the Washington County convention and elected as a Federalist delegate to the constitutional convention. He for the most part voted with the other Washington County delegates.[86] He was appointed to serve on the committee to draft article six on county officials.[87] Unlike the other Washington County delegates, he did not vote for Negro suffrage or civil rights.[88]

---

84   Norris F. Schneider, *Y Bridge City*, The World Publishing Company, Cleveland, 1951, pp. 39-41.

85   Norris F. Schneider, *Y Bridge City*, The World Publishing Company, Cleveland, 1951, pp. 41-46.

86   William T. Utter, *History of the State of Ohio, The Frontier State*, Ohio Archaeological and Historical Society, 1942, Vol. II, p. 7.

87   "Journal of Convention", *Ohio History*, Vol. V, p. 96,

88   Helen M. Thurston, "The 1802 Constitutional Convention and the Status of the Negro", *Ohio History*, Vol. 81, p. 28.

In January, 1804, McIntire and other town leaders persuaded the General Assembly to create Muskingum County, and the County Commissioners to select Zanesville as the county seat.[89] McIntire had a courthouse built which resembled Independence Hall in Philadelphia and used it to persuade the General Assembly to move the capital temporarily to Zanesville, where it remained from October 1, 1810 to May 1, 1812. The population of Zanesville increased from 600 to 1200 during that time.[90]

McIntire completed his stone "mansion house" in 1810.[91] In that year he owned ten tracts totaling 2,405 acres.[92] The first Y Bridge was constructed at Zanesville in 1814.[93]

McIntire died July 29, 1815 at the age of 56.[94] He left a fund to be invested and the income used for poor children.[95] Henry Howe stated, "Mr. McIntire, the founder and patron of Zanesville, was indefatigable in his attention to the interests of his town; no personal or pecuniary sacrifice being considered too great, in his anxiety to promote its prosperity."[96]

Other Founding Fathers from Washington County

Following Jefferson's election as President in 1800, opposition developed to the Federalist anti-statehood leadership of Marietta. The leaders of the opposition were Return Jonathan Meigs Jr., Joseph Buell, and Griffen Greene.[97]

---

89   Norris F. Schneider, *Y Bridge City*, The World Publishing Company, Cleveland, 1951, p. 52.

90   Norris F. Schneider, *Y Bridge City*, The World Publishing Company, Cleveland, 1951, pp. 60-65.

91   Norris F. Schneider, *Y Bridge City*, The World Publishing Company, Cleveland, 1951, p. 71.

92   Lee Soltow, "Inequality Amidst Abundance: Land Ownership in Early 19th Century Ohio", *Ohio History*, Vol. 88, p. 151.

93   Norris F. Schneider, *Y Bridge City*, The World Publishing Company, Cleveland, 1951, p. 71.

94   Norris F. Schneider, *Y Bridge City*, The World Publishing Company, Cleveland, 1951, p. 77.

95   Charles B. Galbreath, *History of Ohio*, Vol I, The American Historical Society, 1925, p. 276.

96   Henry Howe, *Historical Collections of Ohio*, Centennial Edition, Vol. II, p. 330.

97   Andrew R. L. Cayton, *The Frontier Republic*, Kent State University Press, 1986, pp. 78, 79.

Although not elected delegates to the convention, these leaders of the Republicans at Marietta deserve recognition as founding fathers of Ohio because of their contributions before and after the founding of the State. In addition Paul Fearing was the Territory's delegate to Congress at the time of the statehood fight and although he was on the losing side, he deserves recognition for his role in that battle as well as his contributions before and after the statehood fight.

RETURN JONATHAN MEIGS JR.

Return Jonathan Meigs, Jr. was born November 17, 1765, in Middletown, Connecticut. His father Return Jonathan Meigs Sr. was a colonel in the Revolutionary War. The Meigs ancestors arrived in America from Devonshire, England in 1637.[98]

Like many veterans, Meigs Sr. suffered financially from his service during the Revolutionary War. He was attracted by Putnam's call to veterans to join him in making a fresh start in the West. He was employed as one of four surveyors to begin the survey of the Ohio Company's purchase, and arrived at Marietta on April 12, 1788.[99] Recognized as a leader of the community, Governor Saint Clair appointed Meigs Sr. as a justice of the peace and judge of the court of general quarter sessions.[100] In 1801 Colonel Meigs was appointed by President Jefferson as the government's Indian Agent to the Cherokee Nation, where he lived until his death in 1823.

Meigs, Jr. graduated from Yale, studied law and was admitted to the Connecticut bar. He married Sophia Wright, and they rode on horseback to Marietta in 1788 to join his parents. His legal skills were recognized by appointment as first clerk of courts of Washington County in 1788, an office which he held until 1795. He served as the United States Attorney for Washington County from 1794 to 1798. He was appointed as the first postmaster of Marietta in 1794, and judge of the territorial court in 1798. He was elected to the first territorial legislature which convened in 1799.[101]

---

98   Linda Elsie Kolette, *The Papers of Thirteen Early Ohio Political Leaders*, Ohio Historical Society, 1977, p. 79; Martin A. Andrews, *History of Marietta and Washington County, Ohio*, 1902, p. 874.

99   S.P. Hildreth, *Pioneer History*, Cincinnati, 1848, pp. 202, 206.

100   Richard C. Knopf, *Transcription of the Executive Journal of the Northwest Territory*, pp. 34, 35.

101   Linda Elsie Kolette, *The Papers of Thirteen Early Ohio Political Leaders*, Ohio Historical Society, 1977, p. 79.

In 1790 Governor Saint Clair entrusted Meigs with a letter to be delivered to the Governor of Detroit informing him of General Harmar's expedition to pacify the Indians and assuring him that it was not intended to molest the British posts or possessions. Meigs undertook and accomplished the extremely dangerous mission, although narrowly escaping death at the hands of hostile Indians on several occasions.[102] While returning from work in the fields one evening in 1792, Meigs and two assistants were attacked by Indians and Meigs again narrowly escaped with his life.[103]

In 1801 the conflict between the proponents and opponents of statehood flared up, and Putnam came out strongly against statehood. Meigs, who had been part of the leadership in Marietta, broke ranks with Putnam and allied himself with Worthington and Tiffin in support of statehood. Meigs cast his fate with Jefferson and the Republicans at an important time, and although defeated in his bid for delegate to the convention, his decision was richly rewarded when the Federalists were swept from power and influence following adoption of the Constitution.[104]

At the first General Assembly which met in Chillicothe in March, 1803, the oath of office was administered to Governor Tiffin by Meigs and he was elected by the General Assembly as the first chief justice of the Ohio Supreme Court.[105] He resigned the following year in order to accept the President's appointment as commander of federal troops and militia in the St. Charles District of the Louisiana Territory. At the time of the appointment, it was feared that a military expedition might be necessary to take possession of New Orleans. This proved unnecessary and Meigs was then appointed a judge of the Louisiana Territory, presiding at St. Louis. Ill health forced his return to Marietta in the fall of 1806. He was then appointed as a judge of the Michigan Territory on April 2, 1807. [106]

Following his appointment, he was nominated for governor of Ohio and returned from Michigan to Ohio to campaign. In a three way race among

102   S. P. Hildreth, *Pioneer History*, Cincinnati, 1848, pp. 269-270.

103   S. P. Hildreth, *Pioneer History*, Cincinnati, 1848, pp. 312-314.

104   Andrew R. L. Cayton, *The Frontier Republic*, Kent State University Press, 1986, pp. 78-79.

105   William A. Taylor, *Ohio Statesmen and Annals of Progress*, State of Ohio, 1899, p. 37; Linda Elsie Kolette, *The Papers of Thirteen Early Ohio Political Leaders*, Ohio Historical Society, 1977, pp. 79. 80.

106   Linda Elsie Kolette, *The Papers of Thirteen Early Ohio Political Leaders*, Ohio Historical Society, 1977, p. 80.

Meigs, Massie, and Kirker, Meigs received the most votes. However, his election was successfully contested by Massie on the ground that Meigs had not been an inhabitant of the State of Ohio for the past four years due to his judicial service in Louisiana and Michigan as required by Article II, Section 3 of the Constitution. Massie then resigned, and Kirker continued to serve as acting Governor by virtue of his position as speaker of the Senate. Meigs was then again elected by the General Assembly to the Ohio Supreme Court.[107]

When John Smith resigned as United States Senator due to his involvement with the Aaron Burr scandal, Meigs was chosen by the General Assembly to fill his unexpired term and to fill the following six year term.[108] He was elected governor of Ohio in 1810 and resigned his senate seat to accept the governorship. He defeated Thomas Worthington in a hard fought campaign which pitted moderate Republicans and Federalists against the Tiffin/Worthington wing of the Republican Party. Worthington and his allies sought to frame the issue as whether the legislature or the courts were supreme. Meigs and his allies attacked the Tammany Societies organized by the Tiffin/Worthington Republicans as undemocratic "secret societies" which Worthington sought to use to control elections. The vote also reflected growing animosity toward the power exercised by Scioto Valley politicians.[109]

Meigs was reelected governor in 1812 and became Ohio's first war-time governor. Since this was a war fought on Ohio soil and since a good part of the fight was fought with Ohio militia, Meigs was deeply involved in the prosecution of the conduct of the War in Ohio. He worked closely with Major General William Henry Harrison who was the commander of American forces in the Northwest. Although the war in Ohio got off to a very bad start with the surrender of General Hull at Detroit followed by the defeat of the Americans at Frenchtown, momentum turned after Fort Meigs and Fort Stephenson were successfully defended from British and Indian attack and Commodore Perry defeated the British fleet on Lake Erie in 1813. The defeat of the British and Indians by William Henry Harrison's army at the Battle of the Thames later

---

107   Andrew R. L. Cayton, *The Frontier Republic*, Kent State University Press, 1986, pp. 99-100;
       William A. Taylor, *Ohio Statesmen and Annals of Progress*, State of Ohio, 1899, pp. 51-53; Linda Elsie Kolette, *The Papers of Thirteen Early Ohio Political Leaders*, Ohio Historical Society, 1977, p. 80.

108   William A. Taylor, *Ohio Statesmen and Annals of Progress*, State of Ohio, 1899, p. 57.

109   Andrew R. L. Cayton, *The Frontier Republic*, Kent State University Press, 1986, pp. 105-106.

that year removed the threat of Indian attacks from the Ohio frontier and provided the government an opportunity to renegotiate the treaties in northwestern Ohio which opened up this part of the state to settlement.

In March 1814 Meigs resigned as Governor to accept appointment as Postmaster General in President Madison's administration. This appointment shows the high esteem in which he was held among the Republican leadership as well as the growing political stature of Ohio at the national level. He remained in office through the remainder of the Madison administration and continued through the administration of President Monroe, resigning in 1823 due to ill-health. During his nine year tenure, the postal service grew from 3,000 to 5,200 post offices.

Meigs died on March 29, 1825. The epitaph on the monument over his grave in Mound Cemetery at Marietta refers to him as "an ardent patriot, a practical statesman, and an enlightened scholar."[110]

JOSEPH BUELL

Joseph Buell was born February 16, 1760, in Killingworth, Connecticut. He was descended from William Buell who emigrated from England to America in 1630 and was one of the founders of Windsor, Connecticut.[111]

Following Congress' decision to survey and sell lands in the West, America's small military force was sent west for the purpose of asserting federal authority over the Ohio country by driving off squatters, negotiating treaties with the Indians, and protecting surveyors and settlers from Indian attack. Forts were constructed on what had been the Indian side of the Ohio River on the Mingo Bottom at the future site of Steubenville, at the mouth of the Muskingum at the future site of Marietta, at the mouth of the Great Miami at the future site of North Bend, and at the falls of the Ohio across from Louisville. Buell was an orderly sergeant at West Point in November, 1785, when his unit was ordered to march to the western frontiers. He arrived at Pittsburgh on December 21, 1785, and five days later arrived at Fort McIntosh near where Big Beaver Creek

---

110   Linda Elsie Kolette, *The Papers of Thirteen Early Ohio Political Leaders*, Ohio Historical Society, 1977, p. 81

111   Martin A. Andrews, *History of Marietta and Washington County, Ohio*, 1902, p. 881; "Founders of Windsor, Connecticut", Founders of Ancient Windsor, Inc., The Connecticut State Library, June, 1996.

empties into the Ohio River. They discovered the old fort in serious disrepair and set to work making their barracks habitable. They were dispatched to the mouth of the Muskingum where they arrived on May 8. They planted gardens and constructed barracks within the walls of a fortification named Fort Harmar after the Colonel who commanded the regiment. Buell was stationed at Fort Harmar when Rufus Putnam and his associates arrived on April 7, 1788, to establish a settlement across the Muskingum from the fort. He entered in his diary, "General Putnam arrived at this place with fifty men to begin a settlement on the east side of the Muskingum. They commenced with great spirit, and there is a prospect of it becoming a flourishing place in a short time."[112]

Judge Symmes arrived at the Fort on August 27, 1788, on his way to establish his settlement on the land he had purchased from Congress between the Great Miami and the Little Miami Rivers. Buell purchased 400 acres from him and planned to settle on Symmes purchase following his discharge from the army. Upon his discharge in October, he returned to his home in Connecticut. In 1789 he returned to the West with his brother Timothy and an army friend Levi Munsell. They went to North Bend, but soon returned to Marietta.[113]

Buell and Munsell opened a tavern at the point in Marietta at the mouth of the Muskingum in a large frame house which was constructed from boards taken from a boat floated down the Ohio. During the Indian War a garrison was constructed to protect the residences at the point. Because of his military experience, on September 16, 1790, Buell was appointed an ensign in the first regiment of the militia of Washington County.[114]

Buell was a follower of Thomas Jefferson in a town dominated by the Federalists until Ohio became a state. His political career is a prime example of the triumph of the Republicans when Ohio gained statehood. Following the adoption of the constitution, Buell was elected to the Ohio senate where he served for two terms until 1806.[115] He was appointed by the General Assembly to the office of Associate Judge of Washington County.[116] In the second session of the

112   S.P. Hildreth, *Pioneer History*, Cincinnati, 1848, pp. 140-148, 160.

113   S.P. Hildreth, *Pioneer History*, Cincinnati, 1848, pp. 164; Martin A. Andrews, *History of Marietta and Washington County, Ohio*, 1902, p. 882.

114   Martin A. Andrews, *History of Marietta and Washington County, Ohio*, 1902, p. 882; Richard C. Knopf, *Transcription of the Executive Journal of the Northwest Territory*, Ohio Historical Society web page, p. 135.

115   William A. Taylor, *Ohio Statesmen and Annals of Progress*, State of Ohio, 1899, pp. 35, 38, 41, 45.

116   William A. Taylor, *Ohio Statesmen and Annals of* Progress, State of Ohio, 1899, p. 63.

General Assembly the state was divided into four militia divisions and Buell was elected as major general of the third division which included Marietta.[117]

The highpoint of Buell's career was his action in quashing the "Burr Conspiracy." Burr had persuaded Harmon Blennerhasset to assist in organizing an expedition to establish a settlement in the Spanish lands. Blennerhasset owned an estate on an island in the Ohio River located near Marietta. In December, 1806, General Buell received an order from the Governor to arrest Blennerhasset and to seize the boats which were being built at a ship yard at Marietta to carry Burr's expedition down the Ohio. Although Blennerhasset escaped, most of the boats and supplies were seized and the planned expedition was thwarted.[118]

Joseph Buell died on June 13, 1812, and is buried in Mound Cemetery in Marietta.[119]

GRIFFIN GREENE

Griffin Greene was born February 20, 1749, in the town of Warwick, Rhode Island. His Greene ancestors came to Rhode Island from England in 1635.[120] He was a cousin of and grew up with Nathaniel Greene, the famous American General during the Revolutionary War. Griffin married Sarah Greene of Warwick, no relation. At an early age he worked in the smith and anchor-making business. Prior to the Revolution, he and a cousin erected a forge for the manufacture of iron on the Pawtuxet River. During the War it was used to furnish cannon balls and wrought iron which were scarce in the colonies.[121]

He was raised as a Quaker, but was dismissed from membership along with his cousin Nathaniel when they joined the military at the outbreak of the war. The Quakers did not permit members to engage in military activities, although members of that denomination provided valuable services in non combatant roles. He commenced his service as commissary to the Rhode Island troops. In 1777 he was paymaster of a regiment commanded by Christopher Greene. When Nathaniel Greene was appointed by General Washington as quartermaster-general of the army, he selected Griffin Greene as one of his deputies.

---

117   William A. Taylor, *Ohio Statesmen and Annals of Progress*, State of Ohio, 1899, p. 39.

118   Martin A. Andrews, *History of Marietta and Washington County, Ohio*, 1902, p. 883.

119   Martin A. Andrews, *History of Marietta and Washington County, Ohio*, 1902, p. 884.

120   Greenes of the World web page.

121   S. P. Hildreth, *Early Pioneer Settlers of Ohio*, Cincinnati, 1852, pp. 279-280.

Griffin's responsibilities included purchasing supplies for the army, a daunting task because of the government's lack of money and credit.[122]

He became aware of the Ohio Company through General Varnum of Rhode Island, one of the leaders of the enterprise. He sold his interest in his business to his cousin and invested in Ohio Company lands. In 1788 he moved his family to Marietta with three large wagons filled with household goods, all kinds of mechanical and agricultural implements, and a large library of valuable books.[123]

Soon after his arrival Greene was appointed as a justice of the peace and judge of the general court of Quarter Sessions for Washington County.[124] In 1798 he was reappointed and also appointed register of the land office for the county.[125] In 1789 he was appointed as one of the directors of the Ohio Company in place of General Varnum who had died. In 1790 he joined the colony at Belpre and was a leading man in that settlement, solemnizing marriages and settling civil disputes. After the massacre at Big Bottom, he took an active part in the erection of Farmers Castle, the stockade which the settlers at Belpre erected for their protection during the Indian War.[126]

Greene was a mechanical genius. The first anchors made on the Ohio River were made under his direction in 1800. He worked with Captain Jonathan Devol to build a floating mill based on one he had seen in Holland. The mill floated on the River and the current was used to turn a wheel to grind grain. He attempted to build a perpetual motion machine without success. He built a model steam engine and went to Philadelphia in 1796 to have it built, but the mechanic engaged to build it never completed the work.[127]

Griffin Greene, Meigs and Buell were the leaders of the Republican opposition in Washington County. They protested when Putnam organized a town meeting to oppose statehood in January, 1801. Through the influence of Judge Symmes and Thomas Worthington, Greene was appointed postmaster of

122   S. P. Hildreth, *Early Pioneer Settlers of Ohio*, Cincinnati, 1852, pp. 280-286.

123   S. P. Hildreth, *Early Pioneer Settlers of Ohio*, Cincinnati, 1852, pp. 287-288.

124   Richard C. Knopf, *Transcription of the Executive Journal of the Northwest Territory*, p. 45.

125   Richard C. Knopf, *Transcription of the Executive Journal of the Northwest Territory*, p. 514.

126   S. P. Hildreth, *Early Pioneer Settlers of Ohio*, Cincinnati, 1852, p. 288.

127   S. P. Hildreth, *Early Pioneer Settlers of Ohio*, Cincinnati, 1852, pp. 288-290; Joseph Barker, *Recollections of First Settlement of Ohio*, Marietta College, 1958, pp. 41,49.; S.P. Hildreth, *Pioneer History*, Cincinnati, 1848, pp. 375-376.

Marietta by the Jefferson administration in January, 1802 in place of David Putnam and later that year, the administration appointed him collector of revenues at Marietta. He was also the inspector for the Port of Marietta for ships being built there. Although the Washington County Republicans were not successful in electing delegates to the convention, following the convention they were successful in defeating the Federalists in the January, 1803 election for the state's first officers. Greene was rewarded for his efforts by appointment as an associate judge for Washington County by the first General Assembly.[128]

Griffin Greene died in June, 1804 at the age of fifty-five. A pioneer historian described him as follows: "Mr. Greene was a man of intelligent aspect, quick apprehension, and ready, vigorous application of his mind to any subject before him. In person he was tall, of genteel and accomplished manners, having seen and associated with much refined company and men of talents. As a man of genius and intellect, he ranked with the first of the Ohio Company's settlers, abounding as it did with able men."[129]

PAUL FEARING

Paul Fearing was born February 28, 1762 in Wareham, Plymouth County, Massachusetts. His Fearing ancestors arrived at Plymouth from England before 1642. He graduated from Harvard in 1785. He studied law for two years in Wyndham, Connecticut, and was admitted as an attorney in the courts of that state on September 19, 1787.[130]

The glowing reports about the Ohio valley being circulated by the Ohio Company attracted the attention of the young Fearing. On May 1, 1788, he departed on a boat from Boston to Baltimore. From there he commenced the journey across the mountains on foot, arriving in Pittsburgh on June 20. He took a boat to Marietta, arriving on June 16, 1788. On July 4 the villagers celebrated Independence Day by hearing a speech from General Varnum and sharing in a community dinner which included a one hundred pound pike. On

---

128   Randolph Downes, *Frontier Ohio*, Ohio Historical Society, pp. 218-220; Andrew R. L. Cayton, *The Frontier Republic*, Kent State University Press, 1986, pp. 78-79; William A. Taylor, *Ohio Statesmen and Annals of Progress*, State of Ohio, 1899, Vol 1, p. 37; S. P. Hildreth, *Early Pioneer Settlers of Ohio*, Cincinnati, 1852, p. 290.

129   S. P. Hildreth, *Early Pioneer Settlers of Ohio*, Cincinnati, 1852, p. 290.

130   S. P. Hildreth, *Early Pioneer Settlers of Ohio*, Cincinnati, 1852, p. 291; Ancestral File, Family Search web page, Church of Jesus Christ of Latter Day Saints Family History Library

September 2, the first session of the court of common pleas was held in a blockhouse at campus Martius, the stockade at Marietta, and he was admitted as an attorney before that court. On September 9, Judges Parsons and Varnum of the Territorial Court provided him with a certificate authorizing him to practice claw in all courts of the Territory.[131] He was also appointed United States Attorney for Washington County in 1788 and served in this office until 1794.[132]

In January, 1789, Fearing traveled to New England and then returned in the fall by way of Alexandria, Virginia and Redstone, Pennsylvania, on the Monongahela. From Redstone he took a boat back to Marietta. There was little law business in the community so he took a position as deputy contractor for supplying the troops at Fort Harmar with meat. The only attorneys in the county until 1791 were Fearing and Meigs. The Court of Quarter Sessions and Court of Common Pleas met four times a year at Marietta. The Territorial Court also met four times a year but it was a circuit Court rotating between Marietta, Cincinnati, Detroit, and Vincennes.[133]

During the Indian War Fearing lived with his father in a block house at Fort Harmar. Peace was established by the Greenfield Treaty in August, 1795. Fearing married Cynthia Rouse on November 28, 1795, at Marietta. Joseph Gilman officiated.[134]

In 1797 Fearing was appointed probate judge by Winthrop Sargent, acting for Governor St. Clair. He was elected as a representative to the first session of the territorial legislature where he served from 1799 to 1801. When Harrison resigned as the Territory's delegate to Congress to accept the governorship of the Indiana Territory, an agreement was made between the Washington County and Hamilton County representatives in the territorial legislature to elect attorney William McMillan of Cincinnati to serve the remainder of Harrison's term and Paul Fearing for the subsequent two year term. Fearing served as the third representative of the Territory to Congress from March 4, 1801 to March 3, 1803.[135]

After the second Territorial legislature passed the act proposing to divide the Territory at the Scioto in December, 1801, it was Fearing's task to persuade

131   S. P. Hildreth, *Early Pioneer Settlers of Ohio*, Cincinnati, 1852, pp. 292-293.
132   *Biographical Directory of Congress* web site; Martin A. Andrews, *History of Marietta and Washington County, Ohio*, 1902, p. 432.
133   S. P. Hildreth, *Early Pioneer Settlers of Ohio*, Cincinnati, 1852, pp 1789-297
134   S. P. Hildreth, *Early Pioneer Settlers of Ohio*, Cincinnati, 1852, pp. 298-299.
135   S. P. Hildreth, *Early Pioneer Settlers of Ohio*, Cincinnati, 1852, pp. 299-300.

Congress to accept the proposal. Lobbying against him were Thomas Worthington and Michael Baldwin of Chillicothe armed with petitions from throughout the Territory urging rejection of the division law and admission of Ohio to statehood. His problem was compounded by the fact that as a Federalist he was a member of the minority party. Worthington and Baldwin persuaded William Brown Giles, a rabid Jeffersonian Republican from Virginia to lead the effort in the House while Michael Baldwin's brother Abraham Baldwin of Georgia led the effort in the Senate assisted by Senator Mason of Virginia and Senators Brown and Breckinridge of Kentucky, long time friends of Worthington. On January 20, 1802, Fearing presented the division law to the House and urged that it be referred to a select committee for consideration. Giles rose in opposition arguing that the proposal would perpetuate in office an unpopular governor and legislature and pointed out that he had in his hands petitions signed by over a thousand residents of the Territory opposing the measure. He urged action on the proposal as soon as possible. It was referred to a committee of the whole and on January 27, the House voted 81 to 5 not to agree to the proposed division. The fast rejection by the House was totally unexpected by St. Clair and his allies. They did not learn about it in time to send Republican allies of the governor McMillan and Todd to help Fearing. On January 28, Giles moved that a committee be appointed to consider an enabling act authorizing the residents of the Territory to vote on statehood. He was appointed chairman of the committee. The Federalist leaders in Cincinnati and Marietta authorized Fearing to support statehood of two states with a division at the Scioto. This would satisfy the desires of Cincinnati and Marietta to be state capitals and by splitting the Republican vote in the Scioto Valley could lead to Federalist's majorities in the two states, a point no doubt pointed out by Worthington and Baldwin. Worthington, Giles and Albert Gallatin, Jefferson's Secretary of the Treasury, prepared a lengthy report in support of allowing Ohioans to elect delegates to a convention to vote on statehood. The Report was read to the House on March 4 by Congressman Giles. Despite Fearing's attempt to delay the vote and arguments against the bill the Enabling Act was passed in the House on April 9 by a vote of 47 to 29. Fearing argued without success that excluding the Michigan Territory from the new state violated the Ordinance and was unfair to the residents of Michigan. On April 28, 1802 the Senate passed the Enabling Act with minor amendments on April 28, which were agreed to by the House the following day. Jefferson signed the bill on April 30 and the Enabling Act was law. By April 27 Fearing was packing his goods for permanent removal back to Marietta. He had been worsted by Worthington and his Republican allies, but he harbored no ill will. He agreed to take a large parcel of books home for Worthington in his baggage.

Professional throughout, he fought the good fight and gracefully acknowl-
edged defeat. In retrospect, the Division Act enacted by the Territorial
Legislature was extremely ill-considered in that it ignored the political reality
in Washington. Its effect was simply to hasten statehood. Although given the
political realities in Washington, the growing population, the unpopularity of
the Governor, and the sentiments of the people of Ohio, Ohio would certainly
have been admitted within a few years anyway.[136]

Fearing was not a Federalist delegate to the convention from Washington
County. This may have been due to wide spread unhappiness by the Federalists
in Marietta or perhaps due to the fact that his term of office as congressman
had not expired. With the Republican triumph following adoption of the
Constitution, Fearing like other Federalists retired from public life. He practiced law and because of his well-known reputation for honesty and uprightness was popular among the people who referred to him as "Honest Paul." His
practice also included representing eastern land owners in connection with
their Ohio land investments. He improved a farm located a little below the
mouth of the Muskingum where he grew fruit trees. He was one of the early
Ohioans to raise merino sheep and had a herd of several hundred. The merino
was valued because of the fineness of the wool.[137]

On February 15, 1810, the General Assembly elected Paul Fearing to be an
Associate Judge of Washington County. His election is rather remarkable in that
the Republicans in the fall 1809 election ran as anti-court party and then declared
all judicial offices vacant in what was called the "Sweeping Resolution." They then
appointed judges to fill all the vacancies. They defended their action on the
ground that the constitution specified that judges had a seven year term; therefore
all terms expired in 1810 regardless of when the judges were appointed.[138]
Fearing's appointment suggests that Republicans believed that he respected the
authority of the General Assembly and did not subscribe to the view that courts
had the power to invalidate legislative acts. Fearing served for seven years. In 1814
he was appointed master commissioner in chancery.[139]

---

136 Alfred Byron Sear, *Thomas Worthington, Father of Ohio Statehood*, Ohio State
     University Press for the Ohio Historical Society, 1958, pp. 73-85; Randolph
     Downes, *Frontier Ohio*, Ohio Historical Society, pp. 226-232;

137 S. P. Hildreth, *Early Pioneer Settlers of Ohio*, Cincinnati, 1852, pp. 300-301.

138 William A. Taylor, *Ohio Statesmen and Annals of Progress*, State of Ohio, 1899,
     Vol 1, p. 60; Andrew R. L. Cayton, *Frontier Republic*, Kent State University Press,
     1986, pp. 104-105.

139 S. P. Hildreth, *Early Pioneer Settlers of Ohio*, Cincinnati, 1852, p. 301.

Fearing died on August 21, 1822, from an epidemic which swept through the area for two or three years. His wife died the same day. A pioneer historian described Fearing as follows, "In his disposition Fearing was remarkably cheerful and pleasant, much attached to children, and never happier than when in their company. He had great sympathy for the poor and oppressed, and was ever ready to stretch forth his hand, and open his purse for their relief."[140]

---

140   S. P. Hildreth, *Early Pioneer Settlers of Ohio,* Cincinnati, 1852, p. 301.

Chapter 2

FOUNDING FATHERS FROM HAMILTON COUNTY, OHIO

The Miami Purchase

Following Manasseh Cutler's successful negotiation with Congress for a purchase of land by The Ohio Company, John Cleve Symmes persuaded Congress to authorize a sale of land to him and his New Jersey associates in southwestern Ohio for the same price and terms. Symmes was from New Jersey. He argued that what Congress had done for New England with the sale to the Ohio Company should be matched with a similar sale to him and his associates for the benefit of the mid-Atlantic and southern states.

Symmes was a member of Congress in 1785 when the subject of the western lands was discussed and the Land Act of 1785 was enacted which authorized survey and sale of land in the Seven Ranges in eastern Ohio. His interest in the Ohio country was further excited by his friend and neighbor, Benjamin Sites. Sites was engaged in trading on the Monongahela and Ohio Rivers and in 1786 had assumed leadership of an expedition against the Indians in the Miami country. Upon completion of the expedition he returned to New Jersey to interest someone in colonization. Symmes traveled to the West to locate a suitable tract for purchase and at first focused on a tract on the Wabash. Upon returning east, he changed his mind and decided upon a tract north of the Ohio between the Big Miami and Little Miami Rivers. He interested his prominent New Jersey friends General Jonathan Dayton and Dr. Elias Boudinot in assisting with the financing of the venture.[141]

---

141   R. Pierce Beaver, "The Miami Purchase of John Cleves Symmes", *Ohio History*, Vol. 40, p. 287-290.

After Manasseh Cutler persuaded Congress to adopt the Ordinance of 1787 establishing a government for the Northwest Territory and sell a large tract to The Ohio Company on favorable terms, Symmes recognized that the timing was right to seek authorization for a sale of a tract on similar terms to him and his associates. He submitted his proposal to Congress on August 29, 1787, and on October 3, Congress authorized the Board of Treasury to enter into a contract with him for the sale of 2,000,000 acres between the Miamis.[142] The terms of sale were the same as the Ohio Company contract except that only one township was requested for a university, whereas the contact with the Ohio Company provided that two townships be donated by the government for this purpose. When Symmes was unable to make the first payment, he requested that his contract be amended to reduce the acreage to 1,000,000 acres and his down payment be reduced in half. The Board of Treasury agreed to reduce the size of the tract, but refused his request to include all the land fronting on the Ohio between the Miamis in the tract. Without resolving this disagreement, Symmes set out for the West to begin settlement. An amendment to the contract was negotiated in his absence by his agent Jonathan Dayton.[143]

Despite his failure to comply with the terms of his contract with the government, Symmes insisted that he had a right to buy land under his original contract. He sold land and accepted payments for land which he did not own and had no right to buy. His record keeping was terrible. Congress spent many hours and a number of years attempting to unravel the mess created by Symmes actions. Congress eventually authorized a patent to Symmes for all land paid for extending north from the River between the Miamis. It also granted settlers who had purchased land from him which he did not own a preemptive right to purchase the land from the government and appointed commissioners to sort out the claims. When Symmes failed to set aside a township for the university, Congress granted a Township outside the purchase for such purpose upon which Miami University was eventually established.[144]

---

142   R. Pierce Beaver, "The Miami Purchase of John Cleves Symmes", *Ohio History*, Vol. 40, pp. 290-291; William Henry Smith, *The St. Clair Papers*, Cincinnati, 1882, Vol. II, pp. 621-622;

143   R. Pierce Beaver, "The Miami Purchase of John Cleves Symmes", *Ohio History*, Vol. 40, pp. 294-298.

144   R. Pierce Beaver, "The Miami Purchase of John Cleves Symmes", *Ohio History*, Vol. 40, pp. 299-328.

Symmes fell victim to his own incompetence and was financially ruined by the seizure and sale of his assets to satisfy the claims of the many persons who suffered losses at his hands. The Miami purchase was the last attempt by the Federal government to sell lands to a private developer. Despite Symmes short-comings, Cincinnati developed into the leading City and the Miami purchase the most affluent area of the new State. Ironically, the area developed much faster than the Ohio Company purchase which was in contrast with the Miami purchase developed in an organized, orderly, and efficient manner.[145]

Hamilton County

Hamilton County was the second county organized by Governor Saint Clair in the Northwest Territory. The county was established by proclamation on January 2, 1790 and Cincinnati was designated as the county seat.[146]

In appreciation for bringing the Miami country to his attention, Symmes agreed to sell 10,000 of the best acres to Benjamin Stites at the mouth of the Little Miami. Stites organized and led the party which made the first settle-ment in the Miami purchase. They called their settlement Columbia. The party traveled by flat boat from Limestone (now Maysville), Kentucky, on November 18, 1788 and immediately went to work erecting blockhouses for protection against the Indians and then log cabins for the families. For several years Columbia was the most populous and successful settlement in the county.[147]

Early settlers of Columbia included William Goforth, Francis Dunlavy, John Reilly, and John Smith, whose biographies appear later in this chapter.

Mathias Denman of Springfield, New Jersey, purchased 740 acres across from the mouth of the Licking River where he planned to establish a settle-ment and a ferry on the old Indian trail which the Indians had used when invading Kentucky from the north. He enlisted as partners in the venture Col. Robert Patterson of Lexington, a veteran of the Indian wars, and John Filson of Lexington, a surveyor, explorer, and author of the first history of Kentucky. Filson was engaged to survey the town which was named Losantiville. The

---

145   R. Pierce Beaver, "The Miami Purchase of John Cleves Symmes", *Ohio History*, Vol. 40, pp. 284-286, 338

146   Richard C. Knopf, *Transcription of the Executive Journal of the Northwest Territory*, pp. 56, 58-59.

147   Henry Howe, *Historical Collections of Ohio*, Centennial Edition, 1898, Vol I, p. 747.

name was changed at the suggestion of Governor Saint Clair to Cincinnati in honor of the Order of Cincinnati, an organization of former officers in the Revolution. The party explored the area in September, 1788, during which Filson was killed by Indians. The party returned on December 28, 1788, to begin the first settlement. Israel Ludlow took Filson's place in the venture and performed the first survey of the town.[148] In the fall of 1789 Major Doughty was sent from Fort Harmar to erect a fort in the Miami purchase. A location near Losantiville was selected and Fort Washington was constructed. The fort served as the headquarters of the army during the Indian War which lasted until Wayne's victory at the Battle of Fallen Timbers on August 20, 1794, and the Treaty of Greenville was signed the following year. The presence of the army post gave the young town a character of hard drinking, gambling, and fighting, in stark contrast to Marietta. The army's demand for supplies fostered growth of business.

The third settlement in the Miami purchase was established by Symmes at North Bend in February, 1789, near the mouth of the Great Miami. A fort had been erected there at the time of a treaty negotiation. Symmes had persuaded the army to send a military attachment to accompany the settlers. However, when they arrived they discovered the fort had been flooded. Symmes proceeded with establishment of his settlement, however, its prospects suffered when the decision was made to locate Fort Washington at Cincinnati.[149]

According to Jacob Burnet, whose biography follows, he was told by Judge Symmes that the decision to locate the fort at Losantiville rather than North Bend was due to the fact that the officer making the selection became enamored of a beautiful black-eyed married woman who lived at North Bend. Her husband recognizing the danger moved his family to Losantiville. The officer then visited Losantiville and saw the obvious advantages of locating the fort there. As a result of the officers fancy for the black-eyed woman, Cincinnati outpaced its competitors North Bend and Columbia and became the leading metropolis of the future state of Ohio.[150]

---

148   Henry Howe, *Historical Collections of Ohio*, Centennial Edition, 1898, Vol I, pp. 747-748.

149   Henry Howe, *Historical Collections of Ohio*, Centennial Edition, 1898, Vol I, pp. 748-749.

150   Jacob Burnet, "Burnet's Letters" *Transactions of the Historical and Philosophical Society of Ohio*, Cincinnati, 1839, Vol. 1, pp. 17, 19.

Hamilton County Delegates

JEREMIAH MORROW

Jeremiah Morrow was born on October 6, 1771, near Gettysburg, Pennsylvania. His grandfather emigrated from Londonderry, Northern Ireland, in 1730. His father changed his surname from Murray to Morrow, perhaps to avoid the stigma associated with the "Irish" at that time.[151] Like many other early Ohio settlers, he was close enough to his roots that he spoke in a Scotch-Irish dialect.

In the fall of 1794 he decided to settle in the Northwest Territory. He first made his home in Columbia, teaching school, surveying, and raising corn on rented land. A few years later, he purchased land from Symmes on the Little Miami about thirty miles from its mouth in what would later become Warren County. He erected a log cabin and returned to Pennsylvania to marry Mary Parkhill on February 19, 1799. He brought her west and like most of the other settlers of the time undertook the arduous task of felling trees and preparing his land for cultivation.[152]

Morrow was a representative of Hamilton County in the second territorial legislature which convened in Chillicothe on November 23, 1801. Morrow and Dunlavy of Hamilton County joined Tiffin and Worthington of Ross County and Darlinton and Massie of Adams County in opposing Saint Clair's plan to delay statehood by dividing the Territory at the Scioto.[153] Since Cincinnati would have benefited from the plan by being named as capital of the western state, Morrow's opposition was courageous.

Morrow was elected as one of ten delegates from Hamilton County to the convention. There were ninety-nine candidates and he received the third highest vote.[154] Unlike Marietta which was overwhelmingly Federalist prior to statehood and Chillicothe which was overwhelmingly Republican, the politics of Hamilton County was complicated. Most of the Republicans in Cincinnati

---

151   Linda Elise Kolette, *The Papers of Thirteen Early Ohio Political Leaders*, Ohio Historical Society, 1977, pp. 159-160.

152   William Henry Smith, "A familiar Talk about Monarchists and Jacobins," *Ohio History*, Vol 2, p. 199.

153   William Henry Smith, *St. Clair Papers*, Cincinnati, 1882, Vol. II, pp. 544-545.

154   Randolph Chandler Downes, *Frontier Ohio 1788-1803*, Ohio Historical Society, 1935, p. 246.

and Columbia had supported Saint Clair's plan to divide the Territory at the Scioto because it would have made Cincinnati the state capital. On the other hand Republicans in the back country such as Dunlavy and Morrow of Lebanon and John Smith who looked out for the interests of Symmes and his purchasers, had allied with Massie, Worthington and Tiffin.[155] Republicans of Hamilton County organized a committee of correspondence. By 1802 the county had seventeen Republican societies. Each society elected delegates to a county nominating convention. The delegates met on August 13, 1802 at Big Hill and nominated a slate of delegates for the constitutional convention.[156] The campaign for delegates in Hamilton County was fiercely contested. Of the ten delegates elected only John Smith and John Reily were not on the official Republican slate and Smith was a Republican. The Republicans celebrated their victory with a public ox roast. A pedestal was erected on a base labeled "the people" in honor of President Jefferson.[157]

Morrow served as chairman of the committee to draft article four on the qualification of electors.[158] His votes were less antagonistic to Negro rights than the Scioto Valley Republicans, although not very supportive.[159]

After the Republicans swept the Federalists from power following the adoption of the Constitution, Morrow was elected to the Ohio Senate in the first General Assembly which convened on March 1, 1803, at Chillicothe.[160] The delegates to the convention proposed to Congress as one of the conditions of Ohio's admission to statehood that Congress provide for a township to fund a university which under the terms of sale to Symmes was supposed to be located in the Miami purchase. On March 3, 1803, Congress authorized that a township for such purpose be located west of the Great Miami. The General

---

155   Randolph Chandler Downes, *Frontier Ohio 1788-1803*, Ohio Historical Society, 1935, pp. 210-211.

156   Donald J. Ratcliffe, "The Experience of Revolution and The Beginning of Party Politics in Ohio 1776-1816", *Ohio History*, Vol. 85, p. 198; Randolph Chandler Downes, *Frontier Ohio 1788-1803*, Ohio Historical Society, 1935, p. 242.

157   William T. Utter, *The Frontier State, History of Ohio*, Ohio Historical Society, 1942, Vol 2, pp. 8, 9.

158   "Journal of Convention", *Ohio Archaeological and Historical Society Publications*, Vol. V, p. 95.

159   Helen M. Thurston, "The 1802 Constitutional Convention and the Status of the Negro", *Ohio History*, Vol. 81, p. 28.

160   William A. Taylor, *Ohio Statesmen and Annals of Progress*, State of Ohio, 1899, p. 35.

Assembly appointed Morrow as one of three commissioners to locate the college township. He and William Ludlow tracked through the woods and identified what is now Oxford Township in Butler County as the township.[161] He later served as a Trustee of Miami University.[162]

Recognized as one of the leaders of the victorious party, Morrow was nominated as the Republican candidate for Ohio's representative to Congress and was elected on June 21, 1803, as Ohio's first representative to Congress. From October 17, 1803 to March 3, 1813, Morrow served as Ohio's only representative to Congress. During that time only the Governor and U.S. Representative ran for office on a state-wide ballot and he was elected five times.

In 1804 Elias Langham of Ross County, speaker of the Ohio House of Representatives, challenged Morrow and was defeated. In 1806 the Republican Party divided into a faction headed by the old leadership of Worthington, Tiffin, and Morrow and new faction led by Baldwin and Langham of Ross County and James Pritchard of Jefferson County. Morrow was challenged by James Pritchard, a Jefferson County Republican who had served two years as speaker of the Ohio Senate. Morrow won by a vote of 6,735 to 2,364.[163]

Morrow was elected by the General Assembly to the United States Senate in 1813 and served until 1819. One of the most important federal laws governing Ohioans was the federal land law. This law determined the price and terms of public land sales and provided relief for those who were unable to make their payments. It also established the organization to survey and sell public lands and governed how and where sales took place. From the opening of local land offices to 1820, 8,848,152 acres of federal land were sold in Ohio for a price of $17,226,187. This represented approximately one half of all federal land sold during that time period.[164] Morrow served on the committee on public lands in both houses and chairman of the committee in both houses. He was considered an expert on the subject and was involved in the drafting of all the changes in the land laws during that period of time. He was an advocate for the sale of smaller tracts and for lower prices. In 1819 his committee submitted a report which showed unusual care and thought. The Senate passed the recommended legislation that year, and in 1820 the most important amendment to

---

161   *History and Biographical Encyclopedia of Butler County, Ohio*, Cincinnati, 1882, p. 58.

162   William Henry Smith, "A familiar Talk about Monarchists and Jacobins," *Ohio History*, Vol. 2, p. 207.

163   *Steubenville Western Herald*, December 6, 1806.

164   Benjamin Horace Hibbard, *A History of Public Land Policies*, New York, 1939, p. 99.

the public land law was adopted since the first land law of 1785. The credit system was abolished, the minimum size of tracts was reduced to 80 acres, and the price reduced from $2.00 to $1.25 per acre.[165] Henry Clay said of Morrow, "No man in the sphere within which he acted ever commanded or deserved the implicit respect of Congress more than Jeremiah Morrow. There existed a perfect persuasion of his entire impartiality and justice between the old states and the new. A few artless but sensible words pronounced in his plain Scotch-Irish dialect were always sufficient to insure the passage of any bill or resolution which he reported."[166]

Morrow was also a strong advocate in Congress for internal improvements. This was a matter of vital interest to Ohio settlers because of the cost of transporting trade goods to and from the state. When Congress passed the Enabling Act on April 30, 1802, authorizing an election of delegates to a convention to decide if Ohio should became a state, it offered as an inducement to a favorable vote that 5% of the proceeds from sale of lands in Ohio be used to construct a road from Ohio to the east. The delegates at the convention countered with a proposal that 2% of the proceeds be used for the road to Ohio and that 3% be used to construct roads in Ohio. This proposal was accepted by Congress. Worthington in the Senate and Morrow in the House pressed for legislation to begin survey and construction of the road connecting Ohio to the east. In December, 1805, a favorable report was made in the Senate by a committee appointed to study the matter and a law was enacted in March, 1806, establishing a commission to survey the route and appropriating funds for such purpose.[167] The commission rendered its report in 1808 and construction began at Cumberland, Maryland in 1811.[168] While in the Senate Morrow chaired a committee to study the subject of roads and canals which on February 16, 1816, presented an able and lucid report recommending a general system of internal improvements.[169]

---

165   Benjamin Horace Hibbard, *A History of Public Land Policies*, New York, 1939, pp. 97-98.

166   William Henry Smith, "A familiar Talk about Monarchists and Jacobins," *Ohio History*, Vol. 2, p. 200.

167   Archer Butler Hulbert, "The Old National Road—Historic Highway of America", *Ohio History* Vol 9, pp. 417-421; Alfred Byron Sears, *Thomas Worthington, Father of Ohio Statehood*, Ohio State University Press for the Ohio Historical Society, 1958, pp. 125-127.

168   Archer Butler Hulbert, "The Old National Road—Historic Highway of America", *Ohio History* Vol 9, pp. 423-424.

169   William Henry Smith, "A familiar Talk about Monarchists and Jacobins," *Ohio History*, Vol. 2, p. 201.

Morrow contributed valuable service during the War of 1812. He voted for the Declaration of War. President Madison appointed him, Thomas Worthington, and Governor Meigs as Commissioners to hold a conference with the Indians at Piqua in August, 1812, to attempt to keep them from joining Tecumseh and the British. They succeeded in persuading a number of the Ohio Indians to fight along side the Americans or to stay out of the War. Morrow also assisted in organizing the militia and establishing forts to protect the border settlements.[170]

In 1817 Morrow helped organize the first canal company in Ohio. He was one of the eleven directors of The Little Miami Canal and Banking Company. Its purpose was to construct such dams and locks necessary to enable boats to navigate the Little Miami from the Ohio River north to Waynesville.[171] He served as president of a turnpike company which constructed a road to Cincinnati and as president of The Little Miami Railroad Company.[172]

Throughout his career Morrow considered himself as a farmer.[173] There are many stories of important person coming to visit him and finding him dressed like any other farmer in the neighborhood and working in his barn or fields. One of his most endearing qualities was his down-home manners and lack of pretentiousness.[174]

Following his retirement from Congress, Morrow was appointed a Canal Commissioner in 1820 and again in 1822.[175] The Commission was charged by the General Assembly with investigating the feasibility of constructing a canal connecting Lake Erie to the Ohio River. This was of critical important to Ohio because it would provide an inexpensive way of transporting agricultural and

---

170   Linda Elise Kolette, *The Papers of Thirteen Early Ohio Political Leaders*, Ohio Historical Society, 1977, p. 160; Alfred Byron Sear, *Thomas Worthington, Father of Ohio Statehood*, Ohio State University Press, pp. 181-186.

171   Hazel Spencer Phillips, *Banking in Warren County, Ohio*, Oxford Press, 1960, pp. 16-17.

172   Linda Elise Kolette, *The Papers of Thirteen Early Ohio Political Leaders*, Ohio Historical Society, 1977, p. 161.

173   In 1810 the public records showed him to own one tract of 383 acres. 173 Lee Soltow, "Inequality Amidst Abundance: Land Ownership in Early 19th Century Ohio", *Ohio History*, Vol. 88, p. 151.

174   William Henry Smith, "A familiar Talk about Monarchists and Jacobins," *Ohio History*, Vol. 2, pp. 206-208, 211-212.

175   William Henry Smith, "A familiar Talk about Monarchists and Jacobins," *Ohio History*, Vol. 2, p. 201.

manufacturing products to markets outside the state and trade goods into the state. On the other hand, it was an incredibly expensive undertaking for the young state. On January 4, 1823, the Commission rendered a favorable report to the General Assembly on five possible routes and alternative means of financing. Another report was submitted the following year showing that eastern bankers were interested in financing the venture. On February 4, 1825, an act was passed authorizing construction of the canals to begin.[176]

Morrow was a Presidential elector in 1820 and cast his vote for James Monroe.[177]

Morrow was elected Governor of Ohio and served for two terms from 1823 to 1826. During his administration the construction of the canals was begun. Also, the School Act of 1825 was passed which initiated a state system of public education in Ohio supported by taxation. Morrow was a strong supporter of the canal system and state support of public education.[178] The tax system was reformed and established on a more equitable and stable basis providing the financial basis for the other two reforms. The canal systems, public education system, and ad valorem tax system were the most important accomplishments of the state government since formation of the state and all were accomplished while Morrow served as Governor.

During his administration Morrow participated in two events of great importance to the people of Ohio, one looking with reverence and appreciation to the past and the other with confidence and excitement to the future. On May 19, 1825, General Marquis De Lafayette arrived at Cincinnati on his tour of the United States in anticipation of the nation's celebration of fifty years of independence. With the people of Cincinnati and surrounding areas looking on, Morrow met Lafayette at the wharf and in a few touching, unaffected words assured him that a nation's heart greeted him with its love and homage.[179] On July 4, 1825, DeWitt Clinton, Governor of New York and father of New York's Erie Canal, gave the address near Buckeye Lake at the

---

176   Chester E. Finn, "The Ohio Canals: Public Enterprise on the Frontier", *Ohio History*, Vol. 51, p. 7, 11.

177   William A. Taylor, *Ohio Statesmen and Annals of Progress*, Columbus, 1899, Vol. 1, p. 145.

178   Linda Elise Kolette, *The Papers of Thirteen Early Ohio Political Leaders*, Ohio Historical Society, 1977, pp. 160-161; Edward A. Miller, "History of Educational Legislation in Ohio from 1803 to 1850", *Ohio History*, Vol. 27, p. 17.

179   John S. C. Abbott, History of the State of Ohio, Detroit, 1875, p. 746; Andrew Burstein, *America's Jublilee*, Alfred A. Knopf, 2001, p. 27.

groundbreaking for the Ohio Canal and turned the first spade full of earth. New York had just completed its canal linking the Atlantic to Lake Erie. [180]

Morrow represented Warren County in the 1827-1828 session of the Ohio Senate and in the 1829-1830 of the Ohio House of Representatives.[181]

Morrow was a founder of the Whig party in Ohio and presided over the first state convention in 1827. He headed the electoral ticket for John Quincy Adams in 1828. He represented his congressional district at the National Convention in 1831 which nominated Henry Clay for president and his name headed the Clay ticket in Ohio the following year.[182]

Morrow returned to Congress in 1840 when Thomas Corwin resigned to become governor and served for three years. He declined to run for reelection or for election to the constitutional convention on the ground that he lived through his age and generation and served it as best he could. It was now time for younger men, attuned to the needs of the present generation, to assume the responsibilities of public office. He spent the remainder of his life at his beloved farm on the Little Miami and died there on March 22, 1851.[183]

Morrow was a founder, member, and elder of the Sycamore Associate Reformed Church for over fifty years.[184] The Associate Reformed Church was formed by the "seceders" and "covenanters" who split from the Church of Scotland in protest against British reforms. They were theologically conservative and fiercely independent. Many Scots and Scotch-Irish with this background came to America from Scotland or Northern Ireland to avoid persecution. The Scotch-Irish were strongly represented on the frontiers of Western Pennsylvania and Virginia and were among the first Ohio pioneers. Presbyterian ministers followed them into the wilderness. The Associate Reformed Church competed with more traditional Presbyterians for the loyalty of the numerous Scotch-Irish on the Ohio frontier. These churches eventually became part of the United Presbyterian Church.[185]

---

180   George W. Knepper, *Ohio and Its People*, Kent State University Press, 1989, p. 153.

181   William A. Taylor, *Ohio Statesmen and Annals of Progress*, State of Ohio, 1899, pp. 131, 138.

182   Linda Elise Kolette, *The Papers of Thirteen Early Ohio Political Leaders*, Ohio Historical Society, 1977, pp. 160-161.

183   William Henry Smith, "A familiar Talk about Monarchists and Jacobins," *Ohio History*, Vol. 2, pp. 203-205.

184   *History of Sycamore Presbyterian Church*, Sycamore Church web page

185   E. B. Welsh, *Buckeye Presbyterianism*, United Presbyterian Synod of Ohio, 1968, pp. 23-27, 48-50.

Governor Charles Anderson said of Governor Morrow, "If I were compelled to choose and name the one ablest and best of all the Governors whom I knew it would be Jeremiah Morrow of Warren County. I believe I have known but one man who had so little of the spirit 'to show off', of false pretense, of selfish vanity or ambition as he had. And as for his merely intellectual powers and culture, without being as far as I know very profound or original, and surely being neither brilliant nor eloquent, he had so many exact, yet various and extensive knowledge, with such accuracy and aptness of memory and citation, that I am compelled to adjudge him a high place as well in scholarship as statesmanship."[186]

CHARLES WILLING BYRD

Charles Willing Byrd was born at his father's plantation, Westover, in Charles County, Virginia on July 26, 1770. His grandfather William Byrd II was born in Virginia and educated in England. He returned to Virginia upon his father's death to manage the family's 26,000 acre estate. William II founded Richmond and Petersburg. He constructed a Georgian mansion that was completed in 1736 and is still standing. The grandfather was a member of the Royal Governor's Council for thirty-five years and served as president for part of that time. Charles' father William III was a loyalist and supported the British during the Revolution.[187]

Charles grew up in the comfort and culture of Virginia's first families during the turmoil of the Revolutionary period. Well educated, he completed his training to become a lawyer in Philadelphia in 1794. He then traveled to Kentucky where he served as the land agent for Robert Morris. Morris, one of Philadelphia's leading merchants, was a member of the Continental Congress and the financier of the Revolutionary War. In 1797 Byrd returned to Philadelphia to open a law practice. In 1799 he came west and settled in Cincinnati. His wife's sister was married to Nathaniel Massie.[188] He was

---

186 William Henry Smith, "A familiar Talk about Monarchists and Jacobins," *Ohio History*, Vol. 2, pp. 207.

187 W. H. Burtner, Jr., "Charles Willing Byrd", *Ohio History*, Vol 41, p. 237; David Gore, "The House that Byrd Built", William Byrd, British Empire Biography web page; Some Ancestors and Descendants of the Byrd Family of Westover, Va. web page.

188 Morten Carlisle, "Buckeye Station", *Ohio History*, Vol. 40, p. 13.

appointed as Secretary of The Northwest Territory by President John Adams on December 31, 1799, when William Henry Harrison resigned to become governor of the Indiana Territory. He quickly established himself as a leading Republican and political opponent of Governor Arthur Saint Clair.[189] When Saint Clair was out of the Territory, which was frequently, Byrd exercised his authority as acting governor to appoint Republicans to office.[190] Byrd submitted a formal complaint against Saint Clair seeking his removal.

Following the enactment of the Enabling Act by Congress, Byrd played an important role for the Republicans by refusing to call the Territorial Legislature into session. Since Saint Clair was out of the Territory, Byrd had the power as acting Governor to convene the legislature. Leading Federalists wanted the Territorial Legislature to reject the Enabling Act as interference in the affairs of the Territory and a violation of the people's rights under the Ordinance. During the summer and fall of 1802 he helped the cause by attacking Saint Clair and requesting the President to remove him from office.[191]

Byrd was nominated to the Republican slate at the party convention at Big Hill on August 13, 1802, and was elected as a Republican delegate to the convention. He received the fifth highest number of votes.[192] Byrd played a leading role as Hamilton County's representative to the committees appointed to draft article one on the legislature, article two on the executive and article three on the judiciary.[193] His vote on Negro rights was not as anti-Negro as might be expected in view of his Virginia background.[194] Following Saint Clair's speech to the convention attacking Congress, the President removed Saint Clair and appointed Byrd as acting governor until Ohio became a state. The removal was

189   "Charles Willing Byrd", Ohio History Central, Ohio Historical Society web wage; Richard C. Knopf, *Transcription of the Executive Journal of the Northwest Territory*, Ohio Historical Society web page, p. 528; Beverly W. Bond, Jr., *The Foundations of Ohio, History of the State of Ohio*, Ohio Historical Society, 1941, Vol 1, pp. 448-449.

190   Wm. T. McClintock, "Ohio's Birth Struggle", *Ohio History*, Vol. 11, p. 56, 57.

191   Randolph Chandler Downes, *Frontier Ohio 1788-1803*, Ohio Historical Society, 1935, pp. 222-223; 236-237.

192   Randolph Chandler Downes, *Frontier Ohio 1788-1803*, Ohio Historical Society, 1935, p. 246.

193   "Journal of Convention", *Ohio Archaeological and Historical Society Publications*, Vol. V, pp. 88, 92, 93.

194   Helen M. Thurston, "The 1802 Constitutional Convention and the Status of the Negro", *Ohio History*, Vol. 81, p. 28.

particularly painful for Saint Clair because the letter was sent to Byrd, his political enemy.[195]

Upon being informed of the actions of Ohio's constitutional convention, Congress on February 19, 1803, created a United States District Court for the State of Ohio with sessions to be held at Chillicothe. On March 1, 1803, President Jefferson nominated Byrd to be the first federal district court judge for Ohio, and on March 3, 1803, the Senate confirmed the appointment. Byrd's appointment was recommended by Thomas Worthington. Under the United States Constitution federal judgeships are appointed for life. He served until his death on August 25, 1828.[196]

The battle between the Ohio General Assembly and the Second Bank of the United States took place in the federal courts. When the General Assembly levied a tax on the bank, the bank sought an injunction against state officials to enjoin collection. Before the injunction was served, an agent acting for the state auditor entered the vault of the bank at Chillicothe and removed $100,000 for the tax. Judge Byrd was placed in the position of enforcing the supremacy of federal law against a hostile General Assembly.

Byrd lived in Cincinnati until 1807 when he purchased his brother-in-law Nathaniel Massie's six hundred acre estate called Buckeye Station. The estate was located a few miles east of Massie's settlement at Manchester. Massie built a frame residence there in 1797. The residence sat on a high hill overlooking the Ohio River. The Byrds lived there until Mrs. Byrd died in February, 1815. Byrd moved to West Union and on March 8, 1818, married Hannah Miles. He then purchased a farm at Sinking Springs in Highland County where he lived until his death.[197]

Byrd became deeply interested in the Shaker movement and his son William joined the Shaker community at Pleasant Hill, Kentucky.[198]

A descendant of one of the first families of Virginia, Byrd came west and contributed his considerable knowledge, connections to the rich and powerful in the East, and legal skills to the organization of the new State of Ohio.

---

195   William Henry Smith, *The St. Clair Papers*, Cincinnati, 1882, Vol 1, pp. 244-246; Vol. 2, pp. 599-600.

196   History of the Sixth Circuit: A Bicentennial Project p. 36.

197   W. H. Burtner, Jr., "Charles Willing Byrd", *Ohio History*, Vol. 41, pp. 237, 238.

198   Byrd Papers, Manuscripts Department, Lilly Library, Indiana University, Bloomington, IN

JOHN SMITH

John Smith was born in Virginia. By 1790 he was an ordained minister of a Baptist Congregation located at the Forks of the Cheat River, Monongalia County, Virginia. In April, 1791, he moved to Columbia in the Northwest Territory. He became minister of the Church at Columbia, the first Baptist Church in the Territory. The church was organized in 1790 by Rev. Stephen Gano of Providence, Rhode Island, while visiting his father at the new settlement. For a few years Smith served this church and the church at Cincinnati. In 1797 he organized the four Baptist churches in the Cincinnati area into the Miami Association.[199]

Smith was described as of "unusually fine appearance with easy and agreeable manners. He was reserved in character, dignified in deportment and commanded great respect and attention. He was an excellent speaker because of his flow of language and peculiarly sweet, yet powerful voice."[200]

In addition to preaching, Smith owned a farm and operated a store and warehouse where he sold merchandise imported from the east. He held a place among the first circles of Cincinnati society.[201]

Smith was elected to serve in the first Territorial Legislature which met at Chillicothe on November 24, 1799 and recessed January 29, 1801. He also served in the second Territorial Legislature which met from November 23, 1801 to January 23, 1802. He witnessed the conflict between the Governor and the legislature over the power to establish counties and to locate county seats. He participated in the controversy over Saint Clair's plan to postpone statehood by dividing the Territory.[202]

Smith was close to and some say an agent of John Cleves Symmes and very influential in the back country north of Cincinnati. An ally of Worthington and Tiffin on the statehood question, he had enemies among the Republican

---

199   M. Avis Pitcher, "John Smith, First Senator from Ohio and His Connections with Aaron Burr", *Ohio History*, Vol. 45, pp. 68-69; "Ohio and the Western Territories", General Baptist Net web page.

200   M. Avis Pitcher, "John Smith, First Senator from Ohio and His Connections with Aaron Burr", *Ohio History*, Vol. 45, p. 70.

201   M. Avis Pitcher, "John Smith, First Senator from Ohio and His Connections with Aaron Burr", *Ohio History*, Vol. 45, pp. 69-70.

202   William A. Taylor, *Ohio Statesmen and Annals of Progress*, State of Ohio, 1899, pp. 18-21; M. Avis Pitcher, "John Smith, First Senator from Ohio and His Connections with Aaron Burr", *Ohio History*, Vol. 45, p. 71.

leaders of Hamilton County. Although he was not on the Republican slate of delegates nominated at the party convention at Big Hill on August 13, 1802, he was elected as a delegate to the convention.[203]

Smith's stature among the Republican delegates is shown by the fact that he served with Byrd as the representatives from Hamilton County on the committees to draft article one on the legislature, article two on the executive, and article three on the judiciary.[204] He voted with Worthington against slavery and against the suffrage and other civil rights for Negroes.[205]

Following the adoption of the Constitution, the first members of the General Assembly were elected in January and met at Chillicothe on March 1, 1803. On April 1, 1803, the two houses met in joint session and elected John Smith and Thomas Worthington as Ohio's first two United States Senators.[206] When Smith arrived in Washington, he and Worthington drew lots on who would serve the four year term and who would serve the six year term. Smith won the six year term.[207]

While in the U.S. Senate Smith promoted a venture to build a canal around the Falls of the Ohio at Louisville to be financed by a federal grant. He had a financial interest in the venture.[208] In 1805 he secured a defense contract to furnish supplies to the army.[209] He was involved in land speculations in West Florida while advocating that the United States acquire that territory.[210] It was not unusual for Senators and Congressmen in that day to have a financial interest in legislation they were advocating.

While in Washington Smith became a social friend of then Vice President Aaron Burr. President Jefferson and Burr were estranged due to the election

---

203 Randolph Chandler Downes, *Frontier Ohio 1788-1803*, Ohio Historical Society, 1935, pp. 210-211, 246; M. Avis Pitcher, "John Smith, First Senator from Ohio and His Connections with Aaron Burr", *Ohio History*, Vol. 45, p. 72.

204 "Journal of Convention of 1802", *Ohio History*, Vol. 5, pp. 92, 93.

205 Helen M. Thurston, "The 1802 Constitutional Convention and the Status of the Negro", *Ohio History*, Vol. 81, p. 27.

206 William A. Taylor, *Ohio Statesmen and Annals of Progress*, State of Ohio, 1899, p. 36.

207 Alfred Byron Sear, *Thomas Worthington, Father of Ohio Statehood*, Ohio State University Press, p. 115.

208 M. Avis Pitcher, "John Smith, First Senator from Ohio and His Connections with Aaron Burr", *Ohio History*, Vol. 45, pp. 76, 77.

209 M. Avis Pitcher, "John Smith, First Senator from Ohio and His Connections with Aaron Burr", *Ohio History*, Vol. 45, p. 86.

210 M. Avis Pitcher, "John Smith, First Senator from Ohio and His Connections with Aaron Burr", *Ohio History*, Vol. 45, pp. 703-706.

contest over the presidency in 1800. When Burr's term ended and he was dropped from the administration, his interest turned to the West. With others he organized a venture for the ostensible purpose of settling in the Spanish lands west of the Mississippi. Jefferson received information suggesting that Burr was involved in a conspiracy to invade Mexico and to divide the western states from the union. Jefferson alerted Governor Meigs of Ohio and the other western Governors. Smith was accused of being one of the conspirators and was indicted for treason along with Burr and others. Burr was acquitted and the charges against the other conspirators were dismissed, but Smith's career was ruined. The General Assembly of Ohio passed a resolution requesting him to resign. The Senate conducted a hearing to determine if he should be expelled. The vote fell one vote short of the two thirds required for expulsion. On April 25, 1808, Smith sent a letter of resignation to acting Governor Thomas Kirker. He wrote, "I had long before seen enough of the political world, the bitterness of its contests, the malignity of its persecutions, the overbearing arrogance of some and disgraceful compliance and base arts of others to excite my disappointment and aversion."[211]

Historian Daniel J. Ryan after carefully analyzing the evidence against Smith stated, "The bitterest of all political controversies is that of factions within a party. Where partisan opponents refuse to lead in slander, cruelty, and unfairness, the faction fighter will go with the deadliest intent. He spares neither honor, reputation nor gray hairs. This was the character of the fight against Smith; it was waged against him by his own party associates and by men who knew him to be honest and patriotic. He was not the politician his enemies were. His political honor came from sheer personal popularity not through intrigue or power. His place was wanted by others, and the Burr excitement offered the opportunity. The plan to unseat him was developed in the Ohio legislature and soon transferred to the United States Senate."[212] Jacob Burnet, who was no friend of Aaron Burr because of his killing Alexander Hamilton in a duel, shared similar beliefs as to Smith's innocence. He stated, "Mr. Smith was a firm, high minded man—he solemnly affirmed his belief that Colonel Burr was not engaged in a conspiracy against his country, and refused to aid in the prosecution which was carrying on against him. The consequence was fatal to his fame and his fortune."[213]

---

211   M. Avis Pitcher, "John Smith, First Senator from Ohio and His Connections with Aaron Burr", *Ohio History*, Vol. 45, pp. 78-86.
212   Daniel J. Ryan, *History of Ohio*, New York, 1912, Vol. 3, p. 250.
213   Jacob Burnet, "Burnet's Letters" *Transactions of the Historical and Philosophical Society of Ohio*, Cincinnati, 1839, Vol. 1, p. 104.

Smith was not only disgraced, he was financially ruined. The government failed to pay him for the goods he had supplied under his defense contract, and his assets were seized and sold to satisfy creditors. He moved his family to St. Francisville, Louisiana, where he owned property. At the time it was part of West Florida under Spanish control and therefore beyond the jurisdiction of United States Courts. He learned Spanish and resumed preaching. In addition to his other troubles he lost his wife and six children within a few years. He died in St. Francisville, Louisiana July 30, 1824.[214]

Smith's biographer stated, "As politician, preacher, merchant, contractor and land speculator, Smith displayed the usual versatility of a frontiersman of his day. He was evidently attracted to Burr as were many others. How involved and what he knew about Burr's schemes is more difficult to say. Certainly his prosecution was carried out in the same feeling of alarm and excitement that attended the other phases of the Burr Conspiracy. The guilt was in minds of the few and not proven to the many."[215]

FRANCIS DUNLAVY

Francis Dunlavy, sometimes spelled Dunlevy, was born December 31, 1761, near Winchester, Virginia. His father Anthony Dunlavy emigrated from Ireland about 1745. The Dunlavy family had originally lived in Spain, but after becoming Protestants had fled to France. Upon the revocation of the Edict of Nantes, they migrated to Ireland. About 1772 the family settled near Catfish, now Washington, in what is now Washington County, Pennsylvania.[216]

During the Revolutionary War, this area was subject to frequent Indian attack by tribes allied with the British. Dunlavy volunteered as a private on October 1, 1776, when only 14 years old, as a substitute for a family man who had been drafted. The company erected a chain of blockhouses along the Ohio River north of what is now Steubenville and scouted in pairs up and down the River watching for Indians crossing the River. This tour of duty ended in

---

214   M. Avis Pitcher, "John Smith, First Senator from Ohio and His Connections with Aaron Burr", *Ohio History*, Vol. 45, pp. 86-88.

215   M. Avis Pitcher, "John Smith, First Senator from Ohio and His Connections with Aaron Burr", *Ohio History*, Vol. 45, p. 88.

216   C.W. Butterfield, *The Expedition Against Sandusky under Col. William Crawford in 1782*, Cincinnati, 1873, pp. 252-253; *A History and Biographical Cyclopedia of Butler County, Ohio*, Cincinnati, 1882, pp. 253-258.

December of that year. In July of the following year he served fourteen days at Fort Pitt in place of his father who had been drafted. Fort Pitt located at the present site of Pittsburgh was the principal army outpost in the West. In August, 1778 he again served for a month in a company that ranged the woods between Pittsburgh and Wheeling watching for Indians and relieved the company stationed at Wheeling. In October of that year he again entered the service and participated in the construction of Fort McIntosh where Beaver Creek entered the Ohio from the North. The army then marched into the Ohio country and constructed Fort Laurens on the Muskingum River. Fort Laurens was the western most American outpost during the Revolutionary War. It was intended to encourage the Indians on the Muskingum to remain allied with the Americans, but due to difficulty in keeping it supplied it was soon abandoned. Dunlavy returned to Fort McIntosh and was discharged in December. In August 1779 he participated in an expedition commanded by Colonel Brodhead which marched up the Allegheny River attacking Indian Villages. His final military service was in Colonel William Crawford's ill-fated campaign against the Indians on the Sandusky River in 1783. The Americans were defeated at a fierce battle in Wyandot County and Crawford was captured and burned at the stake. Dunlavy was among those who survived the battle and regrouped under Colonel Williamson to make a retreat back to the Ohio.[217]

In the spring of 1782 Dunlavy was a student at Rev. Thaddeus Dodd's log cabin academy for classical and mathematical instruction located on Ten Mile Creek in Washington County. Dodd was a Presbyterian minister and Princeton graduate who established the first such school in the West. Dodd was also the first principal of the Washington Academy which became Washington and Jefferson College at Washington, Pennsylvania.[218] Dunlavy left the school to enlist for the Crawford Expedition and after his return he attended Dickinson College. The College was established by Dr. Benjamin Rush, prominent Philadelphia physician, at Carlisle, Pennsylvania, in 1783, then a town on the western frontier. Rush believed that the promise of America depended upon an educated citizenry and recognized the paucity of educational opportunity in the West.[219] After leaving Dickinson, Dunlavy then received religious

---

217   C.W. Butterfield, *The Expedition Against Sandusky under Col. William Crawford in 1782*, Cincinnati, 1873, pp. 253-256.

218   C.W. Butterfield, *The Expedition Against Sandusky under Col. William Crawford in 1782*, Cincinnati, 1873, p. 255; *Commemorative Biographical Record of Washington County, Pa.*, J. H. Beers & Co., 1893, p. 718.

219   Dickinson College web page.

instruction from his uncle Rev. James Hoge of Winchester, Pennsylvania. He then decided to abandon the ministry and taught at a classical school in that state.[220]

In 1790 Dunlavy moved with his father's family to the vicinity of Washington, Kentucky.[221] The following year he joined John Reily at the school which Reilly had begun the year before at Columbia in the Northwest Territory. Dunlavy taught the classics, Latin and Greek, and higher mathematics while Reily taught the common courses. This school later evolved into an academy under the patronage of Rev. John Smith, William Goforth, John Gano, and Dunlavy.[222] After General Wayne's victory over the Indians in 1794 and the Greenville Treaty the following year, Dunlavy moved his school up the Little Miami to a settlement called "The Island" and in 1798 he moved again to a location where Lebanon would later be established. This became the first school in what later would become Warren County.[223] A student of Dunlavy subsequently conducted the school in Lebanon.

Dunlavy was elected to the second Territorial legislature which met at Chillicothe November 23, 1801 and recessed January 23, 1802.[224] During this session the allies of Saint Clair persuaded a majority to recommend to Congress that the Territory be divided at the Scioto River, a plan intended to postpone statehood. They also changed the meeting place for the Territorial legislature from Chillicothe to Cincinnati. This action resulted in a riot in Chillicothe which was quelled by Thomas Worthington. Following the riot, Dunlavy and others witnessed Governor Saint Clair speak contemptuously of the federal government, the Jefferson Administration, and the militia. The Governor predicted that the government would eventually settle down into an aristocracy and finally a monarchy. Dunlavy prepared a report on what he

---

220   C.W. Butterfield, *The Expedition Against Sandusky under Col. William Crawford in 1782*, Cincinnati, 1873, p. 256; *A History and Biographical Cyclopedia of Butler County, Ohio*, Cincinnati, 1882, pp. 253-258.

221   C.W. Butterfield, *The Expedition Against Sandusky under Col. William Crawford in 1782*, Cincinnati, 1873, p. 256.

222   W. Ross Dunn, "Education in Territorial Ohio", *Ohio History*, Vol. 35, p. 337-339; D. C. Schilling, "Pioneer Schools and School Masters", *Ohio History*, Vol. 25, p. 39.

223   D. C. Schilling, "Pioneer Schools and School Masters", *Ohio History*, Vol. 25, p. 39; W. Ross Dunn, "Education in Territorial Ohio", *Ohio History*, Vol. 35, p. 339.

224   William A. Taylor, *Ohio Statesmen and Annals of Progress*, State of Ohio, 1899, pp. 18-19.

heard and he, Joseph Darlinton, and a third witness signed it. The report was forwarded to President Jefferson as grounds for the Governor's removal.[225] The Republicans hoped to secure the Governor's removal before the election of delegates to the convention so that he could not use his position as Governor to influence the election of anti-statehood delegates. The President waited until after Saint Clair again spoke disparagingly of the Federal Government and the administration at the convention before removing him.

Dunlavy helped lead the campaign in Hamilton County for Republican delegates to the convention and reported to Thomas Worthington on August 12, "We are all Republicans—not a solitary Federalist is now seen thro the whole county...A state government is now the universal cry."[226] Of the ten delegates elected to represent the county in the convention, he received the most votes.[227] He served on the committee appointed to draft a bill of rights.[228] Unlike other leaders of the Republicans, Dunlavy was one of the strongest supporters of civil rights for Negroes.[229] By taking a strong position on this issue, he demonstrated that he would not sacrifice his principles to win favor with the leaders of the party.

At the first election for state officials in January, 1803, Dunlavy was elected to the Ohio Senate. On April 1, 1803, the General Assembly in a joint session elected him President Judge of the Third Circuit of the Court of Common Pleas.[230] The new Constitution provided for common pleas courts comprised of a president and associate judges. The president judges were to be full-time and were required to travel from county to county within their circuit. Each county had two or three associate judges who met with the president judge when he came to the county.[231] All judges were appointed by the General

---

225   William Henry Smith, *The St. Clair Papers*, Cincinnati, Vol 2, pp. 585, 586; Henry Howe, *Historical Collections of Ohio*, Centennial Edition, 1908, Vol 2, p. 758.

226   Alfred Byron Sears, *Thomas Worthington, Father of Ohio Statehood*, Ohio State University Press for the Ohio Historical Society, 1958, pp. 90-91.

227   Randolph Chandler Downes, *Frontier Ohio 1788-1803*, Ohio Historical Society, 1935, 246.

228   "Proceedings of the First Constitutional Convention", *Ohio History*, Vol. 5, p. 90.

229   Helen M. Thurston, "The 1802 Constitutional Convention and the Status of the Negro", *Ohio History*, Vol. 81, p. 27.

230   William A. Taylor, *Ohio Statesmen and Annals of Progress*, State of Ohio, 1899, pp. 35, 37.

231   *Ohio Constitution of 1802*, Article III, Section 3.

Assembly for seven year terms. The Constitution provided for three presidential judges within the state and provided that this number could be increased by the legislature after five years.[232]

At the time of his election as a president judge Dunlavy had received no legal training and had never practiced law or served as a judge. His election reflected the high esteem in which he was held among Republican leaders.[233] Immediately after his election he began earnestly to study law and being well educated and intelligent quickly acquired a fair amount of legal learning. He was strictly honest and had a love of justice which at the time was valued more highly by people on the frontier than legal scholarship.[234]

The first court in Warren County was held in the fall of 1803 at the Black Horse Tavern at Lebanon, owned by Ichabod Corwin, the town's founder and father of Governor and Senator Thomas Corwin. Built in 1798 the log building served as courthouse, tavern, and shop for traveling merchants.[235]

Dunlavy's courage as a judge was displayed in 1810 when he confronted a mob of 1500 who gathered at Union Village to run the Shakers out of the county. The Shakers were an unpopular religious sect whose members gave up their worldly possessions when they joined the society. They also practiced celibacy and adopted abandoned children. The Shakers had established a town at Union Village. The public had been aroused by false statements circulated about them by persons with personal agendas, religious bigots and those who are always ready to exploit the popular prejudice for personal gain. Judge Dunlavy and other responsible leaders, hearing that a mob was being organized, warned the villagers, and were present to keep order. Mounting his horse and pushing to the middle of the crowd, he delivered a solemn injunction that any one who violated the laws would be punished. He was met by verbal abuse and defiance by some, but eventually the crowd dispersed without injury to the villagers.[236] The Bill of Rights drafted by Dunlavy and his committee stated,

---

232   *Ohio Constitution of 1802*, Article III, Section 3, 8.

233   Alfred Byron Sears, *Thomas Worthington, Father of Ohio Statehood*, Ohio State University Press for the Ohio Historical Society, 1958, pp. 111-112.

234   *History of Clinton County, Ohio*, W.H. Beers and Company, 1882, Vol 1, pp. 384-387.

235   "History of Warren County, Ohio", Warren County, Ohio web wite; Hazel Spencer Phillips, *The Golden Lamb*. Oxford Press, 1958, p. 1.

236   J. P. MacLean, "Mobbing the Shakers of Union Village", *Ohio History*, Vol. 11, p. 121; Randy McNutt, "Changed City Retains Its Charm", *Cincinnati Enquirer*, November 19, 2002

"That all men have a natural and indefeasible right to worship Almighty God according to the dictates of conscience."[237] By his courage in the face of the mob, Dunlavy proved that at least for him these were not simply flowery words.

Judge Dunlavy disregarded the Supreme Court's holding that the law increasing the jurisdiction of justices of the peace to fifty dollars was unconstitutional. In his circuit which covered western Ohio, the fifty dollar law was recognized as valid.[238] Following the adoption of the Sweeping Resolution and the election of new judges to fill the vacancies which it created, the associate judges in Greene County refused to recognize the validity of the Sweeping Resolution and the new appointments. Dunlavy refused to participate in their proceedings. The associate judges proceeded without him and their judgments were subsequently set aside by the Supreme Court.[239] The following year a Greene County associate judge who had been replaced by the General Assembly following the adoption of the Sweeping Resolution attempted to forcefully take his place on the bench. Judge Dunlavy found him in contempt and ordered his arrest. When the Sheriff refused, Judge Dunlavy found the Sheriff in contempt and ordered the coroner and several bystanders to make the arrests. One of the associate judges then resigned depriving the Court of a quorum. A heated contest over the vacant seat ensued between Tammany and anti-Tammany voters of the County.[240]

Dunlavy served as president judge of the circuit for southwest Ohio for two terms until 1817. His circuit included ten counties which he traveled on horseback, requiring the swimming of rivers when the water was high. Following his retirement from the bench, he practiced law for ten years.[241]

Although Dunlavy was raised as a Presbyterian, his sentiments lay with the Baptists, and he was one of the founders of the Turtle Creek Baptist Church organized on December 11, 1802. The Church grew out of the Baptist Church

---

237   *Ohio Constitution of 1802*, Article VIII, Section 3.

238   Donald F. Melhorn Jr., *Lest We Be Marsahll'd, Judicial Power and Politics in Ohio*, University of Akron Press, 2003, p. 91.

239   Donald F. Melhorn Jr., *Lest We Be Marsahll'd, Judicial Power and Politics in Ohio*, University of Akron Press, 2003, pp. 153-155.

240   Donald F. Melhorn Jr., *Lest We Be Marsahll'd, Judicial Power and Politics in Ohio*, University of Akron Press, 2003, pp. 159-163.

241   C.W. Butterfield, *The Expedition Against Sandusky under Col. William Crawford in 1782*, Cincinnati, 1873, p. 256; History of Clinton County, Ohio; *History of Clinton County, Ohio*, W.H. Beers and Company, 1882, Vol 1, p. 387.

established at Columbia in 1790. In 1813 its name was changed to the Baptist Church of Lebanon.[242]

Dunlavy maintained his strong convictions against slavery and in 1836 at the age of 75 Dunlavy attended the first annual meeting of the Ohio Anti-slavery Society which was held near Granville, Ohio. He was elected as a vice president.[243]

In 1810 Dunlavy owned four tracts totaling 562 acres.[244]

Francis Dunlavy died on November 6, 1839. Historian C. W. Butterfield, stated, "In many respects he was a remarkable man. His memory was astonishing. He read and wrote the Latin language with ease."[245] A county history described him as "a man of great character and wide influence.... On the bench he was distinguished for diligence and attention. He bent all the faculties of his mind to discover the truth and made his decision conform to it."[246]

WILLIAM GOFORTH

William Goforth was born December 26, 1766, in New York City. His grandfather Aaron Goforth, Jr. came from Yorkshire to Philadelphia.[247] His father William Goforth Sr. was a member of the Committee of Safety and the Committee of One Hundred which governed New York City during the Revolution. William Sr. also served as a captain, major, and lieutenant colonel

242   "Church and Family History Research Assistance for Warren County, Ohio", Primitive Baptist Family History Assistance, Carthage Library web page; "History of the First Baptist Church of Sayville", Sayville Library web page; A History and Biographical Cyclopedia of Butler County, Ohio, Cincinnati, 1882, pp. 253-258.

243   Robert Price, "The Ohio Anti-Slavery Convention of 1836", Ohio History, Vol. 45, p. 182.

244   244 Lee Soltow, "Inequality Amidst Abundance: Land Ownership in Early 19th Century Ohio", Ohio History, Vol. 88, p. 150.

245   C.W. Butterfield, The Expedition Against Sandusky under Col. William Crawford in 1782, Cincinnati, 1873, p. 256.

246   A History and Biographical Cyclopedia of Butler County, Ohio, Cincinnati, 1882, pp. 253-258.

247   Anita Bonin, family web page, Ancestry.com; Barbara McCormick, family web page, Ancestry.com

in the New York Continental Line during the Revolutionary War. He served in the Canadian campaign and at the Battle of Three Rivers.[248]

William Goforth Sr. was among the first settlers at Columbia. When Governor St. Clair arrived at Cincinnati on January 2, 1790, he organized Hamilton County and appointed its first officers. William Goforth Sr. was appointed one of the three judges of the court of common pleas and court of quarter sessions.[249] In 1796 Goforth chaired a meeting of leading citizens in Columbia which adopted resolutions highly critical of the government of the Northwest Territory as administered by Governor St. Clair. They were also critical of Symmes who as judge of the Territory sat in cases in which he was personally interested. The following year he served on a committee of correspondence to correspond with leaders of other counties concerning the taking of a census to show that the Territory had reached five thousand adult white males and therefore a territorial legislature should be established.[250] He was elected as a representative from Hamilton County to the House of Representatives of the First Territorial Legislature which convened on February 4, 1799. In accordance with the Ordinance of 1787 the first duty of the elected Representatives was to nominate ten persons from whom President Adams was to select five to serve in the upper house which was called the Legislative Council. The legislators then reconvened in September after the Council had been selected. They set to work enacting laws for the Territory covering such basic matters as execution of deeds and real estate contracts, partition of real estate, assignment of dower, insolvent debtors, trading with the Indians, militia, relief of the poor, courts for minor offenses, divorce, arbitration, and penalties for crimes. The Governor was no doubt offended when the legislature elected William Henry Harrison over the Governor's son for the Territory's non-voting representative to Congress. The Governor angered many of the members by waiting until the end of the session to veto 11 of 39 bills. A principal issue was his contention that he alone had authority to establish counties and county seats. The legislature met again in November, 1800. Goforth served with Thomas Worthington and Paul Fearing on a committee to draft a response to the Governor's address to the

---

248   Benson J. Lossing, *Pictorial Field Book of the American Revolution*, 1850, Vol. 2, Chapter XX11; James A. Roberts, *New York in the Revolution as Colony and State*, 2nd Ed., 1898

249   Richard C. Knopf, "Transcription of the Journal of the Northwest Territory", Ohio Historical Society, web page, pp. 56, 57.

250   Randolph C. Downes, *Frontier Ohio*, Ohio Historical Society, pp. 181-183.

Legislature. Although conciliatory in tone, it asserted the legislature's right to establish counties and requested that any vetoes be returned in ten days so the legislators could address his objection. The Governor insisted on his power to erect counties and prorogued the assembly on December 9 to coincide with the termination of his term of office. Republicans accused him of doing this to prevent Charles Willing Byrd, Secretary of the Territory and a Republican, from becoming acting Governor. This further incensed members of the legislature.[251] The stage had been set for the political battle which would lead to statehood and the Governor and his allies' removal from power.

William Goforth Jr. studied medicine under Dr. Joseph Young and Dr. Charles McKnight of New York City. While he was studying with Dr. McKnight, the school was attacked by a mob who was upset at its anatomical studies. Goforth decided to accompany his brother-in-law John Gano to the West and on June 10, 1788, he landed at Limestone (now Maysville), Kentucky. He settled in Washington located four miles from the River. It was then the second largest town in Kentucky. He established his practice there and soon became the most popular physician in the county. In 1799 he moved to Columbia where his father resided. In the spring of the following year he moved to Cincinnati where he occupied the Peach Grove house previously occupied by Dr. Allison. He quickly established himself as the leading physician in the area.

Dr. Goforth was a strong Republican and took a keen interest in the politics of the Territory. On January 26, 1802, President Jefferson received a lengthy letter from William Goforth denouncing the administration of the Territory by Governor Saint Clair as "clothed with the power of a British Nabob" who could "convene, prorogue and dissolve" the legislature "at pleasure"; fill all offices "with men of his own political sentiments" and control them by limiting their tenure by appointing them during "his will and pleasure", and keep us out of the Union by getting the legislature to pass a bill dividing the Territory so that neither part would have a sufficient population to qualify for statehood—a bill passed in order to keep St Clair and his allies in power.[252]

Dr. Goforth was elected from the slate of Republican delegates to the Convention. When the delegates convened at Chillicothe on November 1, 1802, its first order of business was to elect Dr. Goforth as temporary chairman.

---

251   Alfred Byron Sears, *Thomas Worthington, Father of Ohio Statehood*, Ohio State University Press for the Ohio Historical Society, 1958, p. 48.

252   Alfred B. Sears, "The Political Philosophy of Arthur St. Clair", *Ohio History* Vol 49, p. 41.

Edward Tiffin was elected president of the convention the following day.[253] Goforth served on the committee appointed to draft the bill of rights and establish a schedule for carrying the new government into operation.[254] Although a strong Republican, Goforth voted with the Federalists in support of Negro suffrage and civil rights.[255]

Dr. Goforth was chosen as a Presidential elector in 1804 and cast his vote with the other two electors for Thomas Jefferson.[256]

Dr. Goforth was keenly interested in natural science. At his personal expense he dug up the bones of a mastodon at Big Bone Lick in Kentucky and shared his findings with Meriwether Lewis of Lewis and Clark fame as well as President Jefferson.[257]

Goforth became enamored of French culture from conversations with émigrés from the French Revolution. In the spring of 1807 he took a flat boat south to the lower Mississippi River where he settled and was made a Parrish judge. He was elected as a delegate of Lafourche County to the convention called to adopt the first constitution of Louisiana. Soon thereafter he moved to New Orleans. During the War of 1812, he served as a surgeon for a Louisiana regiment of volunteers.[258]

On May 1, 1816, he and his family left New Orleans for Ohio on a keel boat. The journey took eight months. During the trip he contracted hepatitis and died May 12, 1817 in Cincinnati.[259]

Daniel Drake came to Cincinnati in 1800 at the age of fifteen to serve as an apprentice to Dr. Goforth.[260] Upon completion of his apprenticeship he

253   "Journal of the First Constitutional Convention", *Ohio History*, Vol. 5, pp. 81, 83.

254   "Journal of the First Constitutional Government", *Ohio History*, Vol. 5, p. 90.

255   Helen M. Thurston, "The 1802 Constitutional Convention and the Status of the Negro", *Ohio History*, Vol. 81, p. 27.

256   William A. Taylor, *Ohio Statesmen and Annals of Progress*, Columbus, 1899, Vol. 1, p. 64.

257   Lewis & Clark Journey of Discovery, Jefferson National Expansion Memorial web page; Letter from William Goforth to Thomas Jefferson 1807

258   Ford, *History of Cincinnati, Ohio*, L.A. Williams & Co., 1881.

259   Ford, *History of Cincinnati, Ohio*, L.A. Williams & Co., 1881; Anita Bonin, family web page, Ancestry.com

260   Elizabeth Faries, "The Miami Country 1750-1815, as Described in Journals and Letters," *Ohio History* Vol. 57, p. 62; "Dr. Drake and his Followers," *Ohio History* Vol 21, p. 338.

became his partner.[261] He subsequently founded the Medical College of Ohio in December, 1818. He described Dr. Goforth as follows, "He had the most winning manners of any physician I ever knew. Yet they were all his own, for in deportment he was quite an original. The painstaking and respectful courtesy with which he treated the poorest and humblest people of the village seemed to secure their gratitude, and the most especially as he dressed with precision and never left the house in the morning until his hair was powdered by our itinerant barber, John Arthurs, and his gold-headed cane was grasped by his gloved hand. His kindness of heart was as much a part of his nature as hair powder was to his costume, and what might not be given through benevolence could always be exacted by flattery, coupled with professions of friendship, the sincerity of which he never questioned. In conversation he was precise yet fluent, and abounded in anecdotes which he told in a way that others could not imitate."[262]

JOHN REILY

John Reily was born in Chester County, Pennsylvania on April 10, 1763, the son of an Irish immigrant.[263] He moved with his family to Staunton, Virginia, when he was five or six years old. The area was on the edge of the frontier. During the Revolutionary War the area was subject to Indian attacks and Reily's family found it necessary at time to seek protection at a small fort near Staunton. When he was seventeen years old, Reily joined General Nathaniel Greene's army which was confronting General Cornwallis in the south. He participated in the battles of Guilford Court House, Camden, Ninety-Six, and Eutaw Springs. Following the last battle the British retreated to Yorktown and were subsequently forced to surrender. After eighteen months of service, Reily returned home to Virginia.[264]

He remained with his family for two years before setting out for Kentucky where he lived with his sister at Danville, Kentucky for five or six years. He

---

261   Adolph E. Waller, "Daniel Drake as a Pioneer in Modern Ecology," *Ohio History*, Vol. 56, p. 364.

262   Ford, History of Cincinnati, Ohio, L.A. Williams & Co., 1881.

263   Dorrit Morgan, Family Tree, Ancestry.Com; Millcreek Valley News, October 24, 1968.

264   *A History and Biographical Cyclopedia of Butler County, Ohio*, Cincinnati, 1882, pp. 77-81.

helped on the farm, performed carpentry work, and made farm implements for the use of the settlers. His last year in Kentucky he taught school.[265]

The settlement of Ohio was just beginning and Reily moved to Columbia on December 18, 1789. The settlement had been established by Benjamin Stites and his associates at the mouth of the Little Miami the year before. On June 21, 1790, Reily opened a school at Columbia. He was joined the following year by Francis Dunlavy who taught the classical courses and higher mathematics. This was the first school in southwest Ohio.[266]

When an Indian attack was made on Dunlap's Station, now Colerain, on January 10, 1791, Reily was part of the group of men from Columbia who set out on horseback to relieve the settlement. They discovered that the settlers had survived the assault. After the defeat of St. Clair's army by the Indians, an expedition was organized by General Wilkinson to bury the dead and recover the cannon left behind. Reily joined a company under Captain John S. Gano of Columbia. They proceeded north up the road cut by St. Clair's army past Ft. Hamilton, Ft. Jefferson, and then on to the battlefield where they were confronted with a melancholy sight. The victims had been scalped, their clothes removed, and their bodies mutilated by wild animals. The ground was covered with deep snow when they arrived which made their job difficult. They dug a large pit, buried the frozen bodies and covered them with a large mound. Due to the limitation of time and the snow, only half of the bodies were interred. They were able to recover and take back only one cannon.[267]

In 1791 Reily purchased a tract of land about seven miles from Cincinnati. Two years later he gave up his interest in the school at Columbia to his friend Francis Dunlavy. He and Mr. Prior sought to improve their neighboring tracts together. However, their horses were stolen by the Indians and then Mr. Prior was killed while on a trip from Fort Washington to Fort Hamilton. Following Prior's death, Reily abandoned farming and returned to teaching at Columbia.[268]

---

265   *A History and Biographical Cyclopedia of Butler County, Ohio*, Cincinnati, 1882, pp. 77-81.

266   W. Ross Dunn, "Education in Territorial Ohio", *Ohio History*, Vol. 35, p. 337-339; D. C. Schilling, "Pioneer Schools and School Masters", *Ohio History*, Vol. 25, p. 39.

267   *A History and Biographical Cyclopedia of Butler County, Ohio*, Cincinnati, 1882, pp. 77-81.

268   *A History and Biographical Cyclopedia of Butler County, Ohio*, Cincinnati, 1882, pp. 77-81.

In April, 1794, he went to Cincinnati and was employed as deputy by John S. Gano, who served as clerk of the territorial courts in the county. As deputy clerk he handled a large part of the business of the office and was highly respected for his accuracy and neatness.[269] When the first Territorial legislature convened in 1799, he was elected clerk of the House of Representatives. He served in the same position for the second Territorial legislature.[270] When Cincinnati's village government was organized, he served as one of the town trustees and was elected clerk and collector of revenue.

An Act of Congress was passed on March 3, 1801 which granted to persons who had purchased land of Judge Symmes not included within his patent first priority to purchase the land from the government. Although they were not given credit for money paid to Symmes, this enabled settlers to protect the value of the improvements which they had made. President Jefferson appointed John Reily, William Goforth, and James Findlay as commissioners to adjust claims under the Act. Reily kept the records for the Commissioners and recorded the location of the claims. The following year he was reappointed for another term.[271]

Despite a vigorous campaign by the Federalists, Reily was the only Federalist from Hamilton County elected as a delegate to the convention.[272] He served on the committee appointed to draft the bill of rights and schedule for bringing the new government into operation and a committee to revise the journal of the convention before it went to press. He chaired the committee of the whole during deliberations on the preamble. He voted with the Federalists on the question of whether the constitution should be submitted to the people for approval.[273] Reily voted for limited suffrage and other civil rights for Negroes.[274]

---

269 *A History and Biographical Cyclopedia of Butler County, Ohio,* Cincinnati, 1882, pp. 77-81

270 *A History and Biographical Cyclopedia of Butler County, Ohio,* Cincinnati, 1882, pp. 77-81; William A. Taylor, *Ohio Statesmen and Annals of Progress,* State of Ohio, 1899, pp. 18, 19.

271 *A History and Biographical Cyclopedia of Butler County, Ohio,* Cincinnati, 1882, pp. 77-81; Broadside Giving Notice to Claimants, Library of Congress, American Memory, Historical Collections from the National Digital Library

272 William T. Utter, *The Frontier State, History of Ohio,* Ohio Historical Society, 1942, Vol. 2, p. 8.

273 "Proceedings of the First Constitutional Convention", *Ohio History,* Vol. 5, p. 90, 94, 98.

274 Helen M. Thurston, "The 1802 Constitutional Convention and the Status of the Negro", *Ohio History,* Vol. 81, p. 29.

Fort Hamilton was constructed by General Arthur St. Clair's army in 1791 on its march north to attack the Indians of northwestern Ohio. Located on the Miami River in what is now Hamilton, Butler County, Ohio, it was the first of a series of forts constructed to protect the supply trains supplying the army. Following Saint Clair's defeat, it continued to be used until after Wayne's victory in 1794 and the signing of the Greenville Treaty the following year. A village sprang up which survived the military's abandonment of the fort.[275]

When the government lands on the west bank of the Great Miami went up for sale a group associated with Jacob Burnet purchased a large tract across the river from Hamilton. John Reily was appointed as the agent for the Burnet group to lay out a town and sell lots. The town was named Rossville. Reily moved to Hamilton in 1803 to carry out his duties for the Rossville venture. When he arrived there were only a few residents. Most of them had been attached to General Wayne's army and stayed on after the army was disbanded.[276]

Butler County was established by the first session of the General Assembly and the three commissioners appointed to locate the county seat selected Hamilton. Under the new constitution the president and associate judges of each county's common pleas court were appointed by the General Assembly, but each court appointed a clerk which kept the office for the court and maintained its records. The appointment was for a term of seven years.[277] When the associate judges met with Reily's old friend presiding Judge John Dunlavy, Reily was appointed clerk. He served as the clerk of the Common pleas court and Supreme Court in Hamilton County until 1842.[278] He also served as the clerk for the county commissioners from 1803 to 1819 and during that time managed the finances of the county.[279] Reily was also the first recorder for the county and served in that office from 1803 to 1811. Although he had been a Federalist, he was also appointed as the first postmaster of Hamilton by the Jefferson administration in 1804 and served until 1832.[280]

---

275   *A History and Biographical Cyclopedia of Butler County, Ohio*, Cincinnati, 1882, pp. 6-10.

276   *A History and Biographical Cyclopedia of Butler County, Ohio*, Cincinnati, 1882, pp. 106-111, 287-291.

277   Ohio Constitution of 1802, Article III, Section 9.

278   *A History and Biographical Cyclopedia of Butler County, Ohio*, Cincinnati, 1882, pp. 253-258.

279   *A History and Biographical Cyclopedia of Butler County, Ohio*, Cincinnati, 1882, pp. 81-86.

280   *A History and Biographical Cyclopedia of Butler County, Ohio*, Cincinnati, 1882, pp. 81-86.

When Reily first became clerk the court met in a building at Fort Hamilton which had been used as the officer's mess. The judges sat at a table which looked like a carpenter's work bench. The clerk's office was located in a small log cabin located south of the fort which had been used as a storehouse or sutler's shop by a trader attached to the garrison. The building served not only as the clerk's office for the common pleas and supreme courts, it also served as the office of the county commissioners, the recorders office, and the post office until 1809. It was also the gathering place for judges, lawyers, and other leading men of the town where they entertained themselves and conversed about politics and news of the day. In 1809 Reily constructed a new residence on the public square and the public offices were moved to a room in his residence until the county erected county offices in 1824.[281]

In explaining why the community entrusted Reily with so many responsibilities for so long, the author of the County History stated, "Mr. Reily was a man of utmost regularity of habits. He came to his room at a certain hour. His papers were all methodically filed away, and he could at any time refer to any paper with which he had anything to do, although it might have been a quarter century before. He trusted nothing to another person which it was possible himself to do. He held office many years, and during the whole course of his life his integrity and veracity were never questioned, nor does the writer recollect in any of the old newspapers whose files he examined an attack upon his character—an exemption which no one else enjoyed. His judgment was excellent, his memory good, his patriotism of the highest."[282]

On December 7, 1807, the County Commissioners organized a new township and named it Reily in honor of John Reily.[283]

Symmes contract with Congress provided for a township to be set aside to fund a university. Symmes failed to reserve a township for this purpose and Congress allowed the State to locate the township in the government lands west of the Great Miami. Jeremiah Morrow served on the committee to locate the township in 1803. Miami University was not chartered by the legislature until 1809 and did not begin operating until 1824. John Reily was appointed as a member of the original board of trustees and served until 1840, holding the

---

281 *A History and Biographical Cyclopedia of Butler County, Ohio*, Cincinnati, 1882, pp. 31-38

282 *A History and Biographical Cyclopedia of Butler County, Ohio*, Cincinnati, 1882, pp. 81-86.

283 *A History and Biographical Cyclopedia of Butler County, Ohio*, Cincinnati, 1882, pp. 31-38.

positions of president and secretary of the board during that time. He served
on the committee which located and laid out the town of Oxford. The former
school master of the first school in southwest Ohio no doubt considered his
work on the board as one of his most worthwhile achievements.[284]

Reily was raised as a Presbyterian and generously contributed to the support of that denomination. He also donated to other churches.[285]

Reily died on June 7, 1850. At the time of his death the second constitutional convention was in session at Columbus. Several delegates offered complimentary remarks about him. One stated, "He was a man of the most strict
and uncompromising integrity.... He discharged his duties with the strictest
fidelity and utmost punctuality."

JOHN KITCHEL

John Kitchel was born November 8, 1756 in Hanover, Morris County, New
Jersey. His ancestor Robert Kitchell emigrated from Kent, England in 1639,
with a group of puritan refugees. While on shipboard they signed the
Plantation Covenant agreeing to remain together on one plantation sharing
their common work. They landed at New Haven, Connecticut, and then settled
at Guilford. After some time, the congregation became unhappy with Guilford
and decided to move to New Jersey where they became the founders of
Newark. In 1667 they signed a Plantation Covenant for their new settlement.
The Kitchells became a large and influential family in New Jersey.[286]

During the Revolutionary War, John Kitchel served in his cousin Obadiah
Kitchell's Company of the New Jersey Militia. Fourteen members of the
Kitchell family of New Jersey served in the Revolutionary War.[287]

---

284   *A History and Biographical Cyclopedia of Butler County, Ohio*, Cincinnati, 1882,
       pp. 81-86, 58-64.
285   *A History and Biographical Cyclopedia of Butler County, Ohio*, Cincinnati, 1882,
       pp. 81-86.
286   H. D. Kitchel, *Robert Kitchel and his Descendants*, 1879; Edward Payson
       Whallon, *Whallon and Kitchell Families*, 1932; Margaret Ellen Kitchell Whallon,
       Kitchell Family Genealogy
287   *The Official Roster of the Soldiers of the American Revolution Buried in Ohio*,
       Daughters of the American Revolution of Ohio, p. 216.

Kitchel was married to Abigail Parkhurst on March 18, 1778 in Hanover, New Jersey.[288]

John's brother Aaron was a republican representative to the state legislature of New Jersey. He also served in the United States House of Representatives for several terms and the United States Senate for a term.[289]

Several members of the Kitchell (sometimes spelled Kitchel) family migrated to Kentucky and then to the Northwest Territory where they settled in and around Cincinnati. Daniel Kitchel, John's cousin, came to Cincinnati in 1788 and was a founder and ruling elder of the First Presbyterian Church established in 1790. John's brothers Asa and Moses were also early settlers of Cincinnati.[290]

John Kitchel purchased land and cleared a farm in what would become Lemon Township, Butler County. Prior to statehood it was part of Hamilton County. Kitchel was nominated on the Republican slate and elected as a delegate to the constitutional convention. He was appointed to the committee to draft article six on county officials. He voted with those supporting the suffrage and other civil rights for Negroes.[291]

The first General Assembly which met on March 1, 1803, at Chillicothe created Butler County and elected John Kitchel as one of three Associate Judges for the county. Francis Dunlavy was elected as the presiding judge for the circuit which included the county. The responsibility for putting the new government under the new constitution in operation in each county fell upon the judges appointed by the General Assembly. Since the area embraced by Butler County was formerly part of Hamilton County, this meant creating a new government for the people of the county. Kitchel and the other two associate judges first met on May 10, 1803, at the house and tavern of John Torrence in Hamilton. This was the first frame house erected in Hamilton outside the garrison. Here they held their first court of quarter session. They elected John Reily as their clerk pro tem, divided the county into five townships, and ordered an election to be held in the townships on June 1 for sheriff and coroner. On July 13, 1803, the first court of common pleas was convened at Torrance's tavern with President Judge Dunlavy and the three associate judges

288   Deloris Kitchel Clem and Dwain L. Kitchel, *Kitchel Family History*, Gregath Company, 1989.

289   Biographical Directory of the United States Congress

290   *The Official Roster of the Soldiers of the American Revolution Buried in Ohio*, Daughters of the American Revolution of Ohio, p. 216.

291   "Proceedings of the First Constitutional Convention", *Ohio History* Vol. 5, p. 96.

in attendance. At this session Reily was appointed clerk and a county treasurer and county recorder were appointed. The magazine of the old fort was designated as the county jail. The Supreme Court met for the first time in the county on October 11.[292]

Kitchel's term as associate judge was cut short by his death on February 8, 1805. He was buried in the cemetery of the Presbyterian Church at Monroe which he founded and served as elder.[293]

JOHN W. BROWNE

John W. Browne was born in England in 1754 and immigrated to the Northwest Territory in 1796. After stopping at Chillicothe, he moved to Cincinnati in 1798. He had been a Congregational minister in England.[294]

In addition to preaching, Browne operated a printing press, sold books, and patent medicines in Cincinnati.

Browne was nominated by the Republican county convention and elected as a delegate to the constitutional convention. He served on the committee appointed to draft the bill of rights and a schedule to carry the government into operation.[295] He supported Negro suffrage and civil rights.[296]

In 1804 Browne commenced publishing a newspaper for Cincinnati titled "Liberty Hall and Cincinnati Mercury". Later the name was changed to just "Liberty Hall." It was the third paper in the town. The first newspaper in Cincinnati was William Maxwell's "Sentinel of the Northwestern Territory." Browne's paper was printed in the loft of a log cabin. In those days newspaper publishers were held accountable for what they said, and Browne was personally attacked on one or two occasions by unhappy readers. After eleven years the paper was combined with the Cincinnati Gazette. In addition to the newspaper,

292   William A. Taylor, *Ohio Statesmen and Annals of Progress*, State of Ohio, 1899, p. 37.

293   Doris Kitchel Clem and Dwain L. Kitchel, *Kitchell Family History*, Gregath Company, 1989, chapter 4; *The Official Roster of the Soldiers of the American Revolution Buried in Ohio*, Daughters of the American Revolution of Ohio, p. 216.

294   Marjorie Byrnside Burress, *A Collection of Pioneer Marriage Records Hamilton County, Ohio, 1789-1817*, Vol I, p. 81; Henry A. Ford and Kate B. Ford, *History of Hamilton County, Ohio*, L.A. Williams & Co., 1881, p. 304.

295   "Journal of the First Constitutional Convention", *Ohio History* Vol. 5, p. 90.

296   Helen M. Thurston, "The 1802 Constitutional Convention and the Status of the Negro", *Ohio History* Vol. 81, pp. 24, 27.

Browne published almanacs and books. He had a bookstore next to his printing shop where he also sold pharmaceuticals.[297]

In his paper Browne took a strong position against slavery. In 1806 he wrote, "Slavery will have a most pernicious effect upon the manners, the habits, and the morals of the inhabitants of the territories…. The effect, therefore, will be, to make the whites indolent, and as their ultimate prosperity must depend upon themselves, to destroy those habits of industry on which alone that prosperity can rest."[298]

In 1811 John Browne was among those who organized the Farmers and Mechanics Bank of Cincinnati.[299]

Beginning in 1804 Rev. Browne preached in the home of Ezekiel Hughes, an immigrant from Wales, who purchased land on the west side of the Great Miami and became the leading citizen of Whitewater Township in Hamilton County. He also preached in the Welsh settlements at Paddy's Run, Dry Creek, and Lee's Creek in Butler County.[300]

In 1810 he owned two tracts of land totaling 316 acres.[301]

In June, 1810, the trustees of Miami University, which at that time had no buildings or money, hired Rev. Browne as the college's missionary to solicit donations. If he was successful, he would become known as the father of the university. Since there was no money in the west, he was sent east. In 1809 the State had chartered the institution and appointed a board of fourteen trustees. In 1803 Congress had donated a township to the state to fund the University and the land was to be rented to provide an income for the University. However, it would be a long time before there were sufficient funds from that source to build and operate the University. The trustees agreed to pay Browne

---

297   Walter Sutton, "Cincinnati as a Frontier Publishing and Book Trade Center", *Ohio History*, Vol. 56, pp. 123, 125, 138; V.C. Stump, "Early Newspapers of Cincinnati", *Ohio History*, Vol. 34, p. 169; Emilius O. Randall, "Newspapers Read by the Ohio Pioneers," *Ohio History*, Vol. 29, p. 45; Robert E. Cazden, "The German Book Trade in Ohio before 1848", *Ohio History*, Vol 84, p. 43.

298   Liberty Hall and Cincinnati Mercury, March 31, 1806.

299   Harry R. Stevens, "Samuel Watt Davies and the Industrial Revolution in Cincinnati", Ohio History, Vol. 70, p. 103.

300   Henry A. Ford, and Kate B. Ford, *History of Hamilton County, Ohio*, L.A. Williams Co., pp. 404-406; *A History and Biographical Cyclopedia of Butler County, Ohio*, Cincinnati, Ohio, 1882, pp. 426-431.

301   Lee Soltow, "Inequality Amidst Abundance: Land Ownership in Early 19th Century Ohio", *Ohio History*, Ohio Historical Society, Vol 88, p. 150.

$50 per month plus expenses out of the donations he received. He visited Washington, Maryland, New Jersey, New York, and New England soliciting books and money for the new college in the wilderness. He left on January 4, 1811 and returned on August 3, 1812. By the time he got back the War of 1812 had broken out. A few weeks after he returned, he went on a preaching mission to Clermont County. While returning on horseback, he drowned while crossing the Little Miami River. The trip was not a financial success, and it was 1824 before the University began operations.[302]

His son Samuel J. Browne, also a clergyman, continued the publishing business, invested in Cincinnati real estate and became very wealthy. At his death in 1872 he bequeathed $150,000 to establish a university, the building of a church, and the establishment of a free school in Cincinnati.

JOHN PAUL

John Paul was born November 12, 1758 in Germantown, Pennsylvania. His father Michael Paul immigrated to Germantown from Holland where he married Ann Parker.[303]

The family moved west to Redstone Old Fort, now Brownsville, Fayette County, Pennsylvania in 1766 or 1767. Redstone Old Fort was located where the old Nemacolin Indian Trail reached the Monongahela River. Fort Burd had been constructed there as a defense against the Indians at the time of the construction of Fort Pitt following the defeat of the French. The trail was improved as Burd's Road so supplies and travelers could travel here from Cumberland, Maryland, and then travel down the Monongahela River by boat to Pittsburgh. In later years this became a boat building center and gateway to the west as pioneers transferred their belongings from wagons or pack horses to a boat and floated down the Monongahela and Ohio Rivers to Kentucky and Ohio.[304]

---

302   Walter Havighurst, "The Beggar on Horseback," *The Miami Years 1809-1814*.

303   Arthur R. Kilner, "Colonel John Paul, Founder of Xenia, Ohio and Madison, Indiana" Greene County, District Library; James Edson, "Edson, Weyer, Neenan, Gier Families," Ancestry World Tree, Ancestry.com; Mrs. Roscoe C. O'Byrne, *Roster Soldiers and Patriots of the American Revolution Buried in Indiana*, Indiana DAR, 1938.

304   Arthur R. Kilner, "Colonel John Paul, Founder of Xenia, Ohio and Madison, Indiana" Greene County, District Library; Solon J. Buck and Elizabeth Hawthorn Buck, *The Planting of Civilization in Western Pennsylvania*, University of Pittsburgh Press, 1939, p. 98.

In 1778 John Paul joined the expedition of George Rogers Clark to drive the British from the Northwest Territory.[305] Clark had persuaded the Governor of Virginia to finance a strike against the British in the west. The men first captured the French towns of Cahokia and Kaskaskia on the Mississippi and then waded across Illinois through freezing swamps to Vincennes where they captured the British Fort in 1779. Clark's success was the basis for America's claim to the Northwest Territory during the negotiation of the treaty with the British following the Revolutionary War.

No doubt due to the urging of John Paul after his adventures with Clark, the family moved to Kentucky in 1781, and eventually settled in what would become Hardin County near Elizabethtown.[306] Kentucky became a state in 1792 and Hardin County was organized the following year. John Paul served as the first clerk and recorder of the county. He married Sarah Thornberry Grover in 1794.[307] He frequently traveled to Cincinnati to purchase merchandise and became enamored of the future prospects of Ohio.

In 1800 Paul moved to Ohio where he settled on Beaver Creek near Belbrook in what was then Hamilton County but is now Greene County.[308] He was nominated by the Hamilton County Republican convention to run as a delegate to the constitutional convention which met at Chillicothe on November 1, 1802. He received the second highest number of votes.

Voting in Hamilton County had previously occurred at the courthouse. In the 1802 election voting was conducted at nine districts throughout the county. Also in 1802 the right to vote for delegates was extended to all male citizens 21 years of age or older who had resided in the Territory for one year and paid a tax. As a result the number of votes cast for delegates in Hamilton County in 1802 was six times the number cast for representatives to the territorial legislature in 1800.[309]

At the convention Paul was recognized as one of the leaders of the Hamilton County delegation. He served on the committees appointed to draft

---

305   "Xenia Founder Paul Born 225 Years Ago", *Xenia, Ohio Daily Gazette*, November 11, 1983.

306   Arthur R. Kilner, "Colonel John Paul, Founder of Xenia, Ohio and Madison, Indiana" Greene County, District Library

307   Arthur R. Kilner, "Colonel John Paul, Founder of Xenia, Ohio and Madison, Indiana" Greene County, District Library

308   R.S. Dills, *History of Greene County, Ohio*, Odell & Mayer, 1881, p. 261.

309   Downes, Frontier Ohio, p. 246; "The Enabling Act for Ohio—1802", *Ohio History* Vol. 5, pp. 75-76.

article one on the legislature, article two on the executive, article three on the judiciary, and article four on the qualification of electors.[310] He voted against slavery and in support of Negro suffrage and civil rights.[311]

In an effort to divide the Republican vote a caucus of Federalists in Hamilton County voted to support Paul for Governor. However, other Federalists nominated Benjamin Gilman of Marietta. Most Federalist simply did not vote for Governor.[312]

Paul was elected as one of Hamilton County's four senators in the first General Assembly which convened at Chillicothe on March 1, 1803. One of the actions taken by the first General Assembly was to create Greene County.[313] He no doubt played an important role in the enactment of that legislation.

The General Assembly directed that the associate justices of each county meet on May 10, 1803, for the purpose of erecting townships and providing for the election of justices of the peace for each township on June 21 at the locations designated by the justices. The General Assembly named three justices for Greene County, and Senator Paul no doubt had a big say in their selection. The Greene County justices met on May 10 at a log house on Beaver Creek owned by Owen Davis. Davis owned and operated a mill nearby and rented the log house in question to Peter Borders who operated a tavern there. It was quite natural that the court would meet at the local tavern near the mill because these were both places frequented by the settlers in the area. The associate justices appointed John Paul as temporary clerk. As clerk it was his duty to keep the records of the court and implement the decisions of the justices.[314]

The first common pleas court of Greene County met on August 3, 1803 at Borders Tavern. The common pleas court consisted of the associate justices plus presiding judge Francis Dunlavy who traveled from county to county in southwest Ohio. Pursuant to Article II of the new Constitution, the Court appointed John Paul as its clerk for a term of seven years. On October 25, 1803, the Supreme Court met in Greene County for the first time and appointed John Paul as its clerk. Paul also served as county recorder with responsibility for keeping the

310   "Journal of First Constitutional Convention", *Ohio History* Vol 5, pp. 89, 92, 93, 95.

311   Helen M. Thurston, "The 1802 Constitutional Convention and the Status of the Negro", *Ohio History* Vol. 81, p. 27.

312   Alfred Byron Sears, *Thomas Worthington, Father of Ohio Statehood*, Ohio State University Press for Ohio Historical Society, 1958, p. 109.

313   William A. Taylor, *Ohio Statesmen and Annals of Progress*, State of Ohio, 1899, pp. 35, 37.

314   R.S. Dills, *History of Greene County, Ohio*, Odell & Mayer, 1881, pp. 212-214.

records of real estate transactions. In 1804 the General Assembly enacted a law which created the office of county commissioners. The first commissioners were elected in April of that year and John Paul was appointed as clerk of the Board.[315] John Paul's role in Greene County was the same as John Reily's role in Butler County and Joseph Darlinton's role in Adams County.

The county seat for Greene County was located at Xenia on land owned by John Paul. The location was determined before the village was laid out and the court appointed a surveyor to lay out the village. Paul agreed to donate land for the public buildings. The first cabin was erected in 1804. Since it was the county seat, the village grew quickly.[316]

In 1809 John Paul, believing there was greater opportunity in Indiana where government lands were coming on the market, sold his land in Ohio and resigned his offices in Greene County. His brother-in-law Josiah Grover was appointed to take his place. Paul purchased land in Indiana from the government in 1809 and in 1810 he laid out a town on the Ohio River. He named it Madison in honor of then President James Madison. It became the county seat of Jefferson County, and he donated the land for the public buildings. Madison became the leading metropolis of the state in the early years until it was eclipsed by Indianapolis. Like Cincinnati, it served as a gateway to the interior. Paul was elected as a representative to the territorial legislature. He was instrumental in the organization of Jefferson County and served as its first clerk and recorder. The county was named after President Jefferson at the recommendation of John Paul. Following the admission of Indiana as a state in 1816, he was elected to the state senate where he was chosen as the presiding officer. Paul established the first newspaper in Madison and the second in the state, "The Western Eagle." His son-in-law William Hendricks was the editor. Hendricks later served as secretary to the Indiana constitutional convention, Congressman, U.S. Senator, and Governor for the State of Indiana.[317] Paul also helped establish the first bank in the Indiana Territory, The Farmers and Mechanics Bank of Indiana, which he served as president.[318]

---

315 R.S. Dills, *History of Greene County, Ohio*, Odell & Mayer, 1881, pp. 207, 926.

316 R.S. Dills, *History of Greene County, Ohio*, Odell & Mayer, 1881, p. 426; Henry Howe, *Historical Collections of Ohio*, Centennial Edition, Vol. 1, p. 700.

317 James Edson, great, great, great grandson of John Paul.

318 Arthur R. Kilner, "Colonel John Paul, Founder of Xenia, Ohio and Madison, Indiana" Greene County, District Library; "Xenia Founder Paul Born 225 Years Ago", *Xenia, Ohio Daily Gazette*, November 11, 1983; Madison Courier, January 4, 1886; *Madison Weekly Herald*, October 24, 1889; "Jefferson County", Indiana Review, State of Indiana, 1838; James Edson, great, great, great grandson of John Paul.

In addition to his service during the Revolutionary War with George Rogers Clark, Paul served as a colonel during the War of 1812. He commanded a regiment which served under General William Henry Harrison in northwestern Ohio during the second siege of Fort Meigs and the attack on Fort Stevenson. By reason of his service, he was always referred to as "Colonel John Paul."[319]

John Paul died on June 6, 1830 and was buried on the grounds of the cemetery which he had donated for use of the town of Madison. The grounds later became the "John Paul Park."[320] He was described by an essayist as "endowed by nature with all the qualities of a leader of men, and he was one. He was tall, with a fine physique, and a commanding appearance. His manner was gentle and he was always ready to befriend the poor and helpless and to help promising young men. Even his enemies respected him and all his friends loved him."[321]

JOHN WILSON

John Wilson was born in 1739 in New Jersey where he married Lydia Amy Thatcher and they began a family. John served in the Continental Army during the Revolutionary War and lost all of his property as a result of the War. The family moved west first settling in Washington County, Pennsylvania. After staying there a few years they moved on to Kentucky in the early 1780s. He served with George Rogers Clark's expedition against the Shawnee towns in Ohio in 1782. Wilson was a delegate from Mason County to the convention which adopted Kentucky's constitution. When Wilson sold his land in Kentucky he was paid with a draft on a Cincinnati firm so he proceeded there to collect his money. The following year he and his sons and their families came to Cincinnati, where they put in a crop on land on Mill Creek north of the village.[322]

---

319   Robert B. McAfee, *History of the Late War in the Western Country*, 1816, pp. 319, 322; Letter from J.C. Bartlett to Brig. General Lewis Cass July 22, 1813, Ohio Historical Society, online documents, War of 1812

320   Ruth Hoggatt, Jefferson County Cemetery List

321   Peggy Bunton, essay, Madison Courier, May 3, 1948.

322   *History of Clinton County, Ohio*, W. H. Beers & Company, pp. 253-255; "James Wilson," Carolyn Johnson Burns' Montgomery County Biographies, Carolyn J. Burns web page; "Thomas J. Wilson Biography", Portrait and Biographical Record of Montgomery Co. Indiana, 1893; John Adkinson, "Descendants of Littleton Adkinson of Maryland", Ancestry.com; "The John Wilson Sr. Family", Greene County District Library.

The Wilsons were the first permanent settlers of what would become Greene County, Ohio. John purchased land from John Cleves Symmes which at the time was in Hamilton County but later would become part of Sugar Creek Township, Greene County. His sons Amos and George Wilson cut a small clearing out of the wilderness. They put in a crop and erected a small cabin on the land in the spring of 1796. They had their horses stolen by Indians, but they pursued the Indians, faced them down, and recovered the horses. In the fall they returned to their families at Mill Creek to help harvest the crop there. They then returned to the woods with their families. Two other brothers Daniel and John and their father John soon followed. The area of their settlement became known as the Wilson settlement.[323]

John Wilson was elected as a delegate to the constitutional convention from Hamilton County which then included what is now Greene County. He was one of the back country delegates nominated by the Republican Hamilton County convention. For the first time voting for convention delegates was conducted in districts rather than at the courthouse. It meant that settlers in the back country would be voting for the first time since it was impracticable for them to go all the way to Cincinnati to cast a vote. The Republicans astutely included people known and respected by the back country settlers on their slate of delegates. Wilson served on the committee appointed to draft article six on selection of county officers.[324] His votes showed strong opposition to slavery and strong support for black suffrage and other civil rights.[325]

Greene County was established by the legislature in 1803 and the first common pleas court convened in August, 1803. John Wilson served on the first grand jury. The only indictments were against persons who had gathered for the occasion and had too much to drink and got into fights on that day. Nine indictments were returned for assaults and batteries committed after the court was organized in the morning. One of those indicted was the local mill owner who owned the tavern in which the court was held. He accused a neighbor of

---

323   R.S. Dills, *History of Greene County, Ohio*, Odell & Mayer, 1881, pp. 259-260, 628-629; *History of Clinton County, Ohio*, W. H. Beers & Company, pp. 253-254; *Greene County 1803-1908*, Committee for the Homecoming Association, Xenia, 1908, 41; George F. Robinson, *History of Greene County, Ohio*, S. J. Clarke Publishing Co., 1902, pp. 67, 217-218.

324   "Transcript of the Proceedings of the First Constitutional Convention", *Ohio History*, Vol. V, p. 96.

325   Helen M. Thurston, "The 1802 Constitutional Convention and the Status of the Negro", *Ohio History* Vol. 81, p. 27.

being a hog thief. A fight ensued, and he was victorious. He then approached the judges who included his son-in-law and said, "I've whipped the hog thief. Now what's the damage?" Then shaking his fist at his son-in-law judge, he said, "If you'd steal a hog, I would whip you too." All persons indicted pleaded guilty and were fined including the father-in-law of the judge.[326] This story of the first day of court in Greene County reveals that the settlers in the back country during the period of territorial government had adopted their own rough and tumble system of justice. Imposing law and order required much more than a written constitution and a statute book. It would be a tough job for tough men.

Although nominated as a representative to the legislature from Hamilton County, Wilson was not elected. Governor Meigs appointed him associate judge on August 15, 1811 to fill the vacancy created by the resignation of an associate judge while the legislature was not in session. The resignation was prompted by the controversy over the Sweeping Resolution. He was the anti-Tammany candidate for the position and was replaced by the Tammany candidate during the next session of the General Assembly.[327] His son John served twenty one years as the clerk of courts of Miami County and served that county in the Ohio legislature.[328] He was also a justice of the peace.

A Baptist church was built in the Wilson settlement in 1799, the first in the county.[329] John's son Amos preached there in 1803. Amos Wilson is credited as being one of the first settlers of Clinton County in what is now Wilson Township. Amos purchased 200 acres and began clearing a spot on what he thought what his land. Two years later he discovered he was on the wrong land and moved to a new location which he believed to be his land. After working for a year clearing that land, he discovered that once again he had been clearing the wrong land. The land owner pitied him and gave him fifty acres for his labor. Finally in the spring of 1802 he began work on his own land.[330]

John Wilson moved to Lost Creek Township, Miami County, where his son John Jr. lived. He died there September 5, 1823, and was buried in the Baptist

---

326   R.S. Dills, *History of Greene County, Ohio*, Odell & Mayer, 1881, p. 220.

327   Donald F. Melhorn Jr., *Lest We Be Marshall'd, Judicial Power and Politics in Ohio*, *University of Akron Press, 2003, p. 163.*

328   "Thomas J. Wilson", Portrait and Biographical Record of Montgomery County, Indiana, 1893; William A. Taylor, *Ohio Statesmen and Annals of Progress*, Vol 1, p. 165.

329   R.S. Dills, *History of Greene County, Ohio*, Odell & Mayer, 1881, p. 640.

330   *History of Clinton County, Ohio*, W. H. Beers & Company, pp. 254-255.

cemetery. He was described in a county history as a man of "intelligence and integrity."[331]

Other Founding Fathers From Hamilton County

ARTHUR ST CLAIR

Although Arthur St. Clair opposed Ohio statehood in 1802, no fair-minded person can deny his considerable influence on the early history of the State. During the territorial period his dominant presence was the center around which all others, supporters and detractors, circled.

St. Clair was born in the town of Thurso, Caithness, Scotland in 1734, of a noble but not wealthy family. He was educated at Edinburgh and indentured to a prominent physician in preparation for a medical career. Following his mother's death, he purchased his freedom, and with the assistance of family friends secured an ensign's commission in the Royal American Regiment of Foot. He saw action during the French and Indian War at Louisburg and Quebec. As a young lieutenant, he participated in Wolfe's victory over Montcalm which was the decisive battle of the War and led to the British taking Canada from the French.[332]

Following the British victory, St. Clair married Phoebe Bayard, daughter of a prominent Massachusetts family. By this marriage, he received 14,000 pounds sterling as a legacy from his wife's grandfather. This sum together with what he had saved of his own fortune made him a wealthy man and prompted his resignation from the army. He received a grant of a thousand acres for his service in the French and Indian War which he located in the Ligonier Valley in western Pennsylvania. Purchasing additional land in the vicinity he became the largest landowner west of the Alleghenies. He served in various county offices by appointment of the colonial Governor and by the time of the Revolution, he was the leading citizen of western Pennsylvania.[333]

331　"James Wilson of Washington Township", Carolyn Johnson Burns, Montgomery County Biographies, Carolyn J. Burns web page; John Adkinson, Descendants of Littleton Adkinson of Maryland, Ancestry.com

332　William Henry Smith, *The St. Clair Papers*, 1882, Vol 1, pp. 2-5; J. Martin West, "Arthur St. Clair", *Timeline*, Ohio Historical Society, Vol. 5, No. 2, pp. 51-55;

333　William Henry Smith, *The St. Clair Papers*, 1882, Vol 1, pp. 5-9; J. Martin West, "Arthur St. Clair", *Timeline*, Ohio Historical Society, Vol. 5, No. 2, p. 52;

In 1774 a contest erupted between Virginia and Pennsylvania over western Pennsylvania. Both claimed jurisdiction over the area under their respective charters. St. Clair played an important role in the contest by arresting Dr. John Connolly who took possession of Fort Pitt in the name of Virginia and demanded that the locals submit to his authority. St. Clair was a magistrate of Westmoreland County, Pennsylvania at the time. The arrest resulted in a demand by Governor Dunmore of Virginia to Governor Penn of Pennsylvania that St. Clair be removed from office. Penn defended St. Clair.[334]

In 1775 St. Clair attended the treaty with the Indians at Pittsburgh as secretary to the Commissioners. The purpose was to persuade the tribes to remain neutral in the coming conflict with Great Britain. Later that year he received a commission as colonel in the Continental Army and recruited a regiment for service in Canada. He participated in the unsuccessful Canadian campaign and retreated with the northern army to Crown Point and then Ticonderoga.[335]

On August 9, 1776, Congress made St. Clair a brigadier general. He left the northern department at Ticonderoga and joined General Washington in New Jersey. He served as one of Washington's most effective commanders during the winter of 1776-1777. He was with Washington when he crossed the Delaware to attack the British at Trenton. When faced with a superior British force, he led the army in its escape to Princeton and routed the British stationed there. As the British approached, he persuaded Washington to retreat to Morristown and covered the army's rear. In recognition of his distinguished service, he was promoted to Major General on February 19, 1777. During this critical period of the War, Washington formed a strong attachment for St. Clair which continued for the remainder of his life.[336]

Ticonderoga was considered the key American western outpost. Located on Lake Champlain, the fort was intended to prevent a British advance from Canada into New York. St. Clair was given command of the fort and arrived on June 12. He immediately discovered that the fort had only a small garrison of 2200 men, badly armed, and worse clad, and that the defenses were in worse condition than when he had been there earlier. He immediately sought reinforcements and supplies and put the men to work improving the fort. General Burgoyne planned to split the colonies in half by taking a British army south to Albany and then joining forces with an army proceeding from the south.

---

334   William Henry Smith, *The St. Clair Papers*, 1882, Vol 1, pp. 10-11.
335   William Henry Smith, *The St. Clair Papers*, 1882, Vol 1, pp. 14-24.
336   William Henry Smith, *The St. Clair Papers*, 1882, Vol 1, pp. 25-44.

Ticonderoga was in the path. He surrounded the fort with an army of 7,800 British, Canadian, and Indian men, and began placing artillery on Mount Defiance which had a commanding view of the fort. Rather than charging the fort, the British planned to blast it apart from Mount Defiance. The Americans had not believed that artillery could be mounted there and were not prepared for this kind of attack. St. Clair after consulting with his officers decided that it was better for his army to escape from the fort and live to fight another day under better circumstances than stay and be destroyed or captured. The army waited for nightfall and then made their escape. Two thousand men were saved. St. Clair was criticized for his decision to abandon the fort, and he demanded a court martial to clear his name. A court martial was eventually held and St, Clair was cleared of any wrongdoing. In the meantime Burgoyne was attacked by an American army of 6,000 near Saratoga, his supply lines were cut, and he was forced to surrender his army. It was a tremendous victory for the Americans and has often been referred to as the turning point in the war.[337]

Although suspended from command for a time by action of Congress as a result of the charges made against him, St. Clair remained with General Washington and served as one of his trusted lieutenants throughout the remainder of the war. He had a horse shot out from under him at Brandywine, endured the hardships of Valley Forge and witnessed the surrender of Cornwallis at Yorktown.[338]

While St. Clair spent eight years at war, he suffered financial ruin. The mill which he had built in Westmoreland County was destroyed, and he lost much of the land which he had owned. Nonetheless, he continued to accept the call to public service. In 1783 he was elected to the Council of Censors which had responsibility for reviewing the constitution adopted by Pennsylvania in 1776 and the operation of the government under it. He wrote a committee report on the problems with that constitution and advocated the calling of a new constitutional convention. He was also elected to the office of vendue-master in Philadelphia and was responsible for public revenues collected there. On February 20, 1786, he first attended Congress as a representative from Pennsylvania and on February 2, 1787, he was elected president of Congress. Under the Articles of Confederation, this was the highest office in the federal government. During his tenure Congress adopted the Ordinance of 1787,

---

337   William Henry Smith, *The St. Clair Papers*, 1882, Vol 1, pp. 53-96.
338   William Henry Smith, *The St. Clair Papers*, 1882, Vol 1, pp. 97-115.

which established a government for the Northwest Territory, and approved the sale of large land tracts to the Ohio Company and John Cleves Symmes and his associates.

The most serious threat facing the new nation was financial bankruptcy. The adoption of the Ordinance and the sale of these tracts were intended to provide the framework for liquidating the national debt through sale of government land in the Northwest Territory. Congress proceeded to elect St. Clair as governor of the Northwest Territory. James M. Varnum, Samuel Holden Parsons, and John Armstrong were elected judges and Winthrop Sargent secretary. Armstrong declined to serve, and John Cleves Symmes was appointed to take his place.[339] These men were entrusted with the responsibility to make the grand plan work. Although it has been suggested by some that St. Clair demanded the office of governor in exchange for his support for the Ohio Company purchase and viewed it as a stepping stone to higher office under the Constitution which had been drafted in Philadelphia, he obviously believed in the vision and welcomed the challenge, or he would not have sought or accepted the office.[340] The Northwest Territory was an untamed wilderness inhabited by hostile Indians, a few unruly and ungovernable squatters, and the inhabitants of three small French villages who had no attachment to the United States. The task of taming this wild land and creating states which could be added to the existing states was indeed daunting and filled with grave risks. St. Clair may well have felt that this was the place where he could do the most good for his country.

On July 9, 1788, Governor St. Clair arrived at Fort Harmar at the mouth of the Muskingum across the river from the newly established settlement of Marietta. He was welcomed with military honors and a fourteen gun salute. On July 15 the Governor joined by Judges Parsons and Varnum and Secretary Sargent met with the citizens of Marietta and organized the civil government of the Northwest Territory amid a speech by the Governor and response by General Putnam. In his speech, St. Clair attempted to articulate the excitement which he and the others shared about the great venture they were undertaking as follows, "Neither is the reducing a country from a state of nature to a state of civilization

---

339   William Henry Smith, *The St. Clair Papers*, 1882, Vol 1, pp. 116-136.

340   Rev. Cutler made clear in his diary that negotiations for the land purchase included discussions on the persons to fill the offices. William Parker Cutler and Julia Perkins Cutler, *Life, Journals and Correspondence of Rev. Manasseh Cutler*, Ohio University Press, Vol 1, pp. 298, 300; William Henry Smith, *The St. Clair Papers*, 1882, Vol 1, p. 126.

so irksome as it may appear from a slight or superficial view; even very sensible pleasures attend it; the gradual progress of improvement fills the mind with delectable ideas; vast forests converted into arable fields, and cities rising in places which were lately the habitations of wild beasts, giving a pleasure something like that attendant on creation; if we can form an idea of it, the imagination is ravished, and a taste communicated of even the joy of God to see a happy world."[341] Perhaps the thrill of creation drew men like St. Clair and Putnam to the wilderness on the northwest banks of the Ohio River. They had gone through hell together while serving under Washington during the dark days of the Revolution and by their efforts helped create a new nation. They were prepared to go through hell together again to bring civilization to a territory which would nearly double the size of the new nation and provide the funds through land sales for paying for the crushing debt of the Revolutionary War.

Washington County was established, laws for organization of courts adopted, and judges and other county officials appointed. On September 2, 1778, the first court was held in Marietta with great fanfare. The Governor, Judges Varnum and Parsons, Secretary Sargent, the county judges and officials, all the residents, the soldiers from Fort Harmar, and visiting Indian chiefs were all present.[342]

Governor St. Clair was given use of the southwest blockhouse of Campus Martius for the use of himself and his family. He was also given fifteen acres of land in the town of Marietta.[343]

Governor St. Clair had been instructed by Congress to convene a council with the Ohio country Indians to reconfirm the cessions made by the Six Nations in the Treaty of Fort Stanwix in 1784. The need for a Treaty was demonstrated by attacks made on surveyors during the survey of the Seven Ranges and attacks made on settlers traveling down the Ohio to Kentucky. Most of the Ohio Indians believed that under previous treaties with the British and reaffirmed by the Americans at the beginning of the Revolutionary War that the Ohio River was the boundary of white settlement. The Americans believed that the Indians by siding with the British during the War had forfeited their rights under prior treaties and that the United States had secured the right to southern and eastern Ohio from the Six Nations who claimed sovereignty over the Ohio tribes. The Ohio Indians denied the right of the Six Nations who were centered in New York to sell Ohio lands occupied by the

341   William Henry Smith, *The St. Clair Papers*, 1882, Vol 2, p. 55.
342   William Henry Smith, *The St. Clair Papers*, 1882, Vol 1, pp. 148-149.
343   William Henry Smith, *The St. Clair Papers*, 1882, Vol 1, p. 150.

Ohio tribes. Although St. Clair successfully concluded a treaty at Fort Harmar on January 9, 1789, the principal chiefs of the Ohio tribes did not participate. Hence, the treaty did not resolve the issue and white settlement north of the Ohio River was not accepted by a majority of Ohio Indians.[344]

St. Clair returned to the east to attend to his family and receive instructions on the settlement of the Indian question. While there he witnessed the inauguration of his old compatriot George Washington as the first President of the United States. While in the east he explored the possibility of resigning the governorship and seeking other political office. His name was circulated as a possible candidate for vice president. He also was advanced as a candidate for governor of Pennsylvania. He was defeated by a vote of 27,188 to 2,869, a humiliating defeat. His association with Ticonderoga and the western part of the state and his strong federalist sympathies, no doubt contributed to the outcome. He was commissioned as major general in command of military operations in the Territory. This was in addition to his office as governor of the Territory.[345]

On January 2, 1790, St. Clair arrived at Fort Washington and on January 4, he established Hamilton County and designated Cincinnati as its county seat. The name of Losantiville was changed to Cincinnati at his suggestion in honor of the Order of Cincinnati, a prominent organization of former Revolutionary War officers, including Washington, St. Clair, Varnum, Parsons, and Sargent. County judges and militia officers were named.[346]

After a short stay in Cincinnati, St. Clair headed down the Ohio River and up the Mississippi to Kaskaskia and Cahokia, old French villages. He found the villages in an impoverished condition. Since they claimed title from the French, the uncertainty of the title to their lands which they occupied was also a major concern. St. Clair County was organized and judges and other county and militia officers appointed. He became a strong advocate for redress of their grievances.[347]

Learning that the Indians on the Wabash were not willing to enter into a treaty with the Americans, St. Clair sent Sargent on to Vincennes, the third French town in the Territory, to complete the organization of government

---

344   William Henry Smith, *The St. Clair Papers*, 1882, Vol 1, pp. 151-158; S. P. Hildreth, *Pioneer History*, Cincinnati, 1848, pp. 234-242.

345   William Henry Smith, *The St. Clair Papers*, 1882, Vol 1, pp. 158-159; J. Martin West, "Arthur St. Clair", *Timeline*, Ohio Historical Society, Vol. 5, No. 2, p. 54.

346   William Henry Smith, *The St. Clair Papers*, 1882, Vol 1, pp. 161-163.

347   William Henry Smith, The St. Clair Papers, 1882, Vol 1, pp. 164-166.

there so that he could focus on the Indian problem. After conferring with General Harmar, it was determined that Harmar would lead an expedition of regular army and militia from Kentucky and Pennsylvania against the Maumee towns. When it left Fort Washington in October, 1790, the expedition consisted of 320 regulars and 1,133 militia. The men succeeded in destroying a Miami town and five villages and 20,000 bushels of corn. However, two smaller detachments were attacked and suffered significant losses, primarily due to the poor performance of the militia. General Harmar was criticized, and although exonerated by a court martial, he resigned from the army.[348]

After reporting to Philadelphia on the situation, St. Clair was instructed to lead a formidable force into the Miami country and while so doing, to build a string of forts northward from Fort Washington. In addition smaller expeditions were to be sent against the tribes on the Wabash. The expeditions sent to destroy villages on the Wabash and Eel Rivers were a success. However, the major expedition led by St. Clair ended in a terrible defeat. Because of delays in recruitment and supplies, the expedition did not get started until September, 1791. Fort Hamilton and Fort Jefferson were constructed. It was late in October, when St. Clair proceeded on with his march. Supplies were short and militia deserted. St. Clair sent back part of his force to capture the deserters and look for the supplies. On November 4, 1791, St. Clair's 1400 man army was attacked at dawn. The camp had not been fortified. The militia immediately fled creating chaos in the camp. 650 were killed, 260 wounded, and some 60 to 200 civilians accompanying the army were killed. The losses were greater than any single battle of the Revolution, and it was the worst defeat that an American or European army ever sustained in a battle with the Indians, before or since. Put differently, it was the greatest Indian battlefield victory. St. Clair demonstrated considerable personal bravery during the battle. He received severe criticism and demanded a court martial. He spent seventeen months in Philadelphia defending his conduct. Although he was eventually exonerated by a committee of Congress, he was never again entrusted with a military command and lived with the stigma of the loss for the remainder of his days.[349]

As a result of their victory, the Indians sensed an opportunity to drive the Americans out of the Territory and back across the mountains. Not only were the settlers north of the Ohio attacked, but settlers in western Pennsylvania, Virginia and Kentucky. The goal was to inflict terror among white settlers, and

---

348   William Henry Smith, *The St. Clair Papers*, 1882, Vol 1, pp. 168-170.
349   William Henry Smith, *The St. Clair Papers*, 1882, Vol 1, pp. 170-182; ; J. Martin West, "Arthur St. Clair", *Timeline*, Ohio Historical Society, Vol. 5, No. 2, p. 54.

to a considerable extent it succeeded. Settlers withdrew into forts and ventured out with armed guards to tend their fields. However, Washington and Congress did not abandon the western settlers. St. Clair resigned his commission and Anthony Wayne was appointed in his place. He was to command an army of five thousand men. Avoiding the mistakes of St. Clair's expedition, Wayne carefully trained his men and proceeded only when the men were ready and the supplies were secured. On August 20, 1794, he attacked and defeated the Indians at Fallen Timbers on the Maumee. A bayonet charge dislodged the Indians and within an hour the battle was over. The fleeing Indians sought refugee in a nearby British Fort and were not admitted, causing them to become disenchanted with the British who had urged them into battle. On August 3, 1795, the Greenville Treaty was signed by which peace was secured and southern and eastern Ohio opened up for settlement free of threat of Indian attack.[350]

Under the Ordinance of 1787, St. Clair as Governor laid out counties, designated county seats, and appointed judges and other county officials, and militia officers. He also had the power to remove them. He also made recommendations to the administration for other federal appointments. He also granted licenses for ferries, taverns, and marriages. The powers conferred upon St. Clair provided the opportunity for abuse. He was accused of using his powers to reward his friends and punish his enemies. It does appear, however, that the leading persons in the counties were appointed by him to offices. In fact many of his loudest critics had received appointments from him. He was also accused of charging fees for licenses to augment his salary without statutory authority. Since fees for such licenses were customary in the eastern states, he may well have thought that such authority was implicit in his office.

Winthrop Sargent had been appointed as Secretary of the Northwest Territory at the same time as St. Clair had been appointed Governor. Sargent had served with Washington and St. Clair during the Revolution. He was a leader of the Ohio Company and had worked with Manasseh Cutler to secure passage of the Ordinance of 1787 and the bill approving the Ohio Company purchase. Like St. Clair he was a strong Federalist. The Ordinance conferred upon him the authority to act for the Governor whenever he was absent from the Territory, which frequently was the case. Although the two men differed in personality, they shared a common vision of the best interests of the Territory,

---

350   William Henry Smith, *The St. Clair Papers*, 1882, Vol 1, pp. 182-184; Hon. Samuel F. Hunt, "Address at the Centennial Celebration of the Treaty of Greenville", *Ohio History* Vol. 7, pp. 229-230.

personal friendship, and mutual trust. Sargent recognized and respected St. Clair's leadership and was loyal to him. St. Clair suffered a severe loss when President Adams appointed William Henry Harrison as secretary of the Northwest Territory on June 28, 1798. He replaced Sargent when Sargent was appointed governor of the Mississippi Territory. Although their relations were no doubt cordial, Harrison was young and ambitious and became an ally of his enemies.[351] After Harrison resigned to become Governor of the Indiana Territory, he was replaced by Charles Willing Byrd who was also an ally and active supporter of the Governor's enemies.

Under the first stage of government, the Governor shared with the territorial judges the authority to enact the laws governing the Territory. Under the second stage of government laws were enacted by the territorial legislature but were subject to his veto. He liberally exercised his veto and refused to recognize the legislature's authority to lay out counties and designate county seats. He received considerable criticism for these actions. After it was determined that the Territory had more than five thousand white male adult inhabitants, St. Clair called for election of representatives to the Territorial legislature as called for in the Ordinance of 1787. Voters were required to own at least fifty acres and representatives must own at least two hundred acres. They met in February 1799 at Cincinnati to elect ten nominees for the upper house of the legislature, known as the Legislative Council. Nominees were required to own at least 500 acres. The ten nominees were forwarded to President Adams who selected five to serve on the Council. Both houses then met in September and at the urging of the Governor set about the important task of reviewing the laws which had been enacted during the first stage of Territorial government. Many were confirmed with changes and additions which experience had shown were necessary. Much of the legislation was the work of Jacob Burnet, a Cincinnati lawyer and member of the Council. Bills for six new counties were vetoed by the Governor who claimed the legislature had no authority to erect new counties or designate county seats. He vetoed eleven acts of the legislature and waited until the end of the session to do it so there was no opportunity to make revisions to address his objections. The Governor was no doubt personally offended when William Henry Harrison was elected by a vote of eleven to ten as the Territory's delegate to Congress over his son Arthur St. Clair Jr.[352]

---

351   William Henry Smith, *The St. Clair Papers*, 1882, Vol 1, pp. 207-208.

352   R. L. Cayton, *The Frontier Republic*, Kent State University Press, 1986, pp. 68-71; William Henry Smith, *The St. Clair Papers*, 1882, Vol 1, pp. 208-214.

While in Congress Harrison rejected the recommendation of Governor St. Clair to have the Territory divided into three territories with the eastern division bounded on the west by the Scioto River. Harrison with the support of the leaders of Chillicothe secured a division of the Territory into two districts with Chillicothe as capital of the eastern Territory. The western division became the Indiana Territory and Harrison was appointed Governor of the new Territory. Harrison while in Washington also worked with Worthington to seek St. Clair's removal or replacement when his term expired for his alleged abuse of power.[353]

The second session of the Territorial legislature met in Chillicothe in November, 1800. The Session was prorogued by the Governor on December 9 on the ground that his term had expired and so their authority also ended. Despite a concerted effort made by the Governor's enemies to secure St. Clair's replacement, President Adams reappointed him Governor, but took the unusual step of forwarding the complaints made against him as well as the petitions supporting his reappointment to the Senate for their consideration when confirming him. His appointment was approved by the Senate with few dissenting votes.[354]

At the fall elections of 1800 a revolution occurred in the Federal government. Because of the closeness of the election and Burr's refusal to defer to Jefferson, the obvious choice of the people for President, the election was decided by the House of Representatives on February 17, 1801. The Jeffersonian Republicans had overthrown the Federalists at the Federal level. The election was bitter and the partisan spirit infected political leaders in Ohio. Ohio statehood became a matter of national interest because the effect it would have on the balance of power in Congress and future elections for President. If Ohio were Republican as Thomas Worthington and his allies represented, its admission to statehood would add two Republicans to the Senate and a Republican Congressman to the House. Ohio's electoral votes could be counted on for Jefferson. Federalists obviously opposed the admission of a Republican state but would be delighted by the admission of two Federalist states. St. Clair and his allies represented that if the Territory were divided at the Scioto the eastern state with its capital at Marietta would be Federalist because of the prevalence of New Englanders in the Ohio Company tract and the Western Reserve in the northern part of the State. The territory west of the

353   William Henry Smith, *The St. Clair Papers*, 1882, Vol 1, p. 215.
354   William Henry Smith, *The St. Clair Papers*, 1882, Vol 1, pp. 222-223.

Scioto would be Federalist because of the strength of that Party in Cincinnati and Detroit.[355]

The second territorial legislature met on November 24, 1801 at Chillicothe. Through the efforts of St. Clair and leaders of Cincinnati and Marietta, an alliance was made which pushed through the legislature a proposal requesting Congress to divide the Territory at the Scioto. The alliance also voted to move the Territory's capital back to Cincinnati. Federalist Paul Fearing of Marietta was elected the Territory's representative to Congress upon the expiration of Harrison's term. McMillan of Cincinnati had been elected to fill the remainder of Harrison term when he resigned to accept the governorship of the Indiana Territory. The actions of the session resulted in a riot at Chillicothe, threats to Federalists members, and the burning of the Governor in effigy. Although St. Clair called for prosecution of the offenders, no action was taken. Worthington had quelled the riot before harm was done by threatening to shoot its leader. St. Clair's victory in this session of the Territorial legislature was the last hurrah of St. Clair and his allies desperately fighting to retain control of the reigns of power in Ohio. They risked all on a bold proposal to Congress, representing their proposal to be the voice of the official representatives of the people of the Territory and therefore the wish of the people of the Territory.[356]

Thomas Worthington and Michael Baldwin of Chillicothe immediately left for Washington. Tiffin, Massie and their allies circulated petitions opposing the division and demanding immediate statehood and forwarded them on to Worthington. Worthington and Baldwin successfully argued to their Republican colleagues in Congress that the Division Act passed by the territorial legislature did not reflect the view of the people, and if Ohio were admitted as a state, it would vote Republican. Congress responded by rejecting the proposed division of the Territory and passing the Enabling Act which called for the election of delegates to a convention to decide whether Ohio should become a state, and if so to frame a constitution. The Act was signed by President Jefferson on April 30, 1802. Worthington and his allies also attempted to get President Jefferson to remove St. Clair from office so he could not use his position to influence the outcome of the election for delegates,

---

355   Randolph Downes, *Frontier Ohio*, Ohio Historical Society, pp. 203-204; Alfred Byron Sears, *Thomas Worthington, Father of Ohio Statehood*, Ohio State University Press for the Ohio Historical Society, 1958, pp. 59-60.

356   William Henry Smith, *The St. Clair Papers*, 1882, Vol 1, pp. 223-224; R. L. Cayton, *The Frontier Republic*, Kent State University Press, 1986, pp. 73-74; Randolph Downes, *Frontier Ohio*, Ohio Historical Society, pp. 199-200.

however, Jefferson in respect for St. Clair's record of public service during the Revolution and in the Territory declined to remove him. However, when St. Clair appeared at the Convention and gave a speech attacking the Act of Congress as illegal, the President promptly removed him.[357]

St. Clair was a strong Federalist, the party of Washington, Adams, and Hamilton. These men and other leading Federalists were among the leaders of the Revolution who had successfully led the fight for independence from Great Britain. They believed a strong national government was necessary to protect the new republic from enemies abroad and dissension within. They believed it must be administered by strong, responsible leaders. They saw the Northwest Territory as a colony of the federal government to be administered by appointees of the federal government until there was sufficient population to support new states. St. Clair had no faith in the ability of the people of the Territory to govern themselves. He believed most Ohio settlers had no interest in or time to devote to self-government and lacked the education and experience to select their own leaders. He believed his enemies intended to create a government democratic in form but oligarchic in substance which they would run for their own personal advantage. In his view government should be entrusted to men of education, character, and property who like himself were motivated by a sense of duty. This philosophy was at odds with the philosophy of most western settlers. The experience of western settlers in creating and running their own communities had made them self-reliant and confident in their ability to run their own affairs. Since the federal government had sold them their land, they expected it to protect them from Indian attacks. Implicit in the land sale was the representation that the federal government had dominion over the land it sold. However, they did not want or expect the federal government or some appointee of the government selecting their leaders or telling them how to run their communities. A war had been fought to rid the country of colonial governors and their aristocratic courts. Since the War a political revolution continued against an aristocracy who because of their education, property, family connections, social status, or revolutionary war rank believed they had the preferential right to hold public offices and to decide what was best for the rest of the people. Aristocrats were viewed as parasites who exploited public office to enrich themselves and protect their business interests and privileged status. They were resented as snobs who thought themselves better than ordinary folk who cleared the wilderness and plowed

---

357   Alfred Byron Sears, *Thomas Worthington, Father of Ohio Statehood*, Ohio State University Press for the Ohio Historical Society, 1958, pp. 73-85.

the fields. The ideas and slogans used by the leaders of the Revolution to arouse the people had accomplished their purpose, but the people had not forgotten those ideas and slogans. Having thrown off the British colonial aristocracy, they were not about to buy the argument that their government was best left to their betters.

A review of St. Clair's actions as Governor suggests that because of his military background or personal predilections, he was a man who had a keen sense of duty and exercised it in a manner which he thought best. He would carry out commands of his superior. However, he simply was not a man who was able to share power. His relationships with the territorial judges was prickly or in some cases hostile. His relationship with the territorial legislators who did not share his viewpoint was hostile. He sometimes treated county officials with lack of respect even though they were leaders of their communities. He appeared to take actions designed to encourage and aggravate confrontations. He had an inflated view of his own opinions and felt threatened by any action which he perceived as questioning or diminishing his authority. During the first stage of Territorial government, a government structure and laws were established which served the needs at the time and provided the foundation for the government of Ohio and four other states which were created out of the Territory. Because of the powers entrusted to him, a man of lesser character could have done much more harm than St. Clair. However, a man of greater wisdom and tact could certainly have made the transition to Ohio statehood much smoother and his own career and reputation more secure. Ironically, St. Clair's most important contribution to the formation of Ohio was convincing early Ohioans to distrust a strong executive and his Federalist party. The drafters of Ohio's first constitution made the governor of the state a largely ceremonial position. The governor was given no power to veto legislation and the power of appointment to public offices was vested in the legislature rather than the governor. In the first elections for state offices St. Clair's Federalist party was overwhelmingly defeated and his supporters replaced by his political enemies. He was removed from public office in disgrace and in the minds of many early Ohioans, he became like King George III, a tyrant overthrown by the people.[358]

After his removal from office, St. Clair retired to his home in Legonier, Pennsylvania, which included a comfortable residence, a mill, an iron smelting

---

358   J. Martin West, "Arthur St. Clair", *Timeline*, Ohio Historical Society, Vol. 5, No. 2, p. 55; William Henry Smith, *The St. Clair Papers*, 1882, Vol 1, p. 248; Jacob Burnet, "Burnet's Letters" *Transactions of the Historical and Philosophical Society of Ohio*, Cincinnati, 1839, Vol. 1, pp. 80-81.

furnace, farm buildings, and a large tract of land which he had received for his service in the Revolution. In 1810, these were all lost at sheriff's sale to satisfy the claim of a government contractor. St. Clair while serving as Indian commissioner had guaranteed payment. The government failed to pay and the creditor pursued the claim against St. Clair. The government also failed to pay a claim for moneys which St. Clair had advanced to pay for the regiment which he had recruited during the Revolutionary War and expenses which he incurred as Governor. Whether St. Clair was the victim of political retribution or his own negligence in failing to present his claims in time is open to debate. It is interesting to note that his old enemy William Henry Harrison was an advocate on his behalf in Congress. Congress did finally award him a pension of $60.00 per month. His old enemy Thomas Worthington supported the pension. However, St. Clair never received any of his pension because it was seized by a creditor. Pennsylvania awarded him a small pension in recognition of his service during the Revolution and his destitute condition. St. Clair spent his last years in a log cabin. He died in August, 1818, at the age of 84, when a wheel fell off the wagon he was driving to a nearby village for supplies. The wagon upset, and he was thrown out on the rocky road and lay there until he was discovered later in the day. He never regained consciousness. In 1857, thirty-nine years after his death, Congress appropriated a considerable sum for the benefit of his surviving heirs.[359]

JOHN CLEVES SYMMES

John Cleves Symmes was born on July 21, 1742, at Riverhead, Long Island, New York. His father Timothy Symmes was a native of Scituate, Massachusetts and a minister. His great grandfather Rev. Zachariah Symmes emigrated from Canterbury, England to America in 1634 and settled in Charlestown, Massachusetts. John Cleves Symmes was raised by his grandfather Captain John Cleves and began his career as a school teacher and surveyor.[360]

---

359   William Henry Smith, *The St. Clair Papers*, 1882, Vol 1, pp.248-254.

360   Rev. Francis M. Symmes, "A Genealogical Tree of the Symmes Family", *History of Butler County, Ohio*, Western Biographical Publishing Co., Cincinnati, 1882; "John Cleves Symmes," *Ohio History Central*, Ohio Historical Society web page; Passenger List for the Griffin 1634, The Great Migration; "John Cleves Symmes", *Appleton's Cyclopedia of American Biography*; *History of Butler County, Ohio*, Odell & Mayer, 1881, pp. 22-31; R. Pierce Beaver, "The Miami Purchase of John Cleves Symmes", *Ohio History*, Vol 40, pp. 284-342.

Symmes moved to Sussex County, New Jersey where he bought a large farm on the Flat Brook and built his homestead "Solitude." He soon became active with those who were opposing Great Britain's arbitrary actions toward the colonies. He became a member of the Committee of Safety for Sussex County and served as chairman in 1774. He became colonel of the county militia, and when General Howe landed on Long Island, his regiment was employed in erecting defenses.[361] He was elected to the New Jersey State Convention in 1776 and served on the committee appointed to draft a constitution for New Jersey. The first legislature of independent New Jersey convened in August, 1776, and a new government was organized. Symmes was appointed a justice of the Supreme Court.[362] During the War Symmes had command of the forts erected to protect New Jersey against Indian attacks, and he participated in a number of engagements with the British. During and following the war, he served six years on the Council, one year as lieutenant governor, and twelve years as judge of the Supreme Court, becoming chief justice. He also served as a member of the Continental Congress in 1785 and 1786. During his period in Congress he became aware of and participated in the deliberations concerning the laws authorizing survey and sale of land in the Northwest Territory.[363] He also was influenced by his friend and neighbor Benjamin Stites who returned home from the west with glowing reports about the land in the Miami country. Symmes went west in the autumn of 1786 to see for himself and was excited by what he saw. While in the west he circulated a flier about a proposed colony before he had even discussed it with Congress. When he returned to the east, having secured the commitment of his friends Jonathan Dayton and Elias Boudinot for financial and political support, he petitioned Congress to allow him to purchase a large tract between the Miamis.[364]

Following Congress's approval of the Ohio Company purchase at the Muskingum River, Symmes was able to persuade Congress to permit him and his associates to purchase a million acres between the Great Miami and the Little Miami Rivers for the same price and terms. He argued that his venture

---

361   *History of Butler County, Ohio,* Odell & Mayer, 1881, pp. 22-31; R. Pierce Beaver, "The Miami Purchase of John Cleves Symmes", *Ohio History,* Vol 40, pp. 284-342.

362   Thomas F. Gordon, *The History of New Jersey from its Discovery by Europeans to the Adoption of the Federal Constitution,* Philadelphia, 1834, pp. 180-181, 236; R. Pierce Beaver, "The Miami Purchase of John Cleves Symmes", *Ohio History,* Vol 40, pp. 284-342.

363   *History of Butler County, Ohio,* Odell & Mayer, 1881, pp. 22-31.

364   *History of Butler County, Ohio,* Odell & Mayer, 1881, pp. 22-31; R. Pierce Beaver, "The Miami Purchase of John Cleves Symmes", *Ohio History,* Vol 40, pp. 284-342.

would do the same thing for New Jersey and the middle states as the Ohio Company was doing for the New England states. The venture was to provide a means for Revolutionary War veterans to redeem their claims in land and also to provide for organization of a colony by responsible gentlemen from the east. Congress named him as one of the three judges of the Territory who along with Governor St. Clair were entrusted with government of the Territory.[365]

Without waiting to complete a purchase contract with the government, Symmes left with a party of settlers for the Ohio valley. When Congress became alarmed, a power of attorney was given to Jonathan Dayton to complete the details. Symmes planned to establish a town at the mouth of the Great Miami which he expected to become the principal town of his purchase. He arrived with his party in February, 1789, and commenced settlement of what would become North Bend. Settlements had previously been begun at Columbia at the mouth of the Little Miami and Losantiville (later Cincinnati) across from the mouth of the Licking River. Due to the location of Fort Washington at Cincinnati, it pulled ahead of Symme's settlement and Columbia.[366]

Despite the fact that he was a lawyer and judge, Symmes legal and business practices were shockingly remiss. The survey of his land was done poorly causing considerable disputes and litigation over boundaries. Records of transactions were not recorded in an organized manner. He failed to meet his commitments under his contract with the Federal government and by so doing lost the right to purchase much of the land which he originally had a right to buy. He sold land which he did not own and sold land that he did own to more than one buyer. He failed to refund purchasers money. He failed to set aside a township for a university as required by the terms of his grant.[367]

Part of his problems was caused by the Indian War which broke out shortly after he began settlement.[368] However, the Ohio Company had the same problem and Congress adjusted the terms for the Ohio Company and was willing to do the same for Judge Symmes. It is difficult not to conclude that most of his problems were self-inflicted due to a deficiency in business organization and skill. He may have also felt that his position as Territorial Judge and his political connections in New Jersey made him unassailable.

---

365   *History of Butler County, Ohio*, Odell & Mayer, 1881, pp. 22-31; R. Pierce Beaver, "The Miami Purchase of John Cleves Symmes", *Ohio History*, Vol 40, pp. 284-342.

366   *History of Butler County, Ohio*, Odell & Mayer, 1881, pp. 22-31.

367   R. Pierce Beaver, "The Miami Purchase of John Cleves Symmes", *Ohio History*, Vol 40, pp. 284-342; Dwight L. Smith, "John Cleves Symmes", *Timeline*, Ohio Historical Society, Vol. 5, No. 2, pp. 20-23.

368   R. Pierce Beaver, "The Miami Purchase of John Cleves Symmes", *Ohio History*, Vol 40, pp. 284-342.

The remarkable thing is that despite all Symme's shortcomings, Symmes purchase was the land which developed the fastest in the Northwest Territory. Cincinnati was the leading town in the Territory, and the Miami country developed faster than any other area of the state. In terms of development, Symmes purchase was far more successful than the much better organized development of the Ohio Company purchase.

Symmes was married three times. His third wife Susanna was the daughter of William Livingston, long time governor of New Jersey, with whom he served before moving west. His daughter Anna married William Henry Harrison, future president of the United States.[369]

Symmes relationship with Governor St. Clair varied between strained and hostile. Symmes highly resented St. Clair's autocratic style, and St. Clair was disgusted by Symmes failure to adhere to the terms of his contract with the government and his sale of lands which he did not own. Symmes also no doubt resented the fact that St. Clair named Cincinnati as county seat. Each no doubt saw the other as a threat to his position in the Territory. Each complained about the other to Congress and the administration in Washington.[370]

In the controversy between the Governor and his Republican adversaries leading up to statehood, Symmes was an ally of the Republican leaders at Chillicothe. He opposed division of the Territory and favored statehood and the overthrow of his old adversary the Governor.

Symmes failures led to protracted litigation, animosity, and financial distress. His house was set fire and as a result of the fire all the records of his land transactions were lost. He died on February 26, 1814, and is buried on a hill near the site of his residence at North Bend.[371]

The sale to Symmes was modeled after the grant of land by the British Crown to a proprietor who then developed a colony. An historian concluded that part of Symmes failure was due to personal shortcomings, but another important part was due to shortcomings in the proprietary system. He stated, "One man could not be a genius in all points necessary to support the system which centered upon him, and the very idea of proprietary was foreign to the democratic spirit of the frontier. Such an enterprise was never again undertaken in the Northwest."[372] Another biographer stated, "Whatever might be

---

369   *History of Butler County, Ohio,* Odell & Mayer, 1881, pp. 22-31.

370   R. Pierce Beaver, "The Miami Purchase of John Cleves Symmes", *Ohio History,* Vol 40, pp. 284-342.

371   Symmes is buried near the tomb of his son-in-law President William Henry Harrison. The site is a state memorial operated by the Ohio Historical Society. See Ohio Historical Society web site.

said of his methods and stewardship and of the consequences to his constituency and his personal fortunes, John Cleves Symmes was one of the movers and shakers of the territorial and early statehood years."[373]

WILLIAM HENRY HARRISON

William Henry Harrison was Governor of the Indiana Territory at the time of Ohio statehood and resided at Vincennes, Indiana. However, he owned an estate at North Bend and returned there after his service in Indiana and the War of 1812. His contributions to the formation of Ohio prior to statehood and his service to Ohio during and after the War of 1812 merit his inclusion among the founding fathers of Ohio. Few men made more important contributions to the early history of Ohio than Harrison.

William Henry Harrison was born February 9, 1773, on Berkley plantation, Charles City County, Virginia. The family plantation was located on the banks of the James River overlooking the seaport of Petersburg and Richmond. He was the son of Benjamin Harrison, signer of the Declaration of Independence, member of the Constitutional Convention, and Governor of the Commonwealth of Virginia. The Harrison family was part of the Virginia planter aristocracy and had provided leadership in the colony for several generations. William attended Hampden Sidney College in Virginia, but left during a Methodist revival. He then began studying medicine at Richmond and left to study under Dr. Benjamin Rush in Philadelphia. Dr. Rush was a signer of the Declaration of Independence and the most prominent physician in the United States. Following his father's death, Harrison inherited 3,000 acres, but he was informed by his brother that there were not sufficient funds for him to continue his medical studies. Upon the advice of a family friend Richard Henry Lee, he decided to join the army.[374]

---

372   R. Pierce Beaver, "The Miami Purchase of John Cleves Symmes", *Ohio History*, Vol 40, p. 342.

373   Dwight L. Smith, "John Cleves Symmes", *Timeline*, Ohio Historical Society, Vol. 5, No. 2, p. 23.

374   Freeman Cleaves, *Old Tippecanoe, William Henry Harrison and his Times*, Charles Scribner's Sons, 1939, pp. 5-8; Andrew R. L. Cayton, *Frontier Indiana*, Indiana University Press, paperback edition, 1998, pp. 172-175; "William Henry Harrison", *Appleton's Cyclopedia of American Biography*; Allen Johnson and Dumas Malone, *Dictionary of American Biography*, Vol. IV, pp 348; Biographical Directory of the United States Congress; Presidential biography, the Whitehouse web page. The home in which Harrison was born and raised has been preserved and is open for visitors. See Berkeley Plantation web page.

President Washington who was a personal friend of Harrison's father encouraged him to join over the advice of his guardian. He received a commission as an ensign and led a company of men from Philadelphia to Fort Washington in 1791 arriving shortly after St. Clair's defeat. He was promoted to lieutenant and made aide-de-camp to General Anthony Wayne in his campaign against the Indians. He took part in the expedition to erect Fort Recovery on the site of St. Clair's defeat and during the Battle of Fallen Timbers carried Wayne's orders into the heat of battle. He was commended by General Wayne for his gallantry during the battle.[375] Wayne's victory at Fallen Timbers in 1794 ended the Indian War which broke out shortly after the first settlement of Marietta and Hamilton County. The victory led to the Treaty of Greenville in 1795 which opened southern and eastern Ohio to settlement free of fear of Indian attack. The treaty unleashed a flood of settlers into southern and eastern Ohio.

Following the disbanding of Wayne's army, Harrison was promoted to captain and given the command of Fort Washington at Cincinnati. While at the fort he fell in love with Judge Symmes' daughter Anna. Judge Symmes refused his consent, but while he was absent, they married at Judge Symmes' home. Symmes soon became reconciled with his son-in-law.[376]

Captain Harrison resigned from the army in 1798 to become register of the federal land office in Cincinnati. At the urging of Judge Symmes, the recommendation of Winthrop Sargent, and his own connections in the east, President Adams appointed him as secretary of the Northwest Territory on June 28, 1798. He replaced Winthrop Sargent who had been appointed governor of the Mississippi Territory.[377] St. Clair was unhappy with the appointment because of his strained relationship with Symmes. Harrison was an ally

---

375   Freeman Cleaves, *Old Tippecanoe, William Henry Harrison and his Times,* Charles Scribner's Sons, 1939, pp. 13-20; Andrew R. L. Cayton, Frontier Indiana, Indiana University Press, paperback edition, 1998, pp. 172-175.

376   Freeman Cleaves, *Old Tippecanoe, William Henry Harrison and his Times,* Charles Scribner's Sons, 1939, pp. 24-25; Andrew R. L. Cayton, *Frontier Indiana,* Indiana University Press, paperback edition, 1998, pp. 172-175; "William Henry Harrison", *Appleton's Cyclopedia of American Biography;* James Huston, *Point Counterpoint Tecumseh v. William Henry Harrison,* Brunswick Publishing Co., 1988, pp. 68-72, 129-134.

377   Freeman Cleaves, *Old Tippecanoe, William Henry Harrison and his Times,* Charles Scribner's Sons, 1939, pp. 26-27; Andrew R. L. Cayton, *Frontier Indiana,* Indiana University Press, paperback edition, 1998, p. 175; Richard C. Knopf, *Transcript of the Executive Journal of the Northwest Territory,* Ohio Historical Society web page, pp. 502-503.

of those who were hostile to St. Clair. When Thomas Worthington arrived in Hamilton County to attend the Territorial legislature on September 16, 1799 he was entertained by the Harrisons at their new home in North Bend.[378] One of the responsibilities of the legislature under the Ordinance of 1787 was to elect a representative to Congress with the right of debating but not voting.[379] At a joint session of the House and Council of the Territorial legislature, Harrison was elected over the Governor's son Arthur St. Clair Jr. by a vote of 11 to 10.[380] He resigned as Secretary of the Territory to assume his duties as the Territory's representative to Congress.

On December 2, 1799, Harrison took his oath as Congressman and on December 24, 1799, he introduced a resolution asking that a committee be appointed to consider alterations in the laws governing sale of lands in the Northwest Territory. The resolution was passed and he was appointed chairman of the committee. Three months later his committee reported a bill which with minor modifications became the Land Law of 1800. The bill dramatically improved the land laws for the western farmer. It provided for sale of lands through local land offices; it reduced the minimum size tract from a section (640 acres) to a half section (320 acres), and it permitted the purchaser to pay for the land in installments. The bill passed over the objection of land speculators.[381]

St. Clair sought Harrison's support for a division of the Territory into three Territories with the eastern most territory to be bounded by the Scioto River. He pointed out that this would permit Cincinnati and Marietta to be capitals of a territory and future states. He assumed that Harrison because of his relationship with Judge Symmes would favor a plan which would make Cincinnati a capital. St. Clair wrote another letter to a Federalist friend stating that the real reason for his proposal was to delay statehood as long as possible. Harrison was successful in getting Congress on May 7, 1800

---

378   Alfred Byron Sears, *Thomas Worthington*, Ohio State University Press for the Ohio Historical Society, 1958, pp. 48-49.

379   Ordinance of 1787, Section 12.

380   Freeman Cleaves, *Old Tippecanoe, William Henry Harrison and his Times*, Charles Scribner's Sons, 1939, pp. 28-29; Alfred Byron Sears, *Thomas Worthington*, Ohio State University Press for the Ohio Historical Society, 1958, pp. 50-51.

381   Freeman Cleaves, *Old Tippecanoe, William Henry Harrison and his Times*, Charles Scribner's Sons, 1939, pp. 29-20; Peter Smith, *A History of the Public Land Laws*, 1939, pp. 69-71.

to pass a Division Act which divided the Territory into an eastern territory which included the area of the present State of Ohio except that it extended west to a point opposite the mouth of the Kentucky River and it included Michigan. The Act further specified that Chillicothe would be the capital of the eastern Territory. The new western territory was called the Indiana Territory.[382] This Act was opposed by the Governor and the leaders of Cincinnati and prompted their efforts to create an alliance between Cincinnati, Marietta and the Governor to defeat the Chillicothe agenda.[383] Both the Land Law and the Division Act were extremely important measures for the future development of the Ohio country.

Harrison resigned his seat in Congress on May 14, 1800 to accept the President's appointment as Governor and Indian Commissioner of the Indiana Territory. He moved to Vincennes where he built a stately brick federal-style mansion "Grouseland" modeled after the home of his youth. When it was completed in 1804, it was the most imposing residence in the Wabash Valley.[384] Governor Harrison's principal achievements were keeping peace with the Indians while negotiating purchases of their lands. His greatest achievement was the Treaty of Fort Wayne in 1809 when the Delaware and other tribes surrendered three million acres. His aggressive land acquisition policy brought him in conflict with the government's Indian agent at Fort Wayne, William Wells, who warned that Harrison's tactics would likely lead to war. There is no question that Harrison's tactics reflected the view of the vast majority of white western settlers and the policy of the Jefferson and Madison administrations. The conflict between Harrison and Wells resulted in Wells removal as Indian agent. Harrison also received criticism for advocating and allowing slavery during his tenure as governor of the Indiana Territory. Although the Ordinance of 1787 prohibited slavery, the prohibition was circumvented by treating slaves as indentured servants for life. Harrison's estate in Indiana was worked by black slaves. He was also criticized for aggressively exercising and jealously guarding his powers as governor. Ironically, the criticism of his exercise of the

---

382   Alfred Byron Sears, *Thomas Worthington*, Ohio State University Press for the Ohio Historical Society, 1958, pp. 54-55.

383   Freeman Cleaves, *Old Tippecanoe, William Henry Harrison and his Times*, Charles Scribner's Sons, 1939, pp. 30-31.

384   Andrew R. L. Cayton, *Frontier Indiana*, Indiana University Press, paperback edition, 1998, pp. 181; Grouseland has been preserved and is open to the public. See Grouseland web page.

powers of the governorship echoed criticisms made by him against Governor St. Clair.[385]

Harrison was a devout practicing Christian, regularly reading the Bible and observing the Sabbath.[386] Raised as an Episcopalian, he left college due to a Methodist revival on campus. He was one of the founders of Christ Church of Cincinnati (Episcopalian) in 1817. The neighborhood adjacent to the church, now known as Lytle Park, was an area where community leaders lived. Other founders included Dr. Daniel Drake, Dr. Philander Chase, General William Lytle, and Nicholas Longworth.[387]

Harrison's aggressive acquisition of land through treaties created growing animosity among the Indians. Tecumseh and his brother "The Prophet" sought to unite the tribes throughout the north, the south and the west to oppose further white expansion. They established an Indian village, "Prophetstown", near the Tippecanoe River's mouth on the Wabash which became the headquarters for their activities. Recognizing the growing threat, Harrison met with Tecumseh in 1810 and 1811 to attempt to reach a resolution. Realizing the threat could not be eliminated through diplomacy, Harrison decided to mount an offensive against Prophetstown. He waited until Tecumseh left on a journey to the south for the purpose of recruiting allies for his united front against white encroachment on Indian lands. Harrison led an army of nine hundred men, which included regular army soldiers and Indiana and Kentucky militia up the Wabash. When the army got within a mile of Prophetstown, the Prophet sent messengers out calling for a council the following day. Before leaving for the south Tecumseh had warned his brother not to engage the whites in military combat while he was away. The Prophet ignored the warning and led an attack on Harrison's camp just before daybreak of the day scheduled for the council. Harrison although wary had not constructed defenses around the camp. The Indians attacked at 4

---

385   Freeman Cleaves, *Old Tippecanoe, William Henry Harrison and his Times,* Charles Scribner's Sons, 1939, pp. 33-68; Andrew R. L. Cayton, *Frontier Indiana,* Indiana University Press, paperback edition, 1998, pp. 187-193, 228-250; Allen Johnson and Dumas Malone, *Dictionary of American Biography,* Vol. IV, pp 348-349; "Treaty with the Delaware, etc. 1809", Indiana Historical Bureau web page; Allan R. Millett, "Caesar and the Conquest of the Northwest Territory, The Harrison Campaign, 1811", *Timeline,* Ohio Historical Society, Vol. 14, No. 4, July, August 1997.

386   Mark Thorburn, *William Henry Harrison, The Hero of Tippecanoe,* self-published, 2000, p. 7.

387   "Our History 1817 to 1830s", Christ Church Cathedral of Cincinnati web page.

A.M. just as the men in the camp were beginning to arise. The initial assault produced a number of casualties. A ferocious two hour battle ensued during which Harrison's courage and leadership held the army together. Recognizing that the Prophet's promise of a quick victory was false, the Indians withdrew and abandoned their town. The Americans burned it to the ground. Tecumseh and the Prophet had created a mystique of invincibility which was destroyed by Harrison's victory at Tippecanoe. The angry Indians stripped the Prophet of his power and threatened to kill him. The battle did not end the Indian threat, but it did undermine Tecumseh's effort to create a united front. Although the victory was widely haled throughout the west, there was also criticism that Harrison's failure to attack the town immediately or to provide adequate defenses against a surprise attack had contributed to needless deaths and injuries. This criticism was forgotten by the time Harrison ran for President in 1840.[388]

Following the battle Harrison recognized that an Indian war was approaching and urged the Madison administration to allocate the resources needed to defend the frontier. The administration was focused on the coming conflict with Great Britain. Seeing that he would receive no help from Washington, Harrison visited his friends in Kentucky to seek assistance. Kentucky was the most populous state in the west at the time, and its history of bloody conflicts with the Indians made it a ripe recruiting ground for troops.[389]

William Hull, Governor of the Michigan Territory, also recognized that a crisis was approaching. Hostile Indians were rallying around the British Fort Malden across the river from Detroit. The American outpost at Fort Detroit was manned by a few hundred men. Hull went to Washington to persuade the administration that the Michigan Territory was in danger of being overrun if a war broke out with the British and the Indians. He secured permission to raise an army of Ohio militia. Governor Meigs of Ohio organized an army of Ohio

---

388   Freeman Cleaves, *Old Tippecanoe, William Henry Harrison and his Times,* Charles Scribner's Sons, 1939, pp. 83-109; Andrew R. L. Cayton, *Frontier Indiana*, Indiana University Press, paperback edition, 1998, pp. 205-225; Allan R. Millett, "Caesar and the Conquest of the Northwest Territory, The Harrison Campaign, 1811" *Timeline*, Ohio Historical Society, Vol. 14, No. 4, July, August 1997; "Tippecanoe Battlefield", Tippecanoe County Historical Association web page. The Association operates a museum at the site of the battlefield.

389   Allan R. Millett, "Caesar and the Conquest of the Northwest Territory, The Second Harrison Campaign, 1813", *Timeline*, Ohio Historical Society, Vol. 14, No. 5, pp. 2-21; Larry L. Nelson, *Men of Patriotism, Courage & Enterprise, Fort Meigs in the War of 1812*, Heritage Books, 1997 reprint.

militia to march to Michigan under Hull's command. They marched northward from Dayton and Urbana through the black swamp to Detroit cutting a road which could act as a vital supply line if the British cut off supplies traveling by boat across Lake Erie. Hull's army arrived at Detroit on July 6, 1812. During the march, War with Britain was declared. Recognizing the weakness of the American position notwithstanding the arrival of the army, the British crossed the river and surrounded Detroit with a vastly larger force of five thousand British, Canadian, and Indian fighters. The British commander demanded surrender and threatened to unleash the Indians on the inhabitants of Detroit if the American army did not surrender. Hull determined his situation was hopeless and in a decision which would bring him disgrace and a demand for court martial surrendered the newly recruited army of the Northwest without a fight. News of the surrender created shock and panic in Ohio.[390]

The American fort at Mackinac Island also fell. The fort at Chicago was abandoned on orders of Hull and its defenders massacred as they attempted to make their way east. One of the casualties was William Wells, the Indian agent who had warned of the consequences of Harrison's aggressive Indian policy. The British had established a strong beachhead in the northwest territory and the British Indian alliance appeared poised to thrust south and drive the Americans out of Ohio and perhaps even out of the west.

Upon hearing that Detroit was besieged, an army of Kentucky militia was raised to come to its defense and Harrison was appointed major general with responsibility for leading the army north to Detroit.[391] Upon learning of Hull's surrender and that Fort Wayne was besieged, Harrison led the army to Fort Wayne. The Indians abandoned their attack as Harrison's army approached. The American line of defense held in Indiana.

After first appointing James Winchester, a Revolutionary War veteran, to take command of the army of the Northwest in place of Hull, the Madison administration put Harrison in command with a rank of brigadier general in the federal army and instructions to take back Detroit.[392] Harrison quickly

---

390   Allan R. Millett, "Caesar and the Conquest of the Northwest Territory, The Second Harrison Campaign, 1813", *Timeline*, Ohio Historical Society, Vol. 14, No. 5, pp. 2-21; Larry L. Nelson, *Men of Patriotism, Courage & Enterprise, Fort Meigs in the War of 1812*, Heritage Books, 1997 reprint.

391   Freeman Cleaves, *Old Tippecanoe, William Henry Harrison and his Times*, Charles Scribner's Sons, 1939, p. 116.

392   Freeman Cleaves, *Old Tippecanoe, William Henry Harrison and his Times*, Charles Scribner's Sons, 1939, pp. 120-122.

went to work organizing the recruitment and supply effort. His army was comprised of militia from Virginia, Pennsylvania, Kentucky and Ohio and troops from the federal army. He planned for them to converge at the rapids on the Maumee near where the Battle of Fallen Timbers had been fought. While Harrison was busy bringing forces forward, Winchester arrived at the Maumee and learning that Frenchtown (now Monroe, Michigan) was undefended, marched his forces into Michigan and took Frenchtown on the River Raisin. The British learning of his action sent a superior force which attacked the American forces, captured Winchester, and secured the surrender of another American army on January 13, 1813. The British left the wounded Americans at Frenchtown where they were massacred, scalped, and butchered by the Indians. Shock and fear once against swept the Ohio frontier.[393]

Recognizing the troops which had been gathering at the Maumee were likely to be attacked, Harrison first ordered them to fall back and then when no attack occurred, he advanced to the rapids on the Maumee where he put the troops to work constructing Fort Meigs, a large stockade overlooking the foot of the rapids.[394] The men worked throughout the remainder of the winter to prepare for an attack the following spring when the ice thawed and the British troops would arrive on their ships to begin their thrust into Ohio. At Fort Meigs the Americans would make their stand to keep the British out of Ohio. As predicted in late April a combined British, Canadian, and Indian army of over two thousand men arrived to attack the fort. Artillery was stationed across the river from the fort as well as in the woods on the same side of the River as the fort and the shelling began. Indians shot into the fort from the trees and charged the fort's walls. The fort held with relatively few casualties. Several days after the attack began a brigade of Kentucky militia approached with instructions to divide into two columns. One column was to attack the Indians surrounding the fort and join the men in the stockade. The second column was to attack the gunners across the river from the fort, spike the cannon, and then cross the river to the fort. The column which attacked the cannon positions across the river quickly captured the cannon but rather than

393   Allan R. Millett, "Caesar and the Conquest of the Northwest Territory, The Second Harrison Campaign, 1813", *Timeline*, Ohio Historical Society, Vol. 14, No. 5, pp. 2-21; Larry L. Nelson, *Men of Patriotism, Courage & Enterprise, Fort Meigs in the War of 1812*, Heritage Books, 1997 reprint.

394   The fort has been reconstructed by the Ohio Historical Society and the fort and visitor's center are operated by the Society. See Ohio Historical Society web page.

follow instructions, they chased the British and Indians into the woods where they were surrounded, counter attacked and forced to surrender. Over six hundred men were killed or captured. Nonetheless, the fort held and the British withdrew. Harrison suspected they would be back.[395]

Taking psychological advantage of the victory at Fort Meigs, Harrison called the Ohio Indians together for a conference at Franklinton (now Columbus). Fifty leaders of the Wyandot, Shawnee, Seneca, and Delaware tribes met with him. He told them that they must demonstrate their friendliness by moving within the American lines or sending warriors to join the American forces. Tarhe, chief of the Wyandots, marched with Harrison in subsequent campaigns. The conference and subsequent American victories did much to quiet the Indian frontier in Ohio.[396]

In July the British and Indians returned for a second attack on Fort Meigs. They attempted to draw the men out of the fort by creating the appearance that a relief column was under attack. The Americans did not fall for the deception, and deciding that further attacks on the fort were futile the British and Indians loaded back on their ships. They sailed to Sandusky where they attacked Fort Stephenson which was commanded by George Rogers Clark's nephew George Croghan. Harrison ordered him to abandon the fort, but by the time Croghan received the order he decided he could not leave without endangering his men so they stayed and fought. After losing ninety-six men in an assault on the fort, the British withdrew. [397]

---

395   Allan R. Millett, "Caesar and the Conquest of the Northwest Territory, The Second Harrison Campaign, 1813", *Timeline*, Ohio Historical Society, Vol. 14, No. 5, pp. 2-21; Larry L. Nelson, *Men of Patriotism, Courage, & Enterprise, Fort Meigs in the War of 1812*, Heritage Books, 1997 reprint; Freeman Cleaves, *Old Tippecanoe, William Henry Harrison and his Time*, Charles Scribner's Sons, 1939, pp. 151-171.

396   William T. Utter, *History of Ohio, The Frontier State, 1803-1825*, Ohio Historical Society, 1942, Vol. II, pp. 105-106; Freeman Cleaves, *Old Tippecanoe, William Henry Harrison and his Times*, Charles Scribner's Sons, 1939, pp. 176-177.

397   Allan R. Millett, "Caesar and the Conquest of the Northwest Territory, The Second Harrison Campaign, 1813", *Timeline*, Ohio Historical Society, Vol. 14, No. 5, pp. 2-21; Larry L. Nelson, *Men of Patriotism, Courage & Enterprise, Fort Meigs in the War of 1812*, Heritage Books, 1997 reprint; Further details on Fort Stephenson and Croghan are found in Sandusky County, Ohio Scrapbook maintained by four libraries of Sandusky County.

The news of the successful defense of Fort Stephenson was followed by news of Commodore Oliver Hazard Perry's defeat of the British fleet near Put-in-Bay.[398] Harrison knew that Perry's victory meant that the British supply line to Detroit and Fort Malden would be cut and the British position would be untenable. He quickly organized an expedition to liberate Detroit and destroy the British/Indian army at Fort Malden. As his army approached, the British vacated Detroit and Fort Malden and retreated up the Thames River. On October 5, 1813, the American army defeated the British and Indian forces near Moraviantown.[399] Tecumseh was killed in the battle. Eight days following the victory Harrison met with chiefs of the tribes that had participated on the British side and dictated the terms of their surrender to the Americans. The war for the Northwest was essentially over and Harrison was widely haled as a hero across the west.[400]

On March 2, 1813, Harrison had been replaced as Governor of Indiana Territory and promoted to Major General in the Army. In May, 1814, he resigned from the army due to disagreements with the Secretary of War.[401] He returned to Cincinnati to undertake the complicated settlement of his father-in-law John Cleves Symmes' estate. He moved back to his home at North Bend near Cincinnati. He cultivated his farm and engaged in several unsuccessful commercial ventures. He was appointed an Indian Treaty Commissioner and presided over councils with the Indians at Greenville in July, 1814, and at Spring Wells in August, 1815.[402]

---

398   The victory is commemorated by Perry's International Peace Monument and Museum at Put-in-Bay on South Bass Island operated by the National Park Service. See National Park Service web page.

399   Freeman Cleaves, *Old Tippecanoe, William Henry Harrison and his Times,* Charles Scribner's Sons, 1939, pp. 188-204. Following the battle, the American troops disgraced themselves by destroying the Christian Indian village nearby. Fred J. Milligan, *Compassionate Revolutionaries, The Moravian Ancestors of George W. Bush,* Heritage Books, 2001, p. 103.

400   Allan R. Millett, "Caesar and the Conquest of the Northwest Territory, The Second Harrison Campaign, 1813", *Timeline,* Vol. 14, No. 5, pp. 2-21

401   Freeman Cleaves, *Old Tippecanoe, William Henry Harrison and his Times,* Charles Scribner's Sons, 1939, pp. 217-223.

402   Freeman Cleaves, *Old Tippecanoe, William Henry Harrison and his Times,* Charles Scribner's Sons, 1939, pp. 225-228; Allen Johnson and Dumas Malone, *Dictionary of American Biography,* Vol. IV., p. 350.

After returning to North Bend, Harrison was not in a position to build another brick mansion like he had done in Vincennes. Instead he added on to the log cabin which he and his wife had lived in following their marriage. Two spacious wings were added and a wide ell from the center creating a commodious dwelling of sixteen rooms. The "Log Cabin", as it was called, became a popular place of entertainment for important personalities in the West and visitors from the East and Europe. His home was located about three hundred yards from the Ohio River and was situated on a 3,000 acre estate.[403]

In 1815 Harrison was elected to Congress to fill the vacancy created by the resignation of John McLean and then reelected for another term. He served from October 8, 1816 to March 3, 1819. He generally supported the policies of his friend and fellow westerner Henry Clay. His chief interest was his work as chairman of the committee on the militia.[404]

Harrison was elected to the Ohio senate in 1819 and served during the 1819-1820 sessions and the 1820-1821 sessions of the General Assembly. During his first session, the question of slavery and its extension to future states gave rise to long and acrimonious debates. Resolutions were proposed to instruct Ohio's congressional delegates to oppose further expansion of slavery. Harrison advocated a conservative middle course. A more radical anti-slavery resolution passed both houses. While in the senate he also served as chairman of a joint committee which considered the judicial proceedings involving the United States Bank. During his campaign for election in 1819 he had waged a campaign against banks and the United States Bank in particular. He stated that the bank was an institution "which may be converted into an immense political engine to strengthen the arm of the general government and which may at some future date be used to oppress and break down the state governments."[405] The legislature had levied a tax on the bank and state officers had forcefully seized the funds from the vaults of the bank. The resulting litigation in Federal court was a major contest of power between the federal and state

---

403   Freeman Cleaves, *Old Tippecanoe, William Henry Harrison and his Times,* Charles Scribner's Sons, 1939, p. 229.

404   Freeman Cleaves, *Old Tippecanoe, William Henry Harrison and his Times,* Charles Scribner's Sons, 1939, pp. 237-249; Allen Johnson and Dumas Malone, *Dictionary of American Biography,* Vol. IV., p. 350; Biographical Directory of the United States Congress.

405   C. C. Huntington, "History of Banking and Currency in Ohio before the Civil War", *Ohio History,* Vol 24, p. 321; Freeman Cleaves, *Old Tippecanoe, William Henry Harrison and his Times,* Charles Scribner's Sons, 1939, pp. 250-251.

government, a contest which Ohio lost. Harrison had owned stock in and been a director of the United States Bank branch at Cincinnati; however, he took a strong position advocating withdrawal of the protection of state laws from the bank. Harrison also chaired a committee which recommended consideration of a canal linking Lake Erie and the Ohio River. Although not a candidate, Harrison in 1820 received 4330 votes for governor coming in third behind popular Ethan Allen Brown who was reelected for a second term and Jeremiah Morrow.[406] He was defeated in a bid for reelection to the Senate in 1821 because he was not sufficiently anti-slavery for his constituents.[407] He was defeated in 1822 in a race for Congress in which he was attacked for his position on slavery, his war record, his association with the Bank of the United States, and his relationship to John Cleves Symmes. He also faced severe financial distress at this time.[408]

Harrison was a presidential elector in 1820 casting his vote for James Monroe and in 1824 casting his vote for Henry Clay.[409]

Harrison was elected by the Ohio General Assembly to the United States Senate on the fourth ballot. despite a slander circulated by his enemies that he had seduced a respectable lady.[410] He served from March 24, 1825 to May 20, 1828, when he resigned to become Minister to Columbia. During his term in the Senate he served as chairman of the committee on military affairs. Harrison lost a bid for appointment as major general of the army to Winfield Scott, but won the consolation prize of ambassador to Columbia.[411] He served as minister to Columbia for only one year due to President Jackson's desire to replace him with one of his supporters. Harrison's tenure as a diplomat was

---

406   Freeman Cleaves, *Old Tippecanoe, William Henry Harrison and his Times*, Charles Scribner's Sons, 1939, p. 253; William A. Taylor, *Ohio Statesmen and Annals of Progress*, Vol I, pp. 94-95, 104-107.

407   Freeman Cleaves, *Old Tippecanoe, William Henry Harrison and his Times*, Charles Scribner's Sons, 1939, pp. 253-254; Allen Johnson and Dumas Malone, *Dictionary of American Biography*, Vol. IV., p. 350.

408   Freeman Cleaves, *Old Tippecanoe, William Henry Harrison and his Times*, Charles Scribner's Sons, 1939, pp. 254-255.

409   William A. Taylor, *Ohio Statesmen and Annals of Progress*, Vol I, p. 145.

410   Freeman Cleaves, *Old Tippecanoe, William Henry Harrison and his Times*, Charles Scribner's Sons, 1939, p. 256; William A. Taylor, *Ohio Statesmen and Annals of Progress*, Vol I, p. 121.

411   Freeman Cleaves, *Old Tippecanoe, William Henry Harrison and his Times*, Charles Scribner's Sons, 1939, p. 260.

controversial because of his involvement with a group which opposed President Bolivar.[412]

After his return from Columbia, Harrison encountered a series of financial reverses and misfortunes, due in part to the indiscretion and misfortune of his sons. Two sons died and he assumed their debts and the responsibility for their widows and children. He sold part of his farm to meet the burden. In 1834 he was appointed clerk of the common pleas court of Hamilton County, which helped relieve the financial strain.[413]

In 1835 Harrison was selected as the Whig candidate for President to run against Martin Van Buren, Andrew Jackson's heir apparent. Although he carried Ohio and ran close in other northern states, Harrison won only 73 votes in the electoral college.[414] Immediately after the election, Harrison and his supporters began planning for the next race. Harrison was picked over Clay at the Whig convention in 1839. Harrison's campaign for president has been called the first modern campaign. Harrison was run as an old war hero under the slogan "Tippecanoe and Tyler too." It was called the "log cabin and hard cider" campaign because Harrison was portrayed as a man of the people. Harrison was assisted by the fact that the country had sustained a severe depression following the panic of 1837. Harrison beat Van Buren by a vote of 234 to 60 in the electoral college. Worn out by the campaign and the strain of meeting with office seekers, Harrison contracted pneumonia and died on April 4, 1841, a month after he took office.[415] His wife who had been ill had remained in North Bend and was not with him at his death. Harrison was the first Ohioan and the first Whig to be elected President. He was the first President to die in office, and before Reagan, the oldest person elected president. He was the President with the shortest term in office.[416]

---

412   Biographical Directory of the United States Congress; Allen Johnson and Dumas Malone, *Dictionary of American Biography*, Vol. IV, p. 350.

413   Francis P. Weisenburger, *The History of Ohio, Passing of the Frontier 1825-1850*, Ohio Historical Society, Vol. 3, p. 317; Mark Thorburn, *William Henry Harrison, The Hero of Tippecanoe*, self-published, 2000, p. 9.

414   Freeman Cleaves, *Old Tippecanoe, William Henry Harrison and his Times*, Charles Scribner's Sons, 1939, pp. 309-310.

415   Freeman Cleaves, *Old Tippecanoe, William Henry Harrison and his Times*, Charles Scribner's Sons, 1939, pp. 341-343; Francis P. Weisenburger, *The History of Ohio, Passing of the Frontier 1825-1850*, Ohio Historical Society, Vol. 3, pp. 326-327, 396-398; Allen Johnson and Dumas Malone, *Dictionary of American Biography*, Vol. IV, p. 351.

416   Mark Thorburn, *William Henry Harrison, The Hero of Tippecanoe*, self-published, 2000, p. 3.

Originally interred in the Congressional Cemetery at Washington, the family later secured approval to bury him in the family cemetery at North Bend. He is buried in a tomb overlooking the Ohio River. In 1887 the Ohio legislature paid for the erection of monument at his grave site.[417]

JACOB BURNET

Jacob Burnet was born February 22, 1770, at Newark, New Jersey. His grandfather Ichabod Burnet was born and educated as a physician in Edinburgh, Scotland. He immigrated to the United States where he settled in Elizabethtown, New Jersey. His father William was educated at the College of New Jersey, now Princeton, and established a medical practice in Newark, New Jersey. With the coming of the Revolutionary War, he became chairman of the committee of safety for Essex County and in 1776 was elected to the Continental Congress. The following winter he was appointed physician and surgeon-general of the army of the eastern department and served in that position for the remainder of the War. Jacob was educated at Princeton and studied law under Richard Stockton and Judge Boudinot for four and a half years and was admitted to the bar of New Jersey in 1796.[418]

In 1796 Burnet went west settling in the village of Cincinnati which at the time was a small village of log cabins. A swamp extended along the base of the second bench which caused the residents, including Burnet during the summer of his arrival, to suffer from what at the time was referred to as "ague" or "fever." The village was located next to Fort Washington which at the time of his arrival was commanded by Captain William Henry Harrison. The population of the village including officers and followers of the army was about five hundred. Because of the proximity of the military post, excessive drinking and gambling were rampant in the town.[419]

Burnet quickly became a leading attorney in Cincinnati. The Territorial Court met in Marietta, Cincinnati, and Detroit. When Court was held at

---

417   Harrison's Tomb is a state memorial administered the Ohio Historical Society. Ohio Historical Society web page.

418   Jacob Burnet, "Burnet's Letters" *Transactions of the Historical and Philosophical Society of Ohio*, Cincinnati, 1839, Vol. 1, pp. 9-10.

419   Jacob Burnet, "Burnet's Letters" *Transactions of the Historical and Philosophical Society of Ohio*, Cincinnati, 1839, Vol. 1, pp. 10-13.

Marietta and Detroit Burnet traveled with the judges to these locations. He also argued cases in the common pleas courts of the counties.[420]

In accordance with the Ordinance of 1787 when the population of the Northwest Territory reached five thousand white mail inhabitants, Governor St. Clair issued a proclamation calling on the people to elect representatives to a territorial legislature. The representatives met on February 4, 1799 in Cincinnati and nominated ten persons for the Legislative Council. These nominations were forwarded to President John Adams who selected five to serve on the Council. One of the five selected was Jacob Burnet. Following the appointment of the Council, the legislature and council convened September 16, 1799, at Cincinnati to review, revise and expand the laws of the Territory. Burnet was offered the position as Ohio's non-voting representative to Congress, but declined, and a majority elected William Henry Harrison over the Governor's son to the position. Since the other members of the Council were not trained in the law, they relied almost entirely upon Burnet to draft the bills which originated or were revised by that chamber. He served in the Legislative Council until 1803 when Ohio was admitted as a state and throughout that time was chosen to serve as presiding officer of the Council. He was the most important member of the legislature during the territorial period.[421]

Burnet was a committed Federalist and his considerable talents were the "brain trust" for that party during the battle with the Republicans leading up to statehood. He provided the legal rationale for the proposed division of the Territory at the Scioto River and the arguments attacking the legality of the Enabling Act passed by Congress calling for the elections of delegates to a convention to vote on statehood and draft a constitution.[422] He was animated not only by the view shared by St. Clair and other Federalists that government must be entrusted to responsible men of property, education, and character but also quite naturally by his view of the best interests of Cincinnati with which his personal interests were aligned.

Writing about the bitter battle with the Republicans thirty-five years later, Burnet stated, "St. Clair was a man of superior talents—of extensive information and of great uprightness of purpose. The course he pursued, though

---

420   Jacob Burnet, "Burnet's Letters" *Transactions of the Historical and Philosophical Society of Ohio*, Cincinnati, 1839, Vol. 1, pp. 54-55.

421   Jacob Burnet, "Burnet's Letters" *Transactions of the Historical and Philosophical Society of Ohio*, Cincinnati, 1839, Vol. 1, pp. 70-71.

422   Jacob Burnet, "Burnet's Letters" *Transactions of the Historical and Philosophical Society of Ohio*, Cincinnati, 1839, Vol. 1, pp. 75-77, 106, 117.

destructive of his own popularity was the result of an honest exercise of his judgment—he not only believed that the power he claimed for the executive belonged legitimately to the executive, but was convinced that the manner in which he exercised it was calculated to advance the best interests of the territory—he placed a high estimate on the powers of his own mind, and though modest and unassuming in his ordinary intercourse in society, he very rarely yielded his opinions....Many of his most active opponents had been his friends—their opposition was attributed to personal ambition and a desire to elevate themselves to political distinction on his ruin; but on a calm review after thirty-five years, many circumstances, over which oblivion has thrown her mantle can be recalled to memory, which may account for their conduct, without ascribing to them, more of self interest, or less of honesty of purpose, than falls to the lot of those who are called consistent politicians of the present day. Some part of the governor's political course was condemned by his best friends and was calculated to excite a warmth of feeling in his opponents which might have led upright men beyond the limits of moderation and even justice. An attentive observer of the conduct of that talented man must come to the conclusion that wisdom and prudence are not synonymous, and that talents of a high order, united with integrity of purpose, are not always sufficient to guide their possessors in the path of duty or safety."[423]

Following the adoption of the Constitution and the route of the Federalists, Jacob Burnet was free to concentrate on his legal practice. Although Cincinnati had lost out in the battle to become a state capital, the town prospered as did his practice, investments, and prominence. He was involved with numerous business ventures in Cincinnati and southwestern Ohio as attorney or investor.

Burnet was among the leading lawyers of the State who volunteered to defend Supreme Court Justice Tod in his impeachment case before the Ohio Senate.[424]

With the War of 1812, the stigma attached to the Federalists had sufficiently waned that he was elected to the Ohio House of Representatives for two terms serving from 1814 to 1816. As he took a seat in the House, his old nemesis Thomas Worthington took office as Governor. During his tenure the state capital was moved to Columbus.[425]

---

423   Jacob Burnet, "Burnet's Letters" *Transactions of the Historical and Philosophical Society of Ohio*, Cincinnati, 1839, Vol. 1, pp. 80-81.

424   Donald F. Melhorn Jr., *Lest We Be Marshall'd, Judicial Power and Politics in Ohio 1806-1812*, Akron University Press, 2003, pp. 98-102.

425   William A. Taylor, *Ohio Statesmen and Annals of Ohio Progress*, Columbus, 1899, pp. 78-83.

On December 24, 1821, the General Assembly elected Jacob Burnet as a Judge of the Ohio Supreme Court. He served until 1828 when he was elected United States Senator to fill the seat vacated when William Henry Harrison resigned.[426] He served until 1831 and did not run for election. Burnet was a strong supporter of the canals, and while in the U. S. Senate he secured legislation to support the construction of the Miami Canal from Dayton to Maumee.[427] He also succeeded in persuading Congress to grant a pension to Simon Kenton, who then lived in poverty in Ohio. Kenton and Daniel Boone were the most important defenders of the Ohio Valley during the time of the Indian wars.

Burnet nominated his old Republican adversary William Henry Harrison for President at the Whig Party's national convention in 1839 and was no doubt thrilled to see his candidate elected President.

Although a strong proponent of the establishment of the second national bank in 1816 and the opening of a branch in Ohio with offices in Cincinnati and Chillicothe, he was highly critical of the policy implemented in Ohio to compel payment of all debts in specie. The actions of the bank caused a severe financial depression in Ohio, and caused him considerable personal hardship. As a result of the severe financial depression from 1819 through 1821, purchasers were unable to pay for their land and faced the risk of losing it. Half the farmers in the state faced bankruptcy. This not only created severe economic hardship, it created an explosive political situation. Burnet proposed a plan by which purchasers could acquire part of the land for the payments made and surrender the balance. In 1821 Congress enacted Burnet's plan into law. Its enactment relieved the people and played an important role in allowing the west to pull itself out of the depression.[428]

Burnet also served as president of the Medical College of Ohio, which was established by Dr. Daniel Drake in 1820.[429]

Jacob Burnet died May 10, 1853. Although he opposed statehood at the time of the 1802 convention, he contributed much to the development of the legal, economic, and social structures of the new state.

---

426   William A. Taylor, *Ohio Statesmen and Annals of Ohio Progress*, Columbus, 1899, p 110, 134.

427   Jacob Burnet, "Burnet's Letters" *Transactions of the Historical and Philosophical Society of Ohio*, Cincinnati, 1839, Vol. 1, pp. 171-175.

428   Jacob Burnet, "Burnet's Letters" *Transactions of the Historical and Philosophical Society of Ohio*, Cincinnati, 1839, Vol. 1, pp. 162-171.

429   "Jacob Burnet", *Ohio History* Central, Ohio Historical Society Web Page; Henry A. Ford and Kate B. Ford, *History of Cincinnati, Ohio*, 1881, p. 300-301.

WILLIAM MCMILLAN

William McMillan was born March 2, 1764, near Abingdon, in Washington County, Virginia. His father William was born in Londonderry, Ireland, and immigrated to America where he settled in Washington County. [430] He was educated at the College of William and Mary at Williamsburg, Virginia, the college which Thomas Jefferson attended. He disappointed his father who was a rigid Scotch Presbyterian by pursuing a career in law rather than the ministry.[431]

McMillan arrived on the first boat of Losantiville settlers and was the first and most prominent attorney in the village.[432] Prior to the organization of the county by Governor St. Clair, the citizens met under a large tree and adopted ordinances and punishments and a court to enforce them. McMillan chaired the meeting and was elected judge of the court. A sheriff was also elected. An offender summoned to come before the court sought the refuge of the commander of Fort Washington. The commandant sent an abusive letter to McMillan ordering him to desist. McMillan sent a spirited reply denying the right of the commandant to interfere. The commandant then sent a sergeant and three men to arrest McMillan. When they came to his door, he refused to go with them. McMillan was young and athletic. A fight ensued which lasted for fifteen or twenty minutes before the soldiers decided to withdraw. He sustained an injury during that fight the effects of which remained with him the remainder of this life.[433]

In January, 1790, Governor St. Clair arrived at Cincinnati and organized Hamilton County. William McMillan was appointed as a judge of the court of common pleas and justice of the peace and court of quarter sessions.[434]

A majority of the early settlers of Losantiville were Presbyterians. McMillan served as a Trustee of the Presbyterian Church organized in the village which

---

430   *Biographical Directory of the United States Congress*; Jo Tice Bloom, "The Congressional Delegates from the Northwest Territory", *Old Northwest 3* (1977), pp. 3-21; Political Graveyard web page; Family Search Ancestral File.

431   Jacob Burnet, "Burnet's Letters" *Transactions of the Historical and Philosophical Society of Ohio*, Cincinnati, 1839, Vol. 1, pp. 101-102.

432   Henry A. Ford and Kate B. Ford, *History of Cincinnati, Ohio*, 1881, p. 310.

433   Jacob Burnet, "Burnet's Letters" *Transactions of the Historical and Philosophical Society of Ohio*, Cincinnati, 1839, Vol. 1, pp. 19-21.

434   *Transcript of the Executive Journal of the Northwest Territory*, Ohio Historical Society web page, p. 57.

erected its first building in 1792. The building was also used by the first courts in the county.[435]

In 1797 McMillan worked with fellow Republican William Goforth to secure census information in Hamilton and other counties showing that the Territory had reached a population of five thousand white male inhabitants and was therefore entitled to elect a legislature. Like Goforth he was at that time critical of the arbitrary actions of the Governor and looked forward to statehood as soon as possible.[436]

McMillan was elected as a representative to the first Territorial legislature which convened at Cincinnati in 1799.[437] Following the separation of the Indiana Territory in 1800, McMillan and other Republican leaders of Cincinnati faced a problem. On the one hand, they wanted Cincinnati to be the state capital. They believed this to be of critical importance to the future of the town, and incidentally to their own careers. On the other hand, they wanted statehood as soon as possible. Cincinnati could be the state capital only if the Territory were divided at the Scioto River as advocated by Governor St. Clair. Otherwise, Chillicothe because of its central location was the obvious choice for state capital. St. Clair and the other Federalists wanted the division at the Scioto in order to delay statehood. McMillan led the effort of Cincinnati Republicans to make an alliance with St. Clair and the Federalists of Washington County to support a division of the Territory at the Scioto. This would enable Cincinnati and Marietta to each become state capitals. As part of the alliance with Marietta against Chillicothe, it was agreed that that the Territory's representative to Congress would alternate between Cincinnati and Marietta. When William Henry Harrison resigned to accept the governorship of the new Indiana Territory, the alliance elected William McMillan to serve the remainder of his term in Congress.[438] He served from November 24, 1800 to March 3, 1801.[439] While in Congress McMillan successfully advocated St. Clair's reappointment as Governor despite President Adams preference for a Federalist from Connecticut.[440] One of the issues which McMillan successfully

435   Henry A. Ford and Kate B. Ford, *History of Cincinnati, Ohio*, 1881, pp. 146-149.

436   Randolph C. Downes, *Frontier Ohio*, Ohio Historical Society, pp. 181-185.

437   William A. Taylor, *Ohio Statesmen and Annals of Progress*, State of Ohio, 1899, p. 18.

438   Alfred Byron Sears, *Thomas Worthington*, Ohio State University Press for the Ohio Historical Society, 1958, p. 58.

439   "William McMillan", *Biographical Directory of the United States Congress*.

440   Alfred Byron Sears, *Thomas Worthington*, Ohio State University Press for the Ohio Historical Society, 1958, p. 61.

advocated was a law granting preemptive right allowing purchasers of land from Judge Symmes outside the boundaries of his purchase to acquire the land from the government. Although he advocated that they only be required to pay $1.00 per acre, the law required them to pay the full government price of $2.00 per acre. Although they would be out the money paid to Symmes, if they had the money to pay the government, they would at least be able to realize the value of their improvements.[441]

In return for supporting the alliance McMillan secured from the Cincinnati Federalists their pledge to support statehood as soon as possible.[442] Judge Symmes, founder of North Bend, had no love for Cincinnati and its leaders. He and his political ally John Smith and back country Republicans like Morrow and Dunlavy believed the Cincinnati Republicans had made an alliance with the devil by joining forces with the Federalists. They remained allied with the Republican leadership at Chillicothe in opposing the division of the Territory. Upon learning that the Republicans had sent Worthington and Baldwin to Washington to lobby against the division of the Territory, the alliance prepared to send Republicans McMillan and George Tod of Trumbull County to lobby in support of the division. However, Congress rejected the proposed division before they left. After Congress rejected the proposal to divide the Territory, the Hamilton County Republicans united to elect a slate pledged to statehood. McMillan remained allied with St. Clair and Burnet in attacking the Enabling Act which Congress had passed calling for an election of delegates to a convention to vote on statehood as an infringement of the rights of the Territory. [443]

Because of his alliance with St. Clair and the Federalists, McMillan is sometimes referred to as a Federalist. Jacob Burnet observed that at the time of the contest between Adams and Jefferson for the presidency in 1800 he recalls only four in Cincinnati who advocated the election of Jefferson. They included Major Ziegler, William Henry Harrison, John Smith, and William McMillan.[444] In December 1799, Governor St. Clair in a letter to Senator James Ross of Pennsylvania, described McMillan as follows, "There is a gentleman of the name

---

441   Randolph C. Downes, *Frontier Ohio*, Ohio Historical Society, pp. 186-200.

442   Alfred Byron Sears, *Thomas Worthington*, Ohio State University Press for the Ohio Historical Society, 1958, p. 78, 89.

443   Randolph C. Downes, *Frontier Ohio*, Ohio Historical Society, pp. 186-200, 208-216, 226-239.

444   Jacob Burnet, "Burnet's Letters", *Transactions of the Historical and Philosophical Society of Ohio*, Cincinnati, 1839, p. 132.

of McMillan, a counselor, spoken of to me in strong terms by the rest of the bar, and I believe they will recommend him to the President. I am personally acquainted with him. He is a man of much application, with a strong and not uncultivated mind, an awkward appearance and address, and is an indifferent speaker, but has fair reputation, and is in great esteem with the people." [445] McMillan was not a Federalist, he was a town booster, and he was on the wrong side at the time of the 1802 convention. The Cincinnati Federalists supported him for Congress at the June, 1803 election. Morrow received 3,701 votes and McMillan ran second in a field of six candidates with 1,887 votes. He was appointed United States District Attorney for Ohio, but due to his declining health did not assume his duties.

McMillan died in May, 1804 and was buried in Spring Grove Cemetery.[446] Jacob Burnet described him as a man of high intellect. He had been one of the early residents of the Territory. His professional and general knowledge of the Territory made him particularly useful as a legislator.[447]

JAMES FINDLAY

James Findlay was born near Mercersburg, Franklin County, Pennsylvania on October 12, 1770. He was of Scotch-Irish descent. Findlay was educated in the neighborhood school. He was the brother of William Findlay, Governor and United States Senator from Pennsylvania and John Findlay, a Congressman from Pennsylvania.[448]

Findlay migrated to Cincinnati in 1793 and opened a store in a log cabin.[449] He invested in real estate and laid out a 52 lot subdivision just north of the City

---

445   William Henry Smith, *St. Clair Papers*, Vol. 2, pp. 483-484.

446   *Biographical Directory of the United States Congress*; Henry A. Ford and Kate B. Ford, *History of Cincinnati, Ohio*, 1881, p. 310.

447   Jacob Burnet, "Burnet's Letters" *Transactions of the Historical and Philosophical Society of Ohio*, Cincinnati, 1839, Vol. 1, p. 101.

448   William A. Taylor, *Ohio in Congress from 1803 to 1901*, Columbus, 1900; James Grant Wilson and John Fiske, "William Findlay", *Appleton's Cyclopedia of American Biography*, New York, 1887-1889; "James Findlay", Biographical Directory of the United States Congress.

449   "Findlay Market", *Cincinnati Post*, April 2, 2001. Findlay Market is located on land donated to the City of Cincinnati following the death of Mrs. Findlay. It had been used as an open air farmer's market. It is the second oldest continually operating public market in the United States.

named Northern Liberties.[450] Findlay was a leading businessman of the town and engaged in a number of business ventures.[451] He was associated with the organizations formed for civic betterment. He was a leader of the Presbyterian Church whose members included many of the town's leaders.[452]

After Governor St. Clair called for election of the first legislature for the Territory, Findlay was nominated by the House and appointed by Adams to the Legislative Council which served as the upper house of the territorial legislature.[453] The first territorial legislature met November 24, 1799 and adjourned January 29, 1801. He served on the Council during the second territorial legislature which met from November 23, 1801 to January 23, 1802.[454] Governor St. Clair appointed him to serve as a justice of the peace and judge of the general quarter sessions of Hamilton County in 1801.[455] He served as United States Marshall of the Territory in 1802.[456]

Following Congress enactment of Harrison's Land law of 1800, a Cincinnati land district was created and a land office was established to handle sales of public lands in the district. Findlay was appointed as Receiver of the Land Office and the first sales in the district were conducted by him at public auction in April, 1801.[457] He held this office until 1824.[458]

---

450   Rev. John H. Lamott, "The Founding of the Roman Catholic Church in Cincinnati, Ohio," *History of the Archdiocese of Cincinnati, 1821-1921*. Findlay sold the land for the first Catholic Church in Cincinnati.

451   Harry R. Stevens, "Samuel Watt Davies and the Industrial Revolution in Cincinnati", *Ohio History* Vol 70, p. 107. He was a founder of the Miami Sheep Company formed to sell and rent Merino rams and ewes. Andrew R. L. Cayton, *Frontier Republic*, Kent State University Press, 1986, p. 114, 119. He was a partner in the Bell Brass and Iron Foundry which employed 120 men. He was a trustee of the Cincinnati Manufacturing Company. He was a member of the board of directors of the Cincinnati branch of the United States Bank.

452   Andrew R. L. Cayton, *Frontier Republic*, Kent State University Press, 1986, p. 140.

453   Henry A. Ford and Kate B. Ford, *History of Hamilton County, Ohio*, Cleveland, 1881, p. 228; Henry A. Ford and Kate B. Ford, *History of Hamilton County, Ohio*, Cleveland, 1881, pp. 37-38.

454   William A. Taylor, *Ohio Statesmen and Annals of Progress*, Columbus, 1899, pp. 18-19.

455   Henry A. Ford and Kate B. Ford, *History of Hamilton County, Ohio*, Cleveland, 1881, p. 239.

456   "James Findlay" *Biographical Directory of the United States Congress*.

457   Benjamin Horace Hibbard, *A History of Public Land Policies*, New York, 1939, pp. 69-70;

458   James Grant Wilson and John Fiske, "William Findlay", *Appleton's Cyclopedia of American Biography*, New York, 1887-1889.

In 1801 Congress passed a law granting purchasers who had purchased land from John Cleves Symmes outside his patent, a preemptive right to buy the land from the government. Findlay along with William Goforth and John Reily were appointed commissioners to receive and decide the claims.[459]

Findlay served as Mayor of Cincinnati in 1805 to1806 and 1810 to 1811.[460]

In 1810 Findlay was appointed to a commission to recommend a permanent location for the state capital. The commission unanimously recommended the present site of Dublin.[461] The General Assembly selected a site on the east bank of the Olentangy across from Franklinton which became Columbus. Findlay also served on the Board of Trustees of Miami University.[462]

As the War of 1812 approached, at the urging of Governor Hull of Michigan, President Madison requested Governor Meigs to call up the Ohio militia to accompany Hull to Detroit. The militia rendezvoused at Dayton. The force was divided into three regiments under Colonels James Findlay, Duncan McArthur, and Lewis Cass. The army had to cut a road through the swamp in northwestern Ohio in order to reach Detroit. On the way north Findlay's troops constructed a stockade which was named Fort Findlay in his honor.[463] When confronted with what he feared was a superior British and Indian force, Hull surrendered. The surrender was opposed by Colonels Findlay, Cass, and McArthur, and led to Hull's court martial. Findlay was eventually exchanged and rejoined the army. Among other duties he led an expedition against the Ottawa towns. He received a commission as brigadier general in the regular army.[464]

Findlay was a director of the Cincinnati branch of the United States Bank. Like other leading Cincinnati citizens including Jacob Burnet, Martin Baum, Daniel Drake, and William Henry Harrison, he suffered severe financial losses

---

459   Henry A. Ford and Kate B. Ford, *History of Hamilton County, Ohio*, Cleveland, 1881, p. 44.

460   "James Findlay" *Biographical Directory of the United States Congress*.

461   E. O. Randall, "Location of State Capital", *Ohio History* Vol. 25, p. 220.

462   *A History and Biographical Cyclopedia of Butler County, Ohio*, Cincinnati, 1882, pp. 58-61.

463   The City of Findlay was subsequently located at the site of the fort.

464   Robert B. McAfee, *History of the Late War in the Western Country*, Lexington, 1816, pp. 52, 55-56, 83-84, 89, 133, 139-140, 149; Henry A. Ford and Kate B. Ford, *History of Hamilton County, Ohio*, Cleveland, 1881, p. 81; William A. Taylor, *Ohio in Congress from 1803 to 1901*, Columbus, 1900, pp. 161-162.

during the economic depression that swept Ohio following the Bank's demand that payments on loans be paid in specie.[465]

The Jacksonian Democrats emerged as a political party in Ohio in 1824. Findlay was elected to Congress as a Jacksonian Democrat in 1824 and served from March 4, 1825 to March 3, 1833.[466] He cooled on the Jacksonians and ran for Governor against the Democratic incumbent Robert Lucas in 1834. He lost in a close vote.[467]

Findlay died in Cincinnati, Ohio on December 28, 1835.[468]

DANIEL SYMMES

Daniel Symmes was born in 1772 in Sussex County, New Jersey. He was the son of John Cleves Symmes' brother Timothy; and was educated at Princeton College.[469] In 1786 he accompanied his uncle John Cleves Symmes to the Ohio Valley to view the country.[470] Daniel's father was the first settler of South Bend, the second settlement established by John Cleves Symmes following his settlement at North Bend. Daniel accompanied his father to the west. At one time John Cleves Symmes hoped that South Bend would be named the county seat instead of Cincinnati. Timothy Symmes died February 20, 1797.[471]

Daniel Symmes served as a clerk of the territorial court of which his uncle sat as judge and as sheriff of Hamilton County from 1795-1796. He studied

---

465 Andrew R. L. Cayton, *Frontier Republic*, Kent State University Press, 1986, pp. 126-128.

466 "James Findlay", *Biographical Directory of the United States Congress*; Homer J. Webster, "History of the Democratic Party Organization in the Northwest", *Ohio History* Vol. 24, p. 16.

467 Francis P. Weisenburger, "Charles Hammond", *Ohio History* Vol. 43, p. 407; William A. Taylor, *Ohio Statesmen and Annals of Progress*, Columbus, 1899, p. 164. The vote was 70,738 to 67,444.

468 James Findlay", *Biographical Directory of the United States Congress*.

469 Marshall, *Courts and Lawyers of Ohio*, p. 234; Henry A. Ford and Kate B. Ford, *History of Hamilton County, Ohio*, Cleveland, 1881, p. 311; Church of Jesus Christ of Latter Day Saints Family History Library web page.

470 R. Pierce Beaver, "The Miami Purchase of John Cleaves Symmes", *Ohio History*, Vol. 40, p. 288.

471 Henry A. Ford and Kate B. Ford, *History of Hamilton County, Ohio*, Cleveland, 1881, pp. 295311.

law and was admitted to practice before the Territorial courts.[472] He served as the first prosecuting attorney of Butler and Greene Counties, Ohio.[473]

Daniel Symmes married Elizabeth Oliver in Cincinnati on April 10, 1796.[474]

The Symmes were enemies of St. Clair and allies of Tiffin and Worthington during the battle for Ohio statehood. In the election following the adoption of the Constitution, Daniel Symmes was elected as one of the representatives of Hamilton County to the Ohio Senate. At the second session which convened in December, 1803, Symmes was chosen as the Speaker of the Senate. During this session he was also appointed Quartermaster of the First Division of the State Militia which included Hamilton County. He was reelected to the Senate in December, 1804 and was again elected Speaker. Following Meigs resignation as Judge of the Supreme Court, Symmes was on February 7, 1805, appointed to fill his vacancy. He served until January 9, 1808, when he resigned to accept the office of the Registrar of the Land Office in Cincinnati.[475]

Although he had served as a judge, Symmes did not support the claim that Judges could declare acts of the General Assembly unconstitutional. When the question of the constitutionality of the fifty dollar act came before the Supreme Court, he dissented from the decision of Justices Todd and Huntington holding that the law was unconstitutional.[476] When the Sweeping Resolution was enacted vacating all the judicial offices of the state, Symmes had a celebration party.[477] Symmes also appreciated the need for an organization such as the Tammany Society championed by Tiffin and Worthington to bring order and discipline to the Republican Party. He joined the chapter in Chillicothe and petitioned to establish a chapter in Cincinnati.[478]

---

472   Henry A. Ford and Kate B. Ford, *History of Hamilton County, Ohio*, Cleveland, 1881, p. 311; Marshall, *Courts and Lawyers of Ohio*, p. 234.

473   *History and Biographical Cyclopedia of Butler County, Ohio*, Cincinnati, Ohio, 1882, pp. 253-258; R. S. Dills, *History of Greene County, Ohio*, Dayton, 1881, p. 926.

474   Ancestry.com web page.

475   William A. Taylor, *Ohio Statesmen and Annals of Progress*, Columbus, 1899, pp. 35-44;

476   Donald F. Melhorn Jr., *Lest We Be Marshall'd, Judicial Power and Politics in Ohio*, University of Akron Press, 2003, p. 45.

477   Andrew R. L. Cayton, *Frontier Republic*, Kent State University Press, 1986, p. 105.

478   Samuel W. Williams, The Tammany Society in Ohio", *Ohio History* Vol. 22, p. 365; Andrew R. L. Cayton, *Frontier Republic*, Kent State University Press, 1986, p. 106.

Symmes was among the leaders of Cincinnati whose names were associated with organizations established for civic and economic improvement of the community.[479] In April, 1803, the Miami Exporting Company was chartered by the General Assembly to promote trade with New Orleans. Symmes was elected a director.[480] When Senator Smith was associated in the Aaron Burr conspiracy, Symmes was among those who convened a public meeting in Cincinnati to demand his resignation.[481] In 1814 when the Cincinnati Lancaster Seminary was organized by the leading citizens of Cincinnati, Jacob Burnet was elected president and Symmes as secretary.[482]

Symmes was named to the first Board of Trustees of Ohio University following it reestablishment after statehood.[483] He also served on the Board of Trustees of Miami University.[484]

Daniel Symmes died May 10, 1817 at Cincinnati.[485]

479   Andrew R. L. Cayton, *Frontier Republic*, Kent State University Press, 1986, p. 140.

480   George A. Katzenberger, "Martin Baum", *Ohio History* Vol. 44, p. 206.

481   M. Avis Pitcher, "John Smith: First Senator from Ohio and His Connection with Aaron Burr", *Ohio History* Vol 45, p. 80.

482   Andrew R. L. Cayton, *Frontier Republic*, Kent State University Press, 1986, p. 143.

483   Thomas N. Hoover, "The Beginnings of Higher Education in the Northwest Territory," *Ohio History* Vol. 50, p. 252.

484   *A History and Biographical Cyclopedia of Butler County, Ohio,* Cincinnati, 1882, pp. 58-61.

485   Henry A. Ford and Kate B. Ford, *History of Hamilton County, Ohio*, Cleveland, 1881, p. 311; *History and Biographical Cyclopedia of Butler County, Ohio*, Cincinnati, Ohio, 1882, pp. 253-258.

Chapter 3

FOUNDING FATHERS FROM ADAMS COUNTY

The Virginia Military District

At the time Virginia relinquished its claim in the Northwest Territory to the federal government, it reserved the lands between the Little Miami and Scioto Rivers to satisfy claims of its Revolutionary War veterans. The veterans' sale of these claims to speculators and their resale to settlers seeking rich farm land was the economic engine which made this the fastest growing area in the five years leading up to statehood. Unlike the federal government's system of surveys which divided the land into arbitrary rectangles and forced buyers to take the bad land with the good, buyers in the Virginia Military District were free to survey by metes and bounds just the land they wanted to buy. Also, unlike the sale of federal lands, where the price of land was arbitrarily established by Congress, the price of land in the District was based on the market. In short, the federal system of land sales served the bureaucratic needs and political goals of the government, while land sales in the District were market driven, hence buyer friendly. This market spawned a number of entrepreneurs who saw the opportunity, capitalized on it, and became very wealthy. The capital they accumulated was not simply invested in more land. To make their land more valuable, they founded towns and to attract settlers to the towns they gave lots away to the first settlers, improved transportation by building roads and establishing ferries, and donated lands and money for courthouses, churches, and schools. They invested in businesses of all kinds. Entrepreneurs of the District were daring and self-confident risk takers and practical visionaries. They reflected the optimism of the settlers rushing into the Scioto Valley

124

and their belief in the wondrous opportunities in the new state which they were creating out of the wilderness.

There were two other factors which gave the District an edge over other areas. The valley of the Scioto and its tributaries contained land which was more attractive for farming than lands in most of the eastern part of the State. Finally, the District was located across the Ohio River from a part of Kentucky which had sustained an earlier surge of settlers seeking opportunity in the West and whose future was clouded with uncertainties arising from disputes over land titles and the institution of slavery. Slavery was promoted and sustained by an aristocratic culture which devalued the effort of the common man trying to better himself through the hard physical labor of himself and his family. Success on the Ohio frontier depended on hard work and good judgment, not how many slaves a person inherited or acquired. These settlers and their offspring were now seeking greater opportunity in the new lands which opened up across the Ohio. A number of men from the Kentucky side of the River had participated in raids against the Indians during the Indian Wars, so it was widely known that potentially rich farm land lay on the other side of the River. However, until General Wayne defeated the Indians at Fallen Timbers and the Greenville Treaty was signed, the lands across the Ohio were forbidden fruit, waiting to be picked once the threat of a burned out cabin and scalped family members was gone.

The entrepreneurs who developed the District are frequently referred to by historians as surveyors. This gives a totally erroneous impression of their role and their skills. Surveying was certainly a skill which most of them needed and possessed, but only one of many skills which made them successful. They were skilled at identifying land which would be attractive to purchasers and which was suitable for future town and mill sites. They had contacts with and the confidence of investors who had purchased or desired to purchase warrants or lands for investment. They were good salesmen, who could sell dreams and inspire trust. They were experts in the legal technicalities of buying and selling warrants given by Virginia to its Revolutionary War veterans and in locating and registering lands to satisfy the warrants. In a business climate where cash was scarce, they developed expertise in selling to buyers with limited cash and in meeting the demands on themselves for cash. They viewed government as an important partner in economic development and their personal financial success, and they possessed the political skills to convince others that the public interest coincided with their private interests. This is not to say that developers of other areas of the future state did not have similar skills and goals. The fact is that because of circumstances unique to the District as well as the talents, efforts and opportunities of the entrepreneurs in the District, the District grew more rapidly than other areas in the years immediately preceding statehood. Twelve thousand settled in the Scioto valley during the late 1790s.

The early surveyor-entrepreneurs of the District also required considerable courage, physical stamina, knowledge of how to survive in the wilderness, and skill at scouting and fighting Indians. Men conducting the early surveys were constantly at risk from injury or sickness, from hunger if their supplies ran low or hunting was unsuccessful, and from attacks by wild animals or Indians. This was a high risk enterprise suitable only for the strong, the quick, the daring, the highly motivated, and the woods-smart. Stories told at Inns in the river towns included many tales of surveying parties which were attacked. Although the danger was great, the rewards were high. Surveyors received as compensation for their services one-fourth, one-third, or even as much as one-half of the land surveyed.

The leading surveyor-entrepreneur of the Virginia Military District was Nathaniel Massie whose biography appears among the delegates of Ross County. Between 1791 and 1801, he surveyed more than 700 tracts of land containing more than 750,000 acres. By 1800 he owned more than 75,000 acres and was one of the largest landowners in the District. Other persons whose biographies appear in this book were close business or political associates of Massie. Duncan McArthur, Joseph Kerr, and Israel Donalson accompanied Massie on surveying expeditions. Charles Willing Byrd, secretary and acting governor of the Territory during the frequent absences of St. Clair, was his brother-in-law. Thomas Worthington, Edward Tiffin, and Michael Baldwin were close political associates.

Massie made surveys in the District throughout the Indian War. To minimize the risk of attack, he organized expeditions for the winter when the Indians were less likely to be in the area. The expeditions included twenty-eight to fifty men, all armed and prepared to defend each other in case of attack. Following their evening meal, the men would sleep in groups away from their campfires and in the morning scouts would reconnoiter the area before they gathered around their campfires for breakfast. They traveled light and depended upon hunting to supply most of their meals. During one expedition after the war, the men were caught in a driving snow storm for four days without shelter or food. On the third day of the storm, two wild turkeys were killed, boiled with head, feet and entrails, and divided into twenty-eight parts for the starving men.

During the first year of the Indian War, Massie founded Manchester on the Ohio River. It was the first white settlement in the Virginia Military District and the only town until the Greenville Treaty was signed in 1795. Manchester became an important stop for riverboats and for cross-country travelers from

Kentucky to Chillicothe. In the early days it was the principal town of what became Adams County. Shortly after Wayne's defeat of the Indians and the Treaty of Greenville, Massie laid out Chillicothe in the heart of what had been Shawnee country. It became the county seat of Ross County and the first capital of the new state.

Adams County

Adams County was established by proclamation of Winthrop Sargent, Secretary and acting Governor in the absence of St. Clair, on July 10, 1797. It was the fourth county established in the Northwest Territory, and at the time of its creation included 6,500 square miles, approximately 15% of the future state. When Ross County was created in 1798, Adams County lost four-fifths of its area. At the time of statehood, it included 1600 square miles. However, immediately following statehood Scioto County was created out of the east end of the county leaving it with 840 square miles. At the time of statehood, Zane's Trace crossed the county, passing through West Union and ending at Aberdeen across from Maysville, then known as "Limestone", Kentucky.

Founded by famed scout and Indian fighter Simon Kenton, Limestone was an important stop on the Ohio River and a gateway to the interior for early immigrants to Kentucky. During the winter of 1790 Nathaniel Massie decided to establish a settlement on the north side of the Ohio River 12 miles up the Ohio River from Limestone across from the southern end of the "Three Islands" to serve as a base for his location of land warrants in the Virginia Military District. He enlisted 19 volunteers to accompany him in the venture by promising them one in lot, one out lot of four acres, and 100 acres if they would remain at the settlement for two years. Cabins were raised by March, 1791. The settlement was enclosed with log pickets connecting block houses at each corner. Although Massie named the place Manchester after the home of his ancestors, the pioneers referred to it as Massie's Station. The settlement was the first in the Virginia Military District and the fourth within the future state. Massie and his associates cleared the lower of the Three Islands and planted it with corn which produced heavy crops. The woods were full of deer, elk, buffalo, bears and turkeys and the river full of fish. With the settlement established, Massie continued to make surveys and locate warrants throughout the Indian War.

Following the organization of Adams County in 1797 and the designation of another location as the county seat by acting governor Winthrop Sargent, Massie was successful in having the local court move the county seat to

Manchester. This decision was overruled by Governor St. Clair who claimed the authority to designate the county seats. Massie then persuaded the territorial legislature to designate Manchester as the county seat, but the act was vetoed by St. Clair. While St. Clair was out of the state, Massie's brother-in-law, Charles Willing Byrd, secretary and acting governor, approved moving the courthouse back to Manchester. This decision was overturned upon St. Clair's return. St. Clair then removed Massie from office as a county judge for holding court in Manchester. The county seat was eventually established at West Union. St. Clair's actions earned him the enmity of a powerful protagonist, and the issue became one of many used by St. Clair's enemies as the basis for seeking his ouster and the establishment of a new state.

In the political controversy between Federalists and Republicans leading up to the vote for statehood at the constitutional convention, Adams County was strongly Republican. The three delegates which it sent to the convention supported statehood and the Republican view of organization of government.

Adams County Delegates

THOMAS KIRKER

Thomas Kirker was born in Tyrone County, Ireland, in 1760, where his father attempted to support his family as a tenant farmer, suffering from poor soil and oppressive landlords. When Thomas was nineteen, the family immigrated to the United States and settled in Lancaster County, Pennsylvania. The father died after a few years leaving his widow and five or six children. When he was thirty, Thomas married Sarah Smith, a young woman of excellent family. Shortly after marrying, the young couple, drawn by tales of great opportunity in the West, moved to Kentucky. In 1792 or 1793 they moved to Manchester, where he became a good friend and political ally of Nathaniel Massie. A year or so later Kirker and his family settled on a farm in Liberty Township, Adams County, where he lived for the remainder of this life. They were the first settlers in the area, but soon the Township was dotted with cabins.[486]

---

486   Nelson W. Evans and Emmons B. Stivers, *History of Adams County, Ohio*, 1900, p. 256; Linda Elise Kolette, *The Papers of Thirteen Ohio Political Leaders*, Ohio Historical Society, 1977, pp. 63-64.

When the County was organized, Secretary Winthrop Sargent, acting for Governor St. Clair, appointed Kirker as a judge of the Court of Quarter Sessions and Justice of the Peace. [487] As such he was a participant in the controversy with St. Clair over the location of the Court House. The Court of Quarter Sessions under the Territorial government served the function performed by county commissioners after statehood.[488]

Kirker was elected as a delegate to the constitutional convention as a prostatehood, anti St. Clair Republican. He served on the committee appointed to draft article one on the legislature, article two on the executive, article three on the judiciary, and article four on the qualifications of electors.[489] Although his votes indicated he opposed slavery, he did not favor granting the suffrage or other civil rights to Negroes.[490]

Following the adoption of the Constitution, Kirker was elected to serve in the House of Representatives in the first General Assembly. He was then elected to the state Senate where he served from 1803 to February 16, 1815. During that time he served as speaker of the Senate in the fifth, sixth, seventh, ninth, tenth, eleventh, and thirteenth sessions. From December 15, 1816 to January 28, 1817, he served in the House where he was elected Speaker. He served in the Senate again from December 13, 1821, to February 8, 1825.[491]

Kirker's legislative service and leadership spanned the first twenty-two years of the history of the State at a time when the legislature was by far the most important branch of government. Under Ohio's first constitution the legislative power was vested in a General Assembly comprised of a Senate and House of Representatives. Representatives were elected annually by the voters of each county. Senators were elected for two year terms from districts which could include more than one county. Each house elected a speaker. The legislature passed laws and appropriated funds for the state government.[492] It also by

---

487   Richard C. Knopf, *Transcription of the Executive Journal of the Northwest Territory*, Ohio Historical Society web page, p. 495.

488   Nelson W. Evans and Emmons B. Stivers, *History of Adams County, Ohio*, 1900, p. 91, 256

489   "Journal of Convention", *Ohio Archaeological and Historical Society Publications*, Vol. V, pp. 92, 93, 95.

490   Helen M. Thurston, "The 1802 Constitutional Convention and the Status of the Negro", *Ohio History* Vol. 81, pp. 15-37.

491   Nelson W. Evans and Emmons B. Stivers, *History of Adams County, Ohio*, 1900, p. 257.

492   Ohio Constitution of 1802, Article I.

joint ballot of both houses elected the secretary of state, state treasurer, and state auditor, judges of the supreme court and presiding and associate judges of the courts of common pleas, and major generals and quartermaster generals of the state militia.[493] It also had the power to impeach and remove the governor and other state officers and judges of the supreme court and courts of common pleas.[494]

In 1824 Kirker was elected as a Presidential elector and cast his vote for Henry Clay.[495]

When Governor Tiffin resigned to enter the United States Senate on March 4, 1807, Kirker became acting Governor by virtue of his position as Speaker of the Ohio Senate. The constitution provided that in the case of the death, resignation or removal of the Governor, the Speaker of the Senate would exercise the power of the Governor.[496] In 1807 Return J. Meigs Jr. was elected Governor; however his opponent Nathaniel Massie challenged his eligibility because of his absence from the state while holding federal judicial appointments in Louisiana and Michigan. The constitution required that a Governor must be 30 years of age, a citizen of the United States for twelve years, and an inhabitant of the state for four years next preceding his election. It further provided that contested elections would be determined by both houses of the General Assembly.[497] After Meigs was ruled ineligible by the General Assembly, Massie declined to accept the office leaving a vacancy which was filled by Kirker as Speaker of the Senate from November 4, 1807 to December 12, 1808, when he was succeeded by Samuel Huntington.[498]

Kirker, Worthington, and Huntington ran for Governor in 1808. The key issue was whether the courts in Ohio had the right to declare acts of the legislature unconstitutional. Huntington, while serving as a justice, had ruled that the act of the legislature which permitted cases under $50.00 to be decided by justices of the peace rather than courts of common pleas was unconstitutional because it violated the right to trial by jury guaranteed by the U.S. and Ohio

---

493   Ohio Constitution of 1802, Article II, Section 16, Article III, Section 8, Article VI, Section 2, Article V, Section 5.

494   Ohio Constitution of 1802, Article I, Section 24.

495   William A. Taylor, *Ohio Statesmen and Annals of Progress*, Columbus, 1899, Vol. 1, p. 145.

496   Ohio Constitution of 1802, Article II, Section 12.

497   Ohio Constitution of 1802, Article II, Sections 2 and 3.

498   Nelson W. Evans and Emmons B. Stivers, *History of Adams County, Ohio*, 1900, p. 257.

Constitutions. Worthington and his allies argued that no provision of the state constitution conferred power upon the courts to declare a law unconstitutional and that the legislature was supreme and should be the judge of whether a law was constitutional. Huntington argued that the legislature's power was limited by the federal and state constitutions and that it was the responsibility of the courts to assure that the legislature did not violate the constitutions, otherwise, the constitutions were meaningless. Worthington and his allies argued that frequent elections were the means by which the people were able to protect themselves from abuse by the legislature. Although taken for granted today, this issue was hotly debated at both the federal and state level at that time. Huntington attracted the votes of the Federalists and the more conservative Republicans who looked to the courts as the protector of property rights. Worthington and Kirker split the vote of the Jeffersonian Republicans and Huntington was elected.[499] This was not the end of the battle over the issue of judicial review, but the campaign of 1808 did show the role of Kirker in the election of Huntington as governor.

From 1808 until his death Kirker was a ruling elder of the Presbyterian Church at West Union. He played an important part in the construction of the church building which was completed in 1810.[500]

Successful in business as well as in government, in 1810 he owned eight tracts of land totaling 1,537 acres.[501]

He died February 19, 1837, and was buried in the family plot on his Liberty Township farm. Despite his busy political life, he and his wife reared thirteen children. The author of the county history describes him as follows: "Not a brilliant man, he was honest, conscientious, and possessed of sound judgment and integrity that was unselfish and incorruptible....No man served his state better or with more credit than he. Called to high offices, he filled them well and went out of office carrying the respect of all who knew him."[502]

499   Andrew R. L. Cayton, *The Frontier Republic*, Kent State University Press, 1986, pp. 95-102.

500   Nelson W. Evans and Emmons B. Stivers, *History of Adams County, Ohio*, 1900, p. 257; Elaine J. Lafferty, "The First Presbyterian Church of West Union Celebrating 200 Years of Faith", The Peoples Defender, September 6, 2000.

501   Lee Soltow, "Inequality Amidst Abundance: Land Ownership in Early 19th Century Ohio", *Ohio History*, Ohio Historical Society, Vol 88, p. 150.

502   Nelson W. Evans and Emmons B. Stivers, *History of Adams County, Ohio*, 1900, p. 257.

JOSEPH DARLINTON

Joseph Darlinton was born July 19, 1765, on a plantation of 400 acres located near Winchester, Virginia, owned by his father Meredith Darlinton. The fourth of seven children, he was educated in the local schools. Six hundred British and Hessian soldiers taken at the surrender of Burgoyne at the Battle of Saratoga were kept at his father's plantation until the end of the War. They were confined in his father's barn and barracks constructed to house them. Through talking with them, young Darlinton developed a desire to see the world. He persuaded his father to advance his patrimony and went to Philadelphia where he embarked on a sea voyage to New Orleans, returning home by land. On March 18, 1790, he married Sarah Wilson of Romney, Virginia, an heiress possessed of land and slaves. The young couple moved to Fayette County, Pennsylvania, to a farm which she owned. While in Pennsylvania, they had two sons and joined the Presbyterian Church. Joseph began a long career of public service by serving as county commissioner of Fayette County.[503]

Becoming discouraged with their future in Pennsylvania, Joseph headed with his family for the new country in the West. Taking a boat down the Ohio, they landed at Limestone, Kentucky, on November 14, 1794. He operated a ferry at the mouth of Cabin Creek for awhile, and then bought land across the Ohio where he settled.[504]

Following establishment of Adams County, Darlinton was appointed probate judge of the County by Secretary Winthrop Sargent acting for Governor St. Clair. In March, 1798, he was appointed by the Governor to the Court of Quarter Sessions, which included Nathaniel Massie, Thomas Worthington, and Thomas Kirker.[505] He was elected a representative from the County to the first and second Territorial legislatures. On June 10, 1802, he was appointed justice of the common pleas court and the general court of quarter sessions for the County by Governor St. Clair.

---

503   Nelson W. Evans and Emmons B. Stivers, *History of Adams County, Ohio*, 1900, p. 251.

504   Nelson W. Evans and Emmons B. Stivers, *History of Adams County, Ohio*, 1900, p. 252.

505   Nelson W. Evans and Emmons B. Stivers, *History of Adams County, Ohio*, 1900, p. 104.

Because of his positions with the County and the Territorial legislature, Darlinton was intimately familiar with and involved in the dispute with Governor St. Clair over location of the Court House in Adams County and his attempts to postpone statehood. Darlinton joined with Massie, Tiffin, Worthington, Dunlavy and Morrow in opposing the Governor's plan to delay statehood by dividing the Territory at the Scioto River.[506]

He and his fellow delegates to the convention from Adams County voted against permitting St. Clair to address the convention. Darlinton served on the committees which drafted article one on the legislature, article two on the executive, and article three on the judiciary. When article one was considered by the whole convention, he chaired the deliberations.[507] Although his votes showed he opposed slavery, he also opposed granting Negroes the suffrage and other civil rights.[508]

Following the adoption of the constitution and admission of Ohio to state-hood, Darlinton served in the first General Assembly as state senator from Adams County after successfully contesting the election of John Beasley.[509] Under the constitution each house was the judge of the qualifications and elections of its members.[510] Therefore, the Senate had the power to determine whether he or Beasley was elected and qualified to serve. He was appointed as an associate justice of the common pleas court under the new constitution an office which he resigned the following year. He served as clerk of that court from state-hood until 1847. Under the new constitution the clerk was appointed by the court for which he served for a seven year term, however, his appointment was subject to certification of a majority of the judges of the Supreme Court that he was qualified for the position.[511] He also served as county recorder from 1803 to 1810 and from 1813 to 1834. He became a lieutenant colonel in the militia in 1804 and two years later, he was promoted to brigadier general. Under Ohio's constitution, captains were elected by the men serving under them, majors were elected by captains, colonels were elected by captains and majors, and brigadier

---

506 William Henry Smith, *The St. Clair Papers*, Cincinnati, 1882, Vol. II, pp. 544-545.

507 "Journal of Convention", *Ohio Archaeological and Historical Society Publications*, Vol. V, pp. 88, 92, 93.

508 Helen M. Thurston, "The 1802 Constitutional Convention and the Status of the Negro", *Ohio History* Vol. 81, pp. 15-37.

509 Nelson W. Evans and Emmons B. Stivers, *History of Adams County, Ohio*, 1900, p. 245; William A. Taylor, *Ohio Statesmen and Annals of Progress*, 1899, p. 35.

510 Ohio Constitution of 1802, Article I, Section 8.

511 Ohio Constitution of 1802, Article III, Section 9.

generals by the officers serving under them.[512] He served as postmaster at West Union from 1804 until 1811. Postmasters were appointed by the Federal government and went to friends of the administration. In 1810 he served on a commission appointed by joint ballot of the houses of the General Assembly to recommend a permanent location for the state capital.[513] The commission recommended that it be located on the farm of John and Peter Sells on the west bank of the Scioto River near Dublin.[514] The legislature ignored the recommendation and decided on the future site of Columbus which at the time was a woods across the Olentangy River from Franklinton.

Darlinton was an elder of the Washington Presbytery organized in 1799 to serve Kentucky and southern Ohio. At his request the presbytery furnished a minister to the first congregation of Presbyterians organized in Adams County at Eagle Creek. When West Union was designated the county seat, the congregation decided to move to town and reorganized as the West Union Presbyterian Church. Joseph Darlinton was elected one of the first ruling elders, and he served as elder of the church for over fifty years. Later Thomas Kirker, who had been instrumental in organizing the congregation before it moved to West Union, became an elder. In 1810 a church building was constructed which has been in continuous use since then.[515]

In 1804 Darlinton built a story and a half log house in West Union. He owned 700 to 800 acres of land east of West Union. The Darlinton house was renowned for its hospitality, and visiting dignitaries usually stayed there rather than at the local inn or hotel.[516]

Darlinton invested in lands of the Virginia Military District. In 1810 he owned 25 properties totaling 2,318 acres.[517] In 1815 Donalson platted the village of Winchester named after the town of his youth. [518]

---

512   Ohio Constitution of 1802, Article V

513   Nelson B. Evans and Emmons B. Stivers, *History of Adams County, Ohio*, West Union, 1900, pp. 251-253.

514   William A. Taylor, *Ohio Statesmen and Annals of Progress*, 1899, Vol. I, pp. 61, 68.

515   Nelson B. Evans and Emmons B. Stivers, *History of Adams County, Ohio*, West Union, 1900, p. 253; Elaine J. Lafferty, "The First Presbyterian Church of West Union Celebrating 200 Years of Faith", The Peoples Defender, September 6, 2000.

516   Nelson B. Evans and Emmons B. Stivers, *History of Adams County, Ohio*, West Union, 1900, pp. 253, 254, 482.

517   Lee Soltow, "Inequality Amidst Abundance: Land Ownership in Early 19th Century Ohio", *Ohio History*, Ohio Historical Society, Vol 88, p. 150

518   Nelson B. Evans and Emmons B. Stivers, *History of Adams County, Ohio*, West Union, 1900, p. 498.

According to the author of the county history, "What distinguished General Darlinton among men and above his fellow men was his unusual amount of good, hard, common sense...He was an entertaining talker, and always had something useful and entertaining to say. He had a wonderful natural dignity of which he seemed unconscious, and which impressed itself on those with whom he came in contact. His life was on a plane above the ordinary and the people who knew him well felt they were looking up to it. But what distinguished his life above everything else, what shone out above all things, was his remarkable Christina life and character...His whole soul, conscience, principles, opinions, worldly interests and everything in his life was made subservient to his religion."[519] Joseph Darlinton was a man of high character and good judgment who people trusted to perform public duties professionally and with dignity. His religious values were part of his daily life and inspired confidence. He was looked up to as a man worthy of emulation. He died August 2, 1851, during a cholera epidemic at the age of eighty-six.

ISRAEL DONALSON

Israel Donalson was born February 2, 1767, in Hunterdon County, New Jersey. When he was a young child, his father moved to Cumberland County, New Jersey, where he grew up and received his education. Although too young to participate in the Revolution, he witnessed the effects of the War on his family and community. In 1787 he left home to seek his fortune in the West. His first stop was the Wheeling area where he remained until the spring of 1790. While there he taught school, engaged in farming, and served as a ranger defending the area against Indian attack. During his military service he was stationed at the old Mingo town about eighteen or twenty miles above Wheeling.[520] This was a time when Indian raids were prevalent in the Virginia panhandle and western Pennsylvania. The rangers were dispatched along the border to intercept Indian parties, to come to the rescue of settlers who were attacked, and to pursue the Indian parties for the purpose of rescuing hostages, recovering stolen property and attacking those responsible for committing outrages. The rangers were experts in woodcraft and Indian fighting.

---

519   Nelson B. Evans and Emmons B. Stivers, *History of Adams County, Ohio*, West Union, 1900, p. 255.
520   Nelson W. Evans and Emmons B. Stivers, *History of Adams County, Ohio*, 1900, pp. 66, 67.

In May, 1790, he took passage on a flatboat for Kentucky and arrived at Limestone on June 1. Indians had been attacking boats on the Ohio, but his boat was part of a fleet of nineteen, and they saw no Indians on the way down. On the night he arrived, he could find no food or lodging so he spent the night at a tavern.[521] Before coming to Ohio, Israel Donalson was the first school teacher at Limestone, Kentucky. While in Maysville he was hired by Simon Kenton, famous Indian fighter, to serve as his secretary. Kenton could not read or write, but he had an extraordinary memory. Kenton was involved in numerous land and business transactions. He remembered what each paper in his files represented even though he could not read it.[522] During the winter of 1790-91, Donalson became acquainted with Nathaniel Massie who was seeking men to join him in establishing a settlement at Manchester. Massie persuaded him to join the expedition, and he arrived at the stockade on April 1, 1791.

On April 21, Donalson shared a cabin with Massie. The next day Massie asked if he and another young surveyor would go up the river to make a survey. He and the other young man carried the chains while Massie worked the compass. During the course of the survey they were spotted by Indians in two canoes. They fled through the woods, but Donalson fell and was captured. He was taken to a Shawnee camp where he was dressed in Indian clothing and his hair cut in the Indian style. There were sixty or more warriors and they had with them over a hundred horses stolen in Kentucky. Fearing pursuit from a party from Kentucky led by Simon Kenton, the Indians headed northward. When it came time to sleep, Donalson was tied up between two Indians. While the Indians slept he managed to loosen his bonds and crawled off through tall grass and then fled through the woods pursued by the Indians. He managed to escape capture and slept one night between two logs and another night in a hollow tree. Finally, he reached the Miami and followed it until he came to the trail Harmar's army had made the previous fall. He followed the trail south toward Fort Washington and Cincinnati until he was spotted by a settler who took him in. His feet were cut and swollen and he was famished. After being fed and clothed, he was taken to the Fort where he was questioned by General Harmar to determine whether in view of his appearance he was a spy. He found an accounting job with a merchant in Cincinnati for three or four

---

521   Nelson W. Evans and Emmons B. Stivers, *History of Adams County, Ohio*, 1900, p. 67.

522   Edna Kenton, *Simon Kenton, His Life and Times 1755-1836*, Ayer Company Publishers, North Stratford, NH, reprint edition 1999, pp. 235-236.

weeks, and then met an acquaintance from North Bend who nursed him back to health and then booked his passage on a contractor's boat to Maysville.[523]

Donalson was the first school teacher in Manchester. The first school house was a log structure built between 1794 and 1796. It had one door and two windows, one of glass and one of oil paper. There was a fireplace at one end of the building where firewood six feet in length was used. Floors and benches were made of split logs.[524]

When the county was organized in 1797, acting governor Sargent appointed Donalson county treasurer. He served until 1800. In June, 1802, Governor St. Clair appointed him as justice of the common pleas court and a justice of the peace.[525]

The first overland mail route in Ohio crossed Adams County over Zane's trace carrying mail from Wheeling, Virginia to Limestone, Kentucky. The first post office in Adams County was established in Manchester in 1801. Israel Donalson was the first postmaster, serving for 12 years.[526]

The Presbyterians organized a congregation in Manchester in 1805 and the first church was a log building constructed in 1805. Donalson was a ruling elder and one of the incorporators when the church was incorporated in 1814.[527] He was clerk of session for years, and attended presbytery nineteen times.[528]

He married Anne Pennyweight on November 15, 1798. They went to Kentucky to solemnize the marriage because there were no legal officials in that part of the Northwest Territory at the time.

In 1810 Donalson owned eight tracts of real estate totaling 807 acres.[529] He started a carding mill in Manchester in 1808.[530] Based on comments made

---

523   Henry Howe, *Historical Collections of Ohio*, Centennial Edition, 1898, Vol. I, p. 224-227; Nelson W. Evans and Emmons B. Stivers, *History of Adams County, Ohio*, 1900, p. 67.

524   Nelson W. Evans and Emmons B. Stivers, *History of Adams County, Ohio*, 1900, p. 442.

525   Richard C. Knopf, *Transcription of the Executive Journal of the Northwest Territory*, pp. 553-554.

526   Nelson B. Evans and Emmons B. Stivers, *History of Adams County, Ohio*, 1900, p. 438.

527   Nelson W. Evans and Emmons B. Stivers, *History of Adams County, Ohio*, 1900, p. 438.

528   Nelson W. Evans and Emmons B. Stivers, *History of Adams County, Ohio*, 1900, p. 550.

529   Lee Soltow, "Inequality Amidst Abundance: Land Ownership in Early 19th Century Ohio", *Ohio History*, Ohio Historical Society, Vol 88, p. 150.

530   Nelson W. Evans and Emmons B. Stivers, History of Adams County, Ohio, 1900, p. 550.

toward the end of his life, he suffered financial reversals as did so many of the early land speculators.

At the constitutional convention, Donalson worked on the committee which prepared the bill of rights and the committee which reviewed and revised the journal before it went to press.[531] His votes on black issues reflected the anti-black sentiments of many of the Virginian residents of Adams County.[532]

He was the last survivor of the convention, dying February 9, 1860, at the age of ninety-three. In the county history he was described as "a man of the strictest integrity, honorable in all his dealings and highly respected by everyone."[533]

---

531   "Journal of Convention", *Ohio Archaeological and Historical Society Publications*, Vol. V, p. 90.

532   Helen M. Thurston, "The 1802 Constitutional Convention and the Status of the Negro", *Ohio History* Vol. 81, pp. 15-37.

533   Nelson W. Evans and Emmons B. Stivers, *History of Adams County, Ohio*, 1900, p. 550.

Chapter 4

FOUNDING FATHERS FROM ROSS COUNTY

Ross County

Ross County was organized by proclamation of Governor St. Clair on August 20, 1798. It was named after the Governor's good friend and confidante James Ross, a member of the Federalist Party who served as a United States Senator representing Pennsylvania from 1794 to 1803.[534] The land west of the Scioto River was part of the Virginia Military District and east of the Scioto was part of the Congress lands.[535] At the time Ross County was established it included approximately 6,700 square miles, approximately 16% of the future state of Ohio. [536]

Nathaniel Massie explored and began surveying the area during the Indian Wars. After Wayne's victory and the Treaty of Greenville brought peace to the Ohio country, Massie laid out the village of Chillicothe in August, 1796. Much of the work was done by Duncan McArthur, one of Massie's assistants. The opening of Zane's Trace shortly afterwards, provided overland transportation to the east. The village grew quickly.

---

534 Henry Howe, *Historical Collections of Ohio*, Centennial Edition, 1908, Vol. 2, p. 491; Richard C. Knopf, *Transcription of the Executive Journal of the Northwest Territory*, Ohio Historical Society web page p. 507; "Edward Tiffin", *Biographical Directory of the Unites States Congress* web page.

535 Henry Howe, *Howe's Historical Collections of Ohio*, centennial edition, 1908, Vol 2, p. 491.

536 "Ross County Boundaries", Scioto.org web site.

Because of its central location, Chillicothe was the logical choice to be state capital of a new state with boundaries as originally delineated in the Ordinance of 1787. The leaders of Cincinnati and Marietta wanted their towns to be state capitals. This led to the proposal by the leaders of Marietta and Cincinnati to divide the Territory at the Scioto River. The competition among the leaders of the three towns was an important part of the political contest leading up to statehood. The leaders of Chillicothe were triumphant, and they no doubt believed that Chillicothe would become a major if not the major city in the state. In the early years their vision seemed correct. Ross County political leaders exercised a dominant influence during the early years of statehood, the town had a vibrant economy, and its population continued to grow. However, after several years, Chillicothe's influence declined because the political leaders of Chillicothe divided into opposing camps within the Republican Party and because of resentment of Chillicothe's influence by leaders from other parts of the state. The state capital was moved to Zanesville for two years from 1810 to 1812. After a brief return to Chillicothe, the capital moved permanently to Columbus in 1816. Chillicothe had its day in the sun, a time when it was the center of power and excitement.

Ross County Delegates

EDWARD TIFFIN

Edward Tiffin was born June 10, 1766, in Carlisle, England. At the age of twelve he was apprenticed to a physician as a student of medicine. He terminated his apprenticeship in the spring of 1783. On July 20, 1783, Tiffin accompanied by his parents, two brothers and two sisters sailed from Liverpool for America. They landed at Norfolk, Virginia that fall. Tiffin, at the age of seventeen, began practicing medicine in Charles Town, Berkley County, Virginia (now a part of West Virginia).[537]

---

537   Linden F. Edwards, "Governor Edward Tiffin: Pioneer Doctor", *Ohio History* Vol. 56, p. 349. Although many biographies refer to his having received further medical education in this country at University of Pennsylvania, Jefferson Medical College, or with Dr. Benjamin Rush, Dr. Edwards did extensive research and was unable to find any evidence of this, and pointed out that no mention of it is found in a letter from Dr. Tiffin relating autobiographical data published in the *Supporter*, a Chillicothe newspaper, on June 15, 1811; S. Winifred Smith, "Edward Tiffin", *The Governors of Ohio*, Ohio Historical Society, 1969, p. 1.

Tiffin married Mary Worthington, sister of Thomas Worthington by 1787. Mary and Thomas were children of Col. Robert Worthington, one of Berkley County's most prominent citizens who died while they were both young leaving a sizeable estate.[538]

In 1790 Edwin who had been reared in the Anglican (Episcopal) Church and his wife joined the Methodist Church during a visit to Charles Town by Thomas Scott who at the time was a Methodist Circuit Rider in Virginia. Both Tiffin and Scott would later become prominent citizens of Chillicothe. Tiffin began to preach and in 1792 he was ordained a deacon by Bishop Francis Asbury and authorized to preach as a lay minister. He continued to preach throughout his career. He saw nothing inconsistent between his role as physician and preacher and ministered to both the physical and spiritual needs of his patients.[539]

While in Berkley County Tiffin not only developed a reputation as a skilled physician, he also was a favorite among the leading men and women of the county as well as among a number of the leading persons of Virginia including George Washington. He had pleasing manners, was an excellent conversationalist, and possessed an engaging personality. He was appointed as a "gentleman justice" by the Governor of Virginia during the years 1795 to 1798 and was a Trustee of Charles Town Academy which was established by the legislature in December 1797.[540]

In the summer of 1797 Tiffin accompanied his brother-in-law Thomas Worthington to Chillicothe. When they arrived they discovered that the village which was laid out the previous year had grown to almost one hundred cabins. There were another one hundred families within a radius of ten miles, and new settlers were arriving daily. The place had the feel of a boom town. Dr. Tiffin and Worthington decided to build log cabin homes immediately. They

---

538   Linden F. Edwards, "Governor Edward Tiffin: Pioneer Doctor", *Ohio History* Vol. 56, pp. 354, 356. The date cited in most biographies is 1789, but Dr. Edwards points to a document signed by the Tiffins in 1787 which shows them to be married.

539   Abel Stevens, *Compendious History of American Methodism*, New York, 1862, pp. 332-334; Linden F. Edwards, "Governor Edward Tiffin: Pioneer Doctor", *Ohio History* Vol. 56, p. 354.

540   Linden F. Edwards, "Governor Edward Tiffin: Pioneer Doctor", *Ohio History* Vol. 56, pp. 356-357; Col. William Edward Gilmore, *Life of Edward Tiffin*, Chillicothe, 1897, p. 6; S. Winifred Smith, "Edward Tiffin", *The Governors of Ohio*, Ohio Historical Society, 1969, p. 2.

returned to Virginia and immediately began preparations for their move the following year. This included freeing their slaves. They left in March traveling by wagon to Pittsburgh and by flatboat to the mouth of the Scioto and then by horseback up the river trail to Chillicothe arriving on April 17, 1798. The party included Tiffin's parents, two brothers and two sisters, Mrs. Worthington's two brothers, and the recently freed slaves who were to be provided homes in the new settlement. Tiffin and Worthington were drawn to the Northwest Territory by a dislike of slavery and the excitement of being part of the development of a new land filled with opportunity.[541]

Dr. Tiffin was the first of two physicians in the settlement, and he was an ordained lay minister. He immediately went to work in both roles tending to the physical and spiritual needs of the settlers in Chillicothe and surrounding areas. He was called out day and night and during good and bad weather and required to travel along Indian trails on horseback and cross swollen streams. Those he called on were often unable to pay him. His patients revered him and no doubt told their neighbors. This and his charming personality no doubt account for his popularity in the area.[542]

Tiffin purchased a four-acre lot on the northeast corner of Water and High Streets in Chillicothe where he constructed a large stone house. This continued to be his residence until his death in 1829, except for brief periods spent on his farm in Union Township or in Washington, D.C.[543]

Dr. Tiffin arrived with a letter to Governor St. Clair from George Washington urging that the Governor consider him for a position and commenting on his character and his knowledge of the law. On September 1, 1798, following his creation of Ross County, St. Clair appointed Tiffin as clerk of the common pleas court, clerk of the court of general quarter sessions, and clerk of the orphans court.[544] As noted in other biographies, the clerk was the person people went to if they had a problem for the courts or county government. He maintained the records of the courts, scheduled matters before the judges, and implemented their decisions. The general court of quarter sessions performed many of the duties later performed by county commissioners.

541   Alfred Byron Sears, *Thomas Worthington, Father of Ohio Statehood*, Ohio State University Press for the Ohio Historical Society, 1958, pp. 27-22.

542   Linden F. Edwards, "Governor Edward Tiffin: Pioneer Doctor", *Ohio History* Vol. 56, pp. 358-360.

543   Col. William Edward Gilmore, *Life of Edward Tiffin*, Chillicothe, 1897, p. 11.

544   Richard C. Knopf, *Transcription of the Executive Journal of the Northwest Territory*, Ohio Historical Society web page, p. 512; Henry Howe, *Historical Collections of Ohio*, centennial edition, 1908, Vol 2, p. 501.

When the population of the Territory reached five thousand voters, St. Clair called for election of representatives to the first Territorial legislature in December, 1798. Both houses met in November, 1799 at Cincinnati, after first meeting in February to nominate ten persons for the Legislative Council. Tiffin was elected as one of four representatives from Ross County. Among the others from Ross County was his brother-in-law Thomas Worthington. Tiffin was selected by his fellow representatives to be the Speaker of the House. This session had much work to do in reviewing and revising the existing laws of the Territory which had been adopted by the Territorial judges. Another matter of interest was the creation of new counties and in the case of Adams County, changing the county seat to Manchester as desired by its founder Nathaniel Massie and the officials of the county. The Territorial legislature enacted thirty-nine bills. Governor St. Clair waited until the end of the session and vetoed eleven of them. During the session, William Henry Harrison was elected as the Territory's first delegate to Congress, defeating the Governor's son by a vote of eleven to ten. The choice of Harrison over Arthur Jr. no doubt angered the Governor, and the veto of eleven acts of the legislature angered many of the legislators. From their perspective St. Clair was acting the way royal governors had acted before the Revolutionary War. His arrogance and contempt for the elected representatives of the people was galling to men whose memories of the War and the ideals for which it was fought were fresh in mind.[545]

In May, 1800, Congress at the urging of William Henry Harrison passed an act dividing the Territory. Before the act the entire Northwest Territory extending all the way to the Mississippi River was under one government. After the Division Act the western part became the Indiana Territory and eastern territory including Ohio, Michigan, and part of Indiana continued under the existing territorial government. The same act specified that Chillicothe would be the capital of the eastern Territory. When the Territorial legislature convened for its second session on November 5, 1800, it met at Chillicothe. All were aware that the Governor's term ended December 9 and there was an active campaign to prevent his reappointment because among other reasons of the actions he had taken during the first session. In the meantime Charles Willing Byrd had been appointed secretary of the Territory in place of Harrison, and it was thought he would be empowered to act as governor if St. Clair was not reappointed and his replacement had not been appointed. Byrd had allied himself with those who opposed the Governor. It was therefore hoped that the

---

545   Col. William Edward Gilmore, *Life of Edward Tiffin*, Chillicothe, 1897, pp. 20-25.

session would not be faced with the veto of a substantial part of its work. St. Clair frustrated this hope by proroguing the legislature when his term expired on December 9, 1800, on the ground that since he had not been reappointed the authority of the legislature terminated. Once again it seemed to those hostile to the Governor that he was behaving liking an arbitrary royal governor, thwarting the representatives of the people from performing the people's business for personal ends. Tiffin had the challenging task of presiding over a legislative body whose members became more and more divided between those who supported and opposed the Governor Notwithstanding the efforts of his opponents, President Adams did reappoint St. Clair on December 22, 1800, and his appointment was confirmed by the Senate on February 3, 1801. However, on March 4, 1801, Thomas Jefferson was inaugurated as President, an event of considerable importance to the future of the Territory and St. Clair's career.[546]

Those upset at the Governor's treatment of the legislature and frustrated by their failure to block his reappointment came to the conclusion their goal should become the admission of Ohio to statehood as soon as possible. Not only would this get rid of St. Clair, it would get rid of a colonial form of government which was demeaning to the people and holding back settlement and development of the state. They firmly believed that statehood would make Ohio more attractive to settlers and speed up settlement and development of the area.[547] Tiffin became a leader of the statehood movement and following the Governor's prorogue of the Assembly addressed a letter to the people of Ohio as chairman of a committee recommending statehood as soon as possible.[548]

Tiffin was reelected to the second Territorial legislature in October, 1801 and he was unanimously reelected as Speaker when the legislature met on November 24, 1801.[549] His selection as Speaker despite the fact that he

546   Col. William Edward Gilmore, *Life of Edward Tiffin*, Chillicothe, 1897, pp. 25-29.

547   William Henry Smith, *The St. Clair Papers*, Cincinnati, 1882, Vol. 1, p. 225-226. The pro-statehood case is set forth in a letter appearing in the Scioto Gazette in October 1801 which Gilmore attributes to Tiffin. The author's name was seldom used in such letters in those days; Archibald Mayo, "State Centennial Address", *Ohio Centennial Anniversary Celebration*, Ohio Historical Society, 1903, pp. 33-34

548   Daniel J. Ryan, *History of Ohio*, New York, 1912, Vol 3, pp. 86-87.

549   William A. Taylor, *Ohio Statesmen and Annals of Progress*, State of Ohio, 1898, pp. 18-19.

obviously opposed the Governor and the plan of the Governor and the Cincinnati and Marietta delegates to divide the Territory at the Scioto is rather remarkable. He must have been highly respected for his parliamentary skills and fairness.[550] This session is best known for the Division Act which proposed to Congress that the Territory be divided at the Scioto River. The act incorporated a plan proposed by the Governor which was supported by representatives from Marietta and Cincinnati because it would result in each of those towns being a state capital. The Governor favored the plan because it would delay statehood. The Federalists also expected that by dividing the Republican vote in the Scioto Valley it would give the Federalists a good chance to control the two states. The Act passed by a vote of twelve to eight. The minority lodged a public protest and immediately implemented a vigorous strategy to persuade Congress to reject the Act and admit Ohio to statehood. The strategy included sending Thomas Worthington and Michael Baldwin to Washington and forwarding to them petitions circulated in the Territory opposing the division and advocating immediate statehood. Tiffin was a leader of this effort.

After Congress rejected the Division Act and enacted the Enabling Act calling for an election of delegates to a convention to vote on statehood and frame a constitution, Tiffin was a leader of the effort to elect Republican delegates to the convention. One of the arguments used by the Federalists against the Republicans was that they sought to introduce slavery into the state. In response Tiffin published a statement in the Scioto Gazette that if the Ordinance did not prohibit slavery, he would regard its introduction into the state as being the greatest injury that could be inflicted on posterity.[551]

The delegates to the convention met at Chillicothe on November 1, 1802, and on the following day elected Edward Tiffin as president. After thanking the delegates, he assured them that he would observe the utmost impartiality.[552] Perhaps the greatest evidence of his skill as presiding officer is the fact that the convention completed its task in twenty-nine days. Three days prior to the end of the convention a motion was made to remove a provision which allowed Negroes to vote. The vote was a tie. Tiffin broke the tie by casting a vote to remove the provision depriving them of the right to vote.[553] Tiffin's vote

---

550   Col. William Edward Gilmore, *Life of Edward Tiffin*, Chillicothe, 1897, p. 29.

551   Archibald Mayo, "State Centennial Address", *Ohio Centennial Anniversary Celebration*, Ohio Historical Society, 1903, p. 33.

552   "Journal of First Constitutional Convention," *Ohio History*, Vol. 5, p. 83.

553   Helen M. Thurston, "The 1802 Constitutional Convention and Status of the Negro", *Ohio History*, Vol. 81, p. 23.

reflected the viewpoint of a majority of Republicans. They opposed slavery, but they also opposed racial equality. They did not want to encourage Negro immigration into Ohio from neighboring slave states.[554]

The delegates of the convention scheduled an election in January, 1803 for the initial state officers. Tiffin was the Republican candidate for Governor. On March 1, 1803 the first General Assembly met at Chillicothe. Both Houses met at 11:00 A.M. to open and declare the result of the ballot for Governor. Tiffin received 4,564 votes. There were no votes cast against him. The oath was administered to him by Return Jonathan Meigs Jr. of Marietta and Tiffin gave a brief address to the Assembly. On March 4 he sent the first state of the state address to the Assembly which again was noteworthy for its brevity. [555] Under the new Constitution the duties of the governor were limited. He did not make appointments except when the General Assembly was in recess and those decisions were subject to review when the Assembly reconvened. The limited authority of the governor was in large measure a reaction to the abuse of power by St. Clair.[556]

Under the new constitution the term of the Governor was two years. Tiffin was reelected for a second two year term receiving 4,783 votes. No votes were cast for any other person.[557] The highpoint of his second term of office was the Aaron Burr affair. Tiffin received information from an envoy from President Thomas Jefferson that Aaron Burr, who was Jefferson's vice president during his first term, was leading a conspiracy with Harmon Blennerhasset and other prominent westerners to organize a group of settlers to settle in lands governed by Spain and then to form a new country. Tiffin promptly convened the General Assembly. The Assembly met in closed proceedings with the Governor, adopted laws to thwart the conspiracy, and authorized the Governor to take action. Tiffin promptly issued orders to the militia in Marietta to seize the conspirators and the boats and supplies associated with the conspiracy. The order was carried out by Joseph Buell whose biography appears in the Washington County chapter and the conspiracy was smashed. An order was also issued to the militia in Cincinnati to keep an eye out for and seize any boats passing by that town. As a result of these actions whatever Burr and

---

554   Alfred Byron Sears, *Thomas Worthington, Father of Ohio Statehood*, Ohio State University Press, 1958, pp. 101-102.

555   William A. Taylor, *Ohio Statesmen and Annals of Progress*, State of Ohio, 1899, p. 36.

556   Jacob Burnet, Letter to the Society, *Transactions of the Historical and Philosophical Society of Ohio*, 1839, Vol 1, p.115.

557   William A. Taylor, *Ohio Statesmen and Annals of Progress*, State of Ohio, 1899, p. 46.

Blennerhasset were planning was thwarted, although there is certainly considerable doubt that what was being planned was as diabolical as was alleged.
Nonetheless, Tiffin received the warm appreciation of Jefferson for his prompt
effective action.[558]

During his terms as Governor, Tiffin also served on the board of trustees of
Ohio University and actively participated in the development of the
University. On February 18, 1804, the Ohio General Assembly passed an act to
establish the University. The board of trustees was to include the Governor of
Ohio. On June 5, 1804, the board met and elected Tiffin its president.[559]

On January 1, 1807, Tiffin was elected United States Senator by joint ballot
of the General Assembly. Upon his resignation as governor to become Senator,
Thomas Kirker, Speaker of the Senate, became acting governor.[560] While in the
Senate, Tiffin secured passage of valuable legislation for the state. He obtained
appropriations for improvements to the Ohio River and funds for the survey
of public lands. He secured better and speedier mail service. He advocated
changes in the laws governing sale of public lands to protect purchasers. He
served on a committee appointed to review a request by William Henry
Harrison, Governor of the Indiana Territory, to allow temporary slavery in the
Territory and recommended disapproval of the request. The Senate followed
the Committee's recommendation and refused to allow slavery in the
Territory. While in the Senate hearings were held to determine if John Smith
should be expelled from the Senate because of his participation in the Burr
conspiracy. Tiffin voted with the majority to expel his fellow senator. However,
since two thirds of the Senators did not vote for expulsion, Smith was not
expelled. He did, however, resign shortly thereafter. Senator Tiffin's wife died
on July 1, 1809. Following her death, he decided to retire from public life. He
returned to Ohio and moved to his farm in Union Township, Ross County,
with his elderly mother, intent upon employing the rest of his life in cultivating
his farm.[561]

His break from public life was short lived, however. He was elected to represent Ross County in the Ohio House of Representatives in October, 1809. The

558   Daniel J. Ryan, *History of Ohio*, New York, 1912, Vol. 3, pp. 77, 229-249.
559   Thomas Nathaniel Hoover, *The History of Ohio University*, Ohio University
Press, 1954, pp. 18-23; Col. William Edward Gilmore, *Life of Edward Tiffin*,
Chillicothe, 1897, p. 103.
560   William A. Taylor, *Ohio Statesmen and Annals of Progress*, State of Ohio, 1899,
pp. 50-51.
561   Daniel J. Ryan, *History of Ohio*, New York, 1912, Vol. 3, p. 77; Col. William
Edward Gilmore, *Life of Edward Tiffin*, Chillicothe, 1897, pp. 108-117.

principal issue in the election was whether the judiciary or the legislature was supreme. The controversy grew out of an attempt by the anti-court Republicans to impeach judges who had declared an act of the legislature unconstitutional. The anti-court party prevailed, and Tiffin was on December 12, 1809 elected Speaker of the House. The legislature promptly declared that all judicial offices would become vacant in 1810. This was called the "Sweeping Resolution" because it swept all the judges out of office. The rationale was that the Constitution provided for a seven year term and the term began with the commencement of the state. The anti-court Republicans then proceeded to fill all judicial offices with men who they believed would recognize the supremacy of the legislature. Tiffin and Worthington viewed the contest over the supremacy of the legislature as a battle to preserve the principles established in the constitution. During this session a decision was made to move the capital temporarily to Zanesville and to appoint a commission to fix a permanent location for the state capital.[562]

Tiffin was reelected to the House in 1810 and was reelected Speaker of the House. His brother-in-law Thomas Worthington was defeated by Return Jonathan Meigs Jr. for Governor. The principal issue in the campaign was once again the supremacy of the legislature or the judiciary. However, the campaign was characterized by bitter personal attacks.

During the 1810 campaign Worthington and Tiffin were attacked because of their association with the Tammany Society, a secret organization which their enemies charged was used to control elections. The Tammany Society was a Republican fraternal organization organized in New York in 1789 to counteract the influence of the Federalists and the Society of Cincinnati. In 1810 an Ohio chapter was chartered and wigwams were established in Chillicothe, Zanesville, Cincinnati, Xenia, Lancaster, Warren, Hamilton, and New Boston. Tiffin was Grand Sachem of the Ohio organization. Tiffin and Worthington did intend to use the organization as a means of encouraging the election of men of character to public office. They feared that demagogues motivated primarily by personal ambition were running for office. However, their enemies attacked Tammany as an undemocratic secret society, and Worthington and Tiffin were accused of being aristocrats, which in those days was like being called a communist during the cold war. In 1811 despite the attacks Tiffin participated in the annual St. Tammany parade in Chillicothe in

---

562   William A. Taylor, *Ohio Statesmen and Annals of Progress*, State of Ohio, 1899, pp. 59-61; Andrew R. L. Cayton, *Frontier Republic*, Kent State University Press, 1986, pp. 104-105.

May, and gave a speech in defense of the organization which was published in the local paper. .He was charged by political enemies in his own church with idolatry for participating in the parade and dismissed from the church. However, the decision was overturned by a higher tribunal.[563] In Ross County the anti-Tammany forces were led by Nathaniel Massie and William Creighton. The anti-Tammany candidates were elected in Ross County, and William Creighton held a mock funeral for St. Tammany. Tiffin was quoted as saying, "The Tammany Hobby Horse" has been ridden "almost to death." Soon all but one of the wigwams had disbanded. The legislature repealed the Sweeping Resolution in 1812, although appointments made under it were preserved. The pro-court moderate wing of the Republican Party allied with the Federalists had triumphed over the Worthington/Tiffin anti-court wing.[564] Although the concept of an independent judiciary and right to judicial review of the acts of the legislature became accepted as part of the constitutional fabric of Ohio, the political contest also established that if the judiciary failed to respect the power of the legislature, it could expect powerful retaliation. Thus neither the legislature nor judiciary is supreme. They are co-equal branches of government between which lies an uneasy truce ready to flare into open warfare when either branch fails to respect the authority of the other.[565]

Congress at the urging of Senator Thomas Worthington created the General Land Office in April, 1812, as a department within the Treasury Department. Its purpose was to consolidate the public land records scattered among various departments into one office and to place responsibility for management of public land in a single office. Madison, who Tiffin had gotten to know while he was a Senator in Washington, appointed Tiffin to be the first commissioner of the office. Tiffin moved to Washington with his new wife Mary Porter Tiffin and their first of five children. He successfully organized the records, established policies for land management, and submitted his first

---

563   Andrew R. L. Cayton, *Frontier Republic*, Kent State University Press, 1986, pp. 105-108.
Dr. Donald D. Shira, "Pioneer Physicians of Ohio", *Ohio History*, Vol 48, pp. 241-242; Samuel W. Williams, "Tammany Society of Ohio", *Ohio History*, Vol. 22, pp. 349-370.

564   Andrew R. L. Cayton, *Frontier Republic*, Kent State University Press, 1986, pp. 107-108; William T. Utter, *History of Ohio, The Frontier State*, Ohio Historical Society, Vol. 2, pp. 55-61

565   The most recent example of flare up is the conflict between the Supreme Court and the Ohio General Assembly over school funding.

report to Congress in December, 1813. Before the British captured and burned Washington in 1814 Tiffin successfully move the records to Loudon County, Virginia so they were saved. The records of his office were the only records which escaped destruction. Later that year Tiffin with the consent of the President and Congress arranged to exchange offices with Josiah Meigs who was serving as Surveyor General of the United States. He did this so he could return to Chillicothe. He served as Surveyor General for 15 years until 1829 when he was removed by President Andrew Jackson shortly before his death. During his tenure in office, Tiffin was active in establishing policies followed in the survey of public lands.[566]

During the time he served as Surveyor General, Tiffin continued to see patients and preach at Methodist meetings. Tiffin died on August 9, 1829 and was buried in Grandview Cemetery at Chillicothe.[567]

Although Thomas Worthington has in recent years been recognized with the title of "Father of Ohio Statehood", at the time of the State's centennial celebration in 1903, Edward Tiffin was recognized as the leader of the battle for Ohio statehood. A medallion portrait of Tiffin was presented to Ross County to be hung in the Court House. Archibald Mayo presented an address describing Tiffin's accomplishments. Mayo stated, "Although Tiffin was in public service during nearly the entire period of his residence in the state, he kept his soul unstained. He utilized no opportunity for private aggrandizement. His industry was unflagging, his fidelity perfect, his tact and wisdom unquestionable."

THOMAS WORTHINGTON

Thomas Worthington was born at his father's estate near Charles Town, Berkley County, Virginia (now West Virginia) on July 16, 1773. Worthington's great, great grandfather John Worthington lived in Cheshire, England, and was

---

566   William T. Utter, *History of Ohio, The Frontier State*, Ohio Historical Society, 1942, pp 117-118; S. Winifred Smith, "Edward Tiffin", *The Governors of Ohio*, Ohio Historical Society, 1969, p. 3; ; *Biographical Directory of the Unites States Congress* web page; *History of Ross and Highland Counties*, Williams Bros, 1880, pp. 223-224; "A Brief History of Illinois Land Surveying" McTigue & Spuwak, Inc. web page; Col. William Edward Gilmore, *Life of Edward Tiffin*, Chillicothe, 1897, pp. 121-131.

567   S. Winifred Smith, "Edward Tiffin", *The Governors of Ohio*, Ohio Historical Society, 1969, p. 3.

one of the earliest followers of George Fox, founder of the Friends or Quakers. His grandfather Robert Worthington emigrated from Ireland to Salem, New Jersey in 1714, and was an active member of the Friends there. He then moved to Philadelphia where he was a merchant, farmer, and land dealer. In 1730 he purchased 3,000 acres in the northern Shenandoah Valley and moved there with his family. He was followed by a number of Quaker families from Philadelphia. His father Robert served in Braddock's campaign against the French and Indians and was awarded two thousand acres for his service. The Quakers disowned him for marrying outside the faith. By diligent effort he built up a substantial estate, and he became a leading citizen of Berkeley County, Virginia. Thomas' father died in 1779 and his mother died the follow-ing year. Each of the six children inherited an equal share (about 1,466 acres) of their father's substantial estate. Thomas lived with his older brother Ephraim until he was fourteen and then moved in with his brother William. After William moved to Kentucky Thomas selected his father's friend Colonel William Darke as his guardian. Darke sent him to school. He had always wanted to go to sea so in May, 1791, with the consent of his guardian Worthington shipped out and served as a common seaman on three boats before returning home on January 18, 1793. He visited islands in the Caribbean and Scotland. The last boat he served on was boarded by the British and he barely escaped being impressed into the British Navy to serve in the Napoleonic War. While Worthington was gone Colonel Darke had served with General St. Clair in his campaign against the Indians and sustained an injury to himself and the death of his favorite son Patrick in St. Clair's defeat. Worthington was happy to get back home and the Darkes were happy to wel-come him back into their family.[568]

Worthington moved to Prospect Hill, the modest home he had inherited, and began farming his land. Due to the Indian problems, he became a lieu-tenant and then captain in the local militia. Following Wayne's defeat of the Indians at Fallen Timbers and the Treaty of Greenville, Worthington caught the "Ohio fever." After purchasing a number of Virginia Military warrants as investments, he proposed to go and locate them in the Virginia Military District north of the Ohio River. On June 26, 1796, he set out on horseback and rode to Wheeling. He left his horse and traveled down stream on the mail boat to Marietta where he secured passage on a sailing boat to the mouth of the Scioto. From there he took a canoe north. He reached Nathaniel Massie's

---

568   Alfred Byron Sears, *Thomas Worthington, Father of Ohio Statehood*, Ohio State University Press for the Ohio Historical Society, 1958, pp. 4-13.

farm at the mouth of Paint Creek and then three miles further came to Chillicothe, which Massie had laid out that year. At that time it consisted of a few scattered cabins. Continuing to explore he found a tract which he liked northwest of the village and employed Duncan McArthur to survey it for him. He visited his brother in Kentucky on the way home. After returning home he married Eleanor Swearingen on December 13, 1796. Eleanor was like him an orphan who had received a sizeable inheritance. The following year, Worthington returned to Chillicothe with his brother-in-law Dr. Edward Tiffin. This time he hired McArthur to locate 7,600 acres for him in the Virginia Military District. Worthington and Tiffin decided to move to Chillicothe the following year. Upon his return to Virginia, Worthington disposed of his Virginia land and manumitted his slaves. On March 14, 1798, the Worthingtons, Tiffins, and related families and recently freed servants set out for the Ohio country, arriving on April 17, 1798.[569]

For a young man endowed with energy, capital, and ambition, Chillicothe was a dream world. Families arrived daily seeking land to settle on. Investors from the east, Kentucky, Virginia and Western Pennsylvania sought lands to invest in or an agent to manage and sell their holdings. Worthington acted as agent for such prominent men as Senator James Ross of Pennsylvania, Thomas Jefferson, Albert Gallatin, Jefferson's Treasury Secretary, Nathaniel Macon, John Breckenridge, Steven Thomas Mason, and Henry Bedinger. Settlers needed mills to cut their timber or grind their grain. Farmers needed to ship their pork and flour down river. Consumers wanted merchandise produced in the east or Europe. Worthington bought and located Virginia military warrants, bought, sold and leased land to settlers, managed investors' land, located mill sites and built and operated mills. He also developed his own farm and raised cattle, hogs, and sheep. He built flat boats and shipped flour and pork to market down the Ohio and Mississippi Rivers. He invested in all kinds of businesses in Chillicothe including rope making and cloth making.[570]

Worthington was always advocating improvements in agriculture. He developed a herd of merino sheep to improve the quality of wool. Through selective breeding he improved the quality of his cattle. His orchards and

---

569   Alfred Byron Sears, *Thomas Worthington, Father of Ohio Statehood*, Ohio State University Press for the Ohio Historical Society, 1958, pp. 13-21.

570   Alfred B. Sears, "Thomas Worthington: Pioneer Businessman of the Old Northwest", *Ohio History*, Vol. 58, pp. 71-79; Alfred Byron Sears, *Thomas Worthington, Father of Ohio Statehood*, Ohio State University Press for the Ohio Historical Society, 1958, pp. 23-28.

vineyards were among the best in the community. .He helped organize the Scioto Agricultural Society in 1819 and served as its first president.[571]

Worthington knew that the essential key to the success of his business and investment activities was making and keeping the Scioto Valley attractive to settlers and investors. In 1798 the valley was the hot area in the Northwest Territory. That is why he settled there. Its attractiveness was due in part to the fertile lands along the Scioto and its tributaries. It was also due to its accessibility by way of the Scioto River and overland by way of Zane's Trace to the East and South. It was the leading town in the Virginia Military District and there was a flourishing market in the buying, selling, and locating of Virginia soldiers warrants particularly among residents of Virginia and Kentucky. Title problems, slavery, and lack of good farm land made Kentucky less attractive to many settlers. The Greeneville Treaty removed the Indian threat which previously held settlers back in Western Pennsylvania and Kentucky. They were now eager to move into the Territory. Chillicothe was a county seat and therefore a market town for the surrounding area. It was well situated to be a gateway to the unsettled land to the north of it. The town was also centrally located and a likely candidate to be the capital of the first state to be erected from the Territory.

Worthington knew business success was intertwined with government protection and promotion. Investments were unsafe unless the law could be relied upon to protect property and contracts. The government was the largest owner and seller of land in the Territory. Government contracts for surveying, road building and military supplies provided cash where cash was in short supply. So did public offices. Public offices also provided access to decisions which could have significant effects on value of investments and enable an investor to influence decisions in a manner helpful to his investments. Public service also brought the opportunity and creative challenge to work with other community and territorial leaders to organize local and state government and the prominence and fame associated with such undertakings.

Prior to arriving in Chillicothe, Worthington received an appointment as a deputy surveyor from Rufus Putnam, the Surveyor General of the United States, and a contract to survey the land between the Ohio Company tract and the Scioto River. This contract was not only an attractive piece of business; it

---

571   Alfred Byron Sears, *Thomas Worthington, Father of Ohio Statehood*, Ohio State University Press for the Ohio Historical Society, 1958, pp. 212-213.

also permitted Worthington an opportunity to identify the best tracts of land on the east side of the Scioto across from Chillicothe.[572]

Governor St. Clair was persuaded to visit Chillicothe and on August 20, 1798, he organized Ross County and designated Chillicothe as its county seat. St. Clair upon learning that Worthington intended to settle in Chillicothe had in 1797 appointed him as a justice of the peace and judge of the court of general quarter sessions of Adams County which at the time embraced Chillicothe. As a member of that court, Worthington voted for the relocation of the county seat to Manchester as desired by Nathaniel Massie. Thus at an early date, Worthington became aware of and associated in the contest between Massie and St. Clair over the location of the county seat of Adams County. On September 1, 1798, Worthington was appointed as justice of the peace and judge of the general court of quarter sessions of Ross County. He was also appointed lieutenant colonel of the militia for Ross County, but later St. Clair appointed Samuel Finley colonel, a decision which offended Worthington and prompted his resignation. This action also may have led to a strained relation between the two men.[573]

On October 29, 1798, Governor St. Clair called for an election of representatives to the first Territorial legislature on the third Monday of December, 1798. Under the Ordinance of 1787, representatives were required to own at least two hundred acres and voters were required to own fifty acres. Voting was conducted at the county seat of each county. Ross County was allotted two representatives and Worthington and his brother-in-law were elected. The representatives first met on February 4, 1799, in Cincinnati to nominate ten candidates for the upper house from whom the President would appoint five. The Territorial Legislature then met in September, 1799 to conduct business. Worthington and his wife and baby were invited by William Henry Harrison to stay with him at Harrison's new residence at North Bend. Harrison had been appointed secretary of the Territory when Winthrop Sargent resigned to accept the governorship of the Mississippi Territory. One of the tasks of the legislature was election of a reprsentative to Congress. Harrison was elected by one vote over the Governor's son. Worthington and Tiffin were supporters of

---

572   Frank Theodore Cole, "Thomas Worthington", *Ohio History*, Vol. 12, pp. 342-343; Richard C. Knopf, *Transcription of the Executive Journal of the Northwest Territory*, p. 535.

573   Frank Theodore Cole, "Thomas Worthington", *Ohio History*, Vol. 12, pp. 342-343; Richard C. Knopf, *Transcription of the Executive Journal of the Northwest Territory*, Ohio Historical Society web page, p. 425, 511-512.

Harrison. The Legislature spent much of its effort reviewing and reaffirming and revising the laws which had previously been adopted by the Territorial judges. The legislature also moved the county seat of Adams County to Manchester which St. Clair had opposed and erected new counties and designated their county seats. These actions were vetoed by the Governor on the ground that he had the exclusive authority to make these decisions. Worthington had persuaded the legislature to enact a law calling for a census to determine if the area was eligible for statehood which the Governor vetoed again claiming the legislature lacked authority. He also vetoed laws on the licensing of marriages and taverns. These were sources of revenue for the Governor which he did not wish to give up, although this was not the reason given for the vetoes. The governor vetoed in total eleven of the thirty-nine bills enacted by the Legislature, and he waited until the last day of the session so that there was no opportunity to revise the bills to address his concerns. Needless to say, this was insulting and offensive to Worthington and other like-minded legislators. Plans were made to get rid of St. Clair.[574]

Worthington left Chillicothe on December 30, 1799, and crossed the mountain to Washington, where he made plans with Harrison to promote a division of the Territory in anticipation of statehood. With Harrison leading the effort on the floor and Worthington assisting in the lobbies, Congress on May 7, 1800, passed the Division Act which created the Indiana Territory. The Act provided that the western boundary of the first state would be line beginning at the mouth of the Great Miami as provided in the Ordinance of 1787. The Act also provided that Chillicothe would be capital of the Territory. Worthington believed the way was cleared for Chillicothe to be the state capital when the area reached a population of sixty thousand voters. Worthington had hoped that St. Clair would be assigned the Indiana Territory, but that governorship went to Harrison so they were stuck with St. Clair for the time being. However, his term expired on December 9, 1800, therefore the next challenge was to see that he was not reappointed.[575]

Harrison's other major accomplishment in Congress was the Land Law of 1800 which allowed sale of government land in smaller parcels and purchase of land on credit. It also created local government land offices including a land office in Chillicothe. On May 12, 1800, Worthington was appointed by

---

574   Alfred Byron Sears, *Thomas Worthington, Father of Ohio Statehood*, Ohio State University Press for the Ohio Historical Society, 1958, pp. 47-54.

575   Alfred Byron Sears, *Thomas Worthington, Father of Ohio Statehood*, Ohio State University Press for the Ohio Historical Society, 1958, pp. 54-56.

President Adams as Superintendent of the Land Office in Chillicothe. He presided over public sales of government land and private sale of land which did not sell at auction. The sales generated substantial sums for the government. However, Worthington was criticized by St. Clair and other political enemies for charging fees not authorized by statute and for some of his decisions interpreting the law. At Worthington's insistence, a hearing was conducted and he was exonerated of all charges. He was also given the position of supervisor of the new internal revenue district north of the Ohio. In both these positions Worthington worked closely with Albert Gallatin, Jefferson's Secretary of the Treasury. By reason of his close association and frequent communications with Gallatin, he was able to keep the administration appraised of political developments in Ohio, during the period leading up to statehood. Following the adoption of the constitution, Worthington resigned these positions.[576]

Petitions were circulated within the Territory supporting and opposing St. Clair's reappointment. In addition letters were sent to President Adams charging St. Clair with abuse of his power. The Territorial legislature reconvened at Chillicothe on November 3, 1800. Because if its increase in population, Ross County was entitled to two additional representatives and Elias Langham and Samuel Finley joined Tiffin and Worthington in the lower House. The legislature met at Abrams Big House, a two story log structure built in 1798. The first floor was used as a courthouse, church, and singing school. The second floor contained a billiard table and was a place of recreation frequented along with Joe Tiffin's and Tom Gregg's taverns by those who liked to drink and gamble. At the beginning of the session St. Clair reminded the members that his term would expire on December 9 and that he might not meet with them again. He complained that the "the vilest calumnies and grossest falsehoods" were being circulated among the people about him. It was soon discovered that in response to the Division Act the leaders of Cincinnati and Marietta had entered into an alliance with the Governor to redress their grievance against what became known as "the Chillicothe junto." The alliance sought to divide the Territory at the Scioto to assure that Cincinnati and Marietta would be state capitals. The alliance agreed to support William McMillan of Cincinnati for representative to Congress to fill the remainder of Harrison's term and then to elect Paul Fearing of Marietta to fill the next term. However, the alliance was

576   Alfred Byron Sears, *Thomas Worthington, Father of Ohio Statehood*, Ohio State University Press for the Ohio Historical Society, 1958, pp. 39-43.

not able to agree upon a new location for the capital. St. Clair brought the session to a quick close on December 9 by proroguing the legislature when his term expired. He took the position that when his term ended their authority ended with it. Worthington and other members assumed that Charles Willing Byrd, as secretary of the Territory, would assume his duties when the Governor's term expired. Byrd was a friend of the Ross County delegation. An unsuccessful attempt was made in the final days of the session to authorize a constitutional convention.[577]

Republicans like Worthington were disappointed to learn that President Adams did reappoint St. Clair for another term, although he took the unusual step of forwarding the petitions and correspondence on to the Senate. Nonetheless, the Senate confirmed the appointment. However, Republicans were elated to learn that Thomas Jefferson was elected President. The election was close and ended up being decided by the House of Representatives. However, with his election, the Republicans controlled the President and both houses of Congress. St. Clair could no longer rely upon protection from the Federal Administration.[578] The Scioto Valley settlers were predominantly from Virginia and Kentucky. They were predominantly Jeffersonian Republicans. Not only were they ideologically and geographically connected with the administration, the leaders of the Valley had strong personal relationships with Virginians in the administration and in the leadership of Congress.

Worthington was elected as a Ross County representative to the House of Representatives in the second Territorial Legislature which convened at Chillicothe on November 25, 1801 at Chillicothe. The legislature met in the courthouse, the first public stone building in the Territory which was erected under the supervision of Worthington. At this session the Marietta/Cincinnati/St. Clair alliance passed an Act on December 18, 1801, giving the Territory's consent to a division of the Territory at the Scioto River. The measure passed by a vote of 12 to 8. The minority protested the action claiming that it violated the rights of the citizens of the Territory under the Ordinance of 1787. The protest was signed by Darlinton, Massie, Dunlavy, Morrow, Langham, Worthington, and Tiffin. The legislature also passed a bill changing the capital of the Territory to Cincinnati with the

---

577   Alfred Byron Sears, *Thomas Worthington, Father of Ohio Statehood*, Ohio State University Press for the Ohio Historical Society, 1958, pp. 56-60.

578   Alfred Byron Sears, *Thomas Worthington, Father of Ohio Statehood*, Ohio State University Press for the Ohio Historical Society, 1958, pp. 60-62.

understanding that it would go to Marietta the following year and alternative between the two towns in future years. The actions of the assembly
prompted a riot and threats to the Federalist representatives which was
thwarted when Worthington threatened to shoot Michael Baldwin, the
leader of the riot. Worthington knew that this kind of activity would be
used by their enemies. St. Clair attempted to exploit the incident politically
by demanding prosecution of its leaders, but his attempt was thwarted by
local officials who blamed the incident on excessive drinking.[579]

The Republicans called a meeting in Chillicothe and decided to send
Thomas Worthington and Michael Baldwin to Washington to oppose the legislature's proposal to divide the Territory. It was also decided to circulate petitions opposing the division in Ross and Adams Counties and to write to urge
Republican committees in other counties to circulate petitions and forward
them to Worthington in Washington.[580]

On December 28, 1801, Worthington left on horseback for Washington,
arriving on January 11, 1802. Letters and petitions opposing the division and
supporting statehood soon arrived. Worthington persuaded an old friend
William Branch Giles, a rabid Virginia Jeffersonian, to lead the opposition in
the House. In the Senate the opposition would be led by Michael Baldwin's
brother Abraham Baldwin of Georgia aided by Mason of Virginia and Brown
and Breckenridge of Kentucky. Worthington also enlisted the aid of William
Duane, editor of the Philadelphia Aurora, the leading Republican newspaper
in attacking the arbitrary actions of St. Clair. When Paul Fearing, the
Territory's delegate to Congress, presented the proposed division to the House
on January 20, 1802, and moved that it be referred to a special committee.
Giles arose in opposition arguing that the measure was intended to delay statehood and perpetuate an unpopular governor and legislature in office. He
urged that it be referred to a committee of the whole. On January 27, 1802, the
measure was considered by a committee of the whole and defeated by a vote of
81 to 5. On January 29 the House passed a resolution to appoint a committee
to draft an enabling act and Giles was appointed Chairman of the committee.
Worthington and Baldwin had succeeded in convincing the Republican leadership that if Ohio were admitted to statehood, it would send three
Republicans to Congress. They had convinced others less partisan that the

---

579   Alfred Byron Sears, *Thomas Worthington, Father of Ohio Statehood*, Ohio State
      University Press for the Ohio Historical Society, 1958, pp. 63-69.
580   Alfred Byron Sears, *Thomas Worthington, Father of Ohio Statehood*, Ohio State
      University Press for the Ohio Historical Society, 1958, p. 66.

delineation of state boundaries laid out in the Ordinance should be adhered to and that the Governor and Territorial legislature did not reflect the sentiments of the vast majority of the voters of the Territory. John Fowler, a Congressman wrote to Nathaniel Massie that Worthington had worked a revolution in the government of the Territory with courage as bold as that of Bonaparte in crossing the Alps. On April 29 an Enabling Act authorizing a vote for delegates to vote on statehood and frame a constitution passed both houses of Congress.[581]

In the meantime Goforth, Massie, Symmes, Worthington and others sent letters to the President delineating charges against St. Clair. They feared that unless removed from office he would use his power over office holders in the Territory to prevent or influence the outcome of an election on statehood. Jefferson did not act on the requests for St. Clair's removal correctly surmising that the people would vote for delegates advocating statehood and that would be the end of St. Clair. He did, however, have Madison write to him reprimanding him for laying out counties and county seats after that function passed to the legislature, collecting illegal fees, and giving his son an illegal tenure of office. However, after St. Clair addressed the convention attacking the constitutionality of the Enabling Act, Jefferson promptly removed him. St. Clair had once again proved that he was his own worst enemy.[582]

Worthington was of course elated by the actions of Congress. Matters had actually gone better than expected. He returned to Ohio amid Republican praise for his efforts and Federalist attacks on his motives. An election for delegates to the convention lay ahead and the summer was spent in virulent campaigning. The Republicans were triumphant and Worthington was elected as a delegate from Ross County. He served a leading role in the convention. He was appointed on a three member rules committee to prepare a report on the rules governing the convention. He also served on the committee appointed to review the qualification of delegates. He served on the committees to draft article one on the legislature, article two on the executive, article three on the

---

581   Alfred Byron Sears, *Thomas Worthington, Father of Ohio Statehood*, Ohio State University Press for the Ohio Historical Society, 1958, pp. 73-78.

582   Alfred Byron Sears, *Thomas Worthington, Father of Ohio Statehood*, Ohio State University Press for the Ohio Historical Society, 1958, pp. 79-81. Alfred Byron Sears, *Thomas Worthington, Father of Ohio Statehood*, Ohio State University Press for the Ohio Historical Society, 1958, pp. 94-106.

judiciary, and article five on the militia.[583] Worthington opposed slavery, but also apposed granting the suffrage and civil rights to Negroes.[584]

Following the adoption of the Constitution Worthington was deputized to carry the constitution and the convention's message to Washington. He left Chillicothe on December 7, 1802, on horseback and arrived in Washington December 19. He called on President Jefferson the following day and delivered the constitution to Congress on December 22. On the following day he dined with the President and his daughters and was pleased to learn that St. Clair had been removed. He remained until Congress adopted acts accepting the convention's proposed modification to the terms of admission and recognized the State by creating a federal district court for the state. During his absence he was elected by the voters of Ross County to the first General Assembly.[585]

The first General Assembly of Ohio met in Chillicothe on March 1, 1803. On April 1 Worthington and John Smith of Cincinnati were elected by the General Assembly to the United States Senate. Worthington drew the short term which ended March 4, 1807. Worthington was present when Congress convened on October 17, 1803. He cast a vote in favor of the Louisiana Purchase which was very popular with westerners because it assured United States control over the Mississippi, the Ohio country's principal trade route to the Caribbean, England and the rest of Europe as well as the Eastern states. He introduced a measure creating a Michigan Territory from the Indiana Territory which passed the Senate but not the House. He reintroduced it in the next session and it won approval. He introduced a bill establishing the boundary of the Virginia Military District which passed. He secured legislation providing lands to support schools in the Virginia Military District and the Connecticut Reserve. He proposed a review of the land laws and secured relief for purchasers who could not make their payments. Worthington won a reputation as the expert in the land laws. He introduced a bill to begin work on a road leading from Cumberland, Maryland to Wheeling, West Virginia, the "National Road." Through his efforts the bill became law. Worthington was a

---

583   "Journal of the First Constitutional Convention", *Ohio History*, Vol. 5, pp. 81-82, 88-89, 92, 93, 96; Frank Theodore Cole, "Thomas Worthington", *Ohio History*, Vol. 12, p. 347-348.

584   Helen M. Thurston, "The 1802 Constitutional Convention and the Status of the Negro", *Ohio History*, Vol. 81, p. 27.

585   Alfred Byron Sears, *Thomas Worthington, Father of Ohio Statehood*, Ohio State University Press for the Ohio Historical Society, 1958, pp. 107-108.

strong proponent of canals, roads and other internal improvements at a time when their constitutionality and wisdom was still a matter of strong debate. John Quincy Adams, who of course was not a Jeffersonian Republican, described Worthington in his diary as follows: "He is a man of plausible, insinuating address, and of indefatigable activity in the pursuit of his purposes. He has seen something of the world and without much education of any other sort, has acquired a sort of polish in his manners and a kind of worldly wisdom which may perhaps more properly be called cunning."[586] This would be considered a compliment by a typical rustic settler in the Scioto Valley, considering the source of the compliment was a New England aristocrat. Worthington through persistence secured legislation which was of practical benefit to Ohio settlers. He also was a strong supporter of the Jeffersonian Revolution. From the point of view of his constituents, "that's what he was thar for."

In 1807 Worthington returned home to Ohio and Tiffin took his place in the United States Senate. Tiffin urged him to run for Governor, but he declined to commit to the race until Massey and Meigs had declared their candidacies. At the last moment Worthington endorsed Massie and offered himself as a candidate for the Ohio House of Representatives. Meigs won the election, but Massie successfully protested his election on the ground that Meigs had not been a resident for four years as required by the Constitution. After winning the protest, Massie declined to accept the office, and Kirker, as Speaker of the Senate, continued to serve as acting governor. Worthington won his race for the House. He also accepted the Governor's appointment as adjutant general and secured passage of a bill arming the 2,443 state militiamen. He also won passage of a law establishing a state bank. Worthington served as a chairman of a committee appointed to consider whether judges had the power to declare laws unconstitutional. The issue had arisen because the courts had declared unconstitutional a law increasing the jurisdiction of justices of the peace to $50 in civil cases. The law was intended to help people resolve disputes without hiring a lawyer. The courts held that it violated the right to jury trial guaranteed by federal and state constitutions because justices of the peace could not conduct jury trials. Worthington's committee recommended that the legislature pass a resolution that courts had no authority to declare a law unconstitutional. For Worthington and many other Republicans the question was one of legislative supremacy. Although the House

---

586   Frank Theodore Cole, "Thomas Worthington", *Ohio History*, Vol. 12, pp. 348-351; Alfred Byron Sears, *Thomas Worthington, Father of Ohio Statehood*, Ohio State University Press for the Ohio Historical Society, 1958, pp. 115-136.

passed the resolution, the senate refused. The issue created a division between the Worthington-Tiffin regular wing of the Republican Party on the one hand and the "quids" or moderate Republican/Federalist alliance on the other. This split would define the political battle ground for the next four years.[587]

In 1808 Worthington, Kirker and Huntington all ran for Governor. Worthington and Kirker split the Scioto Valley and regular Republican vote and Huntington was elected as the moderate Republican/Federalist candidate. Huntington, having served on the Ohio Supreme Court and upheld the authority to declare laws unconstitutional, was obviously the pro-court candidate.[588]

For the next two years Worthington focused his time and energies on business. In addition to his farming and business activities described above, he was a director and shareholder of the State Bank of Chillicothe. He was also a promoter of the Bank of Chillicothe and sat on its first board of directors. When the second National Bank was chartered in 1816, he was instrumental in having a branch located at Chillicothe and sat on it board of directors.[589]

Worthington helped organize the Chillicothe Academy and served as its president. The purpose of the academy was to provide a good education for the young people of the town.[590]

Notwithstanding his focus on business interests, Worthington did continue to serve as adjutant general until 1809. During the 1809-1810 session of the General Assembly Worthington and Tiffin's regular republicans gained temporary ascendancy over the court party, Worthington was only an interested spectator when the sweeping resolution was adopted and the legislature made appointments to every judicial office in the state.[591] In 1810 he owned 11 tracts of land totaling 5,443 acres, one of the larger land owners in the Scioto Valley, but not approaching Nathaniel Massie and Duncan McArthur.[592]

---

587   Alfred Byron Sears, *Thomas Worthington, Father of Ohio Statehood*, Ohio State University Press for the Ohio Historical Society, 1958, pp. 139-145.

588   Alfred Byron Sears, *Thomas Worthington, Father of Ohio Statehood*, Ohio State University Press for the Ohio Historical Society, 1958, pp. 145-147.

589   Alfred B. Sears, "Thomas Worthington" Pioneer Businessman of the Old Northwest", *Ohio History*, Vol. 58, p. 76.

590   Jeffrey P. Brown, "Chillicothe's Elite", *Ohio History*, Vol. 96, p. 151.

591   Alfred Byron Sears, *Thomas Worthington, Father of Ohio Statehood*, Ohio State University Press for the Ohio Historical Society, 1958, pp. 148-150.

592   Lee Solstow, Inequality Amidst Abundance: Land Ownership in Nineteenth Century Ohio, *Ohio History* Vol 88, p. 151.

In 1810 Worthington and Tiffin hoped to reclaim the dominance which they once exercised over the Republicans in Ohio through the Republican Committees of Correspondence. They planned to achieve this through a secret fraternal organization called the Tammany Society of Ohio. Chapters were established in Chillicothe and other towns. The Society's pledged to unite the efforts to elect candidates dedicated to true Republican principles. Their political enemies attacked the Society as undemocratic. Worthington ran for Governor as the Tammany candidate in 1810 against Return Jonathan Meigs. The campaign was nasty. Meigs won and the court party triumphed throughout the state. Despite his defeat, his old friends in the legislature elected him to the United State Senate to fill Meigs unexpired term which would expire March 4, 1815. He was elected in a close vote over former Governor Huntington. After another bitter battle over Tammany in 1811, party divisions disappeared as the state united to fight a second War with Great Britain.[593]

During his term in the Senate he spent much of his time as chairman of the committee on public lands. His expertise on the subject and his sensitivity to the needs of the settlers made him an effective leader of the committee. He advocated a change in policy which would reduce the minimum size tract to 80 acres, the price to $1.00 per acre, and the abolishment of the credit system. His ideas eventually were implemented by the Land Law of 1820. In 1812 he sponsored a law which established the General Land Office to take charge of all records related to the public lands and to render an annual fiscal report to the United States Treasury on the status of land sales. His brother-in-law Edward Tiffin was appointed as the first commissioner of the land office. He was able to secure additional funding for the work on the National Road. He served as chairman of the committee on Indian affairs for awhile.

Worthington's most notable action in the Senate was his opposition to the War of 1812. He felt strongly that the country was not prepared for war and would suffer badly from an engagement with the British and in the West with a British/Indian alliance. His break with the administration over this issue cost him politically for awhile, however, once the War began he was a strong supporter and his original disloyalty was forgiven. In fact he won new respect because his warnings about lack of preparedness proved to be correct. This respect was shown by the fact that he was made chairman of the committee on

---

593   Alfred Byron Sears, *Thomas Worthington, Father of Ohio Statehood*, Ohio State University Press for the Ohio Historical Society, 1958, pp. 150-156.

military affairs in 1813 and chairman of the militia committee in 1814. It is interesting to note that he supported a bill awarding an annuity to St. Clair.[594]

Although Worthington invested in stock in the United States Bank and was a close friend of Albert Gallatin, the Secretary of the Treasury, in 1811 he voted against the renewal of the charter of the United States Bank resulting in a tie vote in the Senate. The tie-breaking vote was cast by Vice President Clinton against the bank. His vote reflected wide-spread sentiment in Ohio that the bank was a monopoly controlled by eastern moneyed interests and a threat to the people. By 1814 the government was in financial distress as a result of the war and the administration urged reestablishment of the bank in order to restore confidence in the government's credit and currency. Worthington now supported the bank; however a law reestablishing the bank did not pass until 1816 after he had returned to Ohio.[595]

President Madison appointed Worthington, Morrow and Meigs as commissioners to negotiate with the Indians of the Northwest. In August, 1812, Worthington attended a council with the Ohio Indians at Piqua. He was highly regarded by Indian leaders because he had always treated them with respect. His influence was important in keeping a number of Ohio tribes out of the British/Tecumseh alliance. Worthington was considered an expert on the Ohio militia in view of his service as adjutant general under Governor's Kirker and Huntington. In the summer of 1812 he assisted Governor Meigs in recruiting and organizing the defenses of the northwestern frontier.[596]

In 1814 Worthington was elected Governor in a lop-sided victory over Othniel Looker of Cincinnati. He immediately took aggressive measures to energize the war effort in Ohio. In February, 1815, he learned the War was over. However, he continued to advocate the importance of maintaining a strong, well-disciplined militia. Worthington also urged the legislature to provide for education and to reform the poor laws by providing for county poor farms under state regulation in place of the existing policy of farming out paupers to contractors. He urged penal reform and the construction of a penitentiary. He urged adoption of a program of public improvements to make roads and

---

594   Alfred Byron Sears, *Thomas Worthington, Father of Ohio Statehood*, Ohio State University Press for the Ohio Historical Society, 1958, pp. 159-191; 594 Frank Theodore Cole, "Thomas Worthington", *Ohio History*, Vol. 12, pp. 353-356.

595   Alfred Byron Sears, *Thomas Worthington, Father of Ohio Statehood*, Ohio State University Press, 1958, pp. 161-162.

596   Alfred Byron Sears, *Thomas Worthington, Father of Ohio Statehood*, Ohio State University Press for the Ohio Historical Society, 1958, pp. 179-186.

rivers more useable. He also urged that measures be taken to regulate banks. In 1816 Worthington was reelected with little opposition. During the summer of 1816 the capital was moved to Columbus. He again urged the adoption of a public school system. During his second term, he established the State Library of Ohio. In addition to the issues he had raised during his first term, he urged that the manufacture and sale of intoxicating liquor be regulated by the state. Little of the legislation which Worthington recommended was adopted. Legislators were primarily concerned about cost. However, several of the ideas whose seeds Worthington planted eventually became law. Laws regulating the establishment and licensing of taverns were enacted after he left office. A school law was eventually enacted. The state undertook a massive internal improvement project in the construction of the canal systems linking Lake Erie to the Ohio River.[597]

Worthington served as a representative to the Ohio House of Representatives in the 1821-22, 1822-23, and 1824-1825 sessions of the Ohio General Assembly. He also served on the commission appointed to investigate and report on the canals and was elected as its first chairman where he served for one year. He also served as a chairman of the finance committee which considered the reforms to the tax laws. During these sessions Worthington worked to push the canal project forward, to reform the tax system, and to establish a state system of common schools. His efforts in all three areas reached fruition in the final session. The legislature embraced the canal project, the tax system was reformed and the state's finances put on a stable and equitable foundation, and the state established a system of common schools. All three measures were of tremendous importance to the future of the state. The 1824-1825 session of the legislature was by far the most productive session since the formation of the state. It is interesting to note that one of his most important partners in this endeavor was his old Federalist adversary Ephraim Cutler.

The key to obtaining legislative approval of the canal system was to develop a plan which would benefit enough areas of the state that it could garner enough support for approval. The winning plan proposed a canal which would connect Lake Erie to the Ohio River by way of the Cuyahoga Valley, Muskingum Valley and Scioto Valley. It proposed a second canal which would connect Cincinnati and Toledo. It should be noted that this plan provided economic benefits for Chillicothe and the Scioto Valley. Like so many things

---

597   Alfred Byron Sears, *Thomas Worthington, Father of Ohio Statehood*, Ohio State University Press for the Ohio Historical Society, 1958, pp. 193-209.

Worthington worked on, a project which served the public interest also helped his own business interests.[598]

During this period Worthington's name was placed in nomination for United States Senator and Speaker of the House, and although he had many friends, he was never able to carry a majority. During his long career in Ohio politics, Worthington had made enemies, and a new generation of political leaders considered him part of the "old guard" just as he had considered St. Clair the "old guard". Furthermore, because of his wealth, he was considered aristocratic by many. His support of the United States Bank had alienated many. His personality offended many. He was obstinate, sarcastic, and with age compounded by financial stress and poor health had become cynical and pessimistic.[599]

During his first four years in the Territory, he lived in Chillicothe. Then he moved to a log house on the high ground northwest of the village which overlooked the Scioto Valley. By 1807 he completed a large stone mansion designed by Henry Latrobe, prominent architect and designer of public buildings in Washington during the administrations of Presidents Jefferson and Madison. At the time it was considered the most magnificent mansion west of the Alleghenies. In this home the Worthingtons entertained not only the important persons of the State, but also dignitaries visiting the state from the east, Europe and other states in the west. The residence was also the headquarters for a large farm operated by Worthington as well as his varied business interests. Worthington's estate was named Adena.[600]

As noted above Worthington's ancestors were Quakers. Worthington attended both the Methodist and Presbyterian churches in Chillicothe and contributed to both. He taught a class in the Methodist Church. He was a friend and strong supporter of Francis Asbury, the Methodist frontier bishop.

---

598   Alfred Byron Sears, *Thomas Worthington, Father of Ohio Statehood*, Ohio State University Press for the Ohio Historical Society, 1958, pp. 224-225.

599   Frank Theodore Cole, "Thomas Worthington", *Ohio History*, Vol. 12, pp. 371-372; Alfred Byron Sears, *Thomas Worthington, Father of Ohio Statehood*, Ohio State University Press for the Ohio Historical Society, 1958, pp. 219-229; John S. Still, "Ethan Allen Brown and the Ohio Canal System", *Ohio History*, Vol 66, p. 36.

600   Alfred Byron Sears, *Thomas Worthington, Father of Ohio Statehood*, Ohio State University Press for the Ohio Historical Society, 1958, pp. 30-33. Adena is a state memorial operated by the Ohio Historical Society. It was recently rehabilitated as an Ohio Bicentennial project.

When traveling, he also attended Quaker meetings. A deeply religious man, he had prayers in the morning and evening in his home, and he attended church regularly wherever he traveled. He opposed gambling and was an advocate of temperance.[601]

When Ohio sank into a depression in 1819, Worthington like all Ohioans suffered financially. His financial problems were compounded by the fact that he had served as surety or bondsman for friends and relatives whose fortunes crashed during the depression. He paid a $6,010 debt for his son-in-law Edward King, and $20,000 on a bond that his old friend Samuel Finley owed to the United States Treasury for moneys collected as receiver of public moneys. His financial worries took their toll on his health. He attempted to bail himself out of his financial troubles through contracts to provide wheat and pork to the military stationed up and down the Mississippi. Notwithstanding his difficulties at the time of his death he owned over 15,000 acres of land and several hundred town lots. His estate was estimated to be worth $146,000 and his debts $38,000 for a net of $108,000 which in those days was considered s sizeable estate.[602]

From 1823 to his death in 1827 Worthington suffered from poor health. Notwithstanding his illness, he accompanied his boats to New Orleans hoping that the change in climate would be helpful. It had the opposite effect. He then took a boat to New York and by the time he arrived, he was in critical condition. Worthington died on June 26, 1827 in New York. His body was shipped back over the mountains to Ohio where he was buried at his beloved Adena.[603]

Writing at the time of Ohio's centennial celebration, Frank Theodore Cole, secretary of the Old Northwest Genealogical Society in summing up Worthington's life stated, "He was clearly the greatest man of the first generation of Ohio statesmen."[604] Alfred Byron Sears, professor of history at the University of Oklahoma and Worthington biographer, stated, "No man did

601   Alfred Byron Sears, *Thomas Worthington, Father of Ohio Statehood*, Ohio State University Press for the Ohio Historical Society, 1958, pp. 43-45, 239.

602   Alfred Byron Sears, *Thomas Worthington, Father of Ohio Statehood*, Ohio State University Press for the Ohio Historical Society, 1958, pp. 231-232; Alfred B. Sears, "Thomas Worthington: Pioneer Businessman of the Old Northwest", *Ohio History*, Vol. 58, pp. 72, 78.

603   Alfred Byron Sears, *Thomas Worthington, Father of Ohio Statehood*, Ohio State University Press for the Ohio Historical Society, 1958, pp. 232-236; Frank Theodore Cole, "Thomas Worthington", *Ohio History*, Vol. 12, pp. 372-373.

604   Frank Theodore Cole, "Thomas Worthington", *Ohio History*, Vol. 12, p. 374.

more that Worthington to make Ohio a state in the Union and a force in the councils of the nation. His services in the Senate were of extraordinary value. During wartime no one carried a heavier load of self-imposed responsibility for the safety of the people of Ohio. As governor, his recommendations to the legislature were simple, straightforward, and reasonable, conciliatory in tone and noble in sentiment. They stimulated the growth of a new philosophy among many of Ohio's legislators. Free education, state control of banking, pauper welfare, reformation of criminals, regulation of the liquor business, stimulation of home manufactures, construction of internal improvements— these were measures too advanced, it is true for immediate realization in their entirety, but they were soon to be achieved."[605]

NATHANIEL MASSIE

Nathaniel Massie was born on the upper James River in Goochland County, Virginia on December 28, 1763. This is located between Richmond and Charlottesville. He was descended from Peter Massie who emigrated from England to Virginia before 1669. Nathaniel's father Major Nathaniel Massie was a wealthy farmer who believed in practical education for his sons. At the age of seventeen Massie served briefly in the Revolutionary War as a substitute for another family member who had been drafted. When he returned home, he studied surveying becoming a master of the subject.[606]

In 1783, at the age of nineteen, he left for Kentucky to take up land which Daniel Boone had located for his father. Family friends had also commissioned him to locate lands for them. Massie quickly developed a reputation as a skilled surveyor and quickly learned the survival skills of a back woodsman. Kentucky was a wilderness. Massie faced threats of wild animals, Indians, harsh weather,

---

605   Alfred Byron Sears, *Thomas Worthington, Father of Ohio Statehood*, Ohio State University Press for the Ohio Historical Society, 1958, p. 237.

606   John McDonald, *Biographical Sketches of General Nathaniel Massie, General Duncan McArthur, Captain William Wells, and General Simon Kenton*, Dayton, 1852, p. 12; Jonathan Bean, "Marketing 'the Great Commodity': Nathaniel Massie and Land Speculation on the Ohio Frontier, 1783-1813, *Ohio History*, Vol. 103, p. 157; Henry Howe, *Historical Collections of Ohio*, Centennial Edition, 1908, Vol. 2, p. 502; Nathaniel Massie Ancestral File, Family Search web page, Jesus Christ of Latter Day Saints Family History Library; Morten Carlile, "Buckeye Station", *Ohio History*, Vol. 40, p. 2.

and lack of food other than what could be found in the woods. He became an agent for James Wilkinson, one of the most active land speculators in Kentucky. With Wilkinson he was involved in speculation in land with salt springs. Salt was scarce in the west and there were few locations where it was found. He also became a deputy surveyor for Richard C. Anderson, the principal surveyor of the Virginia Military District. Virginia soldiers who served in the Revolution were given warrants which entitled them to land in the Virginia Military District. Most soldiers sold their warrants to investors or speculators in the east who then hired someone like Massie to locate and survey land for them. Many of the wealthiest men in America invested in western lands. The investor relied upon the expertise of a surveyor like Massie to find good land that was free of conflicting claims. Massie usually received anywhere from 25% to 50% of the land for his fee.[607]

Under Virginia's agreement with Congress, Virginia's soldiers claims could be located in the land reserved by Virginia in Ohio between the Scioto River and the Little Miami River if it ran out of land in Kentucky for that purpose. In August, 1787, Anderson began accepting surveys of land north of the Ohio. Hoping to get a jump on his competition, Massie made his first excursion into Ohio in 1788. Congress halted the sales north of the Ohio until Virginia could show that its claims could not be satisfied in Kentucky. A report was rendered to Congress showing a two million acre shortfall and on August 10, 1790, the Virginia Military District was opened up for Virginia bounty land claims.[608]

By 1790 the Indian wars had broken out. The Shawnee and Miami refused to accept the American's claimed right to settle north of the Ohio River and attacked the new settlements in Washington and Hamilton County and the squatters on the river bottoms in the eastern part of the state. Massie was not deterred by the danger and in December, 1790, he persuaded nineteen men to join him in establishing a settlement at Massie's Station, later called

---

607   John McDonald, *Biographical Sketches of General Nathaniel Massie, General Duncan McArthur, Captain William Wells, and General Simon Kenton*, Dayton, 1852, pp. 12-19. Jonathan Bean, "Marketing the Great Commodity: Nathaniel Massie and Land Speculation on the Ohio Frontier", 1783-1813, *Ohio History*, Vol. 103, p. 157; Morten Carlile, "Buckeye Station", *Ohio History*, Vol. 40, p. 3.

608   Jonathan Bean, "Marketing 'the Great Commodity': Nathaniel Massie and Land Speculation on the Ohio Frontier, 1783-1813, *Ohio History*, Vol. 103, p. 158-159; John McDonald, *Biographical Sketches of General Nathaniel Massie, General Duncan McArthur, Captain William Wells, and General Simon Kenton*, Dayton, 1852, pp. 26-27.

Manchester after his ancestral home. The settlement was located on the north bank of the Ohio River in what became Adams County. It was twelve miles above Maysville, Kentucky and at the foot of the Three Islands. He promised the men who joined him a free town lot, a four acre out lot, and 100 acres. The men erected cabins and surrounded it with a stockade. They cleared and planted their corn on an island near the town. This was the first settlement in the Virginia Military District and the fourth in what would become the State of Ohio.[609]

Massie used the settlement as his base of operations for exploring and conducting surveys and making land sales in the Virginia Military District during the remainder of the Indian War. This was very hazardous work, but Massie's survey parties were carefully organized to deter and defend against Indian attacks. He and his survey parties had several fights with the Indians. In order to minimize the risk of conflict with the Indians many of his surveys were done in the winter when the Indians were disbursed into their winter hunting camps. The winter surveys created additional hardships and risks due to freezing or frostbite and lack of food. The survey crews were comprised of tough, courageous men, and Massie was highly respected as a skilled woodsman with good judgment who men were willing to trust with their lives. Massie developed strong bonds with the men who worked for him during the Indian Wars and some of them became close political allies in future years.[610]

In 1797 Massie constructed a frame house on a ridge a few miles east of Manchester which had a beautiful view up and down the Ohio River. The ridge was called "Gift Ridge" because Massie gave the first settlers a gift of land there. His house replaced a log cabin which he had earlier erected. He called his residence "Buckeye Station". By the time he built his residence Massie had made

609   John McDonald, *Biographical Sketches of General Nathaniel Massie, General Duncan McArthur, Captain William Wells, and General Simon Kenton*, Dayton, 1852, p. 31-32; Henry Howe, *Historical Collections of Ohio*, Centennial Edition, 1908, Vol. 1, pp. 223-224.

610   John McDonald, *Biographical Sketches of General Nathaniel Massie, General Duncan McArthur, Captain William Wells, and General Simon Kenton*, Dayton, 1852, pp. 34-56; Henry Howe, *Historical Collections of Ohio*, Centennial Edition, 1908, Vol. 1, pp. 224-228, Vol 2, pp. 504-505; Jonathan Bean, "Marketing 'the Great Commodity': Nathaniel Massie and Land Speculation on the Ohio Frontier, 1783-1813, *Ohio History*, Vol. 103, p. 160. Israel Donalson, Joseph Kerr, and Duncan McArthur are examples of men who worked for Massie during the Indian War and later became leaders in their own right.

his principal residence on Paint Creek in Ross County, but he continued to use Buckeye Station occasionally from 1797 to 1802. In 1807 he sold Buckeye Station and the 600 acres surrounding it to his brother-in-law Charles Willing Byrd.[611]

In April, 1796 Massie began clearing and improving a settlement for himself at the mouth of Paint Creek. Later in the summer he located the town of Chillicothe about four or five miles north of the mouth of Paint Creek on a bottom between Paint Creek and the Scioto River. It was located on 3,000 acres of land which he owned. He offered free lots to the first settlers. Many of his first settlers were part of a group of anti-slavery Kentuckians led by Rev. Robert W. Finley. The town settled rapidly and by December, 1796, it had in addition to the settlers' cabins, several stores, taverns, and shops for artisans. Although Massey established over a dozen towns during the next decade, Chillicothe was his greatest success. It quickly became the leading town in the Scioto Valley. By 1801 it had almost 12,000 residents. Massie was successful in attracting good men to the town by selling them on the future of the town and the Valley. Prime examples of this were Thomas Worthington and his brother-in-law Dr. Edward Tiffin who moved their families to the town in 1798, after visiting with Massie the year before.[612]

By 1800 Massie owned over 75,000 acres and was one of the largest landowners in the Virginia Military District. He acquired his land by purchasing warrants and as fees for locating and surveying land for investors who acquired warrants. He had close ties with the other leading landowners in the District. He and his friends were also recognized as the political leaders of the Scioto Valley.[613] In 1800 Massie married a daughter of Colonel David Meade of Kentucky, formerly of Virginia. Following his marriage, he constructed a mansion at the falls of Paint Creek on a large tract of land which he owned. His residence became a place of hospitality and entertainment for business associates,

---

611   Morton Carlisle, "Buckeye Station", *Ohio History*, Vol. 40, pp. 9-13.

612   Jeffrey P. Brown, "Chillicothe's Elite: Leadership in a Frontier Community", *Ohio History*, Vol. 96, p. 143; Jonathan Bean, "Marketing 'the Great Commodity': Nathaniel Massie and Land Speculation on the Ohio Frontier, 1783-1813, *Ohio History*, Vol. 103, p. 161-162; John McDonald, *Biographical Sketches of General Nathaniel Massie, General Duncan McArthur, Captain William Wells, and General Simon Kenton*, Dayton, 1852, pp. 60-63.

613   Jonathan Bean, "Marketing 'the Great Commodity': Nathaniel Massie and Land Speculation on the Ohio Frontier, 1783-1813, *Ohio History*, Vol. 103, p. 162; Andrew R L Cayton, *Frontier Ohio*, Kent State University Press, 1986, pp. 53-56.

prospective purchasers and investors, political and militia leaders, and visitors from the east and other countries.[614]

Adams County was organized in July, 1797, by Winthrop Sargent. He took this action as Secretary and acting Governor of the Territory while St. Clair was in the east. Nathaniel Massie was appointed as a judge of the common pleas court and a justice of the peace and judge of the court of general quarter sessions. He was also appointed lieutenant colonel and commander of the militia of the county. He created the first militia organization in the Scioto Valley. The secretary postponed a decision on the location of the county seat and later fixed it at Adamsville.[615] The Governor subsequently located the county seat at Washington and when the local judges met at Manchester in defiance of the Governor's proclamation, the Governor removed Massie from office.[616] A petition was presented to the first Territorial legislature by residents of Adams County requesting that the county seat be moved to Manchester and in response the legislature named Manchester as the county seat. This action was vetoed by St. Clair.[617]

This conflict over the county seat of Adams County made Massie a bitter enemy of Governor St. Clair. The Governor's decision made Massie's investment at Manchester much less valuable. More importantly, St. Clair's refusal to respect Massie's wishes as the founder and leading citizen of the county as well as the wishes of the county officials, the local residents, and the Territorial legislature confirmed Massie's view that St. Clair was an arbitrary despot. In the case of both Massie and Judge Symmes, St. Clair picked a fight with two of the most powerful men in the Territory. In each case he created bitter personal enemies who used all their influence to bring him down.[618]

---

614   John McDonald, *Biographical Sketches of General Nathaniel Massie, General Duncan McArthur, Captain William Wells, and General Simon Kenton,* Dayton, 1852, pp. 64-65.

615   Richard C. Knopf, *Transcription of the Executive Journal of the Northwest Territory,* pp. 424-427, Ohio Historical Society web page.

616   Richard C. Knopf, *Transcription of the Executive Journal of the Northwest Territory,* p. 517, Ohio Historical Society web page; William Henry Smith, *The St. Clair Papers,* Vol 2, pp. 425-426, 428-431. Massie was subsequently reappointed as judge by Charles Willing Byrd, secretary and acting Governor when St. Clair was out of the Territory. Byrd was Massie's bother-in-law.

617   William Henry Smith, *The St. Clair Papers,* Vol 2, pp. 448, 450, 478.

618   William Henry Smith, *The St. Clair Papers,* Vol 1, pp. 221-222. Smith concludes that Massie's subsequent opposition to the Governor was based on a desire for revenge.

Although the controversy over St. Clair is frequently portrayed as an ideological battle, it can also be viewed as a grudge match among these three strong-willed men and their allies.

Massie was elected as a representative of Ross County to the first and second Territorial legislatures. In the first Territorial legislature, he served on the Ways and Means Committee and the Committee which drafted a bill for levying taxes and regulating revenue. He also served on the committee appointed to draft a militia law. In his address to the legislature, Governor St. Clair stated that these were two of the most important matters with which the legislature must deal.[619] Following St. Clair's veto of eleven of the thirty-nine bills enacted by the legislature, Massie joined with Worthington and Tiffin to form the leadership of the so-called Chillicothe junto committed to blocking reappointment of the Governor and securing statehood as soon as possible. Although Harrison and Worthington blocked St. Clair's first attempt to secure a division of the Territory at the Scioto River, they were not successful in blocking St. Clair's reappointment as Governor by John Adams. Following the Territorial legislature's enactment of St. Clair's plan to divide the Territory at the Scioto, Massie, Worthington, Tiffin and their allies launched a massive effort to secure defeat of the plan in Congress. Worthington and Michael Baldwin were dispatched to Washington while Massie and Tiffin worked feverishly gathering petitions opposing the division.[620] The junto also sought removal of St. Clair by President Jefferson. Massie submitted charges against St. Clair to Secretary of State James Madison urging his removal from office. He accused him of attempting to divide the Territory to delay statehood, of charging oppressive fees unauthorized by law for performing his official duties, of violating the Ordinance of 1787 by refusing to allow the legislature to establish counties and fix county seats, and displaying in his public remarks hostility to the republican form of government.[621] Jefferson sent a letter reprimanding St. Clair for his actions but did not remove him at that time.

Following Congress passage of the Enabling Act calling for an election of delegates to a convention to decide statehood and adopt a constitution, election of delegates favoring statehood became the focus of the Chillicothe junto. Massie was elected as one of the pro-statehood delegates from Ross County. When St. Clair appeared at the convention and asked to address it,

---

619   William Henry Smith, *The St. Clair Papers*, Vol. 2, pp. 447-448, 453-454.

620   William Henry Smith, *The St. Clair Papers*, Vol. 1, pp. 238-240.

621   Letter from Massie to Madison in William Henry Smith, *The St. Clair Papers*, Vol. 2, pp. 563-565, 566-567.

Worthington and other Republicans opposed it, but Massie supported it say-ing, "Give him rope and he will hang himself." He was correct. St. Clair attacked the Enabling Act passed by Congress as unconstitutional. As soon as he learned this, President Jefferson removed him from office.[622]

At the convention Massie was recognized as the leader of the Ross County delegation. He served on the committees appointed to draft article 1 on the legislature, article 2 on the executive, article 3 on the judiciary and article 5 on the militia. He chaired the deliberations on article 2.[623] Massie's votes showed him to be against slavery, but also opposed to Negro suffrage and civil rights.[624]

In the election held in January, 1803 to elect the first officers of the State, Massie was elected as a state Senator from Ross County. When the Senate con-vened in March, he was unanimously elected as Speaker of the Senate. One of the principal issues with St. Clair had been the authority to erect new counties and establish county seats. In its first session the General Assembly erected eight new counties. Another complaint had been that St. Clair had appointed men loyal to him as county judges. The General Assembly enacted a law imple-menting the judicial system outlined in the Constitution and appointed judges to fill the judicial positions created by the new Constitution in the existing and new counties. By so doing they completed the Republican revolution at the county level which had been accomplished in January at the state level. A prin-cipal argument of the Federalists had been that the state could not afford a state government. The session addressed this issue by enacting a law raising revenue for the new state. Another issue with the Governor had been his insis-tence that he issue marriage licenses so that he could collect a fee. The legisla-ture enacted a new marriage law which authorized justices of the peace and ministers to solemnize marriages. An election law was passed. The session was short, lasting only from March 1 to April 16, 1803, and the legislators made no attempt to revise most of the existing laws of the Territory. Except for those which were revised, the existing Territorial laws remained in effect.[625] When

---

622   Jonathan Bean, "Marketing 'the Great Commodity': Nathaniel Massie and Land Speculation on the Ohio Frontier, 1783-1813, *Ohio History*, Vol. 103, pp. 164-165.

623   "Proceedings of the Constitutional Convention of 1802", *Ohio History*, Vol 5, pp. 88, 92-94, 96

624   Helen M. Thurston, "The 1802 Constitutional Convention and the Status of the Negro", *Ohio History*, Vol. 81, p. 27.

625   William T. Utter, *History of Ohio, The Frontier State*, Ohio Historical Society, 1942, Vol 2, p. 27; William A. Taylor, *Ohio Statesmen and Annals of Progress*, State of Ohio, 1899, pp. 35-37.

the Senate reconvened in December, 1803, Massie was again unanimously elected Speaker. This session of the legislature undertook a review and revision of many of the laws adopted during the Territorial period. In this session the state was divided into four militia divisions and Massie was elected major general of the second division. He served in this office until 1810. As a result of this position, Massie was frequently referred to as General Massie.[626]

Massie was elected as a presidential elector for the Republican Party in 1804 and 1808, casting a vote for Jefferson in 1804 and for Madison in 1808.[627]

Massie returned to the legislature during the 1806-1807 session as a Ross County representative to the House of Representatives. When Governor Tiffin sought to address the legislature in secret session concerning the Burr conspiracy, Massie objected on the ground that a secret session would be unconstitutional.[628] Tiffin afterwards wrote to Worthington that Nathaniel Massie while "in liquor" objected so violently to the secret sessions that the House adjourned in disorder.[629] Although the deliberations were delayed for a day, the legislature and governor did promptly address the matter and the militia was dispatched to arrest the conspirators and seize their boats and supplies. Massie reportedly went through periodic drinking binges and became the drinking partner of Elias Langham.[630] Hard drinking was prevalent on the Ohio frontier.

By 1807 a group of Ross County Republicans had formed who were hostile to Worthington and Tiffin. They were led by Elias Langham and Michael Baldwin. Upon Tiffin's resignation to become United States Senator upon the expiration of Worthington's term, this group caucused and nominated Massie for Governor. Meigs was supported by an alliance of Federalists and moderate Republicans. Although Worthington was urged to run by Tiffin, he declined and at the last moment threw his support to Massie. Meigs won by a small margin, but Massie was persuaded to protest the election on the ground that Meigs had not been a resident for four years since he had been serving as a

---

626   William A. Taylor, *Ohio Statesmen and Annals of Progress*, State of Ohio, 1899, pp. 38-41.

627   William A. Taylor, *Ohio Statesmen and Annals of Progress*, State of Ohio, 1899, p. 64.

628   Article I, Section 14 of the Ohio Constitution of 1802 provided that the "doors of each house…shall be kept open, except in such cases, as in the opinion of the house, require secrecy."

629   William T. Utter, *History of Ohio, The Frontier State*, Ohio Historical Society, 1942, Vol 2, p. 72.

630   Jeffrey P. Brown, "Chillicothe Elite", *Ohio History*, Vol. 96, p149.

judge outside the Territory. By a vote of 24 to 20 Meigs was declared ineligible. Worthington who was now in the legislature voted for Massie. Massie then resigned since he had not received the most votes and Kirker as speaker of the senate continued to serve as acting Governor.[631] Why would Massie protest the election and then resign after he won the office? His actions were perfectly understandable to the men of the frontier if not to modern politicians. He bested his adversary, but he would not accept an office that the people had not given him. This would be dishonorable.[632]

Massie returned to the Ohio House of Representatives in the 1809-1810 session. This was the election where the central issue was the power of judges to declare laws unconstitutional. The anti-court Republicans were in the majority and during the session all the judicial offices of the state were declared vacant and new appointments made for all judicial offices.[633]

Massie and William Creighton led the opposition to the pro-Worthington/Tiffin Tammany Society in Chillicothe. They correctly saw the organization as an attempt to control the nomination and election of candidates who were members or allies of the Tiffin/Worthington wing of the Republican Party, which they opposed. They correctly sensed that the exclusiveness and secrecy of the organization as well as its Indian rituals would be unpopular with the public. They organized a mass meeting of protest shortly before Tammany's annual May celebration in 1811. Attacks on the Society continued throughout the summer. In the fall the anti-Tammany Society candidates triumphed resulting in the repeal of the Sweeping Resolution.[634]

During the War of 1812 Massie learned that Harrison's army had been besieged by the British and Indians at Fort Meigs. In 1810 he had resigned as major general of the militia. Even though he held no office, he quickly recruited a company of volunteers who promptly elected him as commander.

---

631   William A. Taylor, *Ohio Statesmen and Annals of Progress*, State of Ohio, 1899, pp. 51-53; Alfred Byron Sears, *Thomas Worthington, Father of Ohio Statehood*, Ohio State University Press, 1958, pp. 139-142.

632   John McDonald, *Biographical Sketches of General Nathaniel Massie, General Duncan McArthur, Captain William Wells, and General Simon Kenton*, Dayton, 1852, p. 68.

633   William A. Taylor, *Ohio Statesmen and Annals of Progress*, State of Ohio, 1899, pp. 59-61; Andrew R.L. Cayton, *Frontier Republic*, Kent State University Press, 1986, pp. 104-105.

634   William T. Utter, *History of Ohio, The Frontier State 1803-1825*, Ohio Historical Society, 1942, Vol. 2, pp. 59-60.

They proceeded as rapidly as possible by horseback north to Sandusky where they learned that the British had lifted the siege and returned to Canada. He and the men then returned to their farms in the Scioto Valley.[635]

Later that year Massie contracted pneumonia and on November 3, 1813, died at his residence leaving a widow and five children. His biographer John McDonald, stated, "His character was well suited for the settlement of a new country; distinguished as it was, by an uncommon degree of energy and activity in the business in which he was engaged. His disposition was ever marked with liberality and kindness."[636]

MICHAEL BALDWIN

Michael Baldwin was born August 26, 1774 in New Haven, Connecticut. His Baldwin ancestors emigrated from England to Connecticut before 1655. He was the half-brother of Abraham Baldwin of Georgia who served in the Continental Congress, the United States Constitutional Convention, the U. S. House of Representatives, and the U. S. Senate. Abraham was instrumental in founding the University of Georgia and served as its president for several years. After the death of his father, Abraham assumed responsibility for the education of his half-brothers and sisters. Michael was also the brother of Henry Baldwin who was elected to three terms in the U. S. Congress and appointed to the United States Supreme Court where he served fourteen years. Michael's father Michael was a blacksmith in Connecticut and invested much of his earnings in his children's educations. All three sons graduated from Yale. After Michael graduated from Yale, he was admitted to the practice of law in Pennsylvania. In 1799 Baldwin arrived in Chillicothe to seek his fortune in the west with letters of recommendation to Nathaniel Massie and Thomas Worthington.[637]

---

635   John McDonald, *Biographical Sketches of General Nathaniel Massie, General Duncan McArthur, Captain William Wells, and General Simon Kenton*, Dayton, 1852, pp. 68-69.

636   John McDonald, *Biographical Sketches of General Nathaniel Massie, General Duncan McArthur, Captain William Wells, and General Simon Kenton*, Dayton, 1852, p. 70.

637   Andrew R. L. Cayton, "The Failure of Michael Baldwin", *Ohio History*, Vol 95, p. 36; Abraham Baldwin, Henry Baldwin, Biographical Directory of the United States Congress web page; International Genealogical Index, Family Search, Jesus Christ of Latter Day Saints Family History Library.

Baldwin was admitted to the practice of law in the Territory in 1799 and received the patronage of Massie and Worthington. He built a good practice and joined Massie and Worthington in attacking Governor St. Clair and advocating statehood. He was quickly accepted into the political and social leadership of the Chillicothe community.[638]

Baldwin became popular with a segment of Chillicothe's population known as the "Bloodhounds." They have been described as a "band of cursing, quarreling, and fighting rowdies" that were obnoxious to the respectable members of the community. These were working men with little if any education and respect for authority. Baldwin was the leader of this group because he excelled at their favorite activities, drinking, gambling, and defying authority. When Baldwin would be judged in contempt for inappropriate conduct in the courtroom and confined to jail, the Bloodhounds would set him free.[639]

Baldwin reflected the egalitarian views of most of the pioneer settlers. They couldn't stand what they called aristocrats, people who thought they were better and therefore entitled to deference. Baldwin stated the political creed of these folks in 1802 when he stated, "all power flows from the people...the people are fully competent to govern themselves; they are the best and only proper judge of their own interests and their own concerns; that in forming governments and constitutions, the people ought to part with as little power as possible."[640]

In December, 1801, the Territorial legislature met in Chillicothe and voted to adopt St. Clair's plan to divide the Territory at the Scioto River and to move the capital of the Territory to Cincinnati. Baldwin and the Bloodhounds viewed St. Clair in the same way as the patriots of Boston viewed King George and proposed to deal with him in the same way. On Christmas Eve a crowd gathered outside the tavern where St. Clair and the other Federalists were lodging. Led by Baldwin the group prepared to burn the Governor in effigy and heated a barrel of tar in anticipation of tarring and feathering him. Thomas Worthington rushed to the tavern and confronted Baldwin. He warned him that if any of the crowd tried to enter the Governor's lodgings, he would shoot him. The crowd broke up, but returned the following evening. Some of them

---

638   Andrew R. L. Cayton, "The Failure of Michael Baldwin", *Ohio History*, Vol 95, pp. 38-39.

639   Andrew R. L. Cayton, "The Failure of Michael Baldwin", *Ohio History*, Vol 95, pp. .39-40.

640   Andrew R. L. Cayton, "The Failure of Michael Baldwin", *Ohio History*, Vol 95, p. 41.

including Baldwin entered the tavern proclaiming that they had as much right to drink there as anyone else. Worthington arrived with a justice of the peace. After an exchange of threats, Baldwin and his followers left. Worthington and his allies refused to cooperate with the Governor's attempts to prosecute Baldwin and other leaders of the mob. In the official report the incident was blamed on excessive drinking, and it was concluded that the crowd had been stopped before any harm was done.[641]

Baldwin accompanied Worthington on his trip to Washington to persuade Congress to reject the plan adopted by the Legislature to divide the Territory at the Scioto River. Baldwin's brother Abraham was persuaded to lead the effort in the Senate. By the end of January, it was clear that Congress would reject the plan and Baldwin left for Ohio while Worthington stayed behind to work for passage of the Enabling Act. When the Bloodhounds learned of the defeat of the Division Act, they led a shouting parade through the streets of Chillicothe.[642]

Baldwin was elected as one of the Ross County delegates to the Convention. He served on the committee to draft the bill of rights and the committee to draft article three on the judiciary.[643] Reflecting the prevalent viewpoint of his constituency, Baldwin did not vote for Negro suffrage or civil rights.[644]

Following the adoption of the Constitution, Baldwin was elected by the voters of Ross County to the Ohio House of Representatives in the January, 1803 election. He received the second highest number of votes behind Worthington. Baldwin was elected Speaker of the House.[645] He was again elected to the House of Representatives in the 1804-1805 session of the General Assembly and was again elected Speaker of the House.[646] Duncan McArthur and Edward Tiffin were highly critical of his performance.[647]

---

641   Andrew R. L. Cayton, "The Failure of Michael Baldwin", *Ohio History*, Vol 95, pp. 42-43.

642   Andrew R. L. Cayton, "The Failure of Michael Baldwin", *Ohio History*, Vol 95, p. 43 Alfred Byron Sears, *Thomas Worthington, Father of Ohio Statehood*, Ohio State University Press, 1958, pp. 73-85.

643   "Journal of the Constitutional Convention of 1802", *Ohio History*, Vol. 5, pp. 90, 94.

644   Helen M. Thurston, "The 1802 Constitutional Convention and the Status of the Negro", *Ohio History*, Vol. 81, p. 28.

645   William A. Taylor, *Ohio Statesmen and Annals of Progress*, State of Ohio, 1899, p. 35.

646   William A. Taylor, *Ohio Statesmen and Annals of Progress*, State of Ohio, 1899, p. 43.

647   Andrew R. L. Cayton, *The Frontier Republic*, Kent State University Press, 1986, pp. 85-86.

Tiffin and Worthington found Baldwin disgusting. Tiffin described Baldwin "to be like the wind, and beats round to every point of the compass in as short a period." He was "too bad to talk about; he publicly has said he will use means to accomplish his purposes foul as well as fair—he is an infamous young man." Worthington described Baldwin as "a quack lawyer who was elected Speaker in consequence of his real character not being known. He may be considered the most finished villain. This man possesses a great share of low cunning and considerable fund of information, added to a strong mind but not a single moral virtue. He is quarrelsome, yet a coward. Arbitrary and tyrannical yet a sycophant and possesses not the smallest spark of sensibility. On the whole if he had a little more courage we might say with Shakespeare that he would be fitted for treasons, stratagems, and usurpations and would cut a respectable figure in a banditti of thieves and robbers. If I could attribute to him one virtue it would give me pleasure." In response to their hostility Baldwin opposed Worthington and Tiffin at every opportunity. During the first session of the General Assembly he voted for Huntington rather than Worthington for United States Senator.[648] In 1806 he supported James Pritchard against Morrow for Congress.[649] The actions of Baldwin, Langham and Pritchard prompted efforts by Tiffin and Worthington to bring greater organization and discipline to the Republican Party ultimately leading to the organization of the Tammany Society.

Baldwin was appointed United States District Attorney on March 3, 1803. and served until December 12, 1804.[650] He was then appointed United States Marshall but was removed in 1807 because of neglect of duties in connection with the Burr affair.[651]

Suffering from alcoholism and poor health, Baldwin faded from public view. He died on March 9, 1810. Before he died, Worthington visited him and reflected "on the miseries this young man has brought on himself and feeling sorrow and regret that the talents he possessed had not been applied to the

648 Andrew R. L. Cayton, "The Failure of Michael Baldwin", *Ohio History*, Vol 95, pp. 43-44.

649 Andrew R. L. Cayton, *The Frontier Republic*, Kent State University Press, 1986, p. 89.

650 Carrington T. Marshall, *A History of the Courts and Lawyers of Ohio*, New York, 1934, Vol. 3, p. 928; Department of Justice, District of Ohio web page

651 Andrew R. L. Cayton, "The Failure of Michael Baldwin", *Ohio History*, Vol 95, p. 46; William T. Utter, *History of Ohio, The Frontier State 1803-1825*, Ohio Historical Society, 1942, Vol. 2, p. 76.

benefit of his fellow mortals and his own good." His life had been "a melancholy instance of the depravity of human nature." [652]

JAMES GRUBB

James Grubb was born in 1771 in Little Britain, Lancaster, County, Pennsylvania. His great grandfather John Grubb emigrated from England in 1677 and settled on the west bank of the Delaware before William Penn established his colony. James' father Thomas served in the French and Indian War and settled just east of the Susquehanna River southeast of Harrisburg. His brother John was one of the early settlers and a prominent citizen of Erie County, Pennsylvania.[653]

James Grubb was an early settler of Ross County and his prominence was recognized by Governor St. Clair's appointment of him as a Justice of the Peace of Ross County on July 10, 1799.[654]

Grubb was prominent among Nathaniel Massie's allies in fighting for the removal of St. Clair and the formation of a new state. Duncan McArthur commended him for his ability, integrity and political zeal. He was described as a "true philanthropist, a lover of his friend, and opponent of every species of slavery, a man possessing good reasoning abilities, modesty and boldness."

In the campaign for election of delegates to the convention the issue of slavery was important because the Federalists accused the Republicans of planning to allow slavery in the new state. In a letter to the Chillicothe paper prior to the convention, Grubb stated, "As to the introduction of slavery,…such a pernicious scheme ought to be guarded against in a particular manner, as I conceive it bad policy, and the principle can not be advocated by any person of humane or republican sentiments." On August 23, 1802, Edward Tiffin stated, "The introduction of slavery, were it practicable, I should view as the greatest national curse we could entail upon our country." Worthington stated, "I was decidedly opposed to slavery long before I removed to the Territory—the prohibition of slavery in the Territory was the one cause of my removal to it. I have

---

652 Andrew R. L. Cayton, "The Failure of Michael Baldwin", *Ohio History*, Vol 95, p. 46; Andrew R. L. Cayton, *The Frontier Republic*, Kent State University Press, 1986, p. 108; Jeffrey P. Brown, The Chillicothe Elite, *Ohio History*, Vol. 96, p. 149.

653 David Grubb, Grubb Family Genealogy Forum, Genealogy.com web page; "Descendants of Thomas Grubb", Joyce Jacobs Gordon genealogy web page".

654 Richard C. Knopf, *Transcription of the Executive Journal of the Northwest Territory*, p. 524, Ohio Historical Society web page.

uniformly adhered to the same opinion and now believe if slavery be admitted into the country, it would be entailing one among the greatest curses on succeeding generations." Nathaniel Massie stated, "I believe the introduction of slavery would ultimately prove injurious to our country. I am clearly of the opinion that it ought not to be admitted in any shape whatever." Michael Baldwin said, "There can be nothing more repugnant to the feelings of a man, not hardened in inequity, than the idea of depriving his fellow of his liberty, and placing him by force and violence into an abject state of slavery and misery."[655] Although these Republicans strongly opposed the introduction of slavery into the state, they were also strongly opposed to granting Negroes the right to vote and other civil rights. They feared Ohio would become a refuge for escaped slaves and if this occurred, the value of the white man's labor would be undermined and the escaped slaves would become financial burdens on the communities where they settled. Although there were Republican delegates from Hamilton and Clermont Counties who were supporters of equal rights for Negroes, there were none from Ross County.[656]

Grubb was elected as a Ross County delegate to the constitutional convention. He served on the committee appointed to draft the bill of rights and the committee appointed to draft article 4 on the qualification of electors.[657] He voted against granting the suffrage and other civil rights to Negroes.[658]

Grubb was an unsuccessful candidate for the legislature in January and October, 1803.[659] He served on the first grand jury convened in Ross County under the new constitution on December 27, 1803.

At the time of his death James Grubb was a resident of Westfall, a village located on the trail along the Scioto River which connected Chillicothe with Franklinton (now Columbus). Although located in Ross County at the time of the convention, it is now in Wayne Township, Pickaway County. It was first settled about 1798. Although at one time it had hopes of rivaling Chillicothe, the location was found to be unhealthy, and the town decayed.[660]

---

655   *Centennial History of Ross County, Ohio*, 1902, pp. 57-58, Chapter XIII, 120.

656   Helen M. Thurston, "The 1802 Constitutional Convention and the Status of the Negro", *Ohio History*, Vol. 81, p. 27-28.

657   "Journal of the Constitutional Convention of 1802", *Ohio History* Vol. 5, pp. 90, 95

658   Helen M. Thurston, "The 1802 Constitutional Convention and the Status of the Negro", *Ohio History*, Vol. 81, p. 28.

659   *Freeman's Journal and Chillicothe Advertiser*, January 15, 1803 and October 22, 1803; *Western Spy* January 26, 1803.

660   Aaron R. Van Cleaff, *History of Pickaway County, Ohio*, Chicago, 1906, pp. 191-193.

Grubbs died in Chillicothe on January 30, 1806 after a short but severe illness. He never married. His will is on file at the Ross County courthouse.[661]

Other Founding Fathers From Ross County

THOMAS SCOTT

Thomas Scott was born on October 31, 1772, at Oldtown, Maryland, on the Potomac River. Oldtown was first settled by Thomas Cresap as a trading post with the Indians. Scott was of Scotch-Irish descent on his father's side and English-Welsh on his mother's side.[662]

As a young man Scott became an itinerant minister traveling for the Methodist Church in western Virginia and Kentucky. Among his converts when he was traveling in Berkley County, Virginia in 1790 were Edward and Mary Tiffin. Tiffin subsequently was ordained a deacon and became a lay preacher. In 1791 Scott was an itinerant minister at Buffalo Creek in Brooke County, Virginia. In 1794 pursuant to instruction of Bishop Francis Asbury he left Wheeling for Kentucky on a flat boat to join the band of other itinerants who were bringing Methodism to the west. Following his marriage in 1796 to Catherine Dorsey Wood, he ceased traveling for the church but continued to preach on Sundays while working during the week to support his family. He learned the tailor's trade and while working at his bench, his wife read Blackstone to him. He was admitted to the practice of law in Lexington, Kentucky in 1800. In 1801 he came to Chillicothe where he was welcomed by Edward and Mary Tiffin whose lives he had changed eleven years earlier. The two of them became the pillars of Methodism in the Scioto Valley.[663]

Tiffin employed Scott to assist him in his duties as clerk of the courts in Ross County, and he was subsequently appointed clerk of the common pleas court, court of quarter sessions, and probate court.[664] Scott became a close ally

---

661   *Freeman's Journal and Chillicothe Advertiser*, January 30, 1806; David Grubb, Grubb Family Genealogy Forum, Genealogy.com web page.

662   Ross County Biographies web page; "Annora's Family", Ancesty.com web page; Irvin Allen/Michael Cresap Museum web page.

663   Ross County Biographies web page; Abel Stevens, LLD, *A Compendious History of American Methodism*, New York, 1868, pp. 332-334; Brooke County, West Virginia Genealogy web page.

664   Carrington T. Marshall, *A History of the Courts and Lawyers of Ohio*, New York, 1934, Vol. 1, p. 236.

of Tiffin and Worthington in the Republican Party in the county. When the delegates gathered at the constitutional convention in November, 1802, the delegates no doubt at the recommendation of Tiffin and Worthington appointed Scott as the Clerk of the convention.[665] On November 29 after all the delegates had signed the Constitution, a jubilant Scott stood on the table and congratulated the delegates.[666]

Scott served as clerk of the Ohio Senate from December, 1803, through February 21, 1809.[667] He also served as prosecuting attorney in half a dozen counties.[668] Following the resignation of Huntington to accept the governorship and Meigs to accept a seat in the United States Senate, there were two vacancies on the Supreme Court. In February, 1909, Thomas Scott was elected by the General Assembly to fill one of the seats and Thomas Morris, leader of the prosecution of the Tod and Pease impeachment cases was the other.[669] This action followed the Tiffin/Worthington wing of the Republican Party's failure to impeach Justices Pease and Tod for declaring an act of the legislature unconstitutional. That wing of the Republican Party elected Scott and Morris because they did not support judicial review.[670] The Sweeping Resolution was adopted the following year after Scott's election to the Bench, and it vacated his as well as the other seats on the Supreme Court. He was reelected to the Court. However, Morris was not. He suffered the same fate as Tod whom he had prosecuted and was very bitter about it.[671] The Sweeping Resolution was repealed in 1812; however, it did not apply to appointments which had been made under it. Scott resigned in 1815 to take a seat in the Ohio House of Representatives.

---

665   "Journal of the Constitutional Convention of 1802", *Ohio History*, Vol 5, p. 84.

666   Betsa Marsh, "Historic Mansion Adena Restored to Former Glory", *Cincinnati Enquirer*, February 23, 2003. The table is on display at the Ross County Historical Society.

667   William A. Taylor, *Ohio Statesmen and Annals of Progress*, State of Ohio, 1899, pp. 38, 41, 45, 48, 51, 55.

668   Carrington T. Marshall, *A History of the Courts and Lawyers of Ohio*, New York, 1934, Vol. 1, p. 236.

669   Donald F. Melhorn Jr., *Lest We Be Marsahll'd, Judicial Power and Politics in Ohio 1806-1812*, Akron University Press, 2003, p. 120.

670   William T. Utter, *History of Ohio, The Frontier State*, 1803-1825, Ohio Historical Society, Vol. 2, p. 94; Andrew R. L. Cayton, *The Frontier Republic*, Kent State University Press, 1986, pp. 104-105.

671   Donald F. Melhorn Jr., *Lest We Be Marshall'd, Judicial Power and Politics in Ohio 1806-1812*, Akron University Press, 2003, pp. 132-133.

As a result of dissension within the Republican Party over the judiciary question, Republicans in the Tiffin/Worthington wing of the party felt the need for better organization and discipline within the party. This had been accomplished in New York and elsewhere through a fraternal organization called the Tammany Society. The first chapter of the Tammany Society in Ohio was chartered in Chillicothe in 1810. Chapters were then begun in other towns around the state. Membership was by invitation only and proceedings were secret. The membership in Chillicothe included Tiffin, Worthington, Scott, Benjamin Hough, Ethan Allen Brown, and other like-minded Republicans. Scott was the first Grand Sachem of Ohio, and he was followed by Tiffin. Tammany was attacked for being undemocratic and became the principal issue in the elections of 1810 and 1811. In 1810 Meigs defeated Worthington for Governor. In 1811 anti-Tammany candidates won seats in the legislature by hammering away at the issue. Tiffin and other Tammany leaders recognized that the organization was a liability and it faded out of existence, particularly as the War of 1812 became the principal issue confronting the State.[672]

As the 1812 election approached Governor Meigs was at first blamed for Hull's surrender at Detroit. Scott was nominated by the Worthington/Tiffin wing of the party to run against him, but was defeated by a vote of 11,859 to 7,903.[673] In 1815 the voters of Ross County elected Scott to the Ohio House of Representatives.[674] He served one term.

Scott was a prominent lawyer in Chillicothe and was retained in many important cases.[675]

Scott died on February 13, 1856 in Chillicothe, Ohio.[676] A county biography states, "During his long career he occupied many public offices, performing his duties with painstaking care, and always finding time to act as "supply" in the pulpit of the Methodist Church. He had a wide reputation for learning and legal ability."[677]

---

672   Alfred Byron Sears, *Thomas Worthington, Father of Ohio Statehood*, Ohio State University Press, 1958, pp. 150-151; Samuel W. Williams, "The Tammany Society of Ohio", *Ohio History*, Vol. 22, pp. 353-356; Andrew R. L. Cayton, *The Frontier Republic*, Kent State University Press, 1986, pp. 106-108.

673   William T. Utter, *History of Ohio, The Frontier State*, 1803-1825, Ohio Historical Society, Vol. 2, pp. 93-94.

674   William A. Taylor, *Ohio Statesmen and Annals of Progress*, State of Ohio, 1899, p. 83.

675   Ross County Biographies web page.

676   Family Tree, Ancestry.com

677   Ross County Biographies web page.

WILLIAM CREIGHTON

William Creighton was born on October 29, 1778, in Berkley County, Virginia. He graduated from Dickinson College at Carlisle, Pennsylvania. He graduated in 1795, a classmate of Roger Taney, later chief justice of the United States Supreme Court who wrote the decision in the Dred Scott case. Although his studies prepared him for the ministry, he studied law in Virginia and was admitted to practice there in 1798. That same year he moved to Chillicothe and was admitted to practice in the territorial courts.[678]

Creighton quickly established himself as a prominent lawyer and worthy adversary of Michael Baldwin who arrived the same year. Like Baldwin Creighton established himself as an effective trial lawyer. Unlike Baldwin Creighton did not cater to the Bloodhounds, the tavern crowd which Baldwin championed. Rather Creighton was quickly accepted among and became a pillar of the most prominent and respectable members of Chillicothe society. Creighton was known for his quick wit and practical jokes. [679]

In September, 1805 Creighton married Elizabeth Meade, daughter of Col. David Meade, a wealthy and prominent Virginia planter who moved to Kentucky in 1796 and established a bluegrass plantation. Elizabeth was the sister-in-law of Nathaniel Massie. Their home at Water and High Street was known for its genial hospitality.[680]

Creighton was an ally of Massie, Tiffin and Worthington in the battle for Ohio statehood. After the Territorial legislature enacted the Division Act proposing to divide the Territory at the Scioto River, Chillicothe Republicans met and agreed to send Worthington and Baldwin to Congress to persuade Congress to reject the proposal. Creighton and others wrote to Republicans

---

678   M. Melissa Wolfe, "William and Elizabeth Creighton", *Timeline*, Vol 15, No. 3 May/June 1998, p. 53; Dickinson College web page; William T. McClintock, "Ohio's Birth Struggle", *Ohio History* Vol. 96, p. 147; David K. Watson, "Early Judiciary, Early Laws and Bar of Ohio", *Ohio History*, Vol. 3, p. 141; Biographical Directory of the U.S. Congress web page.

679   David K. Watson, "Early Judiciary, Early Laws and Bar of Ohio", *Ohio History* Vol. 3, p. 141; William T. McClintock, "Ohio's Birth Struggle", *Ohio History*, Vol. 11, p. 57; Jeffrey P. Brown, "Chillicothe Elite", *Ohio History*, Vol. 96, p. 147; M. Melissa Wolfe, "William and Elizabeth Creighton", *Timeline*, Vol. 15, No. 3, May/June 1998, p. 54.

680   M. Melissa Wolfe, "William and Elizabeth Creighton", *Timeline*, Vol. 15, No. 3, May/June 1998, pp. 52-54.

around the state encouraging them to secure signatures to petitions opposing the division. They also gathered petition signatures in Ross County. When Ohio Congressman Paul Fearing on January 20, 1802, rose in the House of Representatives and sought appointment of a committee to consider the Division Act, Virginian William Branch Giles rose to oppose it and pointed out that he had in his hands petitions signed by over a thousand citizens from the Territory opposing the division. He urged that the question be referred to a committee of the whole. On January 27 the House rejected the proposed division by a vote of 85 to 5. When Creighton forwarded his petitions he specified that the signers not only opposed the division, but also favored statehood. On January 28, Giles requested appointment of a committee to draft an Enabling Act for the Territory to become a state and Giles was appointed Chairman. On April 29, 1802 the Enabling Act was passed by both houses and on the following day signed by President Jefferson.[681]

At the first session of the General Assembly Creighton was at the age of 25 elected as Ohio's first Secretary of State.[682] His selection recognized the service he performed in the Ohio Republican revolution as well as the high stature in which he was held by the Republican leadership. Creighton continued to serve in this office until 1808 when he submitted his resignation to acting Governor Thomas Kirker.[683]

Creighton is credited with the inspiration for the Great Seal of the State of Ohio. After a nightlong meeting at Worthington's home Adena Creighton, Worthington and Tiffin stood on the edge of the hill looking out over the Scioto Valley below and the sun coming up over Mt. Logan on the east side of the valley. Wheat fields had replaced Indian villages in the valley. Mount Logan symbolized the mountains which separated Ohio from the East. The sun rising over the mountains symbolized civilization coming to the Ohio country. Creighton shared with Worthington how the scene symbolized the bright future of Ohio. The thrill of that moment was captured in the Great Seal.[684]

Following a recommendation of Governor Tiffin, the General Assembly of 1804-1805 undertook a review, revision and codification of the criminal law of

---

681   Alfred Byron Sears, *Thomas Worthington, Father of Ohio Statehood*, Ohio State University Press, 1958, pp. 73-75.

682   William A. Taylor, *Ohio Statesmen and Annals of Progress, State of Ohio*, 1899, p. 36.

683   William A. Taylor, *Ohio Statesmen and Annals of Progress, State of Ohio*, 1899, p. 55.

684   Governor Andrew L. Harris, "Address at Ohio Day at the Jamestown Exposition", *Ohio History* Vol. 17, p. 192. The hills which inspired the Great Seal are part of a state park operated by the Ohio Department of Natural Resources. Department of Natural Ohio Resources Great Seal State Park web page.

the state. A committee was appointed to undertake the task and Creighton served as its clerk. He is credited with most of the work in drafting the code which was adopted by the Assembly with minor modifications.[685]

Creighton was appointed U. S. Attorney for the District of Ohio and served from December 12, 1804 to December 19, 1810.[686] In 1808 he secured a grand jury indictment against Aaron Burr and Harmon Blennerhasset. Ironically, Burr had been a guest at his father-in-law's Kentucky home.[687] Creighton supported Tiffin's aggressive action taken against the Burr conspiracy which he described as "a lawless enterprise". He believed that the state had demonstrated "her patriotism and attachment to the general government."[688]

Although Creighton was part of the Republican team, he did not share the faith in the people that Michael Baldwin did. He described Elias Langham, who like Baldwin catered to popular prejudices as "the great author of bustle and confusion" among the people.[689] After the Constitution was adopted, he wrote, "The Sovereign People could not be totally trusted. Too many of them did not like their new constitution because it had no pictures in it."[690] Although said in jest, the comment reflected a philosophical difference which would cause Creighton to split from the Worthington/Tiffin wing of the party. He became a leader of the conservative Republicans which fought with the Worthington/Tiffin wing over the judiciary and the Tammany Society. He later became a friend of Daniel Webster and a supporter of John Quincy Adams.[691]

---

685 William T. Utter, *History of Ohio, The Frontier State*, Ohio Historical Society, Vol. 2, p. 38.

686 Carrington T. Marshall, A History of the Courts and Lawyers of Ohio, New York, 1934, Vol. 3, p. 928; Department of Justice for Southern District of Ohio web site; the following authorities indicate different dates of service: M. Melissa Wolfe, "William and Elizabeth Creighton", *Timeline*, Vol. 15, No. 3, May/June, 1998, p. 54; Biographical sketch published on Federal Judicial Center web site; William T. McClintock. "Centennial Address", *Ohio History* Vol. 12, p. 7.

687 M. Melissa Wolfe, "William and Elizabeth Creighton", *Timeline*, Vol. 15, No. 3, May/June, 1998, p. 54.

688 Andrew R. L. Cayton, *Frontier Republic*, Kent State University Press, 1986, pp. 91-93.

689 Andrew R. L. Cayton, *Frontier Republic*, Kent State University Press, 1986, p. 83.

690 Andrew R. L. Cayton, "The Failure of Michael Baldwin", *Ohio History*, Vol 95, p. 44.

691 David K. Watson, "Early Judiciary, Early Laws and Bar of Ohio", *Ohio History*, Vol. 3, p. 141; Jeffrey P. Brown, Chillicothe's Elite, *Ohio History*, Vol. 96, p. 148; Donald J. Ratcliffe, "The Experience of Revolution and the Beginnings of Party Politics in Ohio, 1776-1816", *Ohio History*, Vol. 85, p. 209.

During the 1808-1809 session of the General Assembly impeachment charges were brought against Supreme Court Justice, George Tod, and Calvin Pease, President of the Third Judicial District, for declaring an act of the legislature to be unconstitutional. The act in question was a law which increased the jurisdictions of justices of peace to $50.00 in civil cases. The law was very popular because it permitted people to resolve disputes without hiring a lawyer. Judge Pease held the law unconstitutional because it violated the provision of the Constitution of Ohio guaranteeing trial by jury. Supreme Court Justices Huntington and Tod agreed with Pease decision. The issue became a principal issue in the 1808 elections. The Worthington/Tiffin Republicans argued that the legislature as the voice of the people was supreme and only the legislature could declare what was and was not the law. They also accused the judges of conspiring with the lawyers of the state to protect their fees. Huntington supported by conservative Republicans and Federalists was elected Governor over Worthington and Kirker who split the Scioto County vote. Huntington was not impeached because he no longer was a judge. Creighton was a member of the legal team who defended Justice Tod and Judge Pease. Impeachment required two thirds vote of the Senate. Tod and Pease escaped conviction by one vote. Creighton split with Worthington and Tiffin on this issue, a split which divided them for the next four years.[692]

The fight between the pro-court and anti-court parties continued in the 1809-1810 session of the General Assembly. A Sweeping Resolution was adopted declaring all the judicial offices vacant seven years after the beginning of state government. Judges were appointed for all offices. In this manner Tod and Pease along with all other judges who thought as they did were removed from office. The split in Republicans over this issue led the Worthington/Tiffin Republicans to organize Tammany Societies in Chillicothe and other towns around the state to enforce discipline within the party. Membership in the societies was by invitation only and their proceedings were secret. Creighton became a leader of the opponents of the Tammany Society. In 1811 Creighton and Massie organized a mass meeting in Chillicothe protesting the society before its annual May Day parade. They stated that the secret aim of the Society was to consolidate and concentrate all power, which rightfully belongs in the people, in the hands of a secret organization. The attacks on the Society and Tiffin as it leader continued throughout the summer. The principal issue

---

692   William T. Utter, *History of Ohio, The Frontier State*, Ohio Historical Society, Vol. 2, pp. 47-51; Donald F. Melhorn Jr., *Lest We Be Marshall'd, Judicial Power and Politics in Ohio 1806-1812*, Akron University Press, 2003, pp. 98-117.

in the elections became the Tammany Society. The anti-Tammany society candidates prevailed. Among the anti-Tammany candidates elected to the House was William Creighton. He held a mock funeral for St Tammany in Chillicothe.[693] The Sweeping Resolution was repealed on January 8, 1812. The Tammany societies faded from existence. Creighton had defied the Worthington/Tiffin political machine and won.[694]

A casualty of the split in the Chillicothe ranks was the location of the state capital. The Ross County leadership's control of the politics of the state had created animosity in other quarters. The fight among themselves strengthened the hand of Republicans in other locales. As a result of the Sweeping Resolution, many vacancies were created in judgeships around the state. Deals were made to procure appointments. A resolution was passed to move the capital temporarily to Zanesville and a commission was appointed to recommend a permanent location. During the 1810-1811 session Columbus was selected as the permanent seat of government and Chillicothe made the temporary seat until the buildings were completed. In 1816 the state capital was moved to Columbus. Chillicothe's status slipped from government center of the state to county seat and regional market town.[695]

The advent of the War of 1812 made defense of Ohio from Indian attack the principal focus of public attention. By the fall of 1812 the public had gone from elation at the prospect of seizing Canada for the Union to the shock of learning that the army which had marched north in glory to defend Detroit and capture Fort Malden across the River had surrendered. General William Hull was considered a coward or a traitor. Fear of Indian attacks swept across the state. Hope was placed in General Henry William Harrison, who had defeated the Indians led by Tecumseh's brother the Prophet at Tippecanoe. In the summer of 1812 Creighton accompanied a regiment commanded by Captain Henry Brush, attorney from Chillicothe. They were escorting 150 horse loads of flour and 300 head of cattle for Hull's army at Detroit. They halted at the River Raisin upon learning that Indians were waiting on the other side. After Hull's surrender a British officer was sent out to accept their

---

693   William A. Taylor, *Ohio Statesmen and Annals of Progress*, State of Ohio, 1899, p.67; Andrew R. L. Cayton, *Frontier Republic*, Kent State University Press, 1986, p. 108.

694   William T. Utter, *History of Ohio, The Frontier State*, Ohio Historical Society, Vol. 2, pp. 52-60.

695   William T. Utter, *History of Ohio, The Frontier State*, Ohio Historical Society, Vol. 2, pp. 53-54; William A. Taylor, *Ohio Statesmen and Annals of Progress*, State of Ohio, 1899, pp. 59, 61.

surrender as well. Creighton, who was serving as an aid to Captain Brush, had the British officer blindfolded and held prisoner until they were ready to make their escape. They then destroyed all their supplies except the whiskey which they left behind. As soon as they departed hastily for home, the Indians arrived and as expected consumption of the whiskey rather than pursuit of the enemy occupied their attention.[696]

As a result of the 1810 census, Ohio became entitled to six congressmen. Prior to that time it had been represented by only one. The General Assembly divided the state into six electoral districts and in the fall of 1812 the congressmen were elected. Duncan McArthur was elected for the third district including Chillicothe, but resigned shortly thereafter after being commissioned a brigadier general in the United States Army. Creighton was elected to complete McArthur's term of office and was then reelected for a second term.[697] In February 1815 Creighton was nominated for U.S. Senator but Benjamin Ruggles was elected.[698]

A principal problem faced by Congress was paying for the cost of the War. Creighton served on the Ways and Means committee which struggled with this problem. The Committee proposed to issue paper money, but when this failed to gain acceptance, a proposal to reestablish a national bank was passed. With other members of the Ohio delegation Creighton advocated strong measures to defend the frontier and payment of claims by Ohioans who advanced funds and supplies for the common defense.[699]

Congress passed an act reestablishing a Bank of the United States. A competition arose between Chillicothe and Cincinnati on the location of its branch in Ohio. As a result a branch was opened in both towns. Creighton served as president of the Chillicothe Branch from 1816 to 1830.[700] This must have

696   Clement L. Martzhoff, "Autobiography of Thomas Ewing", *Ohio History*, Vol. 22, pp. 174-175; Robert B. McAfee, *History of the Late War in the Western Country*, Heritage Books Reprint, 1816, pp. 73, 93.

697   William A. Taylor, *Ohio Statesmen and Annals of Progress*, State of Ohio, 1899, pp. 73, 76, 78; William R. Barlow, Ohio's Congressmen and the War of 1812, *Ohio History* Vol 72, p. 179; "William Creighton", Biographical Directory of the U. S. Congress web page.

698   William A. Taylor, *Ohio Statesmen and Annals of Progress*, State of Ohio, 1899, p. 80; "William Creighton", Biographical Directory of the U. S. Congress web page.

699   William R. Barlow, "Ohio's Congressmen and the War of 1812," *Ohio History* Vol. 72, pp. 157-194.

700   M. Melissa Wolfe, "William and Elizabeth Creighton", *Timeline*, Vol. 15, No. 3, May/June, 1978 p. 54.

caused him no end of distress. As a result of a demand by the parent bank in Philadelphia the Ohio branches in the mid 1818 required payment of notes and government debts in currency and would no longer accept payment in the notes issued by Ohio banks. This action brought on a severe financial depression in Ohio, resulting in the closing of most of Ohio banks, a severe deflation in the price of land and commodities, widespread defaults on government land payments and mortgage payments securing loan from banks, and numerous business failures. The General Assembly attempted to levy a tax on the branches of the United States Bank and seized $100,000 from the vault of the Chillicothe branch. The United States Supreme Court eventually ruled the state's action to be unlawful and ordered return of the money. The General Assembly then withdrew protection of Ohio law from the bank and refused to permit its courts to enforce the Bank's notes. By the mid twenties Ohio's economy began to improve and the punitive laws were repealed.[701]

When Worthington died in 1827 a mass meeting was held in Chillicothe and Creighton was among those appointed to a committee to make preparations for his funeral.[702]

Creighton was again elected to Congress and served from March 4, 1827 until his resignation in 1828 to accept a recess appointment by President John Quincy Adams to the vacancy in the United States District Court caused by the death of Charles Willing Byrd. He was nominated on December 11, 1828, after Jackson had won the election for President. His service terminated on February 16, 1829, after his nomination was not confirmed by the Senate which was now controlled by the Jacksonian Democrats. He was reelected to Congress in 1828 and 1830, serving from March 4, 1829 to March 3, 1833. He witnessed the fury of a popular political revolution which matched the fury of the revolution he had participated in thirty years earlier. Like the Federalists that were banished from power then, he must have felt the insult, anguish and frustration of the people's rejection. He was not a candidate for reelection. Following his retirement from Congress, he resumed his legal practice.

William and Elizabeth Creighton became members of St. Paul's Protestant Episcopal Church in 1834.[703]

---

701 C.C. Huntington, "Banking and Currency in Ohio before the Civil War", *Ohio History* Vol 24, pp. 289-333.

702 Alfred Byron Sears, *Thomas Worthington, Father of Ohio Statehood*, Ohio State University Press, 1958, p. 235.

703 M. Melissa Wolfe, "William and Elizabeth Creighton", *Timeline*, Vol. 15, No. 3, May/June, 1978, p. 54.

Creighton died on October 1, 1851, in Chillicothe and is interred at Grand View Cemetery.

DUNCAN McARTHUR

Duncan McArthur was born on January 14, 1772 in Duchess County, New York. His father John was born in Glenlyon, Perth, Scotland and immigrated to America. Duncan's mother died when he was three and his father remarried. Desperately poor, the family moved to Western Pennsylvania where Duncan grew up on the frontier and became an excellent backwoodsman. As soon as he was old enough he was hired out as a laborer to help support the family.[704].

In 1790 at the age of eighteen McArthur enlisted in a company of Pennsylvania volunteers recruited to serve under General Josiah Harmar in his campaign against the Indians. Harmar's expedition succeeded in destroying Indian villages and corn fields, but one of the companies was ambushed by the Indians, sustained severe losses, and was forced to retreat. As a result the expedition failed in its purpose of intimidating the Indians. Nonetheless, McArthur learned from the experience.[705]

In 1792 McArthur was stationed at Baker's Fort on the Virginia side of the Ohio River. A scouting party on the Indian side was attacked. Fourteen men including McArthur crossed the River and went up to the mouth of Captina Creek where the attack had occurred. They were ambushed by the Indians and their captain killed. McArthur though the youngest man in the group was chosen to direct the retreat. The Indians suffered so many casualties that they gave up the pursuit.[706] The story of the Battle of Captina Creek spread along the Ohio River settlements and McArthur gained a reputation for his bravery and coolness under fire.[707] He was employed by the State of Kentucky as a scout

---

704   Henry Howe, *Historical Collections of Ohio*, Centennial Edition, 1908, Vol 2, p. 505; C.H. Cramer, "Duncan McArthur: First Phase 1772-1812, Ohio History Vol. 45, p. 27; Ancestry World Tree, Ancestry.Com; Ross County Biographies web page.

705   C.H. Cramer, "Duncan McArthur: First Phase 1772-1812, *Ohio History* Vol. 45, p. 27; Alice McGuffey Morrill Ruggles, "The Father of the McGuffeys", *Ohio History*, Vol. 47, pp. 111-117.

706   Henry Howe, *Historical Collections of Ohio*, Centennial Edition, 1908, Vol. 1, p. 307; Alice McGuffey Morrill Ruggles, "The Father of the McGuffeys", *Ohio History*, Vol. 47, pp. 111-117.

707   Ross County Biographies web page.

along the Ohio River to watch for Indian war parties. He had many narrow escapes from pursuing Indians. His knowledge of Indian tactics and warfare increased.[708]

McArthur worked for Nathaniel Massie in his surveying expeditions into the Virginia Military District. He began as a chain bearer and scout. He taught himself surveying and became an assistant surveyor for Massie. He helped Massie layout Chillicothe. The log house which he erected near the village is said to have been the first white man's dwelling in the area. His bride Nancy McDonald joined him there in 1797. He became skilled at locating land for speculators and receiving part of the land as compensation for his services.[709]

McArthur was associated in business with Massie, Worthington, Langham, and his brother-in-law John McDonald, all of whom engaged in locating and surveying land for investors, selling land to new settlers, and speculating in land for their own account. McArthur was one if not the most successful of them all. A study of 1810 land owners showed him ranked third with 111 tracts totaling 35,341 acres.[710] Another author said he owned 90,000 acres.[711] He was reputed to be one of if not the wealthiest man in the state.[712]

In 1804-1805 McArthur constructed a fine mansion overlooking the Scioto Valley on his estate located northeast of Chillicothe. His estate was known as "Fruit Hill." He was a neighbor of Thomas Worthington. Like Thomas Worthington's Adena, his house became a center of hospitality for leaders of the community and state as well as visitors from the east or Europe.[713]

Following the organization of Ross County, McArthur was appointed a captain in the militia.[714] He was an ally of Worthington, Tiffin, Massie, and

---

708   C.H. Cramer, "Duncan McArthur: First Phase 1772-1812, *Ohio History* Vol. 45, p. 28.

709   C.H. Cramer, "Duncan McArthur: First Phase 1772-1812, Ohio History Vol. 45, pp. 28-29.

710   Lee Soltow, "Inequality Amidst Abundance; Land Ownership in Early 19th Century Ohio", *Ohio History,* Vol. 88, p. 13. R. Douglas Hurt, *The Ohio Frontier,* Indianapolis, 1996, p. 167, states Massie owned 28,400 acres and McArthur owned 21,132 acres in the Virginia Military District.

711   Jeffrey P. Brown, "Chillicothe Elite", *Ohio History*, Vol 96, p. 144.

712   *The Governors of Ohio*, Ohio Historical Society, 1969, p. 32; C.H. Cramer, "Duncan McArthur: First Phase 1772-1812, *Ohio History* Vol. 45, p. 29.

713   C.H. Cramer, "Duncan McArthur: First Phase 1772-1812, *Ohio History* Vol. 45, p. 29.

714   "The Executive Journal of the Northwest Territory", Ohio Historical Society web page, p. 513.

Baldwin in the statehood movement.[715] Because of his limited education and rough manners, McArthur was much more a man of the people than any of them. While they were gentlemen, he was an Indian fighter and backwoodsman skilled at locating good land in the wilderness. An English farmer visiting Worthington was introduced to his neighbor McArthur who he described as "a dirty and butcherlike man very unlike a soldier in appearance, seeming half savage and dressed like a backwoodsman." When Worthington spoke to him, he responded with a surly nod. Worthington remarked to the Englishman, "like General Jackson he is fit only for hard knocks and Indian warfare." Whatever McArthur knew, he had taught himself or learned through experience. Whatever he owned, he earned himself. He had no inheritance or rich wife to help him along. Although he drank and gambled "like a man", he unlike Baldwin and Langham was self-disciplined. He was a man of few words, and what he said was plain-spoken and good common sense.

Duncan McArthur was elected to the Ohio House of Representatives in 1804. During this session the Black Laws were enacted requiring black and mulatto persons to file with the clerk of the court where they resided a certificate from a court showing that they were free with a bond by a white property-owner that they would not become a public charge. They were required to reregister every two years.[716] In 1805 McArthur was elected to the Ohio Senate for a two year term. During the 1805-1806 session he participated in the trial and voted for conviction of William Irvin, an associate judge of Fairfield County who was impeached for failing to attend court and speaking slightingly of his duties. This was the first impeachment under the new Constitution.[717] During the 1806-1807 session he participated in the secret session dealing with the Burr Conspiracy. He was reelected for another two year term and during the 1807-1808 session the black laws were amended to prevent a black from testifying against a white or from suing a white person. During the 1808-1809 session he participated in the trial of Judges Calvin Pease and George Tod who were impeached for declaring an act of the legislature unconstitutional. Although McArthur voted with the

---

715   Alfred Byron Sears, *Thomas Worthington, Father of Ohio Statehood*, Ohio State University Press, 1958, pp. 86-87.

716   William A. Taylor, *Ohio Statesmen and Annals of Progress*, State of Ohio, 1899, pp. 43, 45.

717   William A. Taylor, *Ohio Statesmen and Annals of Progress*, State of Ohio, 1899, pp. 45-46; Article I, Sections 23, 24 of Ohio Constitution of 1802. Two thirds vote of all senators required for conviction.

majority for conviction, the vote for conviction was one short of the two thirds vote required for removal from office.[718] McArthur was reelected to the Senate in 1809 as the anti-court candidate against a pro-court candidate. During the 1809-1810 session McArthur was elected Speaker of the Senate. During this session the Sweeping Resolution was adopted declaring all judicial offices vacant and new appointments made to fill the vacant offices. McArthur blamed the resolution and resultant scramble for offices for the vote to move the state capital to Zanesville temporarily and the appointment of a commission to recommend a permanent location near the center of the state.[719] He was reelected in 1811 during the acrimonious campaign against the Tammany Society. McArthur parted company with Worthington and Tiffin during the campaign and came out against the Tammany organization. He blamed them for circulating accusations against him of drinking excessively and cheating at cards.[720] His political instincts were better than theirs. The public didn't like the idea of a secret organization controlling elections and didn't much care about drinking and card playing. An anti-Tammany majority was elected to the legislature. As a result the Sweeping Resolution was repealed in 1812.

In 1805 McArthur became a colonel in the militia. Three years later he was made a major general. In 1812 upon orders of Governor Meigs he recruited a regiment and joined General Hull at Dayton. He was one of three regimental commanders under Hull and accompanied him in his March to Detroit. McArthur was sent on an expedition to meet and escort a supply train and was not present when General Hull surrendered to the British. However, the surrender included him. He was paroled and returned to Ohio. He was later exchanged and released from parole. Hull was considered a traitor or coward for surrendering, but McArthur was considered a hero. Upon his return to Ohio he was nominated for and elected as one of the six new congressmen from Ohio with scarcely any opposition. He resigned shortly after his election in order to enter the military service of

718   William A. Taylor, *Ohio Statesmen and Annals of Progress*, State of Ohio, 1899, pp.55-56;

719   William A. Taylor, *Ohio Statesmen and Annals of Progress*, State of Ohio, 1899, pp. 58-59; Alfred Byron Sears, *Thomas Worthington, Father of Ohio Statehood*, Ohio State University Press, 1958, p. 149; Andrew R.L. Cayton, *Frontier Republic*, Kent State University Press, 1986, p. 105.

720   C. H. Cramer, "Duncan McArthur: First Phase 1772-1812", *Ohio History* Vol. 45, pp. 30-33.

the United States army. He was a witness in the court martial of General Hull and was highly critical of his performance.[721]

McArthur served under Harrison's command. He was in charge of Detroit at the time of the Battle of the Thames. When Harrison resigned McArthur was appointed commander of the army of the Northwest. Like Harrison before him, he became very frustrated with Washington's management of the War and army contractors who overcharged, provided poor quality supplies, and failed to deliver sufficient quantities when needed. He was also frustrated by the failure of the government to provide funds to pay the troops. This led to several threats of resignation. The highpoint of his service was an expedition of seven hundred mounted troops and Indian allies which conducted a raid two hundred miles into upper Canada in the fall of 1814. In March, 1815, a Treaty of Peace was made with Great Britain and McArthur left the army.[722]

McArthur was elected to the Ohio House of Representatives in 1815. The state capital was permanently removed to Columbus.[723] In 1816 he was appointed as a commissioner to negotiate a treaty with the Indians at Springwell near Detroit. The following year he negotiated a treaty at Fort Meigs by which nearly all the remaining Indian lands in Ohio were ceded to the United States. The following year he negotiated the Treaty with the Indians at St. Marys.

In 1817 he was elected to the Ohio House of Representatives and was chosen Speaker of the House.[724] A director of the United States Bank, he opposed the attacks made on it. The bank was widely blamed for the depression which began in 1818. As a result of his position on the bank, he lost a bid for reelection.[725] He was elected to the Ohio Senate in 1821. The following year he was elected to Congress. While in Congress he was a strong supporter of Henry Clay's "American System" for internal improvements and high tariffs. Upon

---

721   William A. Taylor, *Ohio Statesmen and Annals of Progress*, State of Ohio, 1899, pp. 73-74; Andrew R. L. Cayton, *Frontier Republic*, Kent State University Press, 1986, pp. 107-108; C. H. Cramer, "Duncan McArthur: The Military Phase", *Ohio History*, Vol. 46, pp. 128-147; *Governors of Ohio*, Ohio Historical Society, p. 32.

722   C. H. Cramer, "Duncan McArthur: The Military Phase", *Ohio History*, Vol. 46, pp. 128-147

723   William A. Taylor, *Ohio Statesmen and Annals of Progress*, State of Ohio, 1899, pp. 83-84.

724   William A. Taylor, *Ohio Statesmen and Annals of Progress*, State of Ohio, 1899, pp. 88-89.

725   Henry Howe, Howe's *Historical Collections of Ohio*, Centennial Edition, 1908 Vol. 2, p. 506.

completion of his term he returned to Chillicothe to focus on his business interests.[726] In 1826 he was elected to the Ohio House of Representatives.[727]

In 1829 McArthur was again elected to the Ohio Senate. He served in fifteen general assemblies. In 1830 he was elected Governor as a Whig defeating the Jacksonian democrat. He served for two years. During his term the work on the canals progressed and the National Road was completed to Zanesville. In 1830 he sustained a severe injury when an overhanging porch fell on him while he was walking on a sidewalk in Columbus. He never fully recovered from this injury. After completing his term as governor, he ran for Congress but was defeated by the Jacksonian Democrat candidate, thus ending his political career.[728]

McArthur died in Chillicothe on April 29, 1839. He was described as "a strong-minded energetic man and possessed an iron will. He was hospitable, close in business, and had many severe and bitter enemies."[729]

JOSEPH KERR

Joseph Kerr was born of Scotch ancestry in Chambersburg, Pennsylvania in 1765, and was married in that town to Nancy Dougherty in 1788.[730] He migrated to Ohio in 1792 where he served as an assistant surveyor for Nathaniel Massie.[731]

Following the organization of Adams County in 1797, Kerr was appointed a Justice of the Peace and Judge of the Court of Quarter Sessions.[732] He participated in the decision to move the county seat to Manchester which was overruled by Governor St. Clair. He also served as clerk of the county commissioners of Adams County.[733]

---

726   *Governors of Ohio*, Ohio Historical Society, p. 33.

727   William A. Taylor, *Ohio Statesmen and Annals of Progress*, State of Ohio, 1899, p. 128.

728   *Governors of Ohio*, Ohio Historical Society, pp. 33-34.

729   Henry Howe, *Historical Collections of Ohio*, Centennial Edition, 1908, p. 507.

730   William E. Gilmore, "General Joseph Kerr", *Ohio History*, Vol. 12, p. 165; Ancestry World Tree, Ancestry.com

731   Jeffrey P. Browne, "Chillicothe's Elite: Leadership in a Frontier Community", *Ohio History* Vol. 96, p. 144.

732   Richard C. Knopf, "Transcript of the Executive Journal of the Northwest Territory", p. 425, Ohio Historical Society web page.

733   "Joseph Kerr", Biographical Directory of the United States Congress web page.

Following the establishment of Chillicothe, Kerr purchased a large farm on the Scioto River a mile below Chillicothe from Nathaniel Massie where he moved in 1801. Like Worthington, McArthur, and other leading citizens, he constructed a showplace home. The title to his farm was the subject of protracted litigation with a Virginian by the name of Watts who claimed to have purchased the land first. After 18 years of litigation, Kerr lost the case, contributing to his financial ruin.[734]

He was an ally of Massie, Tiffin, and Worthington during the battle for Ohio statehood.

In addition to a land speculator, Kerr was a leading businessman of the Chillicothe area. By 1804 he established a meat packing business and shipped pork and wheat down the river to New Orleans. He was a competitor and sometimes a partner with Worthington in business ventures. By providing an outlet for the agricultural projects produced in the Scioto Valley, Kerr was an important contributor to the growth of the area economy. During the War he sold substantial supplies to the government. His inability to secure payment was another major factor in his eventual ruin. His ventures were risky and depended on the ability to borrow money. Another factor in his financial ruin was the collapse of the local currency and banking system following the decision of the Bank of the United States to demand payment in species. As a result he hated banks and was a leader of the campaign against the Bank. Kerr lost his land and was imprisoned for debt in the fall of 1816 and in 1818.[735]

Recognized as a Republican leader of Ross County, Kerr was elected to the Ohio Senate in 1804 where he served from 1804 to 1806. He was the only senator to vote against impeachment of William Irwin during the first impeachment trial of a judge in the Ohio Senate.[736]

---

734 William E. Gilmore, "General Joseph Kerr", *Ohio History*, Vol. 12, p. 165; Jeffrey P. Browne, "Chillicothe's Elite: Leadership in a Frontier Community", *Ohio History* Vol. 96, p. 150; Andrew R. L. Cayton, *The Frontier Republic*, Kent State University Press, 1986, p. 56.

735 Andrew R. L. Cayton, *The Frontier Republic*, Kent State University Press, 1986, pp. 122-123; Jeffrey P. Browne, "Chillicothe's Elite: Leadership in a Frontier Community", *Ohio History* Vol. 96, p. 144, 150; Alfred B. Sears, "Thomas Worthington: Pioneer Businessman of the Old Northwest", *Ohio History* Vol 58, p. 77; William T. Utter, *History of Ohio, The Frontier State*, Ohio Historical Society, 1942, Vol 2, p. 292.

736 William A. Taylor, *Ohio Statesmen and Annals of Progress*, Columbus, 1899, Vol 1, pp. 41, 45, 47.

As a result of Worthington's efforts, an Act of Congress was passed authorizing President Jefferson to appoint commissioners to lay out the National Road connecting Ohio to Maryland. Kerr was appointed by the President as one of three commissioners. Their first report was presented December 30, 1806.[737]

Kerr served in the Ohio House during the 1808-1809 session of the General Assembly and was a candidate for Speaker coming in second.[738] He did not vote for the impeachment of Pease and Tod.

During the War of 1812, Kerr served as a brigadier general of Ohio volunteers and was subsequently referred to as "General Kerr." He had previously served as the adjutant general of Ohio from 1809 to 1810.[739]

When Thomas Worthington resigned his seat in the U. S. Senate, Kerr was appointed by the General Assembly to fill his unexpired term and served from December 10, 1814 to March 3, 1815.[740] As a Senator he strongly opposed the chartering of the second United States Bank.[741]

Kerr was elected to the Ohio House of Representatives in 1818 and 1819 and was a strong supporter of measures taken against the Bank of the United States.[742] During his term, he was confined to jail at the request of the United States Bank for failure to pay a judgment.

Following the loss of his farm and business, in 1821 Kerr opened an inn in Chillicothe. In 1824 Kerr supported Jackson's candidacy, but Clay carried Ross County and Ohio.[743] Kerr's hopes for a bright future in Ohio were gone, and he left Ohio for the south first settling on land he had purchased near Memphis and then moving to Louisiana, near Lake Providence, where he developed a successful plantation. Kerr died on August 22, 1837, a year after two of his sons were killed by the Mexicans at the Alamo.[744]

---

737   Archer Butler Hulbert, "The Old National Road—The Historic Highway of America", *Ohio History*, Vol. 9, p. 421.

738   William A. Taylor, *Ohio Statesmen and Annals of Progress*, Columbus, 1899, Vol 1, pp. 55, 57.

739   "Joseph Kerr" Biographical Directory of the United States Congress web page.

740   William A. Taylor, *Ohio Statesmen and Annals of Progress*, Columbus, 1899, Vol 1, p. 80. He was elected on the fourth ballot in a close contest with Benjamin Ruggles who was elected to the subsequent term; "Joseph Kerr" Biographical Directory of the U. S. Congress web page.

741   Andrew R. L. Cayton, *The Frontier Republic*, Kent State University Press, 1986, p. 123.

742   Historical Directory of the Ohio House of Representatives, Columbus, 1966, p. 278;

743   Andrew R. L. Cayton, *The Frontier Republic*, Kent State University Press, 1986, p. 123.

744   Andrew R. L. Cayton, *The Frontier Republic*, Kent State University Press, 1986, p. 123; William E. Gilmore, "General Joseph Kerr", *Ohio History* Vol. 12, p. 166.

Chapter 5

FOUNDING FATHERS FROM CLERMONT COUNTY

Clermont County

Clermont County was organized by Governor St. Clair on December 6, 1800, with Williamsburg on the east branch of the Little Miami River as its county seat.[745] The county lay north of the Ohio River in the Virginia Military District with Hamilton County to its west and Adams County to its east.

The original county seat, Williamsburg, was originally called Lytlestown. It was laid out in 1795-1796 by William Lytle whose family came to Kentucky in 1779. He was engaged in several fierce encounters with the Indians while living in Kentucky. Like Nathaniel Massie, he was a surveyor in the Virginia Military District during the Indian wars and was frequently attacked by Indians. He served as a major general of the Ohio militia during the War of 1812 by appointment of the General Assembly, and in 1829 surveyor general of the public lands of Ohio, Indiana, and Michigan.[746]

Some of the first settlers came to the County to get away from the slave culture of Virginia and Kentucky. Reverend Francis McCormack, a Methodist preacher, left Kentucky in 1795 and settled just north of what became Milford, on the Little Miami eighteen miles above Cincinnati. Obed Denham, a Virginian, settled Bethel for the same reason. [747] Ezekiel Dimmit, a Virginian

---

745   Richard C. Knopf, *Transcription of the Executive Journal of the Northwest Territory*, p. 535.

746   Henry Howe, *Historical Collections of Ohio*, 1898, Vol. I, p. 416.

747   Henry Howe, *Historical Collections of Ohio*, 1898, Vol. I, pp. 411, 414.

who migrated to Kentucky and was persuaded to move to the Territory by Reverend McCormack, was the first settler of Batavia in 1797.[748] Batavia subsequently became the county seat.

Francis McCormack is considered as the father of Methodism in the Northwest Territory. He immigrated to Kentucky in 1795, more to preach the Gospel than for personal gain, and wanting to get away from slavery moved to Ohio where he settled near Milford north of Cincinnati. Finding that the local settlers lacked the facilities to practice their religion, he organized the first Methodist class in the Northwest Territory. It met at his cabin. He preached at nearby settlements and organized additional Methodist classes at Lockland and Columbia. He urgently appealed to the Methodist Circuit Riders traveling in Kentucky to send someone to minister to the needs of the settlers north of the Ohio. John Kobler responded and became the first regular Methodist traveling north of the Ohio in 1798. Reverend Philip Gatch arrived with his family shortly after Reverend Kobler began traveling in the area. He had known Kobler in the east. Gatch settled near McCormack at Milford. In 1799 Henry Smith was appointed to the Miami Circuit, the first Methodist Circuit north of the Ohio. Traveling throughout his long circuit, Hunt preached twenty sermons every three weeks and organized small societies in almost every settlement. After firmly establishing Methodism in Milford, McCormack moved to Salem in Hamilton County where he established another Methodist community.[749]

Clermont County was a center of early Methodism in Ohio, and several of the Methodist leaders were very anti-slavery on religious and moral grounds. Its two delegates to the convention were not only pro-statehood, but also adamantly anti-slavery and supportive of civil rights for blacks.[750]

---

748   Abel Stevens, *Compendius History of American Methodism*, New York, 1868, p. 408.

749   Abel Stevens, *Compendius History of American Methodism*, New York, 1868, pp. 334-335, 410-411.

750   Henry Howe, *Historical Collections of Ohio*, 1898, Vol. I, p. 419; Helen M. Thurston, "The 1802 Constitutional Convention and the Status of the Negro", *Ohio History* Vol. 81, pp. 15-37.

Clermont County Delegates

PHILIP GATCH

Philip Gatch was born March 2, 1751, near Baltimore, Maryland.[751] His grandfather brought his family to Maryland from Prussia in 1727 where he purchased a 130 acre farm which was inherited by Philip's father.[752]

In 1772 Philip began attending a Methodist meeting in his neighborhood and was converted. He organized a class which met at his home and was soon preaching at nearby meetings. Church leaders recognized his zeal and talent, made him a traveling preacher, and sent him off to New Jersey in 1773. He was the first itinerant Methodist preacher in that state. He continued this work until the second annual conference of the Methodists at Philadelphia in May, 1774, when he was admitted as a full preacher. In the organizational structure of the church, ministers were assigned to an area where they traveled a circuit preaching at meeting houses, residences, and in the open air. He was one of the first Methodist preachers recruited in America.[753]

He continued his service as a traveling preacher at assignments in Maryland, Delaware, and Virginia until 1778, when due to failing health he discontinued traveling. During his travels, he converted hundreds and perhaps thousands to Methodism. This was a time when Methodist preachers were frequently met with hostility. Since the leaders of the church were English, the Revolutionary period was a difficult time for their representatives in America. One time Gatch was attacked with a chair while conducting a service. Another time he was covered with tar from which he sustained a permanent injury to an eye. Still another time, two men assaulted him and twisted his arms in opposite directions to such an extent that his shoulders turned black. A history of the church states, "He was perhaps the subject of as much or more persecution for his Master's sake than any of his contemporaries."[754]

751   Louis H. Everts, *History of Clermont County, Ohio*, 1880, p. 462.
752   Virginia Gatch Markham. *Descendants of Godfrey and Maria Gatch of Baltimore Maryland. including the development of the Methodist Church and the work of Rev Phillip Gatch*. Allen Press Inc. Lawrence, KS; Byron Williams, History of Clermont and Brown Counties, 1913, Vol II, p. 119.
753   Abel Stevens, *Compendius History of American Methodism*, New York, 1868, pp. 82-85; Nathan Bangs, *History of the Methodist Episcopal Church*, New York, 1839, Vol. I, Book 2, Chapter 1.
754   Abel Stevens, *Compendius History of American Methodism*, New York, 1868, pp. 102, 133-135.

On January 17, 1778, Gatch married Elizabeth Smith and settled down on a plantation in Powhatan County, Virginia. In 1780 he emancipated the nine slaves who came to him through his wife. The deed of emancipation stated, "I do believe that all men are by their nature equally free, and from a clear conviction of injustice of depriving my fellow-creatures of their natural rights, and do hereby emancipate and set free the following persons:" Ten years later he moved to Buckingham County, Virginia. He was a member of an abolitionist society in that state.[755] During his time in Virginia he continued to preach as his health permitted.

Desiring no longer to live in a state where slavery was practiced, on October 11, 1798, he and his brother-in-law Rev. James Smith and friend Ambrose Ransom and others, white and black, totaling 36 persons left Virginia to settle in the Northwest Territory where slavery was prohibited. They came down the Ohio River on a flat boat from Pittsburgh to Cincinnati. Gatch had traded his land in Virginia for land on the Miami River, but when he arrived, he decided that land was not suitable for settlement. They secured a temporary house near Newtown. He then acquired land at the forks of the Miami where they moved as soon as their home was constructed.[756] They located near Rev. Francis McCormick, a local preacher, who had settled near Milford. McCormick had come to the Territory for similar reasons. The first Methodist class in Ohio met at his cabin. Rev. Gatch preached at meetings throughout the area.[757] His home was a meeting place for traveling Methodist preachers.

There were four or five local preachers in the Miami area in 1800, traveling throughout the area, preaching not only on Sundays but on other days as well. Women would walk twenty to thirty miles to attend a meeting at the Gatch home. Women would lodge in the cabins and men in the barns. Mrs. Gatch and wives of other leaders would provide meals for fifty to a hundred persons.[758]

---

755   Abel Stevens, *Compendius History of American Methodism*, New York, 1868, p. 135;, Louis H. Everts, *History of Clermont County*, p. 463.

756   Byron Williams, *History of Clermont and Brown Counties*, 1913, Vol. II, pp. 119-122.

757   Abel Stevens, *Compendius History of American Methodism*, New York, 1868, p. 410-411; Byron Williams, *History of Clermont and Brown Counties*, 1913, Vol. II, p. 467; Ford, *History of Hamilton County, Ohio*, 1881, p. 251; Byron Williams, *History of Clermont and Brown Counties*, 1913, Vol. I, pp. 231-234.

758   Ford, *History of Hamilton County, Ohio*, 1881, p. 251.

In August, 1801 a great revival was held at Cane Creek, Bourbon County, Kentucky, which attracted over 10,000 people from throughout Kentucky, Tennessee and Ohio. For a week, the crowds were treated with Presbyterian and Methodist ministers preaching night and day from tree stumps and wagon beds, singing, and praying. The preachers urged their listeners to save themselves from hellfire and damnation by repenting and accepting Christ as their Savior. Many fainted and others experienced uncontrollable jerking of their bodies as they were overcome with powerful emotions. Thousands were converted. A great awakening had begun in the West.[759]

The first revival in Ohio began at Reverend Gatch's cabin soon after the Cane Ridge revival. Following a sermon on a Sunday afternoon, he discovered a black boy whom he had raised leaning against a wall of his cabin and crying. When asked why he was crying, the boy fell to the floor and begged God for mercy in a loud voice. The congregation heard his cries and gathered around to help him. Soon the service had been resumed. It lasted into the night and resulted in several conversions. Frequent prayer meetings followed, and soon the revival spread throughout the area.[760]

The message of Methodists appealed to settlers on the Ohio frontier. Its message that every soul was important to God and that every person could be saved by repentance and faith resonated with the egalitarian sentiments of the early settlers. Methodist preachers were self-taught, plain speaking, and emotional. They aimed for the heart not the head of the listener.[761]

Gatch was appointed by Governor St. Clair as a judge of the Court of Quarter Sessions and Common Pleas on December 6, 1800, following the organization of Clermont County.[762]

Elected as a delegate to the constitutional convention, he served on the committees appointed to draft article one on the legislature, article two on the executive, and article three on the judiciary. He was one of the strongest advocates of the rights of blacks.[763]

---

759   Charles C. Cole, Jr., *Lion of the Forest, James B. Finley, Frontier Reformer*, University Press of Kentucky, 1994, pp. 4-5.

760   Charles C. Cole, Jr., *Lion of the Forest, James B. Finley, Frontier Reformer*, University Press of Kentucky, 1994, p. 35.

761   Henry A. Ford and Kate B. Ford, *History of Cincinnati*, Ohio, 1881, p. 153.

762   Richard C. Knopf, *Transcription of the Executive Journal of the Northwest Territory*, Ohio Historical Society web page, p. 535.

763   "Journal of Convention", *Ohio History*, Vol. V, p. 88, 92, 93;
       Helen M. Thurston, "The 1802 Constitutional Convention and the Status of the Negro", *Ohio History* Vol. 81, pp. 15-37.

Rev. Gatch was appointed by the General Assembly as an associate judge of Clermont County in 1803 and reappointed in 1810 and 1818, serving a total of twenty-one years.[764] Under Ohio's first constitution, each county had a common pleas court with responsibility for hearing civil and criminal cases in the county. The judges of each court consisted of a president or presiding judge who presided over all the counties in a district. The presiding judge was a full-time judge with legal training who traveled from county to county in his district, of which there were originally three in the state. Francis Dunlavy was the presiding judge for Clermont County. In addition to the presiding judge, each county had at least two and not more than three associate judges who resided in the county. The associate judges were generally not trained in the law, and they met only when the presiding judge came to the county and the court was in session. All the judges were elected by joint ballot of both houses of the General Assembly and served for terms of seven years.[765] One can imagine the dignity, moral tone and confidence which Rev. Gatch's presence on the bench brought to the judicial proceedings of Clermont County during the first two decades of the County's history. The fact that he was reappointed twice after his initial seven year term certainly demonstrates the high esteem in which he was held.

Reverend Gatch is credited with being instrumental in laying the foundation of Methodism in the west.[766] The county history describes him as follows, "Rev. Philip Gatch, a man of deep piety and zeal, strong in the faith of the Gospel, was one of the first ministers to advocate the Methodist belief in America. He was unassuming in manner, quiet, peaceful and harmonious; standing high in the esteem of the community in which he lived. He was a man of strong mind, not easily turned from a course he believed to be right, enduring with gentleness and Christ-like attitude the persecutions that were heaped upon the ministers in those early days, being ready to suffer and die for the truth."[767]

Rev. Gatch preached his last sermon when he was 84 years old and died the following year on December 28, 1835. His son Thomas served four terms in the state legislature and his son Philip like his father was a circuit riding Methodist minister as a young man and then a local preacher.[768]

---

764   William A. Taylor, *Ohio Statesmen and Annals of Progress*, State of Ohio, 1899, pp. 37, 60, 90.

765   Ohio Constitution of 1802, Article III.

766   Matthew Simpson, Editor, *The Encyclopedia of Methodism*, Philadelphia, 1878.

767   Byron Williams, *History of Clermont and Brown Counties*, 1913, Vol. II, p. 119.

768   Louis H. Everts, *History of Clermont County*, 1880, p. 463.

JAMES SARGENT

James Sargent was born in Montgomery County, Maryland, January 25, 1748. His father James Sargent was born and raised on Snow Hill Farm, outside London, England, and migrated to America where he married Ann Taylor in 1735. They settled in Frederick County, Maryland. James Jr. married Philena Pigman in 1773; in 1796 they moved west to Kentucky. He purchased a large tract in what is now the southwestern part of Washington and southeastern part of Franklin Townships, Clermont County, where they moved in 1798. They settled in the southern part of the County near the Ohio River. Before leaving Maryland, he freed his slaves and vowed to live in a land free of that system.[769]

James and his father and brothers participated in the Revolutionary War as associators in Frederick County, Maryland.[770]

James Sargent ground grain into flour for his neighbors with a hand mill using mill irons which he brought from Maryland before 1800. In a few years the mill was converted to water power, and later a large mill was erected known as Sargent's Mill. In subsequent years as many as one thousand barrels of flour per year were shipped down the Ohio from the landing at Chilo nearby.[771]

Sargent was elected to the constitutional convention as a pro-statehood, anti-slavery delegate. He served on the committee to draft article five on the militia.[772] The article which the convention adopted on the militia provided that except for the top officers who were appointed by the General Assembly officers of the militia would be elected by their subordinates.[773] His votes against slavery and for Black civil rights placed him among the four delegates who were most supportive of equal right rights for Blacks.[774]

James Sargent had been converted to Methodism while in Maryland. In 1799 Rev. Lewis Hunt organized a class at Sargent's home. His cabin was twenty foot square, but large enough to accommodate the meetings held there except sometimes on Sunday some of the congregation sat outside the front door. People would walk twenty to thirty miles to attend a meeting. In the

---

769   Louis H. Everts, *History of Clermont County*, 1880, p. 337.

770   *Maryland Historical Magazine*, Vol. II, p. 172.

771   Louis H. Everts, *History of Clermont County*, 1880, p. 341.

772   Journal of Constitutional Convention of 1802", *Ohio History*, Vol. V, p. 96.

773   Ohio Constitution of 1802, Article V.

774   Helen M. Thurston, "The 1802 Constitutional Convention and the Status of the Negro", *Ohio History* Vol. 81, p. 27.

summer they would walk in their bare feet. When Rev. Henry Smith replaced Rev Hunt as the traveling preacher for this area, he stayed at the cabin of James Sargent, an old Maryland Methodist friend.[775] The first Methodist meeting house in the Miami Circuit was a log building known as "Old Hopewell Church" erected in 1805 which the Sargents attended.[776]

Sargent was elected to the state Senate in October, 1803, and served his first term in the second session of the General Assembly which convened on December 5, 1803, and the third session which convened December 3, 1804. He was reelected and served in the fourth and fifth sessions of the General Assemblies in 1805-1806 and 1806-1807. On October 13, 1807, he was defeated for reelection.[777]

According to the County history, Senator Sargent was instrumental in the passage of a law authorizing arrest of persons and seizure of goods engaged in the conspiracy of Aaron Burr.[778] The second day of the legislative session in December, 1806, Governor Tiffin presented to both houses of the Assembly a confidential message which he had received from an envoy from President Jefferson. It was believed that former Vice President Aaron Burr and several prominent western politicians had organized a plan to separate the western states from the national government, seize New Orleans from the Spanish, and establish an independent state which would be protected by the British. According to the information, the conspirators included Harmon Blennerhasset who owned an island below Marietta which was being used as gathering place for boats and supplies. The message urged that Ohio take action to thwart that part of the conspiracy taking place within its boundaries. The Ohio constitution provided that the doors of each house would remain open to the public except in such cases as in the opinion of the house require secrecy.[779] This clearly seemed like a case where secrecy was justified because if news got out, the conspirators would flee before action could be taken. Nonetheless, Nathaniel Massie protested that action taken in secret would violate the constitution. Although his arguments delayed action for a day, a law was promptly passed behind closed doors which authorized the arrest of persons and seizure of goods involved in the conspiracy. As a result the militia in

---

775   Louis H. Everts, *History of Clermont County*, Ohio, 1880, p. 174.

776   Louis H. Everts, *History of Clermont County*, 1880, p. 353; "A Trip Along the Boundaries of my Second Circuit", *Footprints*, Chapter 11.

777   Louis H. Everts, *History of Clermont County*, Ohio, 1880, p. 124.

778   Louis H. Everts, *History of Clermont County*, Ohio, 1880, p. 125.

779   Ohio Constitution of 1802, Article I, Section 15.

Marietta under the command of General Joseph Buell seized several flatboats of the conspirators, and the militia in Cincinnati were alerted to search and seize any boats passing that City.[780]

Sargent was also elected as a justice of the peace for his township.[781]

James Sargent died December 13, 1826, survived by two sons and four daughters.[782]

780   William T. Utter, *History of the State of Ohio*, Vol II, *The Frontier State*, Ohio Historical Society, 1942, pp. 69-73.

781   Louis H. Everts, *History of Clermont County, Ohio*, 1880, p. 124.

782   Louis H. Everts, *History of Clermont County, Ohio*, 1880, p. 337.

Chapter 6

FOUNDING FATHERS FROM JEFFERSON COUNTY

The Seven Ranges

By 1785 the Continental Congress, operating under the Articles of Confederation, had obtained the agreement of the various states to relinquish their claims in Ohio except for Virginia's reserve between the Scioto and the Miami Rivers and Connecticut's reserve along Lake Erie. A law was passed in May, 1785, providing for the survey of lands in eastern Ohio.[783] The land was to be surveyed into six mile square townships, comprised of thirty-six sections of six hundred forty acres each. Each north-south row of townships was called a range. Seven ranges of townships were surveyed; hence the area was called "The Seven Ranges." Thomas Hutchins, the federal "Geographer", directed the surveys, and each of the states was to provide a surveyor. The surveys began in 1786 and between July and the following February, the first four ranges were surveyed. Sales began in 1787 in New York. Public sales were held in New York between September 21 and October 9, 1787, which resulted in completed sales of only 72,974 acres for $117,708.

The disappointing attempt to sell lands in the Seven Ranges was the result of several factors including the fact that the minimum size of tracts for sale was 640 acres, the minimum price of $1.00 per acre plus cost of survey was higher than land could be purchased in the eastern states, Indian hostility, and the

---

783   Land law of May 20, 1785, *A Compilation of Laws Treaties, Resolutions and Ordinances of the General and State Governments which Relate of Lands of the State of Ohio,* Columbus, 1825, reprinted by Arthur W. McGraw, 1996, pp. 15-17.

prevalence of squatters taking unlawful possession of federal land.[784] The situation with the squatters and the Indians created a serious question in the minds of many whether the federal government really had anything to sell. It should also be noted that during 1787 the Continental Congress had authorized the Board of Treasury to enter into contracts for the sale of 5,000,000 acres extending along the Ohio River from the western boundary of the Seven Ranges to the Scioto River, of which 1,500,000 acres was allocated to the Ohio Company and the balance to the Scioto Company. A contract was also made for the sale of 1,000,000 acres between the Miami Rivers to John Cleve Symmes of New Jersey.[785] From the perspective of potential investors in the Seven Ranges this was a classic case of supply far exceeding demand, compounded by uncertainties created by Indian hostility, squatters, and a proposed new government under the framework of the Constitution drafted at Philadelphia which had not yet been ratified by the states.

The absence of legal title to land did not deter settlement along the western bank of the Ohio and its tributaries, nor did resolutions of Congress demanding that trespassers vacate, nor even a detachment of troops dispatched by Colonel Harmar at Fort McIntosh to order them off and burn their cabins. These people were hardy pioneers who followed the border west across western Pennsylvania and Virginia and then across the Ohio. They marked their claim with a tomahawk cut into trees on its boundaries, cleared enough land for a cabin and corn patch, and if forced to leave, simply moved away until the soldiers left and then moved back, or moved on and made a clearing at a new location and erected a new cabin. There were settlements at what later became Tiltonville, Warrenton, Steubenville, and Mingo Junction. The settlers in this forbidden territory even met and adopted a constitution and elected a governor.[786]

---

784   Benjamin Horace Hibbard, *A History of the Public Land Policies*, New York, 1939, pp. 41-43.

785   Benjamin Horace Hibbard, *A History of the Public Land Policies*, New York, 1939, pp. 45-52.

786   W. H. Hunter, "The Pathfinders of Jefferson County," *Ohio History*, Vol VI, pp. 135-139; Robert H. Richardson, *Tilton Territory*, Dorrance and Company, Philadelphia, 1977, pp. 95-113; Joseph B. Doyle, *20th Century History of Steubenville and Jefferson County, Ohio*, Chicago, 1910, pp. 107-122: Charles A. Hanna, *Historical Collections of Harrison County, Ohio*, 1900, p. 43-52; Andrew R.L. Cayton, *The Frontier Republic*, Kent State University Press, 1986, pp. 3-11.

Jefferson County

The surveyors who arrived in 1786 to begin the surveys of the Seven Ranges were accompanied by troops from Fort McIntosh who were dispatched to protect them and their supplies from the Indians. The soldiers constructed a fort consisting of four block houses connected with a tall log fence. Inside the fort were barracks, storerooms, magazine, kitchens, and jail. The fort was named Fort Steuben after the Prussian general who had rendered valuable service to Washington's army during the Revolution. It was located at the future site of Steubenville. The troops left for Fort Harmar at the mouth of the Muskingum in 1787, but the fort was used by the surveyors and residents of the area until it burned down in 1790.[787]

Following the settlement of the Indian question by the Treaty of Greenville, Congress adopted the Land Act of May 18, 1796, which among other matters directed that the unsold lands in the Seven Ranges again be offered for sale. The minimum size of tracts sold was a section (approximately 640 acres) and the minimum price $2.00 per acre. Sales were to be held at Philadelphia and Pittsburgh. On October 4, 1796, at the opening of the sale in Pittsburgh, Bezaleel Wells and James Ross, acting as partners, met with Winthrop Sargent, who represented Governor St. Clair at the sale. They purchased eight sections containing 3,536.5 acres costing $7,077. Ross was a Senator from Pennsylvania and close political ally of Governor St. Clair. Wells was a large land-owner on the eastern side of the Ohio. He was also a surveyor and used money due him for his work to pay for his share of the land. Wells proceeded to survey and lay-out on two hundred acres of the purchase the first legal settlement in the Seven Ranges. It included the old site of Fort Steuben, and so he named the town Steubenville. On July 29, 1797, Winthrop Sargent, Territorial Secretary and acting Governor, visited Steubenville with Wells. Being convinced of the merits of the location, he organized a new county to be known as Jefferson and designated Steubenville as the county seat. Wells then advertised the lots for sale at auction on August 25. Ninety-one lots were sold for $5,607.[788]

---

787   Joseph B. Doyle, <u>2</u>0th Century History of Steubenville and Jefferson County, Ohio, Chicago, 1910, pp. 123-127; W. H. Hunter, "The Pathfinders of Jefferson County," Ohio History, Vol VI, pp. 189-193; S. P. Hildreth, Pioneer History, Cincinnati, 1848, pp. 179-181, quoting from journal of John Mathews.

788   Thornton Heald, Bezaleel Wells, Founder of Canton and Steubenville, Canton, 1948, p. 23.

Although the first houses in Steubenville were log cabins, in 1798 Wells began construction of a manor house on the river front which was completed in 1800. The place was called "The Grove", and for many years it was one of the finest houses in Ohio where Wells' guests were entertained in lavish style. Steubenville was a stop for riverboats traveling from Pittsburgh to Kentucky and a market town for settlers located to the west. It received a boost in 1800 when Congress designated Steubenville as the location of the land office for the Seven Ranges. The Land law adopted by Congress on May 10, 1800, at the urging of William Henry Harrison, encouraged purchase of lands by settlers by reducing the minimum size tract to half a section (approximately 320 acres) and providing for payment over four years. Settlers who still could not afford government terms could buy land from Ross and Wells at a higher price but more favorable terms.[789]

A large proportion of the settlers of Jefferson County were Scotch-Irish from western Pennsylvania and the panhandle of Virginia. Scotch-Irish immigrants had settled along the frontier and as the frontier moved westward across the mountains, the Scotch-Irish were in the forefront. By 1790 the population of the four western counties of Pennsylvania had swelled to sixty-three thousand. The Indian wars had created a dam which held back the tide westward. After Wayne's defeat of the Indians at Fallen Timbers and the signing of the Greenville Treaty, the dam broke and the Scotch-Irish poured into eastern Ohio. They brought their Presbyterian religion with them and their love of independence and hostility to aristocracy.[790]

The Quakers provided another large group of early settlers to eastern Ohio. Most of them came from North Carolina and Virginia. They were seeking a fresh-start in a land free of slavery which they abhorred. Since the Ordinance of 1787 prohibited slavery in the Northwest Territory, the new Ohio lands were attractive to them. Since Quakers had their own distinctive culture and for the most part married within the faith, they congregated in close-knit communities. Mount Pleasant in Jefferson County was an important Quaker community.[791]

---

789 Land Law of May 10, 1800, *A Compilation of Laws Treaties, Resolutions and Ordinances of the General and State Governments which Relate of Lands of the State of Ohio*, Columbus, 1825, reprinted by Arthur W. McGraw, 1996, pp. 40-47; W. H. Hunter, "The Pathfinders of Jefferson County," *Ohio History*, Vol VI, p. 211.

790 W. H. Hunter, "The Pathfinders of Jefferson County," *Ohio History*, Vol VI, p. 95-111; Charles A. Hanna, *Historical Collections of Harrison County, Ohio*, 1900, pp. 1-21.

791 Charles A. Hanna, *Historical Collections of Harrison County, Ohio*, 1900, p. 23-33; W. H. Hunter, "The Pathfinders of Jefferson County," *Ohio History*, Vol. VI, p. 262-264; *History of Belmont & Jefferson County, Ohio*, p. 535.

Jefferson County was organized by Winthrop Sargent acting for the Governor on July 29, 1797. He designated Steubenville as its county seat. It was the fourth county organized in what is now Ohio.[792]

Jefferson County Delegates

BEZALEEL WELLS

Bezaleel Wells was born January 28, 1763, about ten miles northwest of Baltimore, Maryland. He was the son of Alexander Wells, a self-educated surveyor.[793] Alexander migrated west with his wife and Bezaleel's older brothers where they became the first settlers of what would become Cross Creek Township, Washington County, Pennsylvania. In 1775 Alexander purchased fifteen hundred acres on Cross Creek, using soldiers' bounties from the French and Indian War which he had purchased. The British government had in 1754 offered to pay two hundred thousand acres on the east side of the upper Ohio to volunteers who served with the colonial troops.[794]

During the 1770s there was a contest between Virginia and Pennsylvania for control of this area. Each state appointed officials to govern the area which led to conflict and legal uncertainty. The controversy was finally settled by agreement between the two states in 1780. As part of the agreement Washington County became part of Pennsylvania, but Pennsylvania recognized the titles of people such as Alexander Wells who claimed land under Virginia law.

Alexander built the first grist mill in this part of the country in 1775. He also built a saw mill to serve the area. He erected a stockade fort to protect area settlers from Indian attack. He built a log house in 1781. As the settlement grew, he established a general merchandise store, a tannery, blacksmith shop, and distillery.[795]

---

792   Joseph B. Doyle, *20th Century History of Steubenville and Jefferson County, Ohio*, Chicago, 1910, p. 129.

793   Edward Thornton Heald, *Bezaleel Wells, Founder of Canton and Steubenville*, Canton, 1948, p. 1.

794   Edward Thornton Heald, *Bezaleel Wells, Founder of Canton and Steubenville*, Canton, 1948, pp. 6-7.

795   Edward Thornton Heald, *Bezaleel Wells, Founder of Canton and Steubenville*, Canton, 1948, p. 10.

In those days westerners had no way of selling their surplus grain because of the high cost of transportation, so it was converted to whiskey which could be transported and sold. This led to controversy when the federal government enacted a tax on whiskey. In the summer of 1794 the Whiskey Rebellion broke out when western farmers protested the tax and attacked the officials appointed to collect it. The controversy ended when President Washington sent federal troops across the mountains to quash the rebellion. Washington County was a center of the rebellion.[796]

In the late 1780s and early 1790s Alexander began to dispose of his properties on Cross Creek and investing in lots and land in Charlestown (renamed Wellsburg in 1816). In 1792 he moved to Charlestown.[797] Charlestown was located on the east bank of the Ohio River and promised to be an important stop for settlers traveling down the River to Kentucky as well as for settlers moving west across the River.

Bezaleel had been left with an uncle in Baltimore when the family moved west so that he could pursue his education. His education included either graduating or at least obtaining a surveyor's certificate from William and Mary College. When his education was complete, Bezaleel joined his family in the West. He became a prominent surveyor. He returned east to marry his boyhood sweetheart Rebecca Risteau on May 19, 1795.[798]

Bezaleel Wells became acquainted with James Ross, the leading attorney in Pittsburgh, who was the leader of the Federalist Party in western Pennsylvania and a United States Senator. A friend of George Washington, Ross served as his agent for the sale of his extensive holdings in the West. Both Wells and Ross were friends of Arthur St. Clair, governor of the Northwest Territory.

Although the Seven Ranges had been the first land surveyed in Ohio, and the land had been offered for sale in 1787, the sales had been disappointing and no further effort had been made to sell this land until the Indian War ended with Wayne's defeat of the Indians at Fallen Timbers and the Greenville Treaty in 1795. In 1796 Congress passed a new land law which made a second attempt to market land in the Seven Ranges. The law authorized sale of lands at a land office in Pittsburgh. Wells and Ross knew that the Indian War had blocked the westward tide of settlers migrating to the West and that western

---

796   Edward Thornton Heald, *Bezaleel Wells, Founder of Canton and Steubenville*, Canton, 1948, pp. 13-14.

797   Edward Thornton Heald, *Bezaleel Wells, Founder of Canton and Steubenville*, Canton, 1948, p. 11.

798   Edward Thornton Heald, *Bezaleel Wells, Founder of Canton and Steubenville*, Canton, 1948, pp. 3, 10, 16.

Pennsylvania and Northern Virginia were filled with settlers eager to move across the Ohio. They knew that there was an increasing flow of immigrants from the east coming to Pittsburgh and then down the Ohio seeking new land. They knew that the Federal land laws precluded most of these immigrants from purchasing land directly from the government because they did not have the money to buy an entire township or section. This was a perfect opportunity for men with means to buy the best sections of land with the expectation of subdividing it and selling it on terms the incoming settlers could afford. They also believed they had the political connections to assure that political decisions would benefit the value of their holdings.

When the Land Office opened on October 24, 1796, Wells and Ross met Winthrop Sargent, Secretary and acting Governor of the Northwest Territory and purchased eight sections totaling 3,536.5 acres. By November 20, 1799, Wells and Ross had purchased 15,700 acres representing an investment of $31,400 in the Seven Ranges. Ross and Wells signed an Agreement making them equal partners in their land investments.[799] Wells received an advance of his inheritance from his father to assist in his purchase.

Wells promptly surveyed two hundred acres of his land into town lots at a good location on the River. This became the first legal settlement in the Seven Ranges. He named his town Steubenville after Fort Steuben, which had been built there in 1786 to protect the surveyors and had burned in 1790. On July 29, 1797, Winthrop Sargent, acting Governor, established Jefferson County and designated Steubenville as its county seat. Two days later Sargent appointed the county officers, which included Wells as Probate Judge, Prothonotary to the Court of Common Pleas, and Clerk of the Court of General Quarter Sessions of the Peace. This meant that Wells would be responsible for the important records of the new county.[800]

The Steubenville lots were advertised for sale in the Pittsburgh paper and on August 25, 1797, ninety-one lots were sold for $5,607. By 1803 he had sold 12,706 acres of wilderness lands for $48,388.[801] In 1810 he owned 19 tracts in Ohio totaling 5,402 acres.[802]

---

799   Edward Thornton Heald, *Bezaleel Wells, Founder of Canton and Steubenville,* Canton, 1948, pp. 23-24.

800   Edward Thornton Heald, *Bezaleel Wells, Founder of Canton and Steubenville,* Canton, 1948, pp. 25-27.

801   Edward Thornton Heald, *Bezaleel Wells, Founder of Canton and Steubenville,* Canton, 1948, pp. 27-29.

802   Lee Soltow, "Inequality Amidst Abundance: Land Ownership in Early 19th Century Ohio", *Ohio History,* Ohio Historical Society, Vol. 88, p. 150.

Following the death of his first wife, Wells returned to Maryland and in February, 1798, married Sarah Griffith of Rockville, Maryland. During that year Wells began construction of a large manor house on the edge of Steubenville which was completed and occupied in 1800. Called "The Grove", it was a stately mansion rivaling Blennerhassett built by Harmon Blennerhassett on an island near Marietta and Adena built by Thomas Worthington in Chillicothe. For a quarter century Mr. and Mrs. Wells entertained here with lavish hospitality.[803]

Wells donated land for the county courthouse and jail as well as city hall in Steubenville. He constructed a saw mill and grist mill on Wells Run south of town in 1802. He erected the first school building in the village in 1807, called "The Little Red School House" because of its red paint.

Wells was elected as a delegate to the constitutional convention despite the fact that he was a Federalist. Prior to his election he stated that he supported statehood. At the convention he served on the committees to draft article one on the legislature, article two on the executive and article three on the judiciary. He also served on the committee to draft the counteroffer to the terms offered by Congress in the Enabling Act of 1802 for the admission of the state.[804] Although a Federalist, it seems clear that he was respected by Republican leaders of the convention.

Following the adoption of the constitution, elections were held in January for the first General Assembly to be convened on March 1. Wells was elected to represent Jefferson County in the state Senate. All the representatives elected in Jefferson County that January were Federalists. Jefferson County was the only county in the state where Federalists were elected.[805] The Republicans challenged the election without success and claimed that the Federalists had stolen the election. The following fall the Republicans won all the seats; however, Wells had been elected for a two year term and served for another session of the legislature.[806]

On March 26, 1804, Congress passed a new Land Law which made it easier for ordinary settlers to buy land from the Federal Government. The Land Law

---

803   Edward Thornton Heald, *Bezaleel Wells, Founder of Canton and Steubenville*, Canton, 1948, pp. 32-33.

804   "Journal of the Constitutional Convention of 1802", *Ohio History* Vol. 5, pp. 88-89, 92-93, 101.

805   Edward Thornton Heald, *Bezaleel Wells, Founder of Canton and Steubenville*, Canton, 1948, p. 54.

806   William A. Taylor, *Ohio Statesmen and Annals of Progress*, Columbus, 1899, Vol. 1, p. 38.

of 1804 reduced the minimum size tract from 320 to 160 acres and provided for payment in four annual installments. This was a further improvement on Harrison's Land Law of 1800. The Government was now in the retail land business. This did not mean there was no money to be made by a land developer like Wells. He financed those who could not afford the government's terms, and he leased land. He also sought to control the best locations.

From his service in the legislature Wells knew that a county would be split off the west side of Columbiana. He also knew that the county seat would be located near the center. The key to a successful investment was to choose a good location, buy up the land in the area, layout and promote a town and have it designated as a county seat, just as he had done in the case of Steubenville. In 1805 he laid out the town of Canton and began selling lots in 1806. He donated land for a school, a church and cemetery. Stark County was organized and Canton selected as the county seat in 1809.[807]

Wells was not simply a land speculator. He also engaged in a number of business interests. He was the promoter and first president of the first bank in Steubenville. It was the third bank incorporated in the state. He also organized the Steubenville Water Company to provide a water supply to the town. In 1812 he organized a woolen factory, which was the largest west of the Alleghenies and one of the seven most prominent in the country. Recognizing the need for fine wool for his factory and owning open plains west of Canton which were suitable for sheep pastures, Wells invested in merino sheep imported from Spain. At one time he owned a flock of over four thousand head.[808]

The sheep and woolen business was very successful during the War of 1812 because during that time there were no imports from England and the government was a large purchaser of woolen products for soldiers. After the War ended the country was flooded with woolen imports from England. The import problem was compounded by a severe depression which began in 1818 due to the United States Bank requiring payment of debts in United States currency. This meant that notes issued by Ohio banks were no longer acceptable. Bank notes had been the principal currency used in Ohio prior to that time. As a result of these problems Wells woolen business faced severe

---

807   Edward Thornton Heald, The Stark County Story, Vol. I, pp. 1-3; Edward Thornton Heald, *Bezaleel Wells, Founder of Canton and Steubenville*, Canton, 1948, pp. 60-65.

808   Edward Thornton Heald, *Bezaleel Wells, Founder of Canton and Steubenville*, Canton, 1948, pp. 134-164.

financial problems.[809] Nonetheless, from 1815 to 1830 as a result of his and his partner's efforts the Steubenville area became the wool capital of the United States. Wells was considered the most important businessman in southeastern Ohio.

In 1812 and 1814 the Federalists nominated Wells for Congress against the Republican candidate James Caldwell from Belmont County. Both had served in the constitutional convention and both were considered leading business-men in their respective areas. The Republicans were able to win both times.[810]

In 1820 Steubenville was the second most important manufacturing center in the State behind Cincinnati, and it trailed only that city in population. By this time the steam boat had revolutionized river traffic on the Ohio. The first steamboat manufactured in Steubenville was named the Bezaleel Wells in honor of the village's illustrious citizen.

In 1830 Wells' business empire collapsed. Just as the empire had grown with the assistance of Wells political influence through the years, including a gov-ernment loan to build his factory, so his downfall came from a political enemy. When Andrew Jackson was elected President, Wells government loan was called and when payment could not be made a judgment was entered against Wells and his company. Bank loans were also called and reduced to judgment. A total of $232,000 in judgments was entered against Wells and his partner. At that time this was a huge debt. The factory was closed and liquidated, his merino flock was auctioned, and his home and lands were sold at sheriff's sale. He even suffered the humiliation of being put in debtor's prison at Steubenville for a time and taking a pauper's oath.[811]

Wells activities were not limited to business. He organized the Steubenville Academy in 1811 for the purpose of providing advanced education for the young people in the area.[812] He played an important part in the establishment of Kenyon College and the Kenyon Theological Seminary and served as a trustee of those institutions from their incorporation until he retired from business. He was instrumental in the establishment of St. Paul's Parish of the

---

809   Edward Thornton Heald, *Bezaleel Wells, Founder of Canton and Steubenville*, Canton, 1948, pp. 165-167.

810   Donald J. Ratcliffe, "The Experience of Revolution and the Beginnings of Party Politics in Ohio", *Ohio History*, Vol. 85, p. 215.

811   Edward Thornton Heald, *Bezaleel Wells, Founder of Canton and Steubenville*, Canton, 1948, pp. 176-180.

812   Edward Thornton Heald, *Bezaleel Wells, Founder of Canton and Steubenville*, Canton, 1948, p. 181.

Episcopalian Church in Steubenville and served as senior warden almost continuously from its establishment until his death.[813]

After loss of his home and other assets, Wells went to live on a farm owned by his son Alexander, where he lived until his death in 1846 at the age of 83. Despite his financial collapse, he was still regarded as a man of the highest character.[814]

His biographer stated, "Bezaleel Wells was an outstanding representative of the American system of free individual enterprise when it was least trammeled. He exhibited unusual qualities as a promoter and publicist. An uncanny sense for proper timing was an outstanding characteristic. In his large Jefferson and Stark County investments he showed thorough preparation before he acted, but once having adopted an undertaking he carried it through with boldness, imagination, and dispatch.[815]

JOHN MILLIGAN

John Milligan was born May 20, 1762, in Cecil County, Maryland.[816] He was the son of James Milligan, a native of Scotland, and his wife Mary.[817] He grew up in a Scotch-Irish community in colonial Maryland and as a teenager witnessed the hardships of the Revolutionary War. As a young man he witnessed the economic and political turmoil following the War. After the War, his father purchased land which had been confiscated by the State from the heirs of Lord Baltimore where the family lived and developed a three hundred thirty acre farm which was called Fair Hill.[818] John Milligan married Catherine Williams of Cecil County on October 21, 1794. Her family owned slaves.

---

813   Edward Thornton Heald, *Bezaleel Wells, Founder of Canton and Steubenville*, Canton, 1948, p. 192.

814   Edward Thornton Heald, *Bezaleel Wells, Founder of Canton and Steubenville*, Canton, 1948, p. 180.

815   Edward T. Heald, *Bezaleel Wells, Founder of Canton and Steubenville, Ohio*, Stark County Historical Society, 1948, p. 193.

816   Letter from T. V. Milligan to Charles E. Rice dated May 6, 1895, Rice Manuscript Collection, Ohio Historical Society; Fred J. Milligan, *John Milligan of Jefferson County, Ohio*, 1994, Ohio Historical Society Library.

817   Fred J. Milligan, *The Life and Times of James and Mary Milligan of Cecil County, Maryland and Jefferson County, Northwest Territory*, 1994, Ohio Historical Society.

818   patent, Maryland State Archives, MSA S11, Land Office IC#E, p. 493; survey Maryland State Archives, MSA S1194, Land Office Certificate#288.

Following the sale of their farm in Cecil County, Maryland in 1799, the Milligan family headed west to the Village of Steubenville, Jefferson County, Northwest Territory.[819] John Milligan visited Steubenville in 1798, and on June 4, 1799, he purchased a lot there from Bezaleel Wells.[820] John and his father purchased 525 acres five miles west of Steubenville in what would become Island Creek Township, where the family located.[821]

On September 9, 1801, John Milligan was appointed a justice of the Peace and associate judge of the common pleas court by Charles Willing Byrd, Secretary of the Territory, acting for Governor St. Clair in his absence.[822] He was a representative of Jefferson County in the second territorial legislature which met on November 23, 1801, at Chillicothe. He arrived with Thomas McCune. The two of them were leaders of the Scotch-Irish settlers in Jefferson County and politically were Republican. The third representative from Jefferson County was Bezaleel Wells, a Federalist.[823] Milligan voted with Thomas Worthington and his allies against the plan of the Federalists to divide the state at the Scioto. He was in Chillicothe at the time of the riot protesting these actions.

At the time of the convention, Jefferson County was the third most populous county behind Hamilton and Ross. Milligan was elected as a delegate to the convention as a pro-statehood and anti-St. Clair Republican. His stature in the Jefferson County delegation and the Republican leadership is shown by the fact that he served on the rules committee, the committee of privileges and elections, the committee to draft article one governing the legislature, the committee to draft article two on the executive, and the committee to draft article three on the judiciary.[824] On a key vote to strike from the constitution a clause which

---

819   The deed for the sale is recorded at Land Records Vol 21, p. 503, Cecil Co., Md.

820   Letter from T. V. Milligan to Charles E. Rice dated May 6, 1895, Rice Manuscript Collection, Ohio Historical Society; Rev. T. V. Milligan, *History of Jefferson County, Ohio*, published by Fred J. Milligan, 1993, p. 2, Ohio Historical Society Library; Deed Book A, p. 145, Recorders Office, Jefferson County, Ohio.

821   Deed Book A. p. 224, Recorders Office, Jefferson County, Ohio; Account Book I, p. 9, Probate Court, Jefferson County, Ohio; Deed Book B, p. 39, Recorders Office, Jefferson County, Ohio.

822   *Territorial Papers of the United States*, Vol. III, p. 528.

823   *Biographical Annals of Ohio*, 1904, p. 157; *Chillicothe Scioto Gazette*, Nov. 28, 1801, p. 2.

824   "Journal of the Constitutional Convention of 1802", *Ohio History*, Vol 5, pp. 81 et seq.

provided that "no negro or mulatto shall ever be eligible to any office, civil or military or give their oath in any court of justice against a white person", Milligan reversed himself and voted to strike the clause. In so doing he parted from his political ally Thomas Worthington and the two other Republican delegates from Jefferson County and voted with the Federalists. His vote was consistent with strong anti-slavery views which he had expressed in the Territorial legislature.[825] Another issue on which Milligan parted company with Worthington and most of the other delegates was a proposal which read, "no person who denies the being of God or place of future rewards shall hold office in the civil government." The motion was defeated thirty to three with Milligan in the minority.[826] It should be noted that most of those who voted against the proposal were devout Christians and religious leaders in their communities.

Following the adoption of the constitution, an election was held in January, 1803, for the representatives to the first General Assembly under the new constitution. The two senators and t.hree of the four representatives elected were Federalists. Milligan was one of the Republicans defeated. Republicans claimed the Federalists stole the election; however, a protest filed by Jefferson County Republicans was unsuccessful.[827] Elections were again held in the fall of 1803 and this time the Republicans were triumphant, electing Milligan to a two year term in the state Senate and four republicans to the House of Representatives.[828]

The second legislative session was a busy one as the legislature replaced the laws which had governed the Territory under the Ordinance with some of the basic laws which would serve the new state for years. These included laws on such subjects as wills and estates, marriage and divorce, partition of real estate, and taxation. What the Virginians were unable to accomplish at the convention, they did succeed in accomplishing in January 1804, when the "Black Law" was enacted, requiring blacks who came to Ohio to post a bond to assure they would not become dependent on the public, and prohibiting them from testifying against a white. Milligan voted against this law.[829] Another issue which

---

825   "Journal of the Constitutional Convention of 1802", *Ohio History*, Vol 5, pp. 124-125; Cutler, *Life and Times of Ephraim Cutler*, 1890, pp. 75-77.

826   "Journal of Constitutional Convention of 1802", *Ohio History*, Vol. 5, p. 111.

827   William A. Taylor, *Ohio Statesmen and Annals of Progress*, State of Ohio 1899, p. 35.

828   Letter from James Pritchard to Thomas Worthington dated October 31, 1803, Thomas Worthington Collection, Ohio Historical Society.

829   *Journal of Ohio Senate*, Vol. 2, Dec 1803 session, p. 68. This law was subsequently amended and made even more onerous before finally being repealed in 1849. Leonard Erickson, "Politics and the Repeal of Ohio's Black Laws", *Ohio History*, Vol. 82, p. 154-175.

caused Milligan to oppose his fellow Republicans in the Scioto Valley was the distribution of the 3% of the proceeds from land sales which Congress had agreed to allocate to Ohio for road improvements within the state. Milligan joined with four other Senators to formally protest a bill allocating the funds. The protesters objected that no money had yet been received from Congress yet commitments were made to expend the funds long into the future based on political deals rather than the public interest. While serving as Governor Worthington made a similar criticism in 1815. The criticism had no effect on distribution of the funds either time.[830] In October, 1805, Milligan was defeated in his bid for reelection to the Senate by fellow Republican Benjamin Hough.[831] Hough went on to become Auditor of State, a position which he held for a number of years.

In 1806 Milligan sided with Thomas Worthington in opposing his fellow Jefferson County Republican James Pritchard's run for Congress against Jeremiah Morrow. Pritchard was backed by Michael Baldwin and Elias Langham of Ross County, and the race revealed an acrimonious split in the Republicans. Worthington and Milligan characterized the split as one between responsible leadership and ambitious, rabble rousers. Baldwin and Pritchard viewed the contest as between the people and aristocrats. Milligan won the fight with Pritchard, who failed to carry Jefferson County and the state, but in so doing, he made enemies which harmed his future political prospects in Jefferson County. The following year the contest between the two wings of the Republican party in Jefferson County continued when Milligan's wing of the party endorsed Meigs and Pritchard's wing endorsed Massie for governor. Each proposed their own slate of candidates with Pritchard and Milligan on opposing slates. Pritchard's wing of the party endorsed a federalist over Milligan, and both Milligan and Pritchard were defeated in their bids for the legislature. Their attacks on each other did not do either of them any good.[832]

Although Milligan was never successful in running in county-wide elections after that, he was elected as a clerk and justice of the peace of his township, and he did serve in important appointed offices. Under the constitution, justices of the peace were elected for three year terms by township residents and handled minor criminal offenses and small civil claims.[833] Township

---

830   *Chillicothe Scioto Gazette*, July 16, 1804.

831   William A. Taylor, *Ohio Statesmen and Annals of Progress*, 1899, p. 45.

832   *Steubenville Western Herald*, September 20 and 27, 1806, October 11, 1806; December 6, 1806; *Chillicothe Scioto Gazette* November 13, 1806; *Steubenville Western Herald* September 12 and 19, 1807, October 3, 10, and 17, 1807.

833   Ohio Constitution of 1802, Article III, Section 11.

officers were elected annually by the inhabitants of the township.[834] For most citizens town and township officials were the only government officials who they came in contact with, and they were considered the most important in their lives.

In 1813 John Milligan was appointed Associate Judge of Jefferson County by Governor Meigs, while the legislature was not in session.[835] The constitution provided that the governor could appoint officials normally appointed by the General Assembly when it was not in session and they would serve until the end of the next term of the legislature.[836] At the next legislative session in February, 1814, the General Assembly appointed Milligan the non-resident tax collector for the fifth district which included Jefferson County. Under the tax system at that time, taxes on resident and non-resident owners of real estate were not the same, and taxes on non-residents were collected by non-resident tax collectors. He was reappointed by the legislature in 1815 and 1816.[837]

Worthington was governor during this time period.

In 1817 Milligan wrote three lengthy letters to the Steubenville paper on the evils of alcohol and urged that laws be passed to regulate its manufacture, sale and use.[838] He also wrote to Governor Worthington on November 24 urging him to include this subject in his address to the General Assembly.[839] In his address to the Assembly in 1818 the Governor included this topic and urged that laws be passed addressing the problem. A law was adopted in the following session on the subject.

The local school house was built on John Milligan's land and the land on which it was situated was donated to the directors of the school district shortly before he died. As clerk of the township, he was involved in leasing the land which under the land law was reserved for support of the schools.[840]

---

834   Ohio Constitution of 1802, Article VI, Section 3.

835   Letter from David Sloan to Governor Meigs dated May 31, 1813. The appointment was written on the outside of the envelope. Papers of Governor Return J. Meigs Jr., Ohio Historical Society.

836   Ohio Constitution of 1802, Article II, Section 8.

837   *Cincinnati Western Spy* February 19, 1814, March 4, 1815; *Steubenville Western Herald* March 8, 1816.

838   *Western Herald and Steubenville Gazette,* July 25, 1817, November 7, 1817.

839   Letter from Milligan to Worthington November 24, 1817, Thomas Worthington Papers, MIC Roll 11, Ohio Historical Society.

840   *Steubenville Western Herald* February 28, 1817, January 23, 1818; Deed Book 7, p. 147, Recorders Office, Jefferson County, Ohio.

In September, 1819, the grand jury under Milligan's leadership as foreman returned an indictment on the deplorable condition of the county jail.[841] At the time this occurred Ohio and Jefferson County were suffering from a terrible economic depression.

John Milligan served as the first county auditor of Jefferson County from 1820 to 1822.[842] At that time the county auditor was an appointee of the General Assembly not an elected official. Because of the economic depression, it was a difficult time to serve as county auditor.

The Presbyterian Church of Steubenville was organized in the summer of 1801 with John Milligan as one of the three founding elders. He served as elder until his death in 1832.[843] The first preaching was outside in a grove during summer and in the courthouse during the winter. A small brick building was erected and occupied during the winter of 1803-1804. Milligan sold the first minister part of his land, and they were neighbors. In 1823 Milligan was given the assignment of crossing the mountains to Princeton, New Jersey and persuading Rev. Charles C. Beatty to come to the Steubenville church.[844] Not only did Beatty serve the church, but he and his wife established the Female Seminary of Steubenville which was a very highly regarded educational institution for years.

Milligan was also a surveyor and served as surveyor in the land district for a time as well as surveyor of several roads.[845]

In 1817 Milligan helped organize the Jefferson County Association for Promoting Agriculture and Domestic Manufactures. Milligan moved to his Island Creek Township farm in 1816 where like so many of the Scots and Scotch-Irish he raised sheep and the women made woolen cloth in their home.[846] In 1820 he won the prize awarded at the county fair for the best piece

---

841   *Steubenville Western Herald* January 20, 1820.

842   Doyle, *History of Steubenville and Jefferson County, Ohio,* 1910, p. 151; *Steubenville Western Herald* April 8, 1820.

843   *Brief History, Constitution, Rules of the First Presbyterian Church of Steubenville,* 1858, Jefferson County Library.

844   Rev. T. V. Milligan, *History of the Presbytery of Steubenville,* 1888, p. 7, Ohio Historical Society Library.

845   Letter from T. V. Milligan to Charles Rice dated May 6, 1896, Rice Collection, Ohio Historical Society; Doyle, *History of Steubenville and Jefferson County, Ohio,* 1910, pp. 211-212; *Steubenville Western Herald* August 17, 1815.

846   In 1810 he owned a 110 acre farm. Lee Soltow, "Inequality Amidst Abundance: Land Ownership in Early 19th Century Ohio", *Ohio History,* Ohio Historical Society, Vol. 88, p. 150; *Steubenville Western Herald* March 31, 1818.

of woolen cloth and flannel. Jefferson County was the leading producer and manufacturer of wool and wool products in Ohio at the time.[847]

Milligan died in December, 1832. In reporting his death, the Steubenville paper stated, "The deceased was a most useful, enlightened and exemplary man. One of the fathers of the state, having been a member of the convention that framed its constitution—and one of the fathers of the Presbyterian Church in Steubenville, and for many years previous to his decease, an elder thereof; his walk and conversation were in unison with his religious and political beliefs."[848]

NATHAN UPDEGRAFF

Nathan Updegraff was born September 3, 1750, in York County, Pennsylvania. He married Ann Love in July 5, 1780 in York County, and following the death of his first wife, he married Ann Lupton May 14, 1788.

His Updegraff ancestors were among the thirteen Krefelders who came to Philadelphia in 1683 and founded Germantown, Pennsylvania. They came from Krefeld in the Palatinate in response to William Penn's invitation to help establish a city of brotherly love. Two Updegraff brothers signed the first petition in America protesting slavery in 1688. They were Quakers and their petition was directed to their monthly meeting. The petition was eventually considered by the yearly meeting in Burlington, New Jersey, but no action was taken. By the end of the eighteenth century, the Quakers had come to the conclusion that slavery was wrong. Quakers who owned slaves freed them, and Quakers who lived in slave-owning states decided that they no longer wanted to live where slavery was practiced. By 1803 a number of southern Quakers had decided to immigrate to the Northwest Territory where slavery was prohibited. They were joined by Quakers from northern states who wished to make a fresh start in the West.[849]

Although born, reared, and married in York, Pennsylvania, by 1788 Nathan Updegraff had moved to Independence City, near Winchester, Virginia, where he established a hat factory. In 1801 he joined the Quaker migration to the Northwest Territory and moved his family to Short Creek in Jefferson County.

---

847   *Steubenville Western Herald* November 13, 1820.
848   *Steubenville Western Herald* December 5, 1832.
849   James L. Burke and Donald E. Bensch, "Mount Pleasant and the Early Quakers of Ohio", *Ohio History*, Vol. 83, pp. 220-255.

He was a leader of the Quakers in the area, becoming a charter member of the Concord monthly meeting, which was the first in Ohio, and serving as clerk of the Short Creek monthly meeting which was established in 1804.[850]

The village of Mount Pleasant became a center of Quaker activity in eastern Ohio. The Mount Pleasant Quakers built a quarterly meeting house in 1806-1807, which at the time was the largest building in the state. In 1814 a building for the yearly meeting of Quakers was constructed at Mount Pleasant. At that time there were 1,693 families within its jurisdiction, and by 1823 there were 8,873 members.

Updegraff built the first mill in Mount Pleasant Township two miles north of Mount Pleasant where the village of Dillonvale was later established. He also manufactured paper for a number of years. In 1810, he owned three tracts of real estate totaling 1,586 acres.[851]

As a delegate to the convention Updegraff was not identified with either the Republicans or Federalists. He served on the committee to draft the bill of rights.[852] At the Convention he was a staunch opponent of slavery and a defender of the rights of Negroes, and he voted in favor of their right to vote and their right to share in other civil rights in the same manner as whites.[853] He and other Quakers were ahead of their time on this social issue, and his viewpoint did not prevail at the convention.

As a result of the leadership of Nathan Updegraff and other Quakers, Mount Pleasant became a center of the abolition movement. The first newspaper devoted to the abolition of slavery began publication here in 1821. The first anti-slavery convention in Ohio was held in Mount Pleasant in 1837. In 1848 a free labor store was opened which stocked only goods which

---

850 William Wade Hinshaw, *Encyclopedia of American Quaker Genealogy*, Vol. IV, pp. 64, 137, 166. His membership was transferred to the Westland Monthly Meeting at Washington, Pennsylvania, on November, 28, 1801, from Crooked Run Monthly Meeting located nine miles south of Winchester. At the time Westland had jurisdiction over Quakers in Ohio, and was a place where Quakers migrating to Ohio transferred their memberships until monthly meetings were established in Ohio. Charles A. Hanna, *Ohio Valley Genealogies*, 1900, p. xxxv-xxxvi.

851 Lee Soltow, "Inequality Amidst Abundance: Land Ownership in Early 19th Century Ohio", *Ohio History*, Ohio Historical Society, Vol. 88, p. 150.

852 "Journal of Convention", *Ohio Archaeological and Historical Society Publications*, Vol. V, p. 90.

853 Helen M. Thurston, "The 1802 Constitutional Convention and the Status of the Negro", *Ohio History* Vol. 81, pp. 15-37.

were produced by free labor. Mount Pleasant was a leading station on the underground railroad.[854]

Slavery was not the only issue on which Quakers were ahead of their time. They also advocated treating Native Americans with respect and justice, entrusted women with leadership roles in their church, and were early proponents of temperance.

Updegraff died on March 3, 1827 at Mount Pleasant.[855] A county history states, "The business enterprise and energy of Mr. Updegraff was of incalculable benefit to the community. He was one of the earliest and foremost of the Friends in the Short Creek Monthly Meeting."[856]

GEORGE HUMPHREY

George Humphrey was born December 19, 1749, in Northern Ireland. He was a mere toddler when his parents immigrated to America. The family settled first in Chester County, Pennsylvania, where his brother John was born in 1752. He married Jane Wilson on November 2, 1775, and following her death, he married Elizabeth Jolly, sister of Captain Henry Jolly on January 15, 1788.[857] Captain Jolly assumed the command of a company of Virginia militia at Wheeling following the resignation of Lewis Bonnett in 1786.[858]

During the Revolutionary War Humphrey served as a private in the second troop of the first regiment of the Continental Light Dragoons under Captain John Watts during 1782 and 1783. The dragoons were cavalry soldiers. During the early years of the War he served along the Virginia and Pennsylvania frontier.[859]

George Humphrey's younger brother John was among those who established a settlement at the mouth of Short Creek around 1786.[860] John was also a Revolutionary War veteran.[861]

---

854   *Centennial Souvenir of Steubenville and Jefferson County, Ohio*, Herald Publishing Co., 1797, p. 200.

855   Family Search, Jesus Christ Church of Latter Day Saints Family History Library web page.

856   J. A. Caldwell, *History of Belmont and Jefferson Counties*, 1880, p. 531.

857   Thomas Ray McElroy, "Descendants of David Humphrey", web page.

858   Jared C. Lobdell, *Indian Warfare in Western Pennsylvania and North West Virginia at the Time of the American Revolution*, Heritage Books, 1992, pp. 78-79.

859   *Ohio Daughters of the American Revolution Soldiers Roster* Vol 2, p. 188.

860   *Centennial Souvenir of Steubenville and Jefferson County, Ohio*, 1897, p. 199.

861   *Ohio Daughters of the American Revolution Soldiers Roster* Vol 2, p. 188.

On October 25, 1796, Humphrey, who then resided in Ohio County, Virginia, purchased a section of land at the land sale at Pittsburgh. This was on the day following the purchase by Wells and Ross of the land around Steubenville.[862] Humphrey's section was located in the west central part of Warren Township, Jefferson County. He built two grist mills and a saw mill along Short Creek. [863]

After Governor Winthrop Sargent established Jefferson County, on July 31, 1797, he appointed George Humphrey as one of the first Justices of the Common Pleas Court as well as one of the first justices of the Court of Quarter Sessions.[864] The first election held in Warren Township was held at his mill, and he was elected a township trustee.

Humphrey was elected as one of the three republican delegates to the constitutional convention from Jefferson County committed to statehood and the principles of Thomas Jefferson. Although participating in votes coming before the convention, committee assignments went to other delegates from Jefferson County. Although his votes showed he opposed slavery, they did not support granting blacks civil rights.[865] Humphrey was one of the three delegates who supported Milligan's unsuccessful proposal that no person be permitted to hold public office who denied the existence of God or a future state of rewards and punishments.[866]

Humphrey ran for the House in January, 1803, on the Republican ticket and lost to Federalists. On the second day of the first legislative session of the first General Assembly he and Thomas McCune filed a protest and a contest of the election of Zacheus Beatty and Thomas Elliott who had been elected to represent Jefferson County in the House of Representatives. Despite the fact that the House was overwhelmingly Republican and that Humphrey had served with several of them at the convention, upon consideration of the evidence, it overruled the protest and declared Beatty and Elliott elected.[867]

After Ohio became a state, Humphrey was elected a justice of peace of Warren Township. He was elected a representative of Jefferson County to the

---

862   Carol Willsey Bell, *Ohio Lands Steubenville Land Office 1800-1820*, p. 3.

863   Robert H. Richardson, *A Time and Place in Ohio*, Exposition Press, 1983, p. 254.

864   Richard C. Knopf, *Transcription of the Executive Journal of the Northwest Territory*, Ohio Historical Society web page, p. 432.

865   Helen M. Thurston, "The 1802 Constitutional Convention and the Status of the Negro", *Ohio History* Vol. 81, pp. 15-37.

866   "Journal of Convention", *Ohio Archaeological and Historical Society Publications*, Vol. V, p. 111-112.

867   *Ohio Statesmen and Annals of Progress*, 1899, p. 37.

Ohio House of Representatives in 1809 and 1812.[868] The 1809-1810 session was the session where the conflict over the power of the judiciary came to a climax with the adoption of the Sweeping Resolution vacating all the judgeships in the state and reappointing new judges. The session in 1812 was particularly important because of the necessity of dealing with the War. All able bodied men were required to perform military duty when called upon unless excused by the authorities.

In 1810 Humphrey owned 7 tracts totaling 807 acres.[869]

Humphrey died on March 26, 1834, at age 84. He was buried in the Old Seceder Cemetery at Mount Pleasant. His marker commemorates his service as a delegate to the convention and a state representative.

RUDOLPH BAIR

Rudolph Bair, sometimes spelled Baer, was born in 1765 in Northampton County, Pennsylvania. He moved west to Westmoreland County, Pennsylvania and married Margaret Barbara Yerian in 1782. They had seven children.[870]

He came to the Ohio country around 1800 with his brother. He was a pioneer farmer and land speculator who bought wilderness land and sold it to settlers as settlement approached. The records of the Steubenville Land Office show that he made thirty-one purchases of land from the government between April 13, 1801 and December 29, 1815.[871] In 1810 he was the owner of four tracts totaling 786 acres.[872] He financed settlers of limited means allowing payment over an extended period of time.[873]

Bair was elected to the constitutional convention as a pro-statehood, Jeffersonian democrat. He served on the committee to draft the fourth article

---

868   *Historical Directory of the Ohio House of Representatives*, 1966, p. 185.

869   Lee Soltow, "Inequality Amidst Abundance: Land Ownership in Early 19th Century Ohio", *Ohio History*, Ohio Historical Society, Vol. 88, p. 150.

870   This information is based on genealogical information at the Family History Library of the Church of Jesus Christ of Latter Day Saints. The County history refers to his being a native of York County, Pa.

871   Carol Willsey Bell, *Ohio Lands: Steubenville Land Office*, 1983, pp. 8, 135, 166.

872   Lee Soltow, "Inequality Amidst Abundance: Land Ownership in Early 19th Century Ohio", *Ohio History*, Ohio Historical Society, Vol. 88, p. 150.

873   William Henry Perrin, *History of Stark County*, 1881, pp. 486, 502.

designating the qualification of electors.[874] He opposed proposals granting civil rights to Blacks.[875]

Although elected as a delegate to the convention from Jefferson County, he was an early settler of what is now Columbiana County. In January following the adoption of the constitution, he was elected as a representative of Jefferson County to the House of Representatives in the first General Assembly. Bair's fellow delegate at the Convention Thomas Kirker of Adams County on March 10, 1803, presented to the House a petition signed by residents of the northern part of Jefferson County requesting that a new county be created. The petition was assigned to a committee which included Bair. The committee reported a bill to create Columbiana County which was passed by the House and Senate and signed by the Speaker on March 23, 1803. This was one of eight new counties created in that session of the legislature. A principle complaint against Governor St. Clair had been his veto of bills enacted by the territorial legislature creating new counties. With St. Clair gone the legislature moved promptly to rectify the situation.

The creation of new counties and establishment of county seats was of great benefit to land speculators. Not only did it make land at and near the county seat more valuable, but it made land throughout the new county more attractive because it was more accessible to the court house. There is no doubt Bair considered the creation of the new county a top priority not only for himself but other early settlers of that area. When organization of the county was completed, he was elected as Columbiana County's first representative to the House of Representatives in 1804.[876]

Rudolph Bair was an early settler of Salem and Fairfield Townships in Columbiana County.[877] Knowing of the plans of Bezaleel Wells for Canton, he moved west and became one of the first settlers of what became Paris Township, Stark County.[878]

In the summer of 1806, while the first settlers were locating in Canton, Rudolph Bair and his brother Christopher made a trip on horseback through

---

874   "Journal of Convention", *Ohio Archaeological and Historical Society Publications*, Vol. V, p. 95.

875   Helen M. Thurston, "The 1802 Constitutional Convention and the Status of the Negro", *Ohio History* Vol. 81, pp. 15-37.

876   Elliot Howard Gilkey, *The Ohio Hundred Year Book*, p. 186; *History of Columbiana County*, D.W. Ensign & Co., 1879, pp. 24, 25.

877   *History of Columbiana County*, D.W. Ensign & Co., 1879, pp. 140, 141, 236.

878   William Henry Perrin, *History of Stark County*, 1881, pp. 486, 502, 503.

the eastern portion of Stark County to find land to buy. They confined their explorations along each side of what is now the state road, at that time a mere bridal path. They selected a number of quarter sections in Paris and Osnaburg Townships which they entered at the land office at Steubenville. That fall Rudolph Bair built a cabin about a half mile north of the present Village of Paris. After the cabin was erected he moved in with all his household goods before the floor was laid or the door hung. In place of a door a quilt was suspended at the opening from wooden pins. No nails were used in the cabin and windows were made of greased paper. His wife and children were left there for three days while Rudy returned to Columbiana County for supplies. There were Indians encamped on the creek a short distance away. There were no white persons nearer than Osnaburg, five miles away. To frighten the wolves away at night, Mrs. Bair threw out burning sticks.[879]

Bair laid out the state road from Canton to Lisbon, Ohio.[880]

Bair platted the Village of Paris in 1813. He donated two acres of land on which a log building was constructed which was used for the school and for church services by both the Lutheran and Reformed congregations. The land was also used for the village cemetery.[881] Bair also built the first sawmill and gristmill in the township.[882]

In 1818 Rudolph Bair presented a petition to the County Commissioners for the organization of Paris Township to be taken off the east end of Osnaburg Township. The petition was approved.[883]

Bair was the first justice of the peace for Osnaburg Township and according to the county history he conducted the first trial in what is now Stark County. A description of the trial reveals how frontier justice was conducted. Two settlers had swapped horses and one of them feeling cheated brought suit for damages. The parties and three witnesses met at Judge Bair's cabin. The judge opened the proceedings by bringing out a jug of whiskey and proposed that all present take a drink. After these preliminaries were finished, he proposed that they avoid a trial by each stating their view of the case, and he would give his recommendation for settlement. After everyone had another drink, it was

---

879   William Henry Perrin, *History of Stark County*, 1881, p. 503, quoting from the Canton Democrat; Edward Thornton Heald, *The Stark County Story*, Vol. I, p. 52.

880   William B. McCord, *History of Columbiana County, Ohio*, 1905, p. 364.

881   William Henry Perrin, *History of Stark County*, 1881, pp. 507-508; Edward Thornton Heald, *The Stark County Story*, Vol. I, p. 56.

882   Edward Thornton Heald, *The Stark County Story*, Vol. I, p. 55.

883   William Henry Perrin, *History of Stark County*, 1881, p. 505.

agreed to proceed in the manner proposed. After each told his story, Bair proposed that $3.00 be paid to settle the matter. They all had another drink and both sides expressed satisfaction with the decision. The Judge then expressed his pleasure in the settlement because he kept his docket book in the rafters of his cabin and a squirrel had carried it away, so if the case had gone to trial he had nothing in which to record his decision.[884]

Rudolph Bair died in 1819, and he was buried in the graveyard which he donated for church and burial purposes in the Village of Paris.[885]

Other Founding Fathers From Jefferson County

JAMES PRITCHARD

James Pritchard was born November 1, 1763 in Fredrick County, Maryland and served as a private in the Maryland line during the Revolutionary War. He married Tabitha White. They settled first in Pennsylvania before moving to the Northwest Territory.[886]

Pritchard was among the early settlers of Knox Township in Jefferson County.[887] He was among the first members of Sugar Grove Methodist Church, the first church in the township. On September 9, 1801, he was appointed as lieutenant colonel of the county militia.[888] As an associate judge of Jefferson County, he participated in the decision to lay out the county into five townships.[889] He chaired the meeting at which his township government was organized.[890]

---

884   William Henry Perrin, *History of Stark County*, 1881, p. 486.

885   *Canton Ohio Repository*, Nov 12, 1819, p. 3.

886   *DAR Patriot Index*, Centennial Edition, National Society of the Daughters of the American Revolution, 1990, Part 3, p. 2375; *DAR Lineage Book* Vol. XLV 1903, p. 251, genealogical file Public Library of Steubenville and Jefferson County, Schiappa Branch.

887   Rev. T. V. Milligan, *History of Jefferson County, Ohio*. 1876, published by Fred J. Milligan, Jr., 1993, p. 2, Ohio Historical Society Library.

888   *Executive Journal of the Northwest Territory*, p. 544, Ohio Historical Society web site.

889   J. H. Andres, *Centennial Souvenir of Steubenville and Jefferson County, Ohio*, Herald Publishing Co., 1797, p. 544.

890   Joseph B. Doyle, *20th Century History of Steubenville and Jefferson County, Ohio*, Chicago, 1910, pp. 456, 460.

Pritchard was elected as the representative of Jefferson County, Ohio, to the first Territorial House of Representatives which convened at Cincinnati on February 4, 1799, to elect nominees to the Legislative Council. The Territorial legislature including both House and Council convened on September 16, 1799, for the first legislative session.[891] During this session Pritchard developed a relationship with Tiffin, Worthington, and Massie and became a leader of the statehood movement in Jefferson County. He became a correspondent with Worthington and urged the removal of St. Clair before the election for delegates to the constitutional convention. He explained, "Since the governor's pets are chiefly in office, it will give them a greater weight." In case St. Clair should be removed, "a small revolution in this county will be necessary especially with the sheriff Francis Douglas and John Ward the prothonotary".[892]

Following adoption of the constitution, elections were held in January for the first state officers. Jefferson County was the only county in the state where Federalists were elected. The Republican leadership including Pritchard claimed that this was the result of election chicanery by the Federalists who still controlled the county offices. A protest was filed by the Republicans but it was overruled. Another factor may have been the considerable influence which Bezaleel Wells had in the county. In any event the Federalists were soon vacated from office.

Pritchard was elected to the Ohio Senate in 1804 for a two year term replacing Bezaleel Wells. During the first session he was elected Speaker following the resignation of Daniel Symmes and he served as Speaker for the remainder of that session and the next session of the General Assembly.[893] His position as Speaker made him part of the Republican leadership of the state. This was further recognized by his nomination and election as an elector in the presidential election of 1804 where he and the others cast their vote for Thomas Jefferson.[894] During his first term Pritchard secured passage of an act of the legislature incorporating the town of Steubenville which recognized its status as one of the principal towns of the new state.[895]

---

891   Emilius O. Ryan and Daniel J. Ryan, *History of Ohio*, New York, 1912, Vol. 3, pp. 37-39, 44.

892   Randolph Downes, *Frontier Ohio*, Ohio Historical Society, p. 217.

893   William A. Taylor, *Ohio Statesmen and Annals of Progress*, State of Ohio, 1899, pp. 41-42.

894   William A. Taylor, *Ohio Statesmen and Annals of Progress*, State of Ohio, 1899, p. 42.

895   Sandy Day and Alan Hall, *Steubenville Bicentennial 1797-1997*, Steubenville Bicentennial Book Committee, 1992, p. 160.

The election in 1806 saw the Republicans break into factions and in Jefferson County the battle pitted old allies Pritchard and Milligan against each other in a ferocious battle which left both of them bloodied. Pritchard decided to run for Congress against incumbent Jeremiah Morrow. He wrote to Worthington and explained that rotation in office was an important democratic principle and that since Morrow had two terms it was only fair that others be given an opportunity. Since Morrow represented the western part of the state, it was time that there be a representative from the eastern part. Worthington was outraged that Pritchard had come forward on his own. He felt Pritchard was the worst example of the growing tendency of ambitious men seeking positions for which they were not qualified. Democracy was becoming the "wretched practice of self-trumpeting candidates for popular suffrage. The distractions, frauds, and lies associated with popular elections were perverting government."[896]

Pritchard's candidacy was supported by Michael Baldwin and Elias Langham of Ross County. Langham had earlier run against Morrow and lost. Both of them were political enemies of Tiffin and Worthington. The Tiffin/Worthington leadership supported the reelection of Morrow. Pritchard's campaign strategy was to attack Morrow as an ally of land speculators. He focused on Morrow's vote in Congress for a law protecting purchasers of the Yazoo land swindle in Georgia. He attempted to exploit the popular perception that the government was too often controlled by wealthy speculators for their own selfish interests. Worthington's opposition to his candidacy was attacked as an example of this. Although this may have been a popular issue, Pritchard had his facts wrong in the case of Morrow. Morrow had voted to protect the victims of the swindle not the swindlers. The regular Republican organization in Jefferson County conducted a vigorous campaign for Morrow and against Pritchard's candidacy. Pritchard lost state-wide by a vote of 2,364 to 6,735. Interestingly, he won a majority in Ross County, although he failed to carry his own county of Jefferson by a vote of 793 to 367. He had also placed his name in nomination for the Ohio House of Representatives and lost that election as well.[897]

The split in the Jefferson County Republicans continued and the Pritchard wing of the party clashed with the regular Republicans again in the

---

896   Andrew R. L. Cayton, *The Frontier Republic*, Kent State University Press, 1986, p. 83.

897   *Steubenville Western Herald*, September 20, 1806, October 11, 1806, December 6, 1806; *Chillicothe Scioto Gazette*, November 13, 1806.

1807 election. Pritchard ran for the Senate and his wing supported Massie for governor. The regular Republicans supported Meigs for Governor. Although Massie carried Jefferson County, Pritchard's bid for election to the Ohio Senate failed.[898]

Pritchard was elected to the Ohio House of Representatives in 1808. He ran for Speaker and came in second.[899] On December 23, 1808, the House adopted a resolution impeaching Judges Pease and Tod for their decisions holding an act of the General Assembly unconstitutional. Pritchard was appointed one of the managers of the prosecution before the Senate.[900] Two thirds vote was required for conviction. The vote for conviction fell one vote short. Pritchard was reelected to the House in 1809 and he again came in second in a bid for Speaker. This was the session during which the Sweeping Resolution was adopted vacating all judicial offices in the state.[901] Pritchard was elected to the House again in 1810.[902]

In August, 1808 Pritchard's wife Tabitha died leaving her husband with a number of children.[903] He married Sally Huston of Chillicothe in February, 1810.[904]

The General Assembly appointed Pritchard associate judge of Jefferson County on January 27, 1811. In 1811 he was elected to the Ohio Senate for a two year term.[905] His leadership in the Republican Party was again recognized in 1812 when he was chosen as a presidential elector. The electors cast their votes for James Madison.[906]

James Pritchard died in Chillicothe on February 6, 1813.

---

898   *Steubenville Western Herald* September, 12, 1807, September 19, 1807, October 3, 1807, October 10, 1807, October 17, 1807.

899   William A. Taylor, *Ohio Statesmen and Annals of Progress*, State of Ohio, 1899, pp. 56-57.

900   Emilius O. Randall and Daniel J. Ryan, *History of Ohio*, New York, 1912, Vol. 5, p. 118.

901   William S. Taylor, *Ohio Statesmen and Annals of Progress*, State of Ohio, 1899, pp. 59-60.

902   William A. Taylor, *Ohio Statesmen and Annals of Progress*, State of Ohio, 1899, p. 67.

903   *Steubenville Western Herald*, August 12, 1808.

904   *Chillicothe Scioto Gazette and Chillicothe Advertiser*, February 21, 1810.

905   William A. Taylor, *Ohio Statesmen and Annals of Progress*, State of Ohio, 1899, pp. 68-69, 73.

906   William A. Taylor, *Ohio Statesmen and Annals of Progress*, Columbus, 1899, Vol. 1, p. 102.

Chapter 7

FOUNDING FATHERS FROM BELMONT COUNTY

Belmont County

On September 7, 1801, Governor Arthur St. Clair laid out the County of Belmont and designated the town of Pultney to be its county seat. On September 9 he appointed the initial officers of the county.

Settlement of the county had begun long before. Among the first settlers was Captain Robert Kirkwood who served with distinction throughout the Revolutionary War as the captain of the regiment which Delaware provided to the Continental Army. He settled at what is now Kirkwood in 1789. His cabin was attacked by Indians in 1791 and he moved his family back to Delaware. On the way he met with some troops on their way from Delaware to join St. Clair at Cincinnati for the march against the Indians in Northwest Ohio. He accepted command of the company and while leading them was killed by the Indians at St. Clair's defeat.[907]

The first permanent settlement was made about the year 1793 at Dille's Bottom. A fort was erected there the same year. In 1794 a man and woman were killed by Indians within eyesight of the fort.[908]

A settlement was begun by the Quakers in 1795 or 1796 named Concord. This was near Mount Pleasant in Jefferson County. Many of the early settlers were Quakers from North Carolina. They came to the Northwest Territory to avoid slavery.[909]

---

907   J. A. Caldwell, *History of Belmont and Jefferson Counties*, 1880, p.164.
908   Edward Thornton Heald, *The Stark County Story*, Vol. I, p. 164.
909   Edward Thornton Heald, *The Stark County Story*, Vol. I, p. 56.

Additional settlements were made along the creeks which emptied into the Ohio.

The principal road in the county was Zane's Trace which Ebenezer Zane blazed through the wilderness from the west bank of the Ohio River across from Wheeling to Limestone (now Maysville), Kentucky. In 1796 Zane persuaded Congress to contract with him to blaze a trail by which settlers could travel overland through Ohio to Kentucky. He agreed to contribute the service for the work in exchange for three 640 acre tracts of land located where the trail crossed the Muskingum, the Hocking, and the Scioto. These became the sites of Zanesville, Lancaster, and across the Scioto from Chillicothe. As part of the contract he was to provide a ferry at each of these rivers. The Trail became a major artery for settlers traveling west and led to settlement all along the Trail.

St. Clairsville was laid out by David Newell around 1800. It was located eleven miles west of Wheeling on Zane's Trace and was originally called Newellsville. Newell, of Scottish descent, migrated from Westmoreland County, Pennsylvania in 1795-1796. He renamed the town St. Clairsville in honor of his cousin, Governor St. Clair. It became the county seat in 1804.

Belmont County Delegates

JAMES CALDWELL

James Caldwell was born in Baltimore, Maryland on November 30, 1770, the son of James Caldwell Sr. and Elizabeth Alexander. James Sr. and Elizabeth arrived from Castlecaldwell, Fermanaugh County, Ireland in 1769. James Sr. and his son John came to the panhandle of Virginia in 1772 looking for land. He took possession of 800 acres on Wheeling Creek. Son John erected his cabin there the following year. The rest of the family arrived in 1775, settling on Caldwell's Run, a tributary of Wheeling Creek. Following the organization of Ohio County, Virginia in 1776, James Sr. was elected a justice of the peace.[910] Upon learning of Indians in the vicinity, the family left their farm and took shelter at Fort Henry, which was located about a mile and a half away. After

---

910   John Caldwell, Caldwell Genealogy. Com; "James Caldwell of Washington County, Pennsylvania and Ohio County, (West) Virginia", Raymond M. Bell Anthology; History of the Upper Ohio Valley, 1890, Vol. I, pp. 238-239; History of the Panhandle of West Virginia, 1879, pp. 256, 258.

several days two Indians appeared on a hill above the town. They fired a shot or two at the fort and then walked slowly away while taunting the men inside the fort. James Sr. and several other men from the fort ran after them. They soon found that they had fallen into a trap and were surrounded by hostile Indians. They fled for their lives. James Sr. was pursued by a white man who lived with the Indians. Just when his pursuer raised his spear, James Sr. caught his foot and fell and the spear stuck in a tree. James Sr. regained his feet and raced to the fort for safety. He and another man were the only members of the party who survived the trap.[911]

When the Indian War broke out, James Sr. purchased land on Buffalo Creek near Claysville in Blaine Township, Washington County, Pennsylvania. They moved back to Wheeling in 1784.

James Sr. and son John, a surveyor, were active in the land business, and James Sr. was a merchant. James Sr. died in Ohio County in 1800 at age 84.

James Jr.'s older brother John served as a soldier in the area throughout the Revolutionary War.[912] His older brother Samuel became a soldier in the Continental Army when he was only twelve. He was at Fort Henry when it was attacked in 1782, and was wounded while scouting for Indians.[913]

James Caldwell Jr. moved to St. Clairsville, Ohio, shortly after it was laid out. He purchased the first lot in the village, and opened a merchandise store in 1801. He was very successful and became quite wealthy. He was the first president of Belmont Bank of St. Clairsville.[914] In 1810 he owned four tracts in Ohio totaling 476 acres.[915]

Following the organization of Belmont County in September, 1801, Governor St. Clair appointed Caldwell clerk of the court of quarter sessions and prothonitory of the common pleas court, which meant he was responsible for record keeping for the courts of the county. He was one of three persons authorized to administer oaths in the county.[916]

Caldwell was elected as a Republican delegate to the convention pledged to support statehood and Jefferson principles of government. He served on the committees to draft article one on the legislature, article two on the executive and

911   *History of the Panhandle of West Virginia*, 1879, pp. 110, 111.
912   Pension application filed 1832 S9146.
913   Pension application filed 1833 S32168.
914   *History of Belmont and Jefferson Counties, Ohio*, p. 226.
915   Lee Soltow, "Inequality Amidst Abundance: Land Ownership in Early 19th Century Ohio", *Ohio History*, Ohio Historical Society, Vol. 88, p. 150.
916   Richard C. Knopf, *Transcription of the Executive Journal of the Northwest Territory*, p. 540, Ohio Historical Society web page.

article three on the judiciary. [917] Although his father had owned slaves, Caldwell voted against slavery; however he did not support granting civil rights to blacks. [918] Caldwell supported Milligan's proposal for a religious test.[919]

Caldwell served as clerk of courts for Belmont County from 1806 to 1810.[920] He was elected to two terms in the state Senate serving from 1809 to 1813.[921] He was then elected to two terms in the U.S. House of Representatives serving from March 4, 1813 to March 3, 1817.[922] In his campaign for his first term he ran as a captain in the militia supporting the administration and the War against Federalist Bezaleel Wells. This was the first time Ohio would be sending six congressmen to Washington instead of just one. He was a Republican identified with the Tammany wing of the party and the only Tammany candidate to win.[923] Caldwell was elected as a Presidential elector in 1820 pledged to James Monroe and in 1824 pledged to Henry Clay. [924]

Following his retirement from Congress, he resumed business in St. Clairsville. He subsequently moved to Wheeling where he served as president of the Merchants and Mechanics Bank. He died May 5, 1838 in Wheeling and was buried in St. Clairsville.

ELIJAH WOODS

Elijah Woods was born in Rockingham County, Virginia, in 1778. He traveled with his uncle Archibald Woods and other members of the family to the Ohio Valley in 1798.[925]

---

917   "Journal of Convention", *Ohio Archaeological and Historical Society Publications*, Vol. V, pp. 88, 92, 93.

918   Helen M. Thurston, "The 1802 Constitutional Convention and the Status of the Negro", *Ohio History* Vol. 81, pp. 15-37.

919   "Journal of Convention", *Ohio Archaeological and Historical Society Publications*, Vol. V, pp. 111-112.

920   J. A. Caldwell, *History of Belmont and Jefferson County*, 1880, p. 179.

921   William A. Taylor, Ohio Statesmen and Annals of Progress, 1899, pp. 58, 66, 69, 72.

922   "James Caldwell", *Biographical Directory of the United States Congress web page*

923   William R. Barlow, "Ohio's Congressmen and the War of 1812", *Ohio History*, Vol. 72, p. 175.

924   William A. Taylor, *Ohio Statesmen and Annals of Progress*, Columbus, 1899, Vol. 1, p. 145.

925   Karen Ann (Woods) Euritt, "Elijah Woods, Husband of Hester "Hetty" Zane", web page.

Elijah came naturally by his yearning for the frontier. His grandfather Andrew Woods was of Scotch-Irish descent. He settled initially on the Pennsylvania frontier and then migrated to the Shenandoah Valley. Elijah's uncle had enlisted as a soldier in the Revolutionary War when he was only 16 years of age and was wounded at Yorktown. After the War Archibald migrated to the Ohio Valley where he surveyed, acquired and sold lands, and accumulated a substantial estate. He subsequently became a bank president in Wheeling and a Colonel in the Virginia militia.[926]

Elijah was employed by Ebenezer Zane at Fort Henry and acquired land in Belmont County where he settled. He had learned surveying and was considered quite good. Before coming to Ohio, he had spent a winter surveying in Kentucky.

Following the organization of the County in September, 1801, Elijah Woods was appointed County Surveyor of Belmont County.[927] He served as clerk of courts from 1801 to 1806.[928]

Woods was elected to the constitutional convention as a Republican pledged to support statehood and the principles of Jefferson. He served on the committee appointed to draft the bill of rights.[929] He opposed granting civil rights to blacks.[930]

Woods was elected as a representative to the House in the first General Assembly which met at Chillicothe on March 1, 1803. He also represented Belmont County in the House in the session which met December 3, 1810 to January 30, 1811.[931]

In May, 1803, Elijah Woods married Hester "Hetty" Zane, daughter of Ebenezer Zane, founder of Wheeling. In 1804 Zane deeded Elijah and Hetty 320 acres in Belmont County for $500. In 1806 he deeded eight acres to them in Bridgeport after Zane had laid out the town. In 1810 he owned one tract of 320 acres.[932]

---

926   "Background Note on the Woods Family Papers", William L. Clements Library, University of Michigan

927   Richard C. Knopf, *Transcription of the Executive Journal of the Northwest Territory*, p. 541, Ohio Historical Society web page.

928   J. A. Caldwell, *History of Belmont and Jefferson Counties*, 1880, p. 179.

929   "Journal of Convention", *Ohio Archaeological and Historical Society Publications*, Vol. V, p. 90.

930   Helen M. Thurston, "The 1802 Constitutional Convention and the Status of the Negro", *Ohio History* Vol. 81, pp. 15-37.

931   William A. Taylor, *Ohio Statesmen and Annals of Progress*, 1899, pp. 36, 67.

932   932 Lee Soltow, "Inequality Amidst Abundance: Land Ownership in Early 19th Century Ohio", *Ohio History*, Ohio Historical Society, Vol. 88, p. 150.

Woods operated a ferry from Bridgeport on the west bank of the Ohio River to Wheeling Island and his father-in-law operated the ferry from Wheeling Island to Wheeling. Woods built his home in Bridgeport across from the ferry and operated an inn there.

Woods died in 1820. The author of the county history states, "Mr. Woods was a very prominent citizen of Belmont County, especially in its early history in which he figured largely in politics. He was a man that had acquired considerable learning for that day and was far above the great majority of the pioneer settlers of the county."[933]

Other Founding Fathers From Belmont County

CHARLES HAMMOND

Charles Hammond was born September 19, 1779, in Baltimore County, Maryland. His Hammond ancestors immigrated to Maryland before 1643. During the Revolution Charles father George Hammond was a Loyalist, as the British would say, or Tory, as the Americans preferred to call them. An affluent farmer, George moved his family and slaves to the west in 1785 and settled in the vicinity of Wellsburg, Brooke County, Virginia (now West Virginia). George was well educated and Charles a very apt student. Despite growing up in a log cabin on a farm cut out of the wilderness, Charles learned Shakespeare and the other classics. At an early age he demonstrated a remarkable literary talent. George was an avid Federalist, and Charles acquired his father's political view point and passion. He sent poems to the newspaper at Washington, Pennsylvania ridiculing Republican leaders.[934]

Charles studied law with Phillip Dodridge, a prominent attorney in Western Virginia, and was admitted to practice in that state. He proved himself to be a talented and fearless partisan, but his strong Federalist opinions made enemies. He moved to the Ohio side of the River and was admitted to practice in the territorial courts of the Northwest Territory. In November, 1801, he was appointed prosecuting attorney for Belmont County. He served in that office until 1804.[935]

---

933   J. A. Caldwell, *History of Belmont and Jefferson Counties*, 1880, p. 283.

934   Francis P. Weisenburger, "Charles Hammond, the First Great Journalist of the Old Northwest", *Ohio History* Vol. 43, pp. 340-342.

935   Francis P. Weisenburger, "Charles Hammond, the First Great Journalist of the Old Northwest", *Ohio History* Vol. 43, pp. 342-344; J. A. Caldwell, *A History of Belmont and Jefferson Counties*, Wheeling, 1880, p. 229.

During the conflict between the Republicans and St. Clair and his allies over statehood Hammond wrote a series of articles for the Scioto Gazette of Chillicothe. They were considered the most spirited advocacy of the Governor's cause.[936]

Hammond married Sarah (Sally) Tillinghast of Wellsburg on October 23, 1803.[937] In 1804 he moved to Wheeling where he lived for five years. During this time he contributed articles to a Wheeling paper. He also continued to represent clients before Ohio courts and was one of the attorneys in the case where Judge Pease held that the law increasing the jurisdiction of the justices of the peace to fifty dollars was unconstitutional.[938] He became embroiled in the political fight between the anti-court Republicans and the pro-court Republicans and Federalists. He contributed articles attacking anti-court Republican leaders and defending the principle of judicial review.[939]

In 1809 Hammond moved back to Belmont County. In 1813 Hammond began publishing a newspaper in St. Clairsville called "The Ohio Federalist". The paper attacked Republicans and their policies. He was particularly critical of those who were responsible for the War of 1812. By 1819 the paper was abandoned because the Federalist Party by that time had practically disappeared from the state.[940]

While publishing his own paper, he also contributed articles to other papers. His letters in the Chillicothe Advertiser provided powerful arguments against the Sweeping Resolution which no doubt contributed to its repeal.[941]

Hammond represented Belmont County in the Ohio Senate in the 1813-1814 and the 1814-1815 sessions of the General Assembly. In his campaign for

---

936   Francis P. Weisenburger, "Charles Hammond, the First Great Journalist of the Old Northwest", Ohio History Vol. 43, p. 344; Jacob Burnet, Notes on the Settlement of the Northwest Territory, Cincinnati, 1847, pp. 380-381.

937   Francis P. Weisenburger, "Charles Hammond, the First Great Journalist of the Old Northwest", Ohio History Vol. 43, p. 345.

938   Donald F. Melhorn Jr., Lest We Be Marshall'd, Judicial Power and Politics in Ohio 1806-1812, Akron University Press, 2003, pp. 27-28, 44-45.

939   Francis P. Weisenburger, "Charles Hammond, the First Great Journalist of the Old Northwest", Ohio History Vol. 43, pp. 345-346; Donald F. Melhorn Jr., Lest We Be Marshall'd, Judicial Power and Politics in Ohio 1806-1812, Akron University Press, 2003, pp. 77-87. Melhorn describes Hammond's arguments for judicial review as remarkable for their originality as well as eloquence.

940   Francis P. Weisenburger, "Charles Hammond, the First Great Journalist of the Old Northwest", Ohio History Vol. 43, pp. 346-348.

941   Donald F. Melhorn Jr., Lest We Be Marshall'd, Judicial Power and Politics in Ohio 1806-1812, Akron University Press, 2003, pp. 166-169.

the Senate he was highly critical of the Republican administration for its conduct of the War. In the Senate he served as chairman of a committee to draft
Ohio's first criminal code and carry the Penitentiary system into effect. In
order to finance the burden of the war, Congress enacted a direct tax but gave
the states the option of paying it for their citizens. In the 1814-1815 session
Ohio negotiated a loan of $177,055.21 with various banks to pay the tax for the
citizens of Ohio.[942] The Republicans passed a resolution supporting the
administration's war effort which Hammond ridiculed through a doggerel
poem. Many legislators were offended and required him to make a retraction.
He also attacked commander Duncan McArthur with sarcastic comments.
McArthur struck him with his cane. Hammond struck back through articles in
the "Ohio Federalist."[943] Hammond's election and the extent to which his
attack of the war effort was tolerated demonstrates that the War had become
unpopular with a large segment of the population of Ohio. The same year that
Hammond was elected to the Senate Worthington who had originally voted
against the War was elected governor.

Following his retirement from the Senate Hammond continued to work on
drafting legislation. An important example was the law enacted in 1816 which
required state banks incorporated under it to turn over a portion of their stock
to the state. Through this measure the state attempted to exercise some control
over the wildcat banks which were springing up across the state.[944]

Hammond was elected to the Ohio House in 1816, 1817, 1818, and 1820.
James Wilson, editor and publisher of the Steubenville paper, served with him
during part of the time. Wilson, a Republican, had been the subject of
Hammond's vitriolic attacks. However, he described Hammond as a stronger
advocate of the people's interests than many of those who claimed to be
Republicans. He said he never knew a legislator "more fair, honorable and
upright. He was above any kind of trick or double dealing."[945]

Hammond became the leading warrior in Ohio's fight against the United
States Bank. The Bank was blamed for destroying the state's banking system and
bringing on a severe depression in the state's economy by demanding payment

---

942   Francis P. Weisenburger, "Charles Hammond, the First Great Journalist of the
       Old Northwest", *Ohio History* Vol. 43, p. 348.
943   Francis P. Weisenburger, "Charles Hammond, the First Great Journalist of the
       Old Northwest", *Ohio History* Vol. 43, pp. 348-350.
944   Francis P. Weisenburger, "Charles Hammond, the First Great Journalist of the
       Old Northwest", *Ohio History* Vol. 43, pp. 350-351.
945   Francis P. Weisenburger, "Charles Hammond, the First Great Journalist of the
       Old Northwest", *Ohio History* Vol. 43, pp. 351-352.

in specie. The legislature first attacked the bank by levying a tax on its branches at Chillicothe and Cincinnati. When the bank failed to pay, the State Auditor employed an agent to enter the vault of the bank at Chillicothe and remove $100,000, the amount of the tax. Judge Byrd of the Federal Circuit Court ordered the state's agents imprisoned for contempt and set bail at $240,000. The men went to jail. The Federal Court ordered the money returned and a federal marshal seized the money from the state treasury. Hammond chaired the committee which considered these matters and proposed a law which removed the protection of the Ohio laws from the bank. He also served as the attorney for the state and its officials in the suit with the bank which was carried to the United States Supreme Court. In that Court he argued against Henry Clay who represented the bank. One of his principal arguments was that the Federal Constitution prohibits suits against a state, and this should include suits against state officials who are the means by which the state exercises its sovereignty. Although he lost the case, his arguments on behalf of the state were recognized as ably presented. Chief Justice Marshall spoke of Hammond's remarkable acuteness and accuracy of mind. [946]

In 1820 Hammond wrote a series of articles on the relationship between the federal and state governments under the pseudonym "Hampden" which were published in a Washington newspaper and reprinted in other papers throughout the country. The articles were widely discussed at the time and drew the praise of Thomas Jefferson.[947]

The battle between the State of Ohio and the United States Bank was a major test of the Federal system established by the United States Constitution. In testing the limits of its authority the Ohio General Assembly had first clashed with the state courts over the question of whether state courts had the power to declare state laws unconstitutional. It then clashed with the federal courts over the extent to which federal courts had the authority to limit the power of the General Assembly. In both cases the General Assembly learned that there were limits on its power. State and federal judges learned that although they might have the authority to declare laws unconstitutional, such authority must be exercised with prudence and restraint. As the voice of the

---

946   Francis P. Weisenburger, "Charles Hammond, the First Great Journalist of the Old Northwest", *Ohio History* Vol. 43, pp. 352-362; Francis P. Weisenburger, "Charles Hammond, the First Great Journalist of the Old Northwest", *Ohio History* Vol. 43, p. 362.
947   J. A. Caldwell, *History of Belmont and Jefferson County, Ohio*, Wheeling, 1880, p. 229.

people, state legislators were not about to submit easily to judges who assumed the role of a "priesthood".

In 1822 Hammond was defeated in a bid for Congress in a close election. His agricultural pursuits in Belmont County had not been as successful as he had hoped and his political and professional opportunities appeared limited, so in 1823 Hammond moved to Cincinnati. He practiced law and served as an editorial writer for the *Liberty Hall and National Gazette* newspaper.[948]

In the 1824 campaign for President, Hammond served as the Ohio campaign manager for Henry Clay. Despite Clay's representation of the United States Bank Hammond respected his character and his positions on issues affecting Ohio. Hammond was highly critical of Andrew Jackson and his followers seeing in them the same kind of demagoguery which disgusted him about the Jeffersonian Republicans. In Ohio the vote was Clay 19,255, Jackson 18,489, and Adams 12,280. The vote in the electoral college was Jackson 99, Adams 84, Crawford 41, Clay 38. Since Jackson did not have a majority, the question of who would be the next President went to the House of Representatives to decide among those receiving the three highest numbers of votes. Ohio and the other states who had cast their votes for Clay voted for Adams over Jackson and John Quincy Adams became President of the United States.[949]

In 1823 the General Assembly enacted a law which required the Supreme Court to issue written opinions and provided that they be published by an official reporter appointed by the Court. From 1823 to 1839 Hammond served as the first official reporter for the Ohio Supreme Court. As such he was responsible for editing and publishing the decisions of the Court.[950] Prior to his appointment no reports of the decisions were published, and following his resignation no reports were published for ten years.[951]

---

948   Francis P. Weisenburger, "Charles Hammond, the First Great Journalist of the Old Northwest", *Ohio History* Vol. 43, pp. 363-364.

949   Francis P. Weisenburger, "Charles Hammond, the First Great Journalist of the Old Northwest", *Ohio History* Vol. 43, pp. 364-371.

950   Francis P. Weisenburger, "Charles Hammond, the First Great Journalist of the Old Northwest", *Ohio History* Vol. 43, p. 372.

951   Francis P. Weisenburger, "Charles Hammond, the First Great Journalist of the Old Northwest", *Ohio History* Vol. 43, p. 413; Donald F. Melhorn Jr., *Lest We Be Marshall'd, Judicial Power and Politics in Ohio 1806-1812*, Akron University Press, 2003, pp. 184-186.

Hammond's wife died July 31, 1826, after a lengthy illness which took a heavy toll on him. He subsequently married a sister of Thomas and Moses Moorehead of Zanesville.[952]

Hammond continued to practice law. Because of the Bank case, he gained a reputation as a constitutional lawyer and argued additional cases before the United States Supreme Court as well as many cases in lower federal courts and Ohio courts. Jacob Burnet stated, "As a constitutional lawyer he had no superior in the state, and but few if any equals."[953]

In 1825 Hammond became editor of the *Cincinnati Gazette*, a position which he held until his death in 1840. As editor he took strong positions in favor of the Adams administration, against the Jackson administration, and in support of Whig candidates including Henry Clay and William Henry Harrison. He also took a strong position against slavery and defended the right of abolitionists to present their views. These positions were unpopular among many in Cincinnati. He also was a strong advocate of religious toleration which also earned him the enmity of many religious bigots and partisans. During his tenure as editor it was customary for editors to attack each other. Hammond was adept at such attacks and in turn the recipient of many attacks.[954]

As an editor and publicist Hammond was a leader of the attacks on Andrew Jackson personally and against the policies of his administration. He also was a leader of the Whig Party in Ohio. Jackson and his supporters swept into power in 1828, but in 1830 the Whigs elected Duncan McArthur as governor and a majority in the General Assembly. In 1832 Ohio again went for Jackson, but in 1836 and 1840 the state went for its favorite son William Henry Harrison. Hammond did not live to see Harrison elected President.[955]

Hammond considered himself an Episcopalian. When a resident of St. Clairsville, he was involved with the effort to erect an Episcopalian church there and served as a lay delegate of the communion. Although he considered himself a member, he was not a communicant member of the congregation in

---

952   Francis P. Weisenburger, "Charles Hammond, the First Great Journalist of the Old Northwest", *Ohio History* Vol. 43, pp. 376, 425.

953   Francis P. Weisenburger, "Charles Hammond, the First Great Journalist of the Old Northwest", *Ohio History* Vol. 43, p. 414.

954   Francis P. Weisenburger, "Charles Hammond, the First Great Journalist of the Old Northwest", *Ohio History* Vol. 43, pp. 372-412.

955   William A. Taylor, *Ohio Statesmen and Annals of Progress*, Columbus, 1899, pp. 145, 148, 193.

Cincinnati. He engaged in the practice of family prayers. He helped Philander Chase raise money for the establishment of Kenyon College. He encouraged discussion of religious issues, and was critical of those who attempted to suppress such discussion. He defended the Catholics from the Lutherans and the Lutherans from the Catholics and encouraged discussion of the views of Robert Owen, the utopian reformer, who established a community at New Harmony, Indiana.[956]

Hammond died on April 3, 1840, after an extended illness, contributed in part to an excessive use of alcohol.[957] Following his death, a fellow editor stated about him, "That he was singular in his manners, abrupt in his address, and severe in his hostility, will be forgotten, when it is remembered that he was benevolent in disposition, upright in conduct, honest in his opinions, intrepid in their expression; of noble intellect, useful as a citizen, admired as a writer, and respected as a jurist."[958]

---

956   Francis P. Weisenburger, "Charles Hammond, the First Great Journalist of the Old Northwest", *Ohio History* Vol. 43, pp. 420-424.

957   Francis P. Weisenburger, "Charles Hammond, the First Great Journalist of the Old Northwest", *Ohio History* Vol. 43, pp. 425-426.

958   *Cincinnati Chronicle*, April 4, 1840.

Chapter 8

FOUNDING FATHERS FROM TRUMBULL COUNTY

The Western Reserve

Connecticut was the final state to surrender its claim to the Ohio country to the federal government, and in so doing it reserved a strip of land south of Lake Erie known as the "Western Reserve" or "Connecticut Reserve." [959] In 1792 Connecticut set aside 500,000 acres on the western end of the reserve for the inhabitants of Connecticut towns who had suffered severe losses from British raids during the Revolution. This part of the reserve came to be known as the "Fire Lands". It could not be settled until the Indian title was cleared by Treaty in 1805. Following Wayne's defeat of the Indians at Fallen Timbers, Connecticut decided to sell the eastern part of the reserve to create a fund for the use of its schools. In 1796 a deal was struck with a group of investors known as the Connecticut Land Company for $1,200,000.[960]

The Company dispatched Moses Cleaveland west with a surveying party to complete a survey of the Western Reserve so that land sales could begin. Cleaveland was a lawyer, Revolutionary War veteran and substantial investor in the company. On the way he met with Joseph Brant and other chiefs of the Iroquois at their village in upstate New York and secured their agreement not to molest the settlers in the Reserve. He secured this commitment by promising an annuity from the federal government or a payment from the company.[961]

---

959   Connecticut Act of Session, September 13, 1786.
960   Beverly W. Bond, Jr., *History of the State of Ohio*, 1941, Vol. I, pp. 356-362.
961   Beverly W. Bond, Jr., *History of the State of Ohio*, 1941, Vol. I, pp. 362-363.

In addition to surveying the base lines for the division of the land into five acre townships, another task of Cleaveland was to locate the first township to be surveyed and sold off. Cleaveland identified the land at the mouth of the Cuyahoga River as the most promising site for the first township to be sold and established this as the headquarters for the surveyors and the first settlement in the Reserve. Town lots were laid out and the place was named Cleaveland, later shortened to Cleveland. A second settlement was established at what became Conneaut. [962]

Cleaveland and his team returned to Connecticut after three months, and the following spring a new team was sent out to continue the survey under Rev. Seth Hart and Seth Pease. As the surveys were completed settlers began to stream in from New England. They traveled from New England to Albany, New York, from there to Buffalo and from Buffalo west along a trail south of Lake Erie to the Western Reserve.

The New Englanders came to the Reserve from the northeast along the south shore of Lake Erie. However there was another trail into the Reserve which brought an entirely different kind of settler. Scotch-Irish and Germans migrated to the Reserve from western Pennsylvania traveling up the Mahoning Valley from the Ohio River and establishing towns at Youngstown and Warren. By 1800 there were 1,000 families in the Reserve east of the Cuyahoga. The land west of the Cuyahoga was not secured from the Indians until 1805.[963]

Trumbull County

At first there was some question as to whether the Western Reserve would be governed by the federal government through the Governor of the Northwest Territory or by Connecticut. The question was settled when on July 10, 1800, Governor St. Clair created Trumbull County out of the land in the Reserve and designated Warren as its county seat. Like Washington County to the south, Trumbull County was settled predominantly by New Englanders except in the southeast where it was settled by Scotch-Irish and Germans from Pennsylvania.

---

962   Beverly W. Bond, Jr., *History of the State of Ohio*, 1941, Vol. I, pp. 364-366.
963   Beverly W. Bond, Jr., *History of the State of Ohio*, 1941, Vol. I, pp. 368-371…

Trumbull County Delegates

SAMUEL HUNTINGTON

Samuel Huntington was born in Coventry, Connecticut on October 4, 1765. His ancestor Simon Huntington emigrated from Norfolk, England in 1633. As a boy, he was adopted by his uncle Samuel Huntington, a signer of the Declaration of Independence, president of the Continental Congress in 1779-1781 and Governor of Connecticut from 1786 to 1796.[964] As a teenager he accompanied his uncle to Philadelphia where his uncle was one of the most important men in Congress during the Revolution.

He attended Dartmouth and then transferred to Yale where he graduated in 1785. Following a tour of Europe, he studied law, was admitted to the bar in Connecticut, and married a cousin Hannah. He served as his uncle's assistant and law clerk. As part of the Connecticut elite, he was being groomed to succeed his uncle. His world collapsed and his prospects dimmed in 1796 when his uncle died. Increasingly he devoted his energies to western land speculation. He was associated with the Connecticut Land Company, the purchaser of the Western Reserve from the State of Connecticut. In the late 1790s he became identified with the Jeffersonian Republicans which caused hostility among many of his Federalist friends, neighbors and business associates and made any prospect of political office in Connecticut unlikely.[965]

In 1800 Huntington toured the Ohio country on horseback visiting the Western Reserve and the Ohio Valley as far south as Marietta, meeting Governor St. Clair during his trip.[966] Deciding to start a new life in the Ohio country, he brought his family west in the summer of 1801 settling in Cleveland which at that time was a village of a few log houses. Soon after arriving he hired a builder to construct the largest house in town.[967] One night as he was riding home he was attacked by a pack of wolves which he beat off with an umbrella. Indians still lived in the area. The settlers were also threatened by

---

964   *The Governors of Ohio*, Ohio Historical Society, 1969, p. 7; Jeffrey P. Brown, "Samuel Huntington: A Connecticut Aristocrat on the Ohio Frontier", 89 *Ohio History*, Vol. 4, p. 420.

965   Jeffrey P. Brown, "Samuel Huntington: A Connecticut Aristocrat on the Ohio Frontier", 89 *Ohio History*, Vol. 4, pp. 421, 422.

966   *The Governors of Ohio*, Ohio Historical Society, 1969, pp. 7, 8.

967   Jeffrey P. Brown, "Samuel Huntington: A Connecticut Aristocrat on the Ohio Frontier", 89 *Ohio History*, Vol. 4, p. 422.

malaria which arose from the swamps. He later moved to Newburgh where he purchased a grist mill and then to Painesville Township where in 1812 he founded the Village of Fairport at the mouth of the Grand River.[968] He built the first warehouse at the mouth of the river and a large home between Painesville and Fairport.

Through the influence of George Tod, Governor St. Clair's Secretary and a friend of Huntington, Huntington was appointed by Governor St. Clair as a justice of the peace and a justice of the Common Pleas Court of Trumbull County on January 3, 1802.[969] He also was appointed a lieutenant colonel of the Trumbull County militia.[970] Tod like Huntington had come to Ohio as a representative of the Connecticut Land Company. Because of his prior influence in Connecticut, his connection with Tod and Sinclair, and his legal background, Huntington became the political leader of the county.[971] If St. Clair's plan to divide the Territory at the Scioto had gone through, Huntington had a good chance to be appointed Territorial Governor or one of the three judges of the eastern territory.[972]

When Congress rejected the Governor's plan and adopted the Enabling Act calling for a convention to vote on statehood, Huntington recognized which way the wind was blowing and allied with Republican leaders who promised him a judgeship if statehood were achieved.[973] Huntington was elected as a delegate to the constitutional convention and surprised the Federalist delegates by allying himself with Republican leaders in support of statehood and in opposition to the arbitrary rule of Governor St. Clair. He served on the committees to draft article one on the legislature, article two on the executive, and article three on the judiciary.[974] Although Huntington opposed slavery and supported civil rights for Blacks, he did not support their right to suffrage.[975]

968   *The Governors of Ohio*, Ohio Historical Society, 1969, p. 8.

969   Richard C. Knopf, *Transcription of the Executive Journal of the Northwest Territory*, p. 549.

970   *The Governors of Ohio*, Ohio Historical Society, 1969, p. 8.

971   Jeffrey P. Brown, "Samuel Huntington: A Connecticut Aristocrat on the Ohio Frontier", 89 *Ohio History*, Vol. 4, pp. 423, 424.

972   Jeffrey P. Brown, "Samuel Huntington: A Connecticut Aristocrat on the Ohio Frontier", 89 *Ohio History*, Vol. 4, pp. 424, 425.

973   Jeffrey P. Brown, "Samuel Huntington: A Connecticut Aristocrat on the Ohio Frontier", 89 *Ohio History*, Vol. 4, p. 425.

974   "Journal of Convention", *Ohio Archaeological and Historical Society Publications*, Vol. V, pp. 88, 92, 93.

975   Helen M. Thurston, "The 1802 Constitutional Convention and the Status of the Negro", *Ohio History* Vol. 81, pp. 15-37.

Huntington represented Trumbull County in the Senate of the first general assembly. He had hoped to be appointed the federal judge for Ohio by President Jefferson or elected by the General Assembly as one of first U.S. Senators, but he lost both these positions to Cincinnatians. However, the first General Assembly did elect him to serve as one of the first Supreme Court justices of the state along with Return J. Meigs, Jr.[976] From the Republican leadership's perspective, these were prestigious but powerless positions, and therefore, an appropriate reward for their former Federalist allies from the Western Reserve and Marietta. When Meigs resigned as Chief Justice, Huntington was promoted to that position.[977]

Feeling he had reached a dead end in Ohio, Huntington then tried to secure the governorship of the new Michigan Territory. He failed but was offered a judgeship which he declined, preferring to stay on the bench in Ohio.[978]

Huntington continued to pursue his business interests while sitting on the bench. He operated mills and speculated in land in the Western Reserve. By 1807, he owned four thousand acres along Lake Erie, and was one of the wealthier men in the Reserve.[979]

In 1810 he owned nine tracts totaling 2,954 acres.[980]

While sitting on the Supreme Court, Huntington rendered a decision which propelled him to the center of a new division in Ohio politics. He ruled that a law enacted by the General Assembly was unconstitutional. The law permitted justices of the peace to hear cases up to $50. According to Huntington this violated the constitution because, the state's bill of rights guaranteed trial by jury in all cases exceeding $20.[981] This outraged many Republicans who considered the legislature as the supreme power in the State. If a judge could declare a law unconstitutional, then the legislature was subordinate to the courts. They also believed their position reflected public sentiment because the people preferred

---

976   *Ohio Statesmen and Annals of Progress*, 1899, pp. 35, 37.

977   Jeffrey P. Brown, "Samuel Huntington: A Connecticut Aristocrat on the Ohio Frontier", 89 *Ohio History*, Vol. 4, pp. 426, 427, 424.

978   Jeffrey P. Brown, "Samuel Huntington: A Connecticut Aristocrat on the Ohio Frontier", 89 *Ohio History*, Vol. 4, pp. 428-430.

979   Jeffrey P. Brown, "Samuel Huntington: A Connecticut Aristocrat on the Ohio Frontier", 89 *Ohio History*, Vol. 4, p. 431.

980   Lee Soltow, "Inequality Amidst Abundance: Land Ownership in Early 19th Century Ohio", *Ohio History*, Ohio Historical Society, Vol. 88, p. 151.

981   Donald F. Melhorn Jr., *Lest We Be Marsahll'd, Judicial Power and Politics in Ohio*, University of Akron Press, 2003, p. 45-46.

to have smaller claims decided by justices of the peace who were elected by township voters who decided cases at their homes in the township rather than at the county seat and because no lawyers were required. There was a widespread feeling that lawyers and judges opposed the $50 act to protect the fees of lawyers. On the other hand, Federalists and many conservative Republicans feared abuse of power by the legislature and believed that it was important that the courts could protect against such abuses by declaring laws unconstitutional. Huntington was nominated for Governor in 1808 as spokesman for the pro-court alliance of Federalists and conservative and moderate Republicans. Although receiving only 45% of the vote, he was elected because the anti-court vote was split between Thomas Worthington and incumbent Governor Thomas Kirker.[982]

During his term as governor, the battle between the pro-court and anti-court factions continued in the legislature. The pro-court faction won a battle when two supreme court justices were impeached for their decisions declaring legislation unconstitutional, but their conviction and removal failed by one vote. The anti-court faction won a victory by enacting a law, called the Sweeping Resolution which declared all judicial offices vacant in 1810 enabling the legislature to make all new appointments. The pro-court party ultimately prevailed in campaigns which focused on whether the Worthington-Tiffin wing of the party was attempting to control elections through a secret organization known as the Tammany Society. The Governor had no veto at that time and Huntington did not participate in these battles while he served as Governor.[983]

As the 1810 election approached, Huntington and Meigs agreed that Meigs would resign from the Senate and run for Governor, while Huntington would make a bid for the Meigs Senate seat which was at that time filled by vote of the General Assembly. Although Meigs defeated Worthington for Governor, Worthington defeated Huntington for Senator on the sixth ballot by a vote of 35 to 31.[984] The following year he was elected as a representative to the Ohio

---

982   Jeffrey P. Brown, "Samuel Huntington: A Connecticut Aristocrat on the Ohio Frontier", 89 *Ohio History*, Vol. 4, pp. 432-434.

983   Jeffrey P. Brown, "Samuel Huntington: A Connecticut Aristocrat on the Ohio Frontier", 89 *Ohio History*, Vol. 4, pp. 434-436; Donald F. Melhorn Jr., *Lest We Be Marsahll'd, Judicial Power and Politics in Ohio 1806-1812*, Akron University Press, 2003, pp. 94-95, 137.

984   William A. Taylor, *Ohio Statesmen and Annals of Progress*, State of Ohio, 1899, pp. 67-68.

House where he launched an effort to repeal the Sweeping Resolutions which failed by one vote.[985] However, the repeal did pass the following year.[986]

Huntington served as an army paymaster during the War of 1812 under General William Henry Harrison.

He died on June 8, 1817, from injuries suffered while supervising repair of the road from his estate to the harbor at Fairport.[987]

His biography states, "Samuel Huntington was a man of small stature but of abounding energy. He was well educated…His business methods were efficient and ethical. As a lawyer and public servant he was both able and honest, and his influence on the history of Ohio is significant. Perhaps his greatest contribution was his support of the doctrine of judicial review of legislative acts, now a generally accepted judicial principle."[988]

DAVID ABBOT

David Abbot was a native of Brookfield, Massachusetts, born in 1765, and educated at Yale College. His health failed his senior year, and he did not graduate. Deciding to pursue a career in law, he studied law and established his practice at Rome, Oneida County, New York.[989]

He immigrated to the Western Reserve in 1798 and settled in what is now Willoughby. Celebrated as the first permanent settler of what is now that town, he settled at a ford on the Chagrin River and established the first grist mill in the Western Reserve. His settlement was at first known as Chagrin Mill, and then shortened to Chagrin. The name was not changed to Willoughby until 1835.

At the time of Abbot's settlement Indians lived across the River. Mrs. Abbot was the only white woman in the area, and she visited with the Indian women nearby. When her daughter was born, there was no white clergyman to baptize the child. The medicine man at the Indian Village had been raised in a French mission and had been consecrated by the French as a Catholic priest. At the

---

985   Jeffrey P. Brown, "Samuel Huntington: A Connecticut Aristocrat on the Ohio Frontier", 89 *Ohio History*, Vol. 4, pp. 436-437.

986   Donald F. Melhorn Jr., *Lest We Be Marsahll'd, Judicial Power and Politics in Ohio 1806-1812*, Akron University Press, 2003, pp. 170-172, 175.

987   *The Governors of Ohio*, Ohio Historical Society, 1969, p. 10.

988   *The Governors of Ohio*, Ohio Historical Society, 1969, p. 10.

989   Henry Howe, *Historical Collections of Ohio*, 1898, Vol. I, p. 579.

request of the chief, he carried the child to the river and baptized her and named her "Flower of the Forest" in the Indian tongue.[990]

Trumbull County was organized by Governor St. Clair on July 10, 1800, and included all the land in the Western Reserve. Among the county officers appointed by the Governor at the recommendation of the Connecticut Land Company was David Abbot as sheriff.[991] He served in this capacity until the new state was organized.

Abbot was elected as a delegate to the constitutional convention. The convention opened on November 1, but he did not arrive until November 12. He was appointed to the committee responsible for drafting article six designating the manner in which sheriffs, coroners, and other civil officers should be chosen.[992] He voted with the Jeffersonian Republicans. On issues affecting blacks he voted against slavery and in favor of granting them civil rights.[993]

Abbot was elected as one of Trumbull County's two representatives to the House of Representatives in the second General Assembly which convened in December 1803. During that session the General Assembly enacted the first criminal code for the state which included the death penalty for treason, murder, rape, arson, and malicious maiming. A number of lesser offenses were punished by a specified number of lashes.[994]

Abbot represented Portage and Geauga Counties in the Senate of the seventh General Assembly which convened December 5, 1808. During that session Supreme Court justices Calvin Pease and George Tod were impeached for declaring an act of the General Assembly unconstitutional. This is the same decision which Samuel Huntington had made before resigning from the Court to run for Governor. Abbot voted for conviction. Abbot strongly opposed the concept of judicial review. In a letter to Todd, he stated, "if the people allow the judges to set aside the laws, does it not make the judiciary a

---

990   Isabel Sutch, "History of the First Presbyterian Church of Willoughby: The Early Years"

991   Richard C. Knopf, *Transcription of the Executive Journal of the Northwest Territory*, p. 533.

992   "Journal of Convention", *Ohio Archaeological and Historical Society Publications*, Vol. V, pp. 95, 96.

993   Helen M. Thurston, "The 1802 Constitutional Convention and the Status of the Negro", *Ohio History* Vol. 81, pp. 15-37.

994   William A. Taylor, *Ohio Statesmen and Annals of Progress*, Columbus, 1899, pp. 39, 41.

complete aristocratic branch by setting the judges over the heads of the legislature?"[995] Also during this session Huron County was erected on February 7, 1809, out of that part of the Western Reserve known as the "Fire Lands"; however organization of the county was deferred to a later date.[996] Senators being elected for two year terms, Abbot returned for the session which convened December 4, 1809. During this session, the state capital was moved temporarily to Zanesville.[997]

Abbot was returned to the Senate representing Portage, Geauga, and Cuyahoga counties in the ninth General Assembly convening on December 3, 1810. During this session, the Senate passed an act naming Columbus as the permanent capital of the state and Chillicothe as the temporary capital until the necessary buildings were constructed. Cuyahoga was erected as a county with Cleveland as its county seat.[998] Abbot's term also included the session which convened December 10, 1811.[999] He was one of the eight presidential electors for 1812 all of whom voted for James Madison.[1000]

The western part of the Western Reserve was a tract of about 500,000 acres set aside by the State of Connecticut to satisfy the claims of persons whose dwellings and barns were burned by the British during the Revolutionary War. The area could not be settled until title was acquired from the Indians. This occurred at the Treaty at Fort Industry in 1805. [1001] The land was surveyed in 1807 and brought to market in 1808. In the summer of the following year David Abbott purchased 1800 acres lying on both sides of the Huron River in the vicinity of what is now Milan, Ohio. His land was located at the head of navigation on the Huron and was therefore accessible by boats coming across Lake Erie from the east. It was eight miles south of Lake Erie and fifty-miles west of Cleveland. The first white settler, Jarad Ward, purchased part of Abbot's property and moved to the area in 1809. Abbot moved his family to the

---

995   William A. Taylor, *Ohio Statesmen and Annals of Progress*, Columbus, 1899, pp. 55, 56; Donald F. Melhorn Jr., *Lest We Be Marshall'd, Judicial Power and Politics in Ohio, University of Akron Press*, 2003, p. 112.

996   William A. Taylor, *Ohio Statesmen and Annals of Progress*, Columbus, 1899, p. 58

997   William A. Taylor, *Ohio Statesmen and Annals of Progress*, Columbus, 1899, pp. 58, 59.

998   William A. Taylor, *Ohio Statesmen and Annals of Progress*, Columbus, 1899, pp. 66, 68.

999   William A. Taylor, *Ohio Statesmen and Annals of Progress*, Columbus, 1899, p. 69.

1000   William A. Taylor, *Ohio Statesmen and Annals of Progress*, Columbus, 1899, p. 102.

1001   Henry Howe, *Historical Collections of Ohio*, 1898, Vol. I, p. 565.

area the following year. He built the first frame dwelling and frame barn in the area. His settlement was referred for years as "Abbot's Crossing" or "Abbotford." At the commencement of the War of 1812 there were twenty-three families in the township.[1002]

It should be noted that Abbot was in the Senate in 1809 when a law was passed creating the county of Huron; and he no doubt had a considerable part in that legislation. In 1811 commissioners appointed to locate a county seat for the new county located it on or near his farm at Fort Avery, a blockhouse which had been constructed for the protection of the settlers in the area, and which served as a fort during the War of 1812.[1003]

The War of 1812 was primarily an Indian War in Ohio, and there were a number of attacks in the area where Abbot settled. Following Hull's surrender at Detroit at the beginning of the War, many of the settlers of this area fled south or east for safety. Until Oliver Hazard Perry defeated the British fleet, the area was also subject to attack from British soldiers coming up the river from the lake.

Abbot was elected a justice of the peace when the township was organized at his home.[1004] When county officers were elected in 1815, he was chosen clerk of courts.[1005] The construction of a court house was begun on his property in 1817. The following year the county seat was moved to Norwalk, and the court house was never completed.[1006] This was no doubt a severe disappointment to Mr. Abbot.

David Abbot returned to the legislature in 1821 as one of the two representatives from Huron and Sandusky Counties in the House of Representatives. One of the bills passed was to fix the compensation of state officials. Legislators were paid $2.00 per day for each day of attendance plus $2.00 for each 25 miles traveling to and from the state capital.[1007] Abbott's trip to Columbus to attend the legislative session is described in a letter he wrote on November 30, 1821. He took the new "state road" to Columbus, the new capital. He describes a trail through the woods with cabins five or ten miles apart.

1002   Henry Howe, *Historical Collections of Ohio*, 1898, Vol. I, p. 578.

1003   Lewis Cass Aldrich, *History of Erie County*, 1889, p. 53.

1004   Lewis Cass Aldrich, *History of Erie County*, 1889, p. 495.

1005   Lewis Cass Aldrich, *History of Erie County*, 1889, pp. 53, 495.

1006   W.W. Williams, *History of Huron and Erie Counties, Ohio*, 1879, pp. 458-465.

1007   William A. Taylor, *Ohio Statesmen and Annals of Progress*, Columbus, 1899, pp. 108, 110.

He spent the night at cabins along the way.[1008] It should be noted that legislative sessions were in December and January so the trip was long and cold. One of the principal qualifications for a legislator in those days was the willingness to make the trip to Columbus.

According to Henry Howe, the recorder of many stories about early Ohioans, all interesting and some more or less true, Abbot several times traveled the length of Lake Erie in an open boat, of which he was helmsman and commander. One time he was driven by a storm diagonally across the lake a distance of more than one hundred miles and thrown upon the Canadian shore. The other person in the boat spent most of his time bailing out the water with his hat. After the storm was over, they returned across the lake in the same frail boat arriving a week later and were hailed by their friends who had given them up for lost.[1009]

Abbot died in 1822 at the age of 57, leaving one son and three daughters.[1010]

Other Founding Fathers From Trumbull County

GEORGE TOD

George Tod was born December 11, 1773, in Suffield, Connecticut. He was the son of David Tod who immigrated from Perthshire, Scotland to America in 1746. George graduated from Yale College in 1795, studied law at Judge Tapping Reeves' Law School in Litchfield, Connecticut, and was admitted to the bar in that state and practiced for a few years in New Haven, Connecticut.[1011]

1008   "Abbot's Ride", *The Toledo Bee*, Rice Collection, Ohio Historical Society, Box 19, item, 12.

1009   Henry Howe, *Historical Collections of Ohio*, 1898, Vol. I, p. 579.

1010   Henry Howe, *Historical Collections of Ohio*, 1898, Vol. I, p. 579; "Abbot's Ride", *The Toledo Bee*, Rice Collection, Ohio Historical Society, Box 19, item, 12.

1011   William Henry Smith, *The St. Clair Papers*, Cincinnati, 1882, Vol. 2, p. 584; George B. Wright, "Biography of David Tod", *Ohio History*, Vol. 8, p. 107; Carrington T. Marshall, *A History of the Courts and Lawyers of Ohio*, New York, 1934, Vol. 1, p. 234; Jos. G. Butler, Jr., *History of Youngstown and the Mahoning Valley, Ohio*, Chicago, 1921, Vol. 2, p. 220; Donald F. Melhorn Jr., *Lest We Be Marshall'd, Judicial Power and Politics in Ohio*, University of Akron Press, 2003, p. 37.

In 1800 he traveled to Connecticut's Western Reserve with a view to moving there and seeking his fortune in the west. At the opening of the first territorial court in Trumbull County on August 25, 1800, he was appointed by the court as county prosecutor. He was admitted to the practice of law at Warren on September 17, 1800, along with Calvin Pease, Benjamin Tappan, and David Abbot. One of his first cases was the prosecution of a white man for the murder of an Indian. One of the attorneys for the defense was Benjamin Tappan. The jury acquitted the accused, accepting his testimony that he acted in self-defense. In 1801 he moved his family to Youngstown in company with Calvin Pease, John Kinsman and several other immigrants from Connecticut. He purchased land from John Young, the founder of Youngstown.[1012]

By 1802 the settlement at Youngstown and the surrounding area had become sufficiently populated that the court ordered that a township government be formed. On April 5, 1802, the settlers gathered at the village and elected township officers. Tod was elected clerk of the Township and the lister of taxable property.[1013]

George Tod was invited by Governor St. Clair to become his secretary. He readily accepted because this would provide him with access to the center of power as well as the means to support his family. As the battle for statehood warmed up, Tod and his friend Huntington were put in an interesting position. St. Clair and the Territorial legislature favored a division of the Territory at the Scioto River. If this were done, this would provide the opportunity for prominent positions in the eastern Territory. Both Tod and Huntington supported the division of the Territory. However, once the plan was rejected by Congress and the Enabling Act passed, they switched to the Republican band wagon. Huntington, as a delegate to the Convention, was able to secure an appointment as one of the three judges to the Ohio Supreme Court by supporting the Republicans.[1014]

1012   Donald F. Melhorn Jr., *Lest We Be Marshall'd, Judicial Power and Politics in Ohio*, University of Akron Press, 2003, p. 39; Jos. G. Butler, Jr., *History of Youngstown and the Mahoning Valley, Ohio*, Chicago, 1921, Vol. 1, pp. 106-108, 116; *History of Trumbull and Mahoning Counties, Ohio*, Cleveland, 1882, Vol 1, p. 290; Benjamin Tappan, Donald J. Ratcliffe, "Autobiography of Benjamin Tappan", *Ohio History* Vol 85, p. 132.

1013   Jos. G. Butler, Jr., *History of Youngstown and the Mahoning Valley*, Ohio, Chicago, 1921, Vol. 1, pp. 116-117.

1014   Randolph Downes, *Frontier Ohio*, Ohio Historical Society, pp. 220-222.

In December 1801, the Republicans launched an effort to have President Jefferson remove St. Clair from office. St. Clair was accused of speaking contemptuously of the President and the federal government and praising monarchy. The accusers included Francis Dunlavy and Joseph Darlinton. St. Clair wrote to Tod who was present at the time asking if he would write a letter on his behalf. Although Tod was a Republican, he wrote to Secretary of State James Madison refuting the allegations. [1015]

Youngstown and Warren engaged in a spirited competition for the county seat of Trumbull County. The competition spilled over to other areas. When the residents of Warren, believing they had the fastest horse in the area, issued a $1,000 wager that their horse could beat any horse in Youngstown, Tod accepted the challenge and put up the money for Youngstown. People gathered from the two villages and the countryside from miles around to cheer on their respective champions. Youngstown won. The competition for county seat continued until Mahoning County was organized and each town became a county seat.[1016]

Tod was elected to the Ohio Senate in 1804 and served in the 1804-1805 and 1805-1806 sessions of the General Assembly. The Senate sat in judgment of an impeachment brought against Justice William Irvin of Fairfield County. He was convicted by a vote of eleven to four. Tod voted against impeachment.[1017]

In January, 1807, the General Assembly elected Tod justice of the Ohio Supreme Court by a vote of 22 to 21. While sitting on the Court, Todd and Huntington voted to affirm the decision of Calvin Pease holding that a law enacted by the General Assembly was unconstitutional. The law in question had increased the jurisdiction of justices of the peace to $50 in civil matters. This was a popular measure because it allowed people to settle smaller disputes in their townships before an elected justice of the peace without a lawyer. The Judges held the law violated the right to jury trial guaranteed by the federal and Ohio constitutions. While in the legislature Tod had opposed the law on the ground of its unconstitutionality. The decision created a furor and led to impeachment proceedings against Judges Tod and Pease. The Judges escaped the two-thirds vote for impeachment by one vote.[1018] The decision and

---

1015   William Henry Smith, *The St. Clair Papers*, Cincinnati, 1882, Vol. 1, pp. 243-245, Vol. 2, pp. 581-583, 584-586.

1016   *History of Trumbull and Mahoning Counties, Ohio*, Cleveland, 1882, Vol 1, p. 69.

1017   William A. Taylor, *Ohio Statesmen and Annals of Progress*, State of Ohio, 1899, pp. 41, 45-47.

1018   Donald F. Melhorn Jr., *Lest We Be Marshall'd, Judicial Power and Politics in Ohio*, University of Akron Press, 2003, pp. 42-45; William A. Taylor, *Ohio Statesmen and Annals of Progress*, State of Ohio, 1899, pp. 56-57.

impeachments raised a fundamental question under the new constitution. The constitution did not expressly confer on the courts a right to declare a law unconstitutional. The question then was whether that power was implicit in the judicial function. The judges argued that the constitution was a higher law which limited the power of the legislature. If courts had no power to invalidate a law which violated the constitution, then the legislature would be free to ignore the constitution. Jeffersonian Republicans believed the legislature was the voice of the people, and the people were protected because they could remove legislators who violated the constitution. At the same time as this controversy was going on in Ohio, a contest was going on between the Congress and the federal courts. The United States Supreme Court decided that it had the power to invalidate a law which violated the constitution. Jeffersonian Republicans believed that Federalist judges who occupied many of the federal judgeships were thwarting the will of Congress and the President.[1019]

Although Tod was not removed from office by impeachment, he was removed from office in 1810 by the Sweeping Resolution adopted by the General Assembly.[1020] The Assembly declared that all judicial offices became vacant seven years after the formation of the state regardless of when appointments were made. Rather than contest the action, Tod submitted his resignation.

Tod then ran for and was elected to the Ohio Senate in 1810 where he served in the 1810-1811 and 1811-1812 sessions of the General Assembly. Coming shortly after his removal from office, his election showed that in Trumbull County he still had the confidence of the people. The Sweeping Resolution had raised concerns among many Republicans about the independence of the judiciary. They worried whether liberty and property were safe if there was no restraint on the legislature and if judges lacked independence because they were removable at the whim of the legislature. Their worries were compounded when it was revealed that the Worthington/Tiffin wing of the Republican Party was attempting to control elections through a secret organization called the Tammany Society. The public turned against the anticourt party and the Sweeping Resolution was repealed on January 8, 1812.[1021]

1019   William T. Utter, *History of the State of Ohio, The Frontier State 1803-1825*, Ohio Historical Society, 1942, pp. 48-52.

1020   Donald F. Melhorn Jr., *Lest We Be Marshall'd, Judicial Power and Politics in Ohio*, University of Akron Press, 2003, p. 133.

1021   Donald F. Melhorn Jr., *Lest We Be Marshall'd, Judicial Power and Politics in Ohio*, University of Akron Press, 2003, pp. 172-174; William T. Utter, *History of the State of Ohio, The Frontier State 1803-1825*, Ohio Historical Society, 1942, pp. 55-60.

With the outbreak of the War of 1812 Tod volunteered for service and received a commission as a major in the United States Infantry. He played an important part in the defense of Fort Meigs, leading a charge against a British battery. He was promoted to lieutenant colonel and was placed in charge of Fort Malden after it was vacated by the British.[1022]

In February, 1816, the General Assembly elected Tod to the office of presiding judge of the third circuit.[1023] He served in this office until 1829. Following his retirement, he returned to his law practice and management of his Brier Hill Farm.

Tod died on October 11, 1841 at the age of 67. He was the father of David Tod, the Civil War Governor of Ohio.[1024] A biographer of his son described George Tod as follows, "He was a very generous, liberal-minded man, and in the old pioneer times when small salaries were paid to all officials, with a large family to maintain, he did not accumulate any surplus, but fell behind and was compelled to mortgage his Brier Hill farm. But he left to his children a good name, which is better than riches."[1025]

CALVIN PEASE

Calvin Pease was born in Suffield, Connecticut on September 9, 1776. He was descended from Robert Pease who emigrated from Essex, England to America before 1644. Calvin studied law in the office of his brother-in-law Gideon Granger. Granger was a leading Republican in Connecticut and became Postmaster General under President Thomas Jefferson. Pease was admitted to the bar in Connecticut and engaged in the practice of law in New Hartford.[1026]

1022   Donald F. Melhorn Jr., *Lest We Be Marshall'd, Judicial Power and Politics in Ohio*, University of Akron Press, 2003, pp. 177-178, 183; *History of Trumbull and Mahoning Counties, Ohio*, Cleveland, 1882, Vol 1, p. 91. Despite their political differences, Senator Worthington assisted in securing Tod a commission.

1023   William A. Taylor, *Ohio Statesmen and Annals of Progress*, State of Ohio, 1899, pp. 83.

1024   Carrington T. Marshall, *A History of the Courts and Lawyers of Ohio*, New York, 1934, Vol. 1, p. 235.

1025   George B. Wright, "Biography of David Tod," *Ohio History* Vol. 8, p. 108.

1026   *History of Trumbull and Mahoning Counties, Ohio*, Cleveland, 1882, Vol. 1, pp. 174-175.

Pease went west to seek his fortune in the Connecticut Reserve and first set-tled in Youngstown. No doubt through the influence of his brother-in-law he was appointed Postmaster of Youngstown and served in that capacity until he moved to Warren in 1803. When Trumbull County was organized by Governor St. Clair in July, 1800, Pease was appointed clerk of the common pleas court, the court of quarter sessions and the orphans court.[1027] When the township government was organized at Youngstown in 1802, Pease was elected as one of the five trustees of the township. He was also elected to be a constable.[1028]

Following the establishment of the state government, the first General Assembly elected Pease as the President Judge of the common pleas court of the first district.[1029] As president judge he traveled to each county in his circuit and met with the associate judges of the county to hold court. The first circuit originally included Jefferson, Washington, Belmont, Columbiana, and Trumbull Counties[1030]. Pease served in this office until March, 1810, when his term expired, and he was not reappointed.

During his term as presiding judge, Pease rendered a decision holding that a law expanding the jurisdiction of the justices of the peace to civil claims up to $50.00 was unconstitutional. He held that the law violated the United States Constitution and the Ohio Constitution because it deprived litigants of their right to trial by jury. The decision was appealed to the Ohio Supreme Court where it was affirmed by Judges Tod and Huntington. The decision generated a fire-storm of protest by the Worthington/Tiffin wing of the Republican Party. They contended the courts had no authority to refuse to enforce a law passed by the General Assembly. As the voice of the people the General Assembly was supreme. Impeachment proceedings were brought against Pease and Tod and a trial was held in the Ohio Senate. Pease and Tod avoided conviction and removal from office by one vote.[1031] The controversy over this decision

---

1027 *Executive Proceedings of the Northwest Territory*, Ohio Historical Society web page, p. 533.

1028 Jos. G. Butler Jr., *History of Youngstown and the Mahoning Valley, Ohio*, Chicago, 1921, p. 117.

1029 William A. Taylor, *Ohio Statesmen and Annals of Progress*, State of Ohio, 1899, p. 37.

1030 Fletcher Brennan, *Biographical Cyclopedia and Portrait Gallery of Distinguished Men of the State of Ohio*, Cincinnati, 1879, p. 140.

1031 Donald F. Melhorn Jr., *Lest We Be Marshall'd, Judicial Power and Politics in Ohio 1806-1812*, Akron University Press, 2003, pp. 95-98, 106, 115-117; William A. Taylor, *Ohio Statesmen and Annals of Progress*, State of Ohio, 1899, p. 56; Andrew R. L. Cayton, *The Frontier Republic*, Kent State University Press, 1986, pp. 102-104.

divided the Republican Party into the anti-court party led by Worthington and Tiffin and the court party led by Massie and Creighton. The conflict between these two wings of the party dominated politics until the War of 1812 unified the state.

Pease was elected to the Ohio Senate in 1812.[1032] During the War of 1812 Governor Meigs made Pease responsible for establishing and maintaining the lines of communication between the military posts in the Northwest.[1033] He organized the riders who carried dispatches for General William Henry Harrison during the defense of Fort Meigs in May, 1813.[1034]

In February, 1816, Pease was appointed to the Ohio Supreme Court. During this same year the General Assembly increased the number of Supreme Court Justices from three to four. He became the Chief Justice in 1822. Although the Ohio Constitution required the Justices to hold Court in every county, in 1823 they began holding en banc sessions at Columbus as well. Pease was reelected by the General Assembly to the Court in 1823 and served until 1830. Although judicial review eventually was recognized and accepted by the Courts and the Legislature, it was accompanied by deference to the General Assembly's opinion on constitutionality. Only if an act of the legislature's unconstitutionality was plain and palpable would an Ohio Court hold it to be unconstitutional.[1035] Thomas Ewing, United States Senator, U.S. Secretary of the Treasury and Interior and leading lawyer of his day, described Pease as the greatest judge he ever appeared before.[1036] Following his retirement from the Supreme Court, Pease returned to the practice of law in which he engaged for the remainder of his life. He served as attorney for and director of the Western Reserve Bank for many years.[1037] In 1831 he was elected to the Ohio House of Representatives which was his last public office.[1038]

1032   William A. Taylor, *Ohio Statesmen and Annals of Progress*, State of Ohio, 1899, p. 73.

1033   *History of Trumbull and Mahoning Counties, Ohio*, Cleveland, 1882, Vol. 1, p. 91.

1034   Donald F. Melhorn Jr., *Lest We Be Marshall'd, Judicial Power and Politics in Ohio 1806-1812*, Akron University Press, 2003, p. 183.

1035   Donald F. Melhorn Jr., *Lest We Be Marshall'd, Judicial Power and Politics in Ohio 1806-1812*, Akron University Press, 2003, pp. 184-187.

1036   Carrington T. Marshall, *A History of the Courts and Lawyers of Ohio*, New York, 1934, Vol. 1, p. 238.

1037   J. Fletcher Brennan, *Biographical Cyclopedia and Portrait Gallery of Distinguished Men of the State of Ohio*, Cincinnati, 1879, p. 140.

1038   William A. Taylor, *Ohio Statesmen and Annals of Progress*, State of Ohio, 1899, p. 153.

Pease died on September 17, 1839. He was described as, "A man of great strength of character, of keen perceptions and of almost unerring judgment. His purity and integrity as a judge were never assailed or questioned—friends and foes alike placing confidence in his honesty and uprightness."[1039]

BENJAMIN TAPPAN

Benjamin Tappan was born in Northampton, Massachusetts on May 25, 1773. His puritan ancestors came to Massachusetts in 1637. His mother's grandmother was the sister of Benjamin Franklin. His father was a goldsmith and Tappan learned the trade from his father and practiced it as well as several other mechanical trades for several years. He also studied painting under Gilbert Stuart. Tappan reacted against the strict Calvinism of his mother and was hostile to the prevalent religious orthodoxy of New England. When opposition arose to the Federalist political leadership in New England, he became an active participant.[1040]

Tappan studied law for three years under Gideon Granger of Suffield, Connecticut. Granger was the leader of the Republican opposition in that state and most of his students shared his political viewpoint. Despite opposition of some of the Federalist lawyers, Tappan was admitted to the bar of Connecticut.[1041]

His father was a substantial investor in the Connecticut Land Company and needed to liquidate some of his land in the Western Reserve to avoid financial embarrassment. The most substantial tract was two-thirds of a township named Ravenna. Benjamin agreed to go west to develop and sell the land. His father agreed to split with him whatever he realized from the sale. Tappan left for the west in April 1799. He traveled part of the way with David Hudson, founder of Hudson, Ohio. He made camp at the mouth of the Cuyahoga. At the time only one settler lived at the location of Cleveland. He then cut a trail

---

1039 J. Fletcher Brennan, *Biographical Cyclopedia and Portrait Gallery of Distinguished Men of the State of Ohio*, Cincinnati, 1879, p. 140.

1040 Donald J. Rattlciffe, "The Autobiography of Benjamin Tappan", *Ohio History*, Vol. 85, pp. 112-113, 114-115; Gary S. Williams, *Gliding to a Better Place, Profiles from Ohio's Territorial Era*, Buckeye Books, Caldwell, Ohio, 2000, pp. 197-198.

1041 Donald J. Rattlciffe, "The Autobiography of Benjamin Tappan", *Ohio History*, Vol. 85, pp. 112-113, 120-122.

through the wilderness to his father's land where he erected a cabin and became the first settler of Ravenna.[1042]

Tappan was present when Trumbull County was organized in July, 1800, and St. Clair offered to appoint him as justice of the peace. He declined, telling the Governor that he could not accept an appointment from a government he was trying to change. He was already involved with those seeking to replace the Territorial government with a state government. Tappan observed at the time that St. Clair's drinking capacity was phenomenal.[1043] He was admitted to practice law before the Territorial Courts that summer and participated in the defense of a white man accused of killing an Indian. It was his first jury trial. The white man was acquitted on the ground of self-defense, and as a result Tappan developed a reputation as an effective advocate. However, there was not enough legal business on the frontier to keep him busy.[1044]

At the election for delegates to the Constitutional Convention Tappan lost to Huntington by one vote. When Huntington resigned his seat in the Ohio Senate to accept a seat on the Ohio Supreme Court, Tappan ran for the vacant seat and represented Trumbull County at the session which began in December, 1803. Among the laws which he drew up was a bill establishing county commissioners to replace the court of quarter sessions, a bill governing partition of real estate, and a bill for organizing and disciplining the militia. He was not reelected because of a false accusation that he had opposed a tax on non resident land-owners. [1045]

Tappan was appointed aid to major general Elijah Wadsworth and commissioned as a major. He assisted in organizing the militia of the northeast area of the state.[1046]

Tappan was elected justice of the peace of his township. Court was held at his cabin. Because his nearest neighbor lived a mile away, he felt obliged to feed

---

1042 Donald J. Rattlciffe, "The Autobiography of Benjamin Tappan", *Ohio History*, Vol. 85, pp. 122-131; Henry Howe, *Historical Collections of Ohio*, Centennial Edition, 1908, Vol. 2, pp. 433-434.

1043 Donald J. Rattlciffe, "The Autobiography of Benjamin Tappan", *Ohio History*, Vol. 85, p. 134.

1044 Henry Howe, *Historical Collections of Ohio*, Centennial Edition. 1908, Vol 2, pp, 660-662; Donald J. Rattlciffe, "The Autobiography of Benjamin Tappan", *Ohio History*, Vol. 85, p. 132.

1045 Donald J. Rattlciffe, "The Autobiography of Benjamin Tappan", *Ohio History*, Vol. 85, pp. 138-140.

1046 Donald J. Rattlciffe, "The Autobiography of Benjamin Tappan", *Ohio History*, Vol. 85, pp. 140.

the parties, witnesses and their horses. Due to the burdens of the office, he resigned after a year.[1047]

In 1806 Tappan moved to Canfield. While there he was visited by an agent for Aaron Burr who attempted to recruit him for his expedition. Tappan suspected villainy, but was unable to determine the details of the plot. He reported his suspicions to the government in Washington and learned that they were watching Burr's activities and warning official in the west.[1048]

Tappan bought his father's land in 1806. When Portage County was organized in 1807, he laid out the town of Ravenna and was successful in having it designated as the county seat. This greatly increased the value of his land, and he soon became relatively wealthy.[1049]

In 1809 Tappan moved to Steubenville. There was much more opportunity for him as an attorney, and he and his wife desired to live in a town with more amenities than offered by the Village of Ravenna.[1050]

Tappan attended the 1809-1810 session of the General Assembly as a lobbyist for John Bever, the proprietor of Wooster, to secure the designation of Wooster as the county seat of Wayne County. Commissioners had recommended another location. While at the session, Tappan participated in the drafting of the "Sweeping Resolution" which declared all judicial offices vacant seven years after the formation of the State. The Resolution was adopted by the Republicans and passed. Although subsequently repealed, the Resolution was an important event in the battle between the General Assembly and the courts for supremacy.[1051]

When the War of 1812 broke out and Hull's surrender became known, fear spread that the British and Indians would attack Cleveland. Tappan was assigned responsibility for organizing, equipping and marching a unit north to Cleveland. Although he participated in the early part of the War, he became so

---

1047   Donald J. Rattlciffe, "The Autobiography of Benjamin Tappan", *Ohio History*, Vol. 85, pp. 140.

1048   Donald J. Rattlciffe, "The Autobiography of Benjamin Tappan", *Ohio History*, Vol. 85, pp. 141.

1049   Donald J. Rattlciffe, "The Autobiography of Benjamin Tappan", *Ohio History*, Vol. 85, pp. 142.

1050   Donald J. Rattlciffe, "The Autobiography of Benjamin Tappan", *Ohio History*, Vol. 85, pp. 142-143.

1051   Donald J. Rattlciffe, "The Autobiography of Benjamin Tappan", *Ohio History*, Vol. 85, pp. 143-146; Donald F. Melhorn Jr., *Lest We Be Marsahll'd, Judicial Power and Politics in Ohio*, University of Akron Press, 2003, pp. 130-131.

disenchanted with the poor system of providing supplies though defense contractors that he resigned and refused to rejoin the war effort until the system was reformed.[1052]

The General Assembly elected Tappan president judge of the fifth circuit in 1816 and he served for seven years. He prepared summaries of his decisions which were published as Tappan's Reports. It was the first publication of court decisions in Ohio.[1053]

Tappan was one of the first seven Canal Commissioners appointed in 1822 to investigate the feasibility of a canal. The group also included Thomas Worthington and Jeremiah Morrow. Worthington was elected the first chairman but resigned a year later. Tappan was elected chairman in his place and served for thirteen years. Morrow resigned when he was elected governor and used his office as a bully pulpit to push for the project. The first task of the Commission was to formulate a report and recommendation as to location and feasibility which would win the support of a majority of the General Assembly at a time when the state was slowly emerging from a severe financial depression which had crippled the economy of the state. The location of the canal would have huge financial implications for landowners and towns located along its route so the politics was intense. The project would also have huge financial implications for contractors providing labor to build the canals and firms selling materials used in its construction. On February 4, 1825, the General Assembly authorized financing and construction of the canal system recommended by the Commission. Although Alfred Kelley and Micajah Williams are given primary credit for the canal system, Tappan also played an important role.[1054]

While on the bench, Tappan had denied the constitutionality of the act chartering the national bank. At a Democratic Party convention he drafted and proposed a resolution attacking the bank which became a rallying issue for Jacksonian democrats.[1055] Tappan became a leader of the Jacksonian

---

1052   Donald J. Rattlciffe, "The Autobiography of Benjamin Tappan", *Ohio History*, Vol. 85, pp. 147-153.

1053   Donald J. Rattlciffe, "The Autobiography of Benjamin Tappan", *Ohio History*, Vol. 85, pp. 153-155.

1054   Donald J. Rattlciffe, "The Autobiography of Benjamin Tappan", *Ohio History*, Vol. 85, pp. 110, 155-156; "Alfred Kelley and the Ohio Business Elite", *Ohio History* Vol 87, pp. 365-392; George White Dial, "The Construction of the Ohio Canals", *Ohio History*, Vol. 13, p. 460-482. Ethan Allen Brown is also credited with playing a major role. John S. Still, "Ethan Allen Brown and the Ohio Canal System", *Ohio History*, Vol 66, p. 22.

1055   H. H. Hunter, "The Pathfinders of Jefferson County", *Ohio History* Vol. 6, p. 226.

Democrats of Ohio. He was a presidential elector pledged to Jackson in 1832.[1056] In recognition for his service he received a recess appointment from President Jackson to be Judge of the United States District Court on April 12, 1833, and served until May 29, 1834, when his nomination was not confirmed by the Whig controlled Senate.[1057]

On December 20, 1838, the General Assembly elected Tappan as United States Senator. He served from March 4, 1839, to March 3, 1845.[1058] Tappan became a confidante and adviser of President Martin Van Buren. However, his opposition to slave power caused him to leak to the press confidential documents relating to the proposed annexation of Texas as a state. He was censured by the Senate. Tappan became a Free Soiler in 1848 and a Republican in 1856.[1059]

In 1839 Edwin Stanton, Secretary of War under Abraham Lincoln, became a law partner of Tappan in Steubenville. After retiring from the Senate, Tappan returned to full-time legal practice in Steubenville.[1060]

Tappan's interest in art caused him to recognize the talent of Thomas Cole. Tappan encouraged and assisted him while he was a teenager in Steubenville. He went on to become one of America's foremost portrait painters. Tappan was also interested in science and published articles on geology. He was also a founder and president of the Historical and Philosophical Society of Ohio.[1061]

Tappan's brother Arthur Tappan was a distinguished abolitionist and philanthropist, president of the American Anti-Slavery Society and founder of the American Tract Society and Oberlin College. Benjamin's son Eli Tappan was president of Kenyon College, School Commissioner of Ohio, and one of the first presidents of the National Education Association.[1062] Tappan's brother

---

1056   William A. Taylor, *Ohio Statesmen and Annals of Progress*, Columbus, 1899, Vol. 1, p. 193.

1057   Donald J. Rattlciffe, "The Autobiography of Benjamin Tappan", *Ohio History*, Vol. 85, pp. 110-111; Biography of Benjamin Tappan, Federal Judicial Center web page.

1058   William A. Taylor, *Ohio Statesmen and Annals of Progress, State of Ohio*, 1899, Vol. 1, p. 181; Biographical Directory of the United States Congress web page.

1059   Donald J. Rattlciffe, "The Autobiography of Benjamin Tappan", *Ohio History*, Vol. 85, p. 111.

1060   Wyman W. Parker, "Edwin M. Stanton at Kenyon", *Ohio History*, Vol. 60, p. 243; H. H. Hunter, "The Pathfinders of Jefferson County", *Ohio History* Vol. 6, p. 227.

1061   Gary S. Williams, *Gliding to a Better Place, Profiles from Ohio's Territorial Era*, Buckeye Books, Caldwell, Ohio, 2000, pp. 206-207.

1062   Henry Howe, *Historical Collections of Ohio*, Centennial Edition, 1908, Vol. 1, p. 978.

Lewis was also a leading abolitionist and played a major role in the Amistad affair, providing financial and legal assistance to the African slaves who had taken over a slave ship.[1063]

Tappan died April 20, 1857 at Steubenville. According to H.H. Hunter, "His career as a pioneer, as a lawyer, as a judge and statesmen made his name a household word throughout the west."[1064]

1063 Gary S. Williams, *Gliding to a Better Place, Profiles from Ohio's Territorial Era*, Buckeye Books, Caldwell, Ohio, 2000, p. 212.

1064 H. H. Hunter, "The Pathfinders of Jefferson County", *Ohio History* Vol. 6, p. 227; Biographical Directory of U. S. Congress web page.

Chapter 9

FOUNDING FATHERS FROM FAIRFIELD COUNTY

Zane's Grant, Congress Lands, Military District, Refugee Tract

Fairfield County created by Governor St. Clair in 1800 was four times as large as the present county and included all of present Fairfield and Licking and parts of present Knox, Richland, Pickaway, and Perry Counties.[1065] Access to Fairfield County from the east was overland from Wheeling by way of Zane's trace which was laid out by Ebenezer Zane in 1797. From the south, access was up the valley of the Hocking River from the Ohio River or up Zane's Trace from Limestone, Kentucky. From the west access was across the Trace from Chillicothe.

Prior to the Greenville Treaty the land within the original Fairfield County was still occupied by Indian villages. A village of Wyandots was located at the site of Lancaster and named after its chief Tarhe which means Crane in English. After the Treaty, the tribe moved north to Upper Sandusky north of the Treaty line; however, several Indian families continued to live in the area for several years after white settlement.[1066] Isaac Zane, brother of Ebenezer, married Chief Tarhe's daughter and lived with the Wyandots.

1065   A.A. Graham, *History of Fairfield and Perry Counties*, 1883, p. 38; 1065 Richard
       C. Knopf, *Transcription of the Executive Journal of the Northwest Territory*, p.
       536, Ohio Historical Society web page.
1066   Henry Howe, *Historical Collections of Ohio*, 1898, Vol. I, pp. 587, 588.

Original purchases of land in the original Fairfield County came from one of four different tracts authorized by Congress. The first tract was a one mile square grant awarded to Ebenezer Zane located where Zane's Trace crossed the Hocking River. This was one of three such grants which Congress awarded to Zane by law dated May 17, 1796, as compensation for his services in laying out the road between Wheeling and Limestone.[1067]

The second tract was part of the Congress Lands, Ohio River Survey. This survey began with the Seven Ranges on the eastern boundary of the State, and proceeded westward. Fairfield County included range fifteen on the east to range twenty on the west. The land area within the original boundaries of Fairfield County extended from the east bank of the Scioto at Chillicothe to about five miles west of Zanesville. This land was sold at the Federal land office at Chillicothe pursuant to the terms of sale of federal land under the land acts.[1068] The survey of this land was authorized by Congress in the Land Act of 1796 enacted shortly after the Treaty of Greenville brought peace to the Ohio country.

The original Fairfield County also included a tract called the Refugee Lands. This tract included 103,527 acres set aside by Congress for refugees from Nova Scotia, who had abandoned their homes and fled to the United States to aid the Americans during the Revolutionary War.[1069]

The fourth tract was called the United States Military Lands. It included 2,650,000 acres set aside by Congress to satisfy the bounty land warrants awarded to veterans of the Revolutionary War under the Act of July 9, 1788. The survey of this tract was also authorized by the Land Act of 1796 and began in March, 1797.[1070]

Fairfield County

Fairfield County was created by Governor St. Clair on December 9, 1800, and Lancaster was designated at its county seat.[1071] Lancaster had just been

---

1067   Ohio Lands, A Short History, Thomas E. Ferguson, State Auditor, pp. 30-31.
1068   A.A. Graham, History of Fairfield and Perry Counties, 1883, p. 29;
1069   Ohio Lands, A Short History, Thomas E. Ferguson, State Auditor, pp. 29-30.
1070   Ohio Lands, A Short History, Thomas E. Ferguson, State Auditor, pp. 23-24.
1071   Richard C. Knopf, Transcription of the Executive Journal of the Northwest Territory, p. 536.

surveyed by Zane and there were not more than two or three cabins at the place.[1072]

The first settler was Joseph Hunter who came from Kentucky in April 1798 and settled on the Hocking River about a half mile west of present day Lancaster just north of Zane's Trace. A few more settlers came later that year and many more the following year.[1073] The Trace was not wide enough for wagons at that time so settlers had to bring their goods by pack horse.

Lancaster was laid out by Ebenezer Zane's sons John and Noah in November, 1800, on the grant awarded to him where his Trace crossed the Hocking River. Lots were dedicated for a church, school house, graveyard, and public buildings. Lots were given to a blacksmith, carpenter, and tanner who would remain for four years. Originally called New Lancaster, the town's name was changed to Lancaster. The name was chosen by Zane at the suggestion of Emanuel Carpenter because he and a number of other early settlers were from Lancaster County, Pennsylvania.[1074]

Fairfield County Delegates

EMANUEL CARPENTER

Emanuel Carpenter was born October 2, 1744, in Earl Township, Lancaster County, Pennsylvania. He married Maria Smith in 1764. His grandfather Heinrich, a native of the Village of Wattenwyl, Canton Berne, Switzerland, took an exploratory trip to America in 1698 where he stayed at Germantown, Pennsylvania. In 1700 he returned to Switzerland full of enthusiasm for America to recruit a party to immigrate with him to the new country. After returning home, he married, practiced medicine and began his family. He was identified with an armed rebellion against the government and found it necessary to escape with his family to America. They arrived at Germantown in 1706 where he practiced medicine. He invested in land sixty miles west of Philadelphia in the present limits of Lancaster County, Pennsylvania, where

---

1072   A.A. Graham, *History of Fairfield and Perry Counties*, 1883, p. 135.

1073   A.A. Graham, *History of Fairfield and Perry Counties*, 1883, p. 32; Henry Howe, *Historical Collections of Ohio*, 1898, Vol. I, pp. 588, 589.

1074   A.A. Graham, *History of Fairfield and Perry Counties*, 1883, pp. 133-134.

the family moved in 1717. As was common in those days, the family's name was anglicized from Zimmerman to Carpenter.[1075]

Emanuel's father was a prominent citizen of Lancaster County, Pennsylvania, serving as a representative to the Provincial Assembly from 1756 to 1771 and judge of the court of common pleas from 1759 to the date of his death in 1780. During the Revolutionary War, he was a member of the Committee of Safety of his township.[1076] Emanuel was also a veteran of the Revolutionary War.

Emanuel Carpenter immigrated to Fairfield County in 1798 with a party of relatives and friends from Lancaster County. They came west across the newly established Zane's Trace and met Ebenezer Zane at what would later become Zanesville. They were looking for a good mill site and Zane encouraged them to proceed on to the Hocking River.[1077] They purchased four sections of land south of Zane's tract and became the first settlers of Berne Township. The township was named after the Carpenter's ancestral home.[1078] Emanuel was one of the first purchaser's of Zane's lots and as stated above recommended the name of the town. The Carpenters brought machinery from Pennsylvania and erected a saw mill and grist mill about a mile south of Lancaster. [1079]

Following the organization of the county in December, 1800, Governor St. Clair appointed Emanuel Carpenter as a judge of the court of quarter sessions and the court of common pleas.[1080] The first court of quarter sessions was held in a log school house on January 12, 1801. Emanuel was presiding judge and his cousin Samuel was one of the associate judges.[1081] On September 9, 1801, Carpenter was appointed treasurer of the county. At the same time

---

1075   A. Y. Casanova, "A Carpenter Family of Lancaster", *The Pennsylvanian German*, Vol XI, No. 2, February, 1910.

1076   A. Y. Casanova, "A Carpenter Family of Lancaster", *The Pennsylvanian German*, Vol XI, No. 2, February, 1910.

1077   Herbert M. Turner, *Fairfield County Remembered*, Ohio University Special Publications, Athens, 1999, pp. 36-37.

1078   A.A. Graham, *History of Fairfield and Perry Counties*, 1883, p. 205-206; Harvey Scott, C.M.L. Wiseman, *Pioneer Period and Pioneer People of Fairfield Co., Ohio*, 1901, p. 100.

1079   C.M.L. Wiseman, "The Carpenter Family", *Centennial Lancaster*, 1897; C.M.L. Wiseman, *Pioneer Period and Pioneer People of Fairfield Co., Ohio*, 1901, p. 36.

1080   Richard C. Knopf, *Transcription of the Executive Journal of the Northwest Territory*, p. 536.

1081   Harvey Scott, *A Complete History of Fairfield County, Ohio*, 1877, p. 78.

Emanuel's cousin Samuel Carpenter was appointed lieutenant colonel of the militia of Fairfield County.[1082]

The first election in the County was for delegate to the constitutional convention and Carpenter received 228 votes, the largest number of votes, and Henry Abrams, the other delegate elected received 181 votes. There were ten candidates.[1083] Carpenter served on committees to draft article one on the legislature, article two on the executive, and article three on the judiciary.[1084] Although his votes show he was against slavery, he did not support granting civil rights to blacks.[1085]

In 1810 the records showed that Carpenter owned three tracts totaling 850 acres.[1086] He owned a large tract in what is now Madison Township. His son Sebastian manufactured a good quality of gun powder for rifles in a water-powered powder-mill for many years.[1087]

Emanuel's son Emanuel III was elected sheriff of the county and was elected to the Ohio House of Representatives in 1813. In 1814 Emanuel III bought the south half of Ebenezer Zane's tract. From this land he created Carpenter's addition to Lancaster. He donated lots to the Methodists for a church and a graveyard and a lot to the African Methodists for a church.[1088] After the bank crisis and the collapse of the western economy following the War of 1812, Emanuel III's assets were seized by creditors and he became ill and died in 1818.[1089]

Emanuel's cousin Samuel Carpenter was elected an associate judge by the General Assembly in 1803 for a seven year term and was reappointed in

---

1082   Richard C. Knopf, *Transcription of the Executive Journal of the Northwest Territory*, p. 545.

1083   A.A. Graham, *History of Fairfield and Perry Counties*, 1883, p. 84; Harvey Scott, *A Complete History of Fairfield County*, 1877, p. 106.

1084   "Journal of Convention", *Ohio Archaeological and Historical Society Publications*, Vol. V, pp. 88, 92, 93.

1085   Helen M. Thurston, "The 1802 Constitutional Convention and the Status of the Negro", *Ohio History* Vol. 81, p. 27.

1086   Lee Soltow, "Inequality Amidst Abundance: Land Ownership in Early 19th Century Ohio", *Ohio History*, Ohio Historical Society, Vol. 88, p. 151.

1087   A.A. Graham, *History of Fairfield and Perry Counties*, 1883, p. 233.

1088   A.A. Graham, *History of Fairfield and Perry Counties*, 1883, p. 136; C.M.L. Wiseman, "The Carpenter Family", *Centennial Lancaster*, 1897.

1089   C.M.L. Wiseman, "The Carpenter Family", *Centennial Lancaster*, 1897; *Scioto Gazette*, New Series No. 17, Vol. II, November 28, 1816 and New Series No. 2, Vol. 4, August 28, 1818.

1810.[1090] He was appointed to the Board of Trustees of Ohio University in 1804 where he served until his death in 1821. He built the first brick house in the county.[1091]

Emanuel died March 20, 1822. A county historian described the Carpenter family as one of the largest, wealthiest, most prominent, and influential of the pioneer period.[1092]

HENRY ABRAMS

Henry Abrams was born in 1752 in Augusta County, Virginia. His father was born in Wales and immigrated to Pennsylvania where he married Rhonda Taylor. He served as a second lieutenant in the Pennsylvania Militia during the Revolutionary War. Henry married Ruth Beall Tannehill in 1795.[1093]

In 1800 Henry Abrams brought his family from Chillicothe to what is now Greenfield Township approximately three miles from Lancaster. He built the first hewed log house in the township.[1094]

Following the organization of the county in 1800, Abrams was appointed a justice of the peace by Governor St. Clair.[1095]

He was elected as a delegate to the constitutional convention on October 12, 1802, at the first election held in the county. He did not serve on any committees. He voted with the Ross County Republicans and voted against granting civil rights to blacks.[1096]

During the fourth General Assembly which convened December 2, 1805, Abrams was appointed an associate judge of the common pleas court. His appointment followed the impeachment and conviction of associate judge William Irwin of Fairfield County for willfully failing to meet with the other

---

1090   William A. Taylor, *Ohio Statesmen and Annals of Progress*, 1899, pp. 37, 61.

1091   C.M.L. Wiseman, "The Carpenter Family", *Centennial Lancaster*, 1897

1092   C.M.L. Wiseman, "The Carpenter Family", *Centennial Lancaster*, 1897.

1093   A.A. Graham, *History of Fairfield and Perry Counties*, 1883, p. 307; Chris Mowery web page, Gencircles.com; Juanita Maxine Andreasen, Ancestral File, Familysearch.com; DAR File #201934

1094   A.A. Graham, *History of Fairfield and Perry Counties*, 1883, pp. 217-218.

1095   Richard C. Knopf, *Transcription of the Executive Journal of the Northwest Territory*, p. 548, Ohio Historical Society web page.

1096   Helen M. Thurston, "The 1802 Constitutional Convention and the Status of the Negro", *Ohio History* Vol. 81, p. 28.

judges and speaking slightingly of his duties.[1097] The constitution provided that the House of Representatives could impeach any civil officer in the state by majority vote of all its members for any misdemeanor in office. A case of impeachment was tried in the Senate and required two thirds vote of all members for conviction.[1098] Irwin's case was the first impeachment case tried in the General Assembly. Abrams was reappointed associate judge on February 15, 1810.[1099]

Abrams was a farmer.[1100] The records showed that in 1810 he owned two tracts totaling 762 acres.[1101] He was also a surveyor. He assisted Thomas Worthington survey the lands lying south of Lancaster and extending south into Hocking County.[1102]

Abrams was a horse fancier and rode with the hounds. He was fond of hunting. He brought a huge bear into Lancaster in 1810.[1103] He lost his life on a hunting trip when a hunting companion shot him for game as he crept through the bushes.[1104] He died November 26, 1821, the father of twenty children.[1105]

1097   William A. Taylor, *Ohio Statesmen and Annals of Progress*, Columbus, 1899, pp. 46, 48.

1098   Ohio Constitution of 1802, Article I, Sections 23, 24.

1099   William A. Taylor, *Ohio Statesmen and Annals of Progress*, 1899, p. 60.

1100   Letter from Jacob Beck to Dr. Charles E. Rice dated Oct. 20, 1894, Rice Collection, Ohio Historical Society.

1101   Lee Soltow, "Inequality Amidst Abundance: Land Ownership in Early 19th Century Ohio", *Ohio History*, Ohio Historical Society, Vol. 88, p. 151.

1102   Harvey Scott, *A Complete History of Fairfield County, Ohio*, 1877, pp. 261-262.

1103   Harvey Scott, *A Complete History of Fairfield County, Ohio*, 1877, p. 262.

1104   Letter from Jacob Beck to Dr. Charles E. Rice dated Oct. 20, 1894, Rice Collection, Ohio Historical Society.

1105   A.A. Graham, *History of Fairfield and Perry Counties*, 1883, p. 307; Chris Mowery, Gencircles.com; Juanita Maxine Andreasen, Ancestral File, Familysearch.com

Chapter 10

SUMMING UP

The public service of the founding fathers included one U.S. President, seven U. S. Senators, nine U. S. Congressmen, one Postmaster General, two U.S. Surveyor Generals, one Commissioner of the Federal Land Office, one foreign diplomat, seven Ohio Governors, eighteen state Representatives, twenty-four state Senators, seven Ohio Supreme Court Justices, four Presiding Justices of the Common Pleas Court, nine Associate Justices of the Common Pleas Court, twelve Clerks of Court, one Secretary of State, two Adjutant Generals, six Postmasters, and nine Presidential Electors. Two participated in the French and Indian War, fourteen in the Revolutionary War, twelve in the Indian Wars, and sixteen in the War of 1812. Six were involved in negotiating treaties with the Indians. Fifteen were militia officers. Sixteen were originally or directly from Pennsylvania, thirteen from New England, six from New Jersey, eight from Maryland, three from New York, and seven from Kentucky. Twenty-one were from families that had been in America since at least 1700. Twenty-four were from prominent families. Two were born in England, one in Scotland, and one in Ireland. Fifteen were from Scots or Scotch-Irish ancestry, one from Welsh ancestry, four from German, Dutch or Swiss ancestry, and the rest from English or unknown. Twenty-six were surveyors, land developers, or specula-tors, five were teachers, fifteen were lawyers, four were inn or tavern keepers, two were ferry keepers, two were meat packers and shippers, one was a woolen manufacturer, eleven were bank officers or directors, five were storekeepers, one was a book publisher and seller, two were newspaper editors and publish-ers, ten were mill owners, two were physicians, one was a pharmacist, five were ministers, and all or practically all were farmers. At least fourteen were strong advocates of civil rights for Blacks. Three were Baptists, four were Episcopalians, four were Methodists, eleven were Presbyterians, and three were

Quakers. Five of the founders attended Yale, one Harvard, two William and Mary, one Phillips-Exeter Academy, two Princeton, and two Dickinson College. Fourteen had served in the Territorial legislature and twenty-nine had served as judges or clerks of the Territorial Courts before Ohio became a state. The founders included Federalists and Jeffersonian Republicans who later became Whigs and Jacksonian Democrats.

During their lifetimes the founders witnessed Ohio change from a wilderness beyond the control of the United States government to a Territory subject to colonial rule, then to a frontier state based on a subsistence economy, and finally to a state integrated economically, politically, and culturally with the eastern states.

The founding fathers created a plan of government which placed most governmental power in the legislature. In addition to the law making function, the legislature appointed the judges, the militia leaders, U. S. Senators, and executive officers except the Governor. Legislators were made responsive to the public by requiring annual elections of House members and biennial elections of Senators. Because so much power was vested in the legislature, service in the legislature was considered more prestigious then than now when it is frequently viewed as a stepping stone to higher office. In the early days former Governors, U.S. Senators, and Supreme Court Judges served in the legislature. Judges were appointed by the legislature for seven year terms but could be and were in some cases removed by impeachment during their terms. The Governor was a figure head with no power to veto or make appointments except for temporary appointments while the legislature was not in session. Yet political leaders competed vigorously for the office.

When the plan of government conceived by the founders was put into practice, it worked. A Wild West frontier was transformed with time into an organized society where law and courts and other governmental institutions were for the most part respected. The county courthouses throughout the state were not just seats of government. They were memorials to the high respect and pride which the people felt for their government. In retrospect, the success of the plan conceived by the founders was due in large part to its instilling in the people a sense of ownership. For better or worse they believed it was their government. If it was not responsive to the people's needs and aspirations, the people were fully conscious of their power to change their leaders and did not hesitate to do so. The success of the plan also had much to do with the character and practical wisdom of the political leaders at that time. The Ohio frontier attracted some outstanding leaders from very diverse backgrounds. It is somewhat remarkable to compare the backgrounds of Samuel Huntington, William Henry Harrison and Charles Willing Byrd who were from very prominent, wealthy families in the east with self made men like Jeremiah Morrow, Duncan McArthur, Thomas Kirker, and Francis Dunlavy. The selection of outstanding leaders reflects well on the people who selected them. Many of the frontier folk were not well-educated but most of them took the selection of their political leaders seriously and participated in the discussions in the taverns, mills, militia musters, churches, and other gathering places on the frontier which preceded every election. The frontiersman might not understand all the fine points of the law or public policy, but he was for the most part a good judge of character.

Once the plan of government was put into practice it evolved and adapted in response to political, military and economic crisis. The concept of judicial review and an independent judiciary as a check on the power of the legislature evolved from a bitter political battle. The legislature's power to thwart economic policy carried out through the United States Bank established by Congress was tested. The legislature and Governor's power and ability to deal with internal and external threats were challenged during the Burr Conspiracy and the War of 1812. The role of state government in promoting the economy was clarified through the banking crisis, the financing of roads and other internal improvements, and the development of the canal system.

By the latter half of the 19th century Ohio had evolved into one of the most powerful political and economic states in the Union. This was in no small matter due to the firm foundations laid by the founding fathers of Ohio described in this book.

About the Author

The author is an attorney who has served as general counsel of the Ohio Historical Society for over 25 years. He learned a love of history from his father who served as a member of the board of trustees, president, and general counsel of the Society. The author and his wife are descended from Ohio pioneer families. He researched and prepared a family history on each of their pioneer families as an Ohio family bicentennial project. His discovery that his wife was descended from an early Moravian family from whom the President is also descended led to his writing *Compassionate Revolutionaries, The Moravian Ancestors of George W. Bush,* published by Heritage Books. It includes a history of the Moravians who established the first European settlements in Ohio and traces the President's ancestors to one of the early Moravian families. His research also led to his discovery that his ancestors were the parents and brother of John Milligan, a delegate to the 1802 constitutional convention from Jefferson County. This aroused his curiosity about the other delegates to the convention which led to the research and writing of this book. The author believes that every family's history is important and interesting if sufficient time is taken to understand how each life related to what was going on around it. He hopes that the recent interest in family history will help Americans rediscover what is important in life and what is important for America as a nation.

INDEX OF BIOGRAPHIES BY COUNTY

ALPHABETICAL INDEX OF BIOGRAPHIES

Nathaniel Massie – Ross Co. delegate   168

Duncan McArthur – Ross Co.   193

John McIntire – Washington Co. delegate   23

William McMillan – Hamilton Co.   115

Return Jonathan Meigs Jr. – Washington Co.   26

John Milligan – Jefferson Co. delegate   220

Jeremiah Morrow – Hamilton Co. delegate   42

John Paul – Hamilton Co. delegate   74

Calvin Pease – Trumbull Co.   263

James Pritchard – Jefferson Co.   233

Rufus Putnam – Washington Co. delegate   9

John Reily – Hamilton Co. delegate   65

James Sargent – Clermont Co. delegate   207

Thomas Scott – Ross Co.   183

John Smith – Hamilton Co. delegate   52

Arthur St. Clair – Hamilton Co.   81

Daniel Symmes – Hamilton Co.   121

John Cleves Symmes – Hamilton Co.   94

Benjamin Tappan – Trumbull Co.   266

George Tod – Trumbull Co.   260

Edward Tiffin – Ross Co. delegate   140

Nathan Updegraff – Jefferson Co. delegate   226

Bezaleel Wells – Jefferson Co. delegate   214

John Wilson – Hamilton Co. delegate   78

Elijah Woods – Belmont Co. delegate   240

Thomas Worthington – Ross Co. delegate   150

INDEX OF BIOGRAPHIES BY SUBJECT

0-595-29322-0

Printed in the United States
29373LVS00003B/22